CANADA AND JAPAN

IN THE TWENTIETH CENTURY

Edited by John Schultz and Kimitada Miwa

CANADA

AND

JAPAN

IN THE

TWENTIETH

CENTURY

**Edited by John Schultz
and Kimitada Miwa**

Toronto   Oxford   New York
OXFORD UNIVERSITY PRESS
1991

F
1029.5
J3
C363
1991

Oxford University Press, 70 Wynford Drive, Don Mills, Ontario M3C 1J9

Toronto Oxford New York
Delhi Bombay Calcutta Madras Karachi Petaling Jaya
Singapore Hong Kong Tokyo Nairobi Dar es Salaam
Cape Town Melbourne Auckland

and associated companies in
Berlin Ibadan

Canadian Cataloguing in Publication Data

Main entry under title:

Canada and Japan in the twentieth century

Includes bibliographical references and index.
ISBN 0-19-540860-8

1. Canada — Relations — Japan. 2. Japan — Relations — Canada.
I. Miwa, Kimitada, 1929– . II. Schultz, John A.

FC251.J3C35 1991   327.71052   C91-094723-6
F1029.5.J3C35 1991

Copyright © Oxford University Press Canada 1991
OXFORD is a trademark of Oxford University Press
1 2 3 4 — 94 93 92 91
Printed in Canada by John Deyell Company

1/6/95

TABLE OF CONTENTS

DEDICATION

For those who have gone before us, for those who are with us, but especially for those who are yet to come who will continue to build a bridge across the Pacific and a rewarding community of humanity, despite the distances and differences between our two countries.

PREFACE

Unlike much of the contact between West and East, relations between Canada and Japan have been marked from the outset by a remarkable degree of mutuality. On 30 June 1873, two pioneer Canadian missionaries, George Cochran and Davidson McDonald arrived in Yokohama to begin the Christian work that was to establish one of the enduring ties between the two Pacific nations; at almost the same time a young carpenter named Kuno Gihei left his village in Wakayama Prefecture to establish a second *furusato*, or home place, at the British Columbia fishing settlement at Steveston, where a community of Japanese-Canadians would grow and flourish. From these early beginnings evolved over more than a century a relationship that grew steadily closer and more complex as trade, diplomacy, investment, and cultural ties were added to those of immigration and religion. Always pragmatic, sometimes uncomfortable, generally cordial but occasionally hostile, the interchange took on a growing importance to both countries as its elements multiplied.

That the relationship should have broadened and deepened is hardly surprising, for the two countries are in many ways complementary. Japan is densely populated; Canada, filled with empty spaces. Japan is heavily industrialized and a leader in technology; Canada is a primary producer, rich in the resources that Japan lacks. Both have export economies heavily dependent on the United States market, and both are greatly influenced by U.S. politics and culture. Both are countries at the geographical margin. Both grapple, albeit in different ways, with the problem of 'internationalization': Canada, with new immigrants arriving daily, struggles to integrate the world into its multicultural mosaic; Japan, with its more homogeneous population, strives to integrate itself into the world community. Both seek a role in the world which emphasizes peaceful influence rather than military might. In some ways the cooperation that has made Japan Canada's second largest trading partner and Canada a leading destination for Japanese investment and tourism has been a natural consequence of practical utility, mutual advantage and shared concerns. Given the strength of past ties and the promise of future benefits, a continuing expansion of the working partnership seems inevitable.

Yet the relationship continues to be marked on both sides by a certain ambivalence. Despite the long-standing historical connections, Japan has for most Canadians remained a far-away place in the 'mysterious East' easily confused with one of its neighbours. Despite the expansion of trade and investment and cultural exchange, Canadian political leaders and senior civil servants are, as Charles McMillan has noted, far more likely to be conversant with the art galleries and museums of Europe than with the Kabukiza of Tokyo or the robotics factories of Nagoya.[1] The national television networks keep no news teams in Tokyo. Canada's traditions orient it toward Britain and France, while its geography pulls it toward the United States. Few Canadians outside the western provinces are inclined to think of Canada as a Pacific nation, and many continue to regard Japanese companies, tourists, and investment uneasily, as a somehow strangely foreign presence. Seen from Japan, on the other hand, Canada too often appears inconsequential—a safer, if less prosperous, extension of the United States. To the extent that the average Japanese thinks of Canada at all, it is most likely to be in geographical and sentimental terms: the majestic mountains of Banff and the innocent world of *Anne of Green Gables*. Middle-power status conveys little prestige. Despite Canada's membership in the G-7, it is not generally regarded as a leading economic power. Rather, its role as a supplier of resources tends to reinforce the view of Canada that sees it, in the words of one official report, as a third-world country with an artificially high standard of living. At least a part of the ambivalence can be accounted for by mutual ignorance: like distant relations they know little of each other. More important to the skew between reality and perception, however, is the asymmetry which marks the relationship.

John Saywell argues that understanding its asymmetry is the key to grasping the nature of the relationship, and in a sense that is true. Certainly the first thing that emerges as one considers the relations between Canada and Japan is the overwhelmingly obvious differences between the two countries. Japan is small in area, Canada sprawls. Japan has a long history, Canada is relatively young. Japan has a homogeneous population, Canada is a multiethnic mosaic. Politically, Japan is one of the most highly centralized and nationally cohesive countries in the world, while Canada's federal structure holds together a loose collection of autonomous provinces. Yet despite this lengthy list of superficial differences (which could be extended almost indefinitely), there are moments when the Japanese feel at one with Canadians. A poet from New Brunswick, Alden Nowlan, speaks of long-awaited spring thus:

> Spring is distrusted here, for it deceives—
> snow melts upon the lawns, uncovering
> last fall's dead leaves.[2]

The form and spirit, if not the content, are strikingly similar to Japanese *haiku*: geography, climate and seasonal change may differ, but the poet's involvement with nature and the form chosen to express it echo Japanese counterparts.

The similarity is suggestive: in spite of manifest dissimilarities and asymmetries, there are areas of subtle but significant consonance. In the sphere of metaphysics and values, Japanese and Canadians share common aspirations; attitudes and understandings are more symmetrical. In spite of industrialization and urbanization, the Japanese easily hark back to their nature-worshipping Shintoist traditions. Both societies tend to emphasize co-operation and community. Both have a tradition of concern for the group, rather than the individual. Both accept the notion of an active role for the state in organizing and directing the economy and society. Such fundamental commonalities hold the promise for deepening and extending the bilateral relationship.

With little stretching of the imagination, for example, it is possible to see in their concern for nature the source of both peoples' search for peace in world politics. In the case of Canada, popular support for the role of 'peacekeeper' is rooted in part in a national psyche conditioned by an awareness of nature. Meanwhile, it has become more and more apparent in recent years that in Japan the anti-nuclear weapons pacifism of the Hiroshima and Nagasaki vintage has given way to an environmental concern which in turn is related to the profound awareness on the part of the Japanese of human life as part of nature. Hence the Japanese find encouragement as they discover in Canada not simply a less-powerful version of the United States, but instead a distinctive nation that has pursued a different and constructive policy even during the years of superpower confrontation.

Why has Japan not responded more positively to such Canadian initiatives as then Canadian External Affairs Minister Joe Clark's call for the establishment of a Pacific-rim counterpart of the Conference on Security and Co-operation in Europe? Why has Japan not emulated Canada's pursuit of 'middle-power' diplomacy and international co-operation? The answer is not that Canada and Japan are vastly different, separated by an unbridgeable gulf of conflicting interests and objectives in world affairs. Rather, the lack of imaginative and creative leadership on the part of the Japanese establishment and press has meant this and other similar possibilities have been stillborn. Despite the common perception of Japan as a closely-knit society of consensus content to rest on its economic accomplishment, it is in reality a society in ferment as a new generation and a new awareness replaces what has gone before. These changes, taken together with the mutual understandings and shared concerns that draw Canada and Japan together, offer a golden opportunity to both peoples. Will it be seized before it slips away?

ACKNOWLEDGEMENTS

While it is impossible to repay the many individuals who contribute in important ways to a volume of this kind, the editors would like to acknowledge their
debt to the Japanese and Canadian scholars who have contributed to the growing
awareness in both countries of the ties which link them together. We are grateful
to Richard Teleky of Oxford University Press Canada for encouraging us to
pursue the project as well as to Olive Koyama, our English-language editor, for
making the book a better one than we could have done. Paul Henry and the staff
of the Canadian Embassy, Tokyo gave generously of their time and assistance, as
did Ivan Bumstead and the staff of the Government of Alberta Office.

A special thanks is owed to Yuki Yamazaki of the Institute for American and
Canadian Studies and to Reiko Yanagisawa of the Institute of International
Relations at Sophia University, to Yasuko Tadenuma of the School of Area Studies
at the University of Tsukuba, and to Mary Clarke of the Nikkei International
Center, all of whom met unreasonable demands on their time and energy with
patience and good humour. A similar thanks is owed to Peter Currie, who
painstakingly translated the Japanese language text. We are grateful to the Japan-
Canada Educational and Cultural Exchange Foundation for their assistance with
translation costs involved with the Japanese language edition.

Publication of this book was made possible through the generous support of
External Affairs and International Trade Canada and The Japan Foundation, and
the editors are deeply indebted to those organizations for their contribution.

Kimitada Miwa
John Schultz

EDITORS' NOTE

For the convenience of readers of the English language edition, Japanese
names when they appear in the table of contents, running heads, and introductory essays are rendered in Western style—i.e., given name followed by family
name. Elsewhere in the text they are rendered in the normal Japanese manner
which places the family name first.

A selection of photographs follows page 84.

○

Strangers in a Strange Land

The arrival of Japanese immigrants constituted one of the first contacts between Canada and Japan, and the tensions and dilemmas that immigration posed would play a significant part in animating and shaping relations between the two countries. Until World War II, most Japanese in Canada lived along the British Columbia coast. With the rare exception, that province never welcomed them. The Japanese immigrants who began arriving in the 1890s came to a place that had a well-established hostility to earlier and more numerous immigrants from Asia, the Chinese. Moreover, white British Columbians realized quickly that the Japanese came from a more powerful nation and were more ambitious than the Chinese. Thus, the imin *became a greater threat to the notion of British Columbia as a 'white man's province'. The provincial government tried repeatedly to restrict immigration from Japan and to curtail the activities of Japanese already in the province; these efforts usually ran afoul of Canadian and British diplomatic considerations.*

In 1907, an unusually large influx of Japanese helped cause an anti-Asian riot in Vancouver. Subsequently, Canada and Japan negotiated the Gentlemen's Agreement whereby Japan voluntarily curtailed emigration. Japan scrupulously honoured the agreement but a large proportion of the post-1907 immigrants were young women and the Japanese birth rate in Canada rose. White British Columbians seldom distinguished between issei *and* nisei *and demanded that all Japanese immigration be halted. Then, as tensions mounted in East Asia in the 1930s, rumours of large-scale illegal Japanese immigration abounded in British Columbia. The Canadian government found little evidence of such immigration but the rumours contributed to strong anti-Japanese feeling in coastal British Columbia which led to the evacuation of all persons of Japanese origin from the coast in 1942 and the ultimate dispersal of these approximately 22,000 people across Canada. Not until 1962 did Canada again permit immigration from Japan. Today, there are no special regulations for would-be Japanese immigrants but few Japanese have sought to come to Canada while those of Japanese descent already in Canada are scattered throughout the country.*

Patricia Roy is the author of A White Man's Province: British Columbia Politicians and Chinese and Japanese Immigrants 1858-1914 *(Vancouver: University of British Columbia Press, 1989) and recently published, with J.L. Granatstein, Masako Iino and Hiroko Takamura,* Mutual Hostages: Canadians and Japanese During the Second World War *(Toronto: University of Toronto Press, 1990). Professor Roy currently teaches Canadian history at the University of Victoria in Victoria, British Columbia.*

NOT ALL WERE WELCOME:
CANADA AND THE DILEMMA OF IMMIGRATION

Patricia E. Roy

From the 1880s until the outbreak of World War I, a flood of propaganda poured out from the government of British Columbia and private real estate promoters. Books, pamphlets, magazine articles, and advertisements emphasized the province's rich natural resources and its attractions for immigrants and investors. The opportunities in Canada's Pacific coast province were indeed great. While the mountains which cover much of the province are not suitable for agriculture and impede internal communication, many of them are covered with merchantable timber, and within the mountains lie significant deposits of valuable minerals—gold, silver, lead, zinc, copper and coal. Agricultural land occupies only about three per cent of the province's 948,600 square kilometres, but some of that land, particularly in the Fraser and Okanagan Valleys, is of excellent quality. And two major rivers that flow within the province, the Fraser and the Skeena and their tributaries, enjoy abundant runs of north Pacific salmon.

Immigration propaganda constantly promoted these resources. It appealed to 'the enterprising capitalist, the enlightened farmer, the skilled artisan, the frugal and industrious labourer, and all who understand the use of hands and brains, to enter and participate in the work of developing her dormant resources.' Although the invitation was extended to 'the intelligent, industrious and law-abiding of every nation', it was implicit that that meant every European nation.[1] Immigration literature was circulated only in eastern North America and Europe. The 'establishment' of British Columbia, themselves mainly immigrants from the United Kingdom and eastern Canada, wanted to make their new home a 'white man's country'; they did not want immigrants from Asia no matter how intelligent or industrious they might be. On the contrary, the very intelligence and industry of the Japanese made them people to fear rather than to welcome.

The welcome for Asians had never been warm. In the wake of the gold rush which began in 1858, Chinese men had joined thousands of others from all parts of the world, especially California, to form the first large modern wave of immigration. As the gold rush faded and the economy declined in the late 1860s, white British Columbians, who simultaneously viewed the Chinese as an inferior people and as serious competitors in the labour market, became increasingly less tolerant. They accused the Chinese of being sojourners who, by working as cheap labour, living frugally, and sending their earnings home to China, did not contribute to the local economy. Shortly after British Columbia became a province of Canada in 1871, the provincial legislature tried to prevent further Chinese immigration and to limit the activities of Chinese already within the province. In the early 1880s, the chief contractor for the Canadian Pacific Railway in British Columbia claimed that to meet construction deadlines he needed to import Chinese labourers. British Columbia politicians were temporarily persuaded to set aside their anti-Chinese agitation but as the railway neared completion, they convinced the government of Canada to impose a $50 head tax on all Chinese immigrants. For some years, that tax checked Chinese immigration.[2]

Meanwhile a second influx of Asian immigration, this time from Japan, was slowly developing. Nagano Manzo, who jumped ship at New Westminster in 1877, is considered to be the first Japanese immigrant to Canada. He worked variously as a fisherman, longshoreman and merchant. The lack of detailed information about him and the handful of other Japanese immigrants suggests they initially generated little concern. When some British Columbians proposed applying existing anti-Chinese legislation to the Japanese, others noted great commercial prospects in Japan and observed that because of 'the extraordinary enterprise, the readiness to receive European ideas and the wonderful social and political change'[3] in Japan in recent decades, the Japanese were not like the Chinese. But that 'extraordinary enterprise' of Japan and its *imin* made Japanese immigrants highly unpopular in British Columbia.

During the 1880s and early 1890s a few more Japanese arrived. Unfortunately, their coming coincided with one of the many brief downturns which characterize resource-based economies such as that of British Columbia. Like the Chinese, the Japanese were perceived as 'cheap' or 'unfair' labour. The Vancouver *Daily News-Advertiser*, for example, complained that 'the flooding of one of the best districts of the Province with unassimilative Asiatic labour, spending little for the benefit of general trade and by no means developing the civilization of the Province, is gradually raising a problem more and more difficult to solve save on the basis that a large part of B.C. is to become Little China-Japan.[4] This indiscriminate categorization of the Japanese with the Chinese, grouping both under the general term 'Asian' or such less polite names as 'Mongolian', meant that Japanese newcomers experienced the prejudices and disabilities the Chinese had long endured, including, after 1895, disfranchisement.

In Vancouver the Japanese consulate, established in 1889, took pains to argue that the Japanese were a superior people to the Chinese and that their number in British Columbia was small. In 1896 Nosse Tatsugoro, the consul, estimated the maximum number of Japanese in British Columbia had been 1100, and that the average was only about 300. He explained that numbers were exaggerated because many Japanese en route to the United States landed briefly at British Columbia ports.[5] Moreover, he asserted, Japan had no 'desire to see a large emigration of her subjects'.[6] His comment that 'population is needed in British Columbia which has a great future . . . and the Japanese come because there is great opportunity',[7] though reflecting immigration propaganda, did not reassure white British Columbians.

During 1896 and 1897 an Anti-Mongolian Association called for restrictions on Chinese and Japanese immigration. Because there was less hostility to the Japanese than to the more numerous Chinese, and some recognized that Japanese traders could benefit British Columbia, the Association circulated separate anti-Chinese and anti-Japanese petitions. After the Japanese petition had accumulated six thousand signatures, the provincial legislature unanimously asked the Canadian government to ensure that provisions in a proposed Anglo-Japanese treaty would prevent 'the unrestricted immigration here of the lower classes of Japanese labourers'.[8]

Significantly, the agitation was still primarily directed only at working-class Japanese. As the Vancouver *News-Advertiser* explained, 'we readily welcome the settlement of Japanese traders and professional men' but 'we have a natural right to see to it that our own western labour has a fair opportunity in its own domain'.[9] In an effort to halt that competition, the legislature began trying to forbid the employment of 'Chinese or Japanese' in mines and transportation companies incorporated under provincial law. Such regulations offended the government of Japan, ran afoul of federal jurisdiction over trade and commerce and aliens, and upset British diplomatic considerations. Thus, the federal government regularly disallowed such legislation.

Marginal labourers had first felt Japanese competition. Prominent among them were native Indians—themselves the descendants of people who had emigrated from Asia some ten to twenty thousand years earlier.[10] Many lived in remote areas, had been shunted off to precisely defined and limited areas known as Indian Reserves, and played a useful role in the local economy as a pool of unskilled labour. Chief Joseph of Capilano Creek told a government inquiry in 1901, 'We cannot get work and cannot get any money because of the Japanese.'[11]

Thus from time to time the native peoples joined the angry protests against the Japanese, especially in the fisheries where the Japanese first made their economic mark. Their presence in the Fraser River industry was initially noted in the summer of 1890;[12] by 1893 Japanese held about twenty per cent of the total fishing licences issued on the river. An angry protest developed against these alleged 'serfs' of the canners who had been naturalized (a qualification for fishing licences) under false pretences and who accepted lower prices for fish.[13] Meanwhile the Japanese continued to enter the fisheries. By 1901, they held about forty-one per cent of the licences on the Fraser River. Tensions were exacerbated in the 1900 and 1901 seasons, years of unusually good fish runs, by disputes over the price of fish and the decision of the Japanese fishermen to accept lower prices. Japanese penetration of the fisheries increased: by 1905 they held 85% of the licences on the Fraser, dominated the Skeena River, and had developed new possibilities for the industry such as the salting of dog salmon. Moreover, the Japanese had 'practically' taken over the building of fishing boats.[14] Their success in the fishery seemed to demonstrate that the Japanese could easily take over any industry they sought to master.

At the turn of the century, British Columbia, like most of the rest of Canada, was enjoying unusual prosperity. Japanese labourers appeared in a variety of industries. Francis Carter-Cotton, the provincial Minister of Finance and Agriculture, warned the cabinet that an influx of Japanese in the forests, fisheries and mines had 'materially and injuriously interfered with white labour'. He noted 'many indications' that the influx of Japanese would 'become large and that Japanese labour would—if some restrictive measures be not adopted—entirely supplant white labour in many important industries.'[15]

The danger appeared imminent. Between April 1 and June 30, 1900, 7,682 Japanese arrived in B.C.,[16] which then had a total population of about 150,000. Although many were en route to the United States, even the Victoria *Colonist*, which hitherto had been sympathetic to Japanese immigrants, complained that 'steps must be taken to prevent the province being overrun by Japanese.'[17] All three governments recognized a problem. Japan said it would limit emigration permits and then announced it was forbidding the emigration of labourers;[18] Prime Minister Wilfrid Laurier promised that a federal royal commission would investigate Chinese and Japanese immigration, and provincial politicians passed 'An Act to Regulate Immigration Into British Columbia'. This act, popularly known as the Natal Act, included a language test which required prospective immigrants, on request, to fill out a simple application form in 'some language of Europe.'[19] Such a test would allow provincial immigration officers to admit Japanese merchants but deny entry to most labourers. The Japanese consul promptly protested this 'unfriendly action.'[20] In due course, the federal government disallowed the legislation. The provincial government re-enacted it; Japan protested; Ottawa again disallowed it. What the *Japan Times* rightly described as a farce[21] became an almost annual event and, until the province finally abandoned the game in 1908, a regular grievance in federal-provincial relations.

The Natal Act also applied to Chinese but Japanese immigrants continued to be its main target despite the repeated declarations of Japanese diplomats that Japan was banning most emigration, and the release of Canadian government statistics indicating that fewer than 500 Japanese had entered Canada between 1901 and 1905 inclusive. Moreover, according to Japanese Consul Nosse, most of those were merchants, professionals, students, and families of Japanese already resident in Canada. Nevertheless, white British Columbians, who had little faith in Japan's ability to regulate immigration, still feared a large-scale influx. Not all Japanese stayed; although 13,913 arrived between 1896 and 1901, the 1901 census recorded only 4,578 Japanese in British Columbia. Most were 'adult males of the labouring class.'[22] The public, however, did not distinguish among actual immigrants, Japanese in transit to the United States or Mexico, those returning to British Columbia after visits to Japan, or those who stayed in the province only long enough to earn some money. The seasonal sojourners (*dekasegi*) were, in any case, especially unpopular because they spent their earnings in Japan and not in British Columbia. According to the leading provincial newspaper, the Vancouver *Province*, 'whether the Mikado is trying to prevent the emigration of Japanese from Japan to Canada or not, the fact remains that they succeed in getting here—which they generally do about the time of the fishing season.'[23]

Of course, what really worried white British Columbians was the fact that Japanese immigrants were effective competitors. The 'virile, civilized and intellectual Japanese', argued the Victoria *Colonist*, 'is even a more dangerous rival than the Chinese. He can live as cheaply, can work as cheaply, and he is more aggressive and adaptable as a rival. He is more desirable as a citizen, it is true, but not less disturbing as a factor in the labour market.'[24] Premier Richard McBride similarly claimed, during the 1903 provincial election, that 'the Japs were, if anything, worse than the Chinamen, as the latter were content with occupying menial positions, while the former had higher ambitions and were ousting the whites from higher fields of work.'[25] Specifically, he told another election audience,

In the logging camps, sawmills, carpenter shops, machine shops and in other industries where you formerly saw white men you now see the Japs. And the

Japs' hold in the province is getting stronger all the time. . . . This inroad of the Japanese will become a very serious matter indeed, unless some action is immediately taken against them.[26]

For the time being, no immediate action was necessary; no immigrants were coming. Japan was honouring its promise to halt emigration. After the conclusion of the Russo-Japanese War, that situation changed. A handful of Japanese began arriving from Hawaii and, after Canada adhered to the Anglo-Japanese Treaty of Commerce and Navigation in 1905, Japan sought to relax her voluntary emigration restrictions. In the first seven months of 1907, 5,571 Japanese landed at British Columbia ports; more were to come.[27]

In 1907 British Columbia was booming. Employers complained of a labour shortage aggravated by an increase in the head tax to $500, which had almost eliminated Chinese immigration. Enterprising emigration agencies in Japan prepared to meet the needs of such British Columbia employers as Lieutenant-Governor James Dunsmuir, the proprietor of a large colliery and a major employer of Asian labour. Although Japan still restricted the issue of passports for prospective emigrants to Canada, emigration agents routed labourers via Hawaii.

The influx began to build in the spring. By July newspapers featured headlines such as 'Jap Invasion. Little Brown Men Swarming into Province.'[28] On July 26, the steamer *Kumeric* arrived with about 1200 Japanese passengers and rumours circulated that another twelve thousand were on the way. 'Every development', argued the Vancouver *Province*, 'points to the belief that the Japanese Government has broken faith with Canada in the matter of this immigration.'[29] Politicians, the press, and labour leaders openly advanced racial arguments against the new arrivals and warned that white British Columbians could be swamped. The Nanaimo *Free Press*, for example, contended that the 'Japanese are of a different colour from us, of different ambition, can never be intelligent citizens, use our ballot, or intermarry. In fact, they cannot assimilate with us in any way. . . . If their incoming is not checked inside of two or three years we could have twenty to thirty thousand able-bodied Japs. That will give us, with 80,000 males in British Columbia, one Jap to every three or four in the population.'[30] A Vancouver *Province* cartoon captured the common fear. It portrayed a white working man, his neatly clad wife, an infant and a toddler at the door of their modest cottage. The dominant feature of the drawing was an ominous shadow, in the shape of a Japanese labourer, covering the side of the house.[31]

Although all parts of the province were concerned about the influx, the main opposition centred in Vancouver. There, during the summer of 1907, some local labour leaders and politicians organized a branch of the American-based Asiatic Exclusion League. The League called for the prohibition of all immigration from Asia but especially the Japanese: 'one of the races now coming here is excessively aggressive, and we fear that they look forward to ultimately controlling this part of Canada. . . . In time when these men are not only labourers but merchants and manufacturers with large material interests in the country their ingress can only be prevented at the expense of the peaceful relations now existing between this country and Japan.'[32]

To draw attention to itself the League sponsored a parade and public rally on Saturday, September 7. It was, for Vancouver, an unusually hot and humid night. Because not all the audience could be accommodated in the meeting room at the City Hall, the speakers repeated their harangues outside. Then, someone in the crowd called for a march on nearby Chinatown and the adjacent 'Little Tokyo' district. The mob responded, smashing shop windows in Chinatown; by the time it got to 'Little Tokyo' the residents there had prepared defences and forced the mob back but not before more windows were broken. Although the mob had attacked Chinatown, its main targets were the Japanese. Consul General Nosse advised Governor General Grey that continued widespread agitation had 'created a feeling of very grave apprehension on the part of my countrymen, resident in British Columbia, that further disturbances may arise which might lead to the loss of life or property . . .'[33]

News of the riot had spread quickly around the world, much to the embarrassment of the government of Canada, which acted swiftly to compensate for damages to Japanese-owned property and to negotiate an immigration agreement with Japan. To accomplish the first goal it sent William Lyon Mackenzie King, the Deputy Minister of Labour, to Vancouver with authority to investigate claims and to pay for damaged property. After almost two months of investigating the whole Asian immigration question in Vancouver, King informed a British friend that he had decided the 'agitation against the Japanese' was more than a labour agitation:

> The people of British Columbia of all classes are pretty generally in favour of restricting the immigration of Japanese simply because they not only fear Japanese competition, but the possibility of complications in the future should the Japanese ever secure too strong a hold in that Province. There is a good deal . . . to indicate that Japan is desirous of becoming a great power on the Pacific, and it is only natural . . . [that] . . . her statesmen should have an eye upon the western coast of this continent. . . . The people of the whole western coast from Mexico to Alaska are feeling a common concern in this problem. If it were a question tomorrow between treaty and restriction of immigration it would soon become impossible for a government in this country to retain office and advocate the maintenance of the treaty.[34]

Similarly, Morikawa Kishiro, the new Japanese consul in Vancouver, observed that 'the difficulty . . . was not that Japanese are undesirable immigrants, rather that their thrift and capacity for work is dwelt upon as their only fault, qualities which are generally understood as necessary for good citizenship. . . .'[35]

In the meantime, the Canadian Minister of Labour, Rodolphe Lemieux, had gone to Tokyo to negotiate what became the Lemieux-Hayashi or 'Gentlemen's' Agreement. Although the details of the agreement were secret, British Columbians understood that Japan would permit the emigration of no more than four hundred labourers per year. Almost simultaneously, Canada passed an order-in-council requiring immigrants to come direct from their country of origin. Although directed principally at emigrants from British India, the order also effectively cut off Japanese immigration from Hawaii. A few newspapers questioned the idea of allowing Japan to be 'the judge of the number of coolies which shall be sent to this province,'[36] but otherwise the response to the so-called Gentlemen's Agreement was generally favourable.

Yet, neither the new restrictions on Japanese immigration nor attempts by Japanese already in British Columbia 'to melt the hostile feeling of your workingmen and certain politicians' eased concerns about the Japanese presence. Indeed, Fred Yoshy who worked as a translator for the Department of Immigration in Vancouver told Mackenzie King that 'sometimes I felt myself as though I was living in a close-door country like China, where the humanity, freedom and civilization are not known.'[37]

That Yoshy and other Japanese should have such feelings is hardly surprising. Although the press and politicians frequently coupled their complaints about the Japanese with compliments for them, racist ideas about inassimilability increasingly surfaced along with the old objections about economic competition. G.H. Cowan, the Conservative Member for Vancouver, told Parliament: 'I yield to no man in my admiration of the Japanese as a nation and as individuals, but the danger to Canada lies in that very fact that we have to accord to them our admiration in many respects. They are aliens and will remain so.'[38] More explicitly, after visiting the prosperous and largely Japanese fishing village of Steveston at the mouth of the Fraser River, a magazine reporter remarked that the Japanese fisherman 'is a hard worker and he has no bad habits. The only thing you can say about him is that he is not white, but brown, and is the product of the East not the West. That's the white man's objection to all Orientals because he wants to keep British Columbia a white man's country. . . . He starts you thinking what would happen if the Japanese came to British Columbia in very great numbers.'[39] In practice, once the Gentlemen's Agreement came into effect, the number of immigrants dropped dramatically. While not falling below the 400 limit which British Columbians thought the agreement had ensured, the numbers were usually well below 1,000. During the Great War, Japan was allied with Great Britain. Under the terms of the alliance, Japan temporarily assumed part of the responsibility for the naval defence of the British Columbia coast. Given this circumstance and their preoccupation with the war in Europe, British Columbians said relatively little about Japan or the Japanese in their midst. But when the British Ambassador in Tokyo sought evidence to combat an anti-British campaign in the Japanese press, Canadian officials could produce no 'speeches, newspaper articles or publications tending to show . . . much improvement in feeling in Canada towards Japanese.'[40]

During the war, some Japanese settlers in British Columbia, seeking alternative livelihoods in anticipation of restrictions on their fishing activities, took advantage of a depressed real estate market to establish small retail shops in white neighbourhoods and to purchase small farms, especially in the Fraser Valley. Once the war was over, farmers' organizations, fearing further Japanese competition, took the lead in persuading the provincial legislature to ask Prime Minister Robert Borden to oppose Japan's demand for a racial equality clause in the Covenant of the League of Nations. They wanted to ensure that Canada could prohibit 'the immigration of races that will not assimilate with the Caucasian races.'[41] Such a request meant 'no imputation of race inferiority', claimed the Vancouver *Province*, 'only a recognition of race differences.'[42] This attitude contributed to demands that the Anglo-Japanese alliance not be renewed, as did the idea that 'wherever the Japanese establish themselves sooner or later the Anglo-Saxons are driven out. Thrifty and industrious and, generally speaking, excellent citizens as they are, it is nevertheless impossible for the English-speaking peoples to contemplate with equanimity a Japanese Pacific Coast . . .'[43]

In the years immediately after the Great War, British Columbia, like most of Canada, suffered from economic depression and high unemployment. Tough times touched off renewed agitation. Most was not directed specifically against the Japanese but against Asian immigration in general. During the summer and fall of 1921 a new Asiatic Exclusion League emerged in Vancouver. Its impact and that of anti-Asian agitation generally was so great that in the federal election campaign that fall, almost all British Columbia candidates tried to outdo themselves in blaming the other party for allowing Asian immigration in the first place, and in promising to halt Asian immigration if they were elected. Thus, when the British Columbia members of Parliament got to Ottawa in the spring of 1922, they set aside party differences to argue as one for a law to exclude 'the immigration of all alien orientals.'[44] Their motion was defeated but the following year Parliament passed what was effectively a Chinese exclusion act.[45] To avoid the embarrassment of a parliamentary debate on a similar Japanese bill proposed by A.W. Neill, the Independent M.P. for Comox-Alberni, the federal government in 1923 persuaded Japan to permit a maximum of 150 household servants and agricultural labourers to emigrate to Canada annually.[46] The British Columbia public, however, took little note of the new policy and observed only that the Japanese population was increasing. It had been 8,587 in 1911; in 1921 it was 15,006.

Before 1908 the majority of the *imin* had been young men; after, they sent for their wives and brides. In 1914, the assurance of a Japanese government official that Canada need not worry about a Japanese influx since 'the number of Japanese in the Dominion is being increased rather by families joining their successful male heads than by a movement of the adult male population westward' prompted the response, 'That's exactly what we ARE worrying about.'[47] The main explanation of population growth was, as the Vancouver *Sun* explained, 'the fecundity of the Japanese race.'[48] Provincial statistics released in 1923 indicated that the Japanese in British Columbia had a birth rate three times that of whites.[49] 'The real menace in the Japanese invasion of Canada', a Department of Immigration official concluded, 'is the female immigration.'[50] Similarly, the New Westminster *British Columbian* complained that such immigration had resulted in an 'embarrassing and abnormal' increase in the Japanese population.[51]

Meanwhile, a small amount of Japanese immigration continued. That, and the knowledge that the United States was about to replace its Gentlemen's Agreement with an exclusionary law, inspired British Columbians to press for more stringent immigration regulations. There were calls for legislation on the pattern of the Chinese Immigration Act of 1923. Prime Minister Mackenzie King was well aware of the problem. The British Columbia members of Parliament constantly reminded him of it, and late in 1924 the provincial legislature called for an amendment to the Immigration Act of Canada 'to completely prohibit Asiatic immigration.'[52] King, who headed a minority government throughout the 1920s, was anxious to placate British Columbia and had been informed by the Department of Immigration that the Japanese government's control of emigration had not been 'effective',[53] yet he recognized the need to move slowly through diplomatic channels.

But British Columbians were growing impatient. In 1928, when Canada and Japan announced they would initiate full diplomatic relations by exchanging ministers, the provincial legislature responded by passing an even stronger resolution complaining of the undesirability of intermarriage with certain races; competition in agriculture, commerce, the professions, and industry; the high Japanese birth rate; and Japan's restrictions on the economic activities of Canadian nationals in Japan. The Legislature unanimously called for more restrictions on Chinese and Japanese immigration, the repatriation of many of the Chinese and Japanese resident in British Columbia, and a new treaty with Japan which would allow British Columbia to legislate as it wished concerning property and civil rights.[54] The last clause sought to give British Columbia the power to follow the California precedent of limiting the right of Japanese to acquire land. In Parliament, meanwhile, British Columbia members had continued to demand exclusionary legislation. Early in 1926, for example, H.J. Barber, the Conservative member for Fraser Valley, proposed to introduce a motion for an 'oriental' exclusion law. He referred specifically to the increase in the Japanese population, including, he claimed, a 70% increase in the enrolment of Japanese children in the public schools between 1923 and 1925.[55]

In response to such pressures, the King government initiated a series of discussions with the Japanese Consul General in Ottawa. Implicit in the Canadian argument was the warning that if Japan did not voluntarily concede further restrictions, Canada might have to legislate and thus cause embarrassment all round.[56] Canada wanted to reduce the number of immigrants generally and particularly to tighten the restrictions on the immigration of women and children. Japan, of course, also had to consider the opinion of its public which would consider a proposed time limit on the entry of wives and children to be 'discriminatory and anti-humanitarian'.[57] The negotiations moved slowly but in the spring of 1928, Japan agreed to revise the Gentlemen's Agreement. Once the Tokyo legation was established, Canada would take control of such matters as issuing visas; Japan for its part would limit the total number of emigrants to Canada, including agricultural labourers and domestic servants, to 150 per year and would put a stop to the practice of 'picture brides'.[58] It was understood that Japan would allow no more than 75 women to emigrate per year but, out of respect for public opinion in Japan, Prime Minister King agreed not to mention a specific number publicly but merely to say that 'Japan understood Canada did not wish the preponderating number to be women'. Prime Minister King was delighted with the new arrangement. He told his faithful confidante, his diary, that the agreement was 'a real triumph in diplomacy' since it avoided 'exclusion & on all else (save this few) we have everything in our own hands'.[59] In British Columbia the response was mixed. A Liberal newspaper described the announcement of the revisions as 'pleasant reading'[60] but in the provincial election campaign which was just beginning, the Conservatives argued it was necessary to continue 'efforts for a white British Columbia'.[61]

Despite the persistent idea that British Columbia must be white, there was some appreciation of the value of Japanese settlers. Shortly before taking up his post as Canadian minister to Japan, H.M. Marler made a twenty-seven-day tour of the province. He reported that many people had raised the question of Japanese immigration but he observed:

> those who speak against the Japanese do not sufficiently take into consideration their distinct value to that Province as a whole. They do, it is true by their industry, create an active competitive factor in some places. In the fishing and lumber industries they are of great value. Without them I doubt if these two industries would be as successful as they are. In no place, however, did I hear one word against the Japanese as individual citizens. All agreed that they were most intelligent, thrifty, industrious and splendid heads of families.[62]

The revision of the Gentlemen's Agreement and the onset of severe economic depression in late 1929 sharply reduced Japanese immigration. In 1928, 535 Japanese immigrants had arrived in Canada; in 1935, only 70. As immigration declined so too did agitation. An illegal immigration scandal in 1931 involving Fred Yoshy and occasional rumours of illegal immigrants aroused little excitement.

The situation changed abruptly after the beginning of the Sino-Japanese War in July 1937. British Columbia newspapers regularly carried news of that war and considerable sympathy developed for the Chinese. Then, in November 1937, Archdeacon F.G. Scott, an Anglican clergyman based in Montreal, told the Toronto *Star* that he had been informed on 'good authority' that Japanese naval officers in disguise were living in the 'so-called Japanese fishing villages in British Columbia'.[63] Rumours of Japanese spies in the province had circulated intermittently since at least 1907, but, given the tense international situation and allegations that Japanese interests were acquiring strategic sites, timber and mineral resources, Scott's 'revelations' revived stories of illegal Japanese immigration and encouraged British Columbia politicians to call for a complete ban on Japanese immigration. Premier T.D. Pattullo advised his fellow Liberal, Prime Minister King, that 'in view of the activities of Japan public feeling is becoming very much aroused'. He reported how 'a Conservative member charged that many Japanese had been bootlegged into British Columbia, that is the quota of one hundred and fifty a year was very much exceeded by Japs coming in surreptitiously'. The premier urged the federal government to make 'a most careful survey' to ascertain if any Japanese 'should not be here'.[64]

In Ottawa, A.W. Neill proposed to apply the Chinese Immigration Act to Japanese; that is, to repeal the Gentlemen's Agreement and to ban immigration from Japan. The idea had wide support in British Columbia but Prime Minister King feared that some of the things that might be said in a Parliamentary debate on Neill's bill 'would occasion misunderstanding beyond the boundaries of Canada' and embarrass British diplomats.[65] King could not forestall the debate but he did limit it and, for diplomatic purposes, put on record the fact that Japan had 'been perfectly loyal' to the Gentlemen's Agreement.[66] This may have avoided embarrassing British diplomats; it did not please British Columbians. To assuage their sensitivities, the King government appointed a Board of Review under H.L. Keenleyside, an official of the Department of External Affairs who had once served in the Tokyo legation, to investigate illegal immigration and assigned a special interdepartmental committee of civil servants in Ottawa to re-examine the 'general problem of Orientals in Canada'.[67]

The announcement of these investigations ended public discussion of illegal immigration. Indeed, after conducting extensive investigations, the Board found little evidence of such immigration. In the meantime, British Columbians revived old demands for a total ban on immigration from both China and Japan. In asking Parliament for such legislation, the Vancouver City Council explained the 'Orientals' already here were 'not capable of assimilation', did 'not conform to Canadian traditions', and had 'gained an ascendancy over our own people in many lines of business by employing unfair methods of competition and through low standards of living.'[68] When the federal Royal Commission on Dominion-Provincial Relations visited Victoria in mid-March 1938, Premier Pattullo called for a better financial deal from Ottawa, for the prohibition of 'Oriental immigration into Canada . . . upon grounds of ethnological differences of race', and for the return of 'as many Orientals as possible . . . to the land from which they came.'[69]

In Parliament, Neill introduced another bill to curtail Japanese immigration. 'Much more moderate'[70] than Pattullo desired, it was a throwback to the old Natal Acts, namely a requirement that intending immigrants should be able to demonstrate knowledge of a European language. The bill was defeated. Nevertheless, Prime Minister King asked former Consul General Matsunaga and Consul General Tomii to help him 'stop migration from Japan to Canada, so I would not have to enact an exclusion measure.'[71]

After studying the question and, especially British Columbia opinion, the special interdepartmental committee concluded that barring 'further immigration from the Orient would produce a psychological result in British Columbia altogether out of proportion to its actual and numerical effect on the growth of the oriental population in the Province' and was therefore 'an essential factor in any final solution of the problem . . .'. But the special committee also realized that any termination of the Gentlemen's Agreement must be made 'without injury to the good official relations existing between the two countries'. Therefore, it suggested a reciprocal arrangement whereby Canada and Japan would accept people in specified businesses and professions and tourists as temporary residents but not as permanent immigrants.[72] The proposal would also apply to China as there was considerable pressure within Canada to treat China and Japan equally. Such an arrangement would halt Japanese immigration to Canada without interfering with Canadian business people and missionaries who wished to go to Japan. However, Randolph Bruce, the Canadian minister in Japan, reported that ending the Gentlemen's Agreement would create 'a strong anti-Canadian feeling in Japan'[73] and that, because of the 'incident' in China and the appointment of Mr Arita to the Foreign Ministry, the time was not opportune to raise the matter.[74] Indeed, Baron Tomii advised King that Japan would regard the proposed reciprocal agreement as 'a reflection on the way in which they had lived up to their agreement of voluntarily reducing numbers'.[75] In the meantime, King used the difficult diplomatic situation as an excuse to persuade Premier Pattullo not to press for an exclusionary law.[76] Although anti-Japanese agitation did not disappear, it was directed more at the

Japanese already in Canada rather than at new immigrants of whom, in 1941, there were only four. The outbreak of war in December 1941, of course, completely halted immigration.

In August 1944, at the same time as he announced that Japanese in Canada could choose to disperse themselves across Canada or go back to Japan after the war, Prime Minister King declared that 'in the years after the war the immigration of Japanese should not be permitted'. That policy could be altered in future,[77] but post-war Parliaments were in no rush to reconsider it since many British Columbia members had not changed their minds about Japanese immigration. When Parliament debated the treaty of peace between Canada and Japan in 1952, Howard Green, a Conservative who had been one of the most outspoken British Columbia political opponents of Japanese immigration before the war, pointed to a news report that the Japanese Canadian Citizens Association was seeking a new immigration policy. He claimed any new Japanese immigration could again cause 'friction' in British Columbia. Lester Pearson, the Minister of External Affairs, agreed that Canada had 'no desire . . . to ease in any way the possibility of Japanese immigration to Canada; to make it any easier in the future for them to get here than it has been in the past—and it has not been very easy in the past.'[78] In fact, the Department of Citizenship and Immigration made only a few individual exceptions on humanitarian or compassionate grounds for near relatives of Canadian citizens.[79] As late as 1956, the Department of External Affairs—while recognizing the changing international situation, Canada's desire to develop trade, and Japan's desire for 'prestige'—advised C.D. Howe, the Minister of Trade and Commerce, that when visiting Japan he should not 'give any encouragement to the press in Japan to foresee increased immigration to Canada' because 'the main requirement for migrants is ability to assimilate'.[80]

But opinion was changing in Canada. In 1958 a CCF M.P. from Saskatchewan noted ironically that Canada was 'encouraging people to come from Germany' but not from Japan. He expressed the hope that the new Progressive Conservative Minister of Immigration would try 'to erase the damage done to the prestige of Canada in Asia . . . by making the people of Japan understand that we do not now share the views of his predecessors when they were in office during the war'.[81] In fact, the new government made some slight concessions. Prime Minister Diefenbaker told the Japan-Canada Trade Council and Canada-Japan Society that Canada would allow the permanent admission of a few key personnel of Japanese mining and manufacturing enterprises that were establishing operations in Canada.[82] Eventually, in 1962, Canada revised its immigration policy to eliminate race as a criteria for admission.[83] Henceforth, the skill of an individual, not his racial origin, would determine his acceptability as an immigrant. The Liberals under Lester Pearson, who returned to power in 1963, continued the policy.

There was little immediate effect in Japan. After he visited Japan in the summer of 1964, Rene Tremblay, the Minister of Citizenship and Immigration, explained to the House of Commons that emigration from Japan had been negligible and that Japanese had shown little interest in emigration because of Japan's booming economy and a tradition of group rather than individual emigration. Because Canada was now anxious to have 'qualified Japanese professional and technical workers and their families', he promised that the Canadian immigration service would assist such people in finding jobs and homes.[84] Canada followed up by publicizing its 'new policy' in Japan, and, after ascertaining that the British Columbia Liberal members of Parliament would favour the idea,[85] established an immigration office in Tokyo. There was no great rush of applicants. The Japanese government did not allow the new office to advertise and the highly skilled professional and trades people that Canada wanted often lacked language skills and were reluctant to leave the security of a Japanese employer for the insecurity of work in Canada.[86] Although 1,105 Japanese emigrated to Canada in 1973, a peak trade year, that was exceptional; in most years the number was significantly less.[87]

In a sense, the story of Japanese immigration to Canada had come full circle. The very first *imin*, traders and professional people, had been welcomed. Although it was soon realized that Japanese labourers were also 'intelligent and industrious', that welcome was not extended to those Japanese with limited skills. Indeed, their very intelligence and industry as well as their Asian origins made them unpopular. Canadian immigration policy no longer has racial barriers but ironically, now that Canada would admit them, the 'intelligent and industrious' Japanese prefer to stay in Japan.

○

Despite the hostility of the British Columbia government, the racial discrimination of white Canadians, and the hardships of the struggle to put down roots in a strange land, the Japanese who migrated to Canada managed to establish new homes in towns like Steveston, British Columbia where, thanks to determination and endurance, Japanese-Canadian communities gradually took shape. But resentment continued to smoulder, especially during the Depression years of the 1930s. Jealousy, scorn and occasional abuse were a condition of life. Japan's attack on Pearl Harbor and the outbreak of war inflamed tempers again. Under pressure from local opinion, the federal government rounded up the Japanese, first generation and Canadian-born alike, and moved them to remote and desolate relocation camps in the interior where they waited for peace and wondered at the future. More than forty years later the Canadian government at last moved to redress the impact of the injustice and compensate those who suffered for their shattered lives.

In the fall of 1958, Ronald P. Dore, then Professor of Asian Studies at the University of British Columbia, invited a team of Japanese researchers led by the late Professor Gamō of Meiji University to join him in collecting the life histories of residents of Steveston, a fishing village about fifteen miles from Vancouver. The results of that research were published in Japanese as Umio Watatta Nihon no Mura *[The Japanese Village That Crossed the Ocean], Masao Gamō, ed. (Chūōkōron-sha, 1962) and* Sutebusuton Monogatari *[Steveston Stories] (Chūōkōron-sha, 1962), written by Kazuko Tsurumi, a member with then graduate student Kiyotaka Aoyagi of the Japanese team. In the following chapter Professor Tsurumi returns to that work to describe the effect of the war-time experience on the subsequent lives of the Steveston residents, and their sense of identity both as Japanese and as Canadians, and to reflect on the recent effort by Canada to offer redress.*

Born in Tokyo, Kazuko Tsurumi graduated from Tsuda College and received her MA from Vassar College and her PhD from Princeton University. Visiting Professor of Sociology at the University of Toronto in 1973-74 and Visiting Professor of East Asian Studies at Princeton in 1976, she is the author of many books and papers in both English and Japanese, among which are Social Change and the Individual: Japan before and after Defeat in World War II *(Princeton: Princeton University Press, 1970),* Minakata Kumagusu; Chikyū-shikō no Hikakugaku *[Minakata Kumagusu: A Global Comparativist] (Tokyo: Kodansha, 1978) and, co-edited with Tadashi Kawata,* Naihatsuteki Hatten-ron *[The Theory of Endogenous Development] (Tokyo: Tokyo University Press: 1989). She is currently a member of the Institute of International Relations and Professor Emeritus at Sophia University.*

JAPANESE CANADIANS:
THE WAR-TIME EXPERIENCE

Tsurumi Kazuko

As of 1959, out of approximately 580 households in Steveston, about 260 were Japanese Canadian with a total population of about 1,200, including immigrants from Japan and their descendants. Before the war, the population of Japanese origin had numbered roughly 3,000; in 1959, when we visited there, the Japanese-Canadian population had decreased to less than half that. The highest percentage of the male population was at that time engaged in fishing, while most of the women worked in canneries and offices.[1] According to our survey, out of 1,207 Japanese Canadians, 763 held Canadian citizenship, 378 had dual citizenship (citizenship in both Canada and Japan), while 66 retained

Japanese citizenship. The Japanese Canadian Citizens Associations (JCCA) were then assisting holders of dual citizenship to withdraw their Japanese citizenship and become full-fledged Canadian citizens.[2]

Generally speaking, the attitudes of first-generation immigrants are 'bi-focal', in the sense that their loyalties are split between the country of their origin and the country to which they have immigrated.[3] So it was not peculiar for first-generation Japanese Canadians to identify themselves more strongly with the Japanese than with the Canadians. Within the context of Canadian society, composed of immigrants from various countries many of whose identities tend to be bifocal, we shall consider the changing attitudes of the Japanese Canadians before, during, and after World War II.

The first-generation Japanese Canadians in Steveston, whom I interviewed, may be classified into five types:

(1) The consistently-Canada-oriented: those who, ever since they arrived in Canada, have consistently and persistently, before, during, and after the war, hoped to stay in Canada.

(2) The consistently-Japan-oriented: those who, ever since they arrived in Canada, have consistently and persistently, before, during, and after the war, wished eventually to return to Japan.

(3) The *chinjimari* I (this is a Japanglish expression actually used by first-generation Japanese Canadians, meaning to 'change one's mind', or 'mind changer'): those who before and during the war wished to return to Japan, but changed their minds after the war to stay permanently in Canada.

(4) The *chinjimari* II: those who before the war intended to stay permanently in Canada, but changed their minds during and/or after the war to return to Japan.

(5) The undecided: those who had been undecided whether to return or not to return to Japan, before and during the war, and were still undecided after the war.

Among those first-generation immigrants with whom I had relatively intensive interviews, the consistently-Canada-oriented were very few. The consistently-Japan-oriented were practically nil, since by that time, they would have already returned to Japan. Most of those who stayed in Steveston in 1959 belonged to the *Chinjimari* I type. Let me trace their changing attitudes with reference to Canadian policies toward the Japanese Canadians during and immediately after the war and the implementation of those policies.

Before Japan's attack on Pearl Harbor, the treatment of Japanese Canadians was a controversial political issue in Canada. One extreme group advocated an exclusionist policy toward them, regardless of whether or not they held Canadian citizenship. Another group, in contrast, argued that those who held Canadian citizenship should be assured of their civil rights. After Pearl Harbor, the exclusionist policy prevailed. In February 1942, the federal government ordered all Japanese Canadians evacuated from the Pacific coast. The British Columbia Security Commission was created to carry out the task of moving 21,079 Japanese Canadians, including not only the first generation with Canadian citizenship but also the second generation, to inland camps, one hundred miles away from the Pacific coast. According to La Violette, the evacuees were allocated to the following different types of projects and areas (Table 1).

The heads of the Steveston Japanese-Canadian household were distributed among different projects (Table 2).

In January, 1943, the federal government decided to liquidate all the properties left behind by the evacuees. Fishing boats, automobiles, houses, and land were auctioned and sold by the custodian at low prices, without the consent of the owners.[4]

In the case of forced evacuation, the Japanese Canadians were not given any choice whether to leave or to stay. But a choice was given in March, 1945, while the war was still going on. The evacuees in the internment camps and other project areas were visited by relocation officers accompanied by Mounted Police, and were asked whether or not, after the approaching end of the war, they wished to return to Japan. The government claimed that freedom of choice either to stay in Canada or to leave was given to the individuals. But from the point of view of the Japanese Canadians, it was a very difficult

Table 1

TYPES	NUMBER OF PERSONS
Road Camp Projects	986
Sugar-beet Projects	
Alberta	2,585
Manitoba	1,053
Ontario (males only)	350
Interior Housing	11,694
Self-Supporting Projects	1,161
Independent and Industrial Projects	431
Special Permits	1,337
Reparation to Japan	42
Evacuated voluntarily prior to March, 1942	579
Internment Camps	699
In Detention, Vancouver	57
Hastings Park Hospital	105
Total:	21,079[5]

Table 2

TYPES OF PROJECT	NUMBER OF HOUSEHOLD HEADS
Internment Camps	15
Road Camps	3
Interior Housing	46
Self-Supporting Projects	67
Sugar-beet Projects	106
Not Clear	10
Total:	247[6]

decision to make. In retrospect, Tomekichi Mio writes: 'To those who stated their wish to return to Japan, travelling expenses and other "preferential treatment" were provided by the government. In contrast, those who stated their wish to stay in Canada were told that they had to prove that they had found some stable job east of the Rocky Mountains. So it is too cruel to call those repatriates voluntary returners.'[7] In October, 1945, immediately following Japan's defeat, Clause G of the National Emergency Powers Act, Bill 15 was introduced in the House of Commons. Clause G, as explained by La Violette, 'proposed to control, as an emergency power, the "entry into Canada, exclusion and deportation, and revocation of nationality".'[8] There was an up-surge of protest against the bill led by the CCF (the Canadian socialist party), supported by the press and public opinion. So in place of the bill, the government issued orders-in-council that would make it possible, without parliamentary approval, to deport Japanese nationals and Canadian citizens of Japanese origin, who had made a written request for repatriation which was not revoked in writing prior to September 1, 1945—the day before the unconditional surrender paper was signed by Japan and the allied powers. Confronted with public protest, the Government, by an Order of Reference, asked the Supreme Court whether or not the orders-in-council were *ultra vires* of the Governor-in-Council. The judgement of the Supreme Court was split and not conclusive, which meant that the case should then be appealed to the Privy Council in London. Finally, in January, 1947, the Government decided to withdraw the orders-in-council. Thus, except for those who consistently expressed their intention to return to Japan and/or those 'recognized to be clearly and positively disloyal to Canada', no Japanese Canadians, including Japanese nationals, were to be deported against their will.[9]

As a result, it was made clear that a great number of the Japanese Canadians actually changed their minds. According to the statistics of the Department of Labour, 9,891 persons filed requests for repatriation before Japan's defeat, but only 3,964 persons actually returned after the war.[10] That is, two-thirds of those who signed for repatriation had changed their minds.

Three major reasons for Japanese Canadians to change their life-orientation from Japan to Canada may be pointed out: first, Japan's defeat; second, the betterment of living conditions in Canada; and third, the better prospects of their children in Canada. Let me describe those factors with reference to the life-history materials of the Steveston inhabitants:

(1) Japan's defeat—freedom from taboo

Although Japanese Canadians, during the war, were prohibited from owning or listening to short-wave radios, some of them, in secret, listened to the news given by the Japanese Imperial Headquarters, and shared the information thus acquired with fellow Japanese Canadians. 'Ninety per cent of us', in this way, 'expected that Japan should win.' The decision of seventy per cent of the Japanese Canadians to sign up for repatriation, before the end of the war, was presumably premised upon Japan's victory. Informed of the news of Japan's defeat, therefore, some of them were so utterly disappointed that they 'could not swallow anything but water for about a week'. Gradually, however, they came to accept the fact of defeat. Then they put portraits of George VI and Queen Elizabeth in place of those of the Emperor and the Empress, and eventually abandoned the rising-sun flag. This does not mean a sudden and conscious shift of loyalty from Japan to Canada. It was a more complex and subconscious process.

The Canadian high school principal whom I interviewed in Richmond, a town near Steveston, told me what he saw, during the war, when he visited one of the labour camps where Japanese Canadian men were interned: 'Around the camp, there was a fence neatly made of logs. Upon close scrutiny, I found that the logs were woven together in such an intriguing way as to show the Union Jack and the rising sun alternatingly.' The fence, made by the inmates, symbolized their bifocal attitudes of loyalty, before and during the war. We call it bifocal. That does not necessarily mean, however, that their loyalty is equally split between Canada and Japan. Let me quote the following story.

Urashima-san, born in 1890 in Mio village in Wakayama prefecture, arrived at Steveston in 1906, and had settled there until the Pacific War broke out. He was a fisherman and his wife worked in a cannery. They had no children:

> One day immediately before the war, the Japanese Consul, Mr Ukita, made a speech to the Japanese-Canadian group in Steveston. Should a war break out, he said, between Japan and Canada, those who had acquired Canadian citizenship would surely have an evil intention to fight against Japan. 'I do not', he continued, 'wish to speak to those "black-haired white men". If it were in Japan, their heads would be cut off. I, for myself, however, am a Japanese. I, therefore,

feel sorry for the "black-haired white men". So I advise you to sign your application to the Immigration Office for departure.' In order to acquire a fishing licence, one had to get Canadian citizenship. So all of us fishermen had Canadian citizenship. So we were all stunned and silenced by the consul, who, to us then, was just as supreme as the Emperor.

From the Japanese emigrants' point of view, they felt that they were under the constant surveillance of the Emperor system, through the medium of the government organization abroad. Although they were out of Japan, they still felt that they were bound by the taboo of Emperor worship. It was only through Imperial permission, they felt, that they were able to 'pledge loyalty' to Canada. A bartender in Steveston told me: 'It was an utter mistake to say that the Japanese Canadians here [before the war] were disloyal to Canada. It was our sincere intention to be loyal to the King. It was the Meiji Emperor that commanded us to be loyal to whatever country we might go and live in.' The Japanese Canadians, before and during the war were unifocal, rather than bifocal: the centre of loyalty was the Emperor, from whom loyalty to everything else emanated.

After Japan's defeat, however, a leading figure in the Buddhist church in Steveston reflected: 'We used to overworship the consul.' It was the impact of Japan's defeat that emancipated the minds of the emigrants from the psychological constraints of the Emperor and the consul, the Imperial government agency. They were thus free from the taboo. They became free to choose between the principle of loyalty to the Emperor (by going back to Japan) and the desire to be better off (by staying Canada).

(2) Betterment of living conditions—a gradual process of enforcing the decision to stay

When in 1946 the Japanese Canadians were given the final choice whether to return to Japan, with travelling expenses provided by the Canadian Government, or to stay in Canada, they were not certain what their prospective life might be like in Canada. In fact, it was not until 1947 that all the war-time regulations against them were lifted. It was only in April, 1949 that fishing licences equivalent to those of other Canadians were given to Japanese Canadians; legal discrimination in occupation was abolished, and they acquired the right to vote. Former residents gradually came back from their places of evacuation to Steveston around 1949. Before the war, the living standard of Japanese Canadians was reported to be relatively better than that of Chinese Canadians but among the lowest in comparison to Canadians in general.[11] In comparison, by 1959, their average income had increased to such an extent as to be placed in the middle or upper middle brackets in relation to the income distribution of Canadians in general.[12] Before the war, the Japanese Canadians mostly used to send money back to support their families or to deposit for prospective retirement in their native villages in Japan. But after the war, they stopped sending money to Japan, except to support their elderly parents, if necessary. This also increased the amount of money available for their own expenditures.

The change in living standards occurred gradually within some ten years after the war. In 1946 when the Japanese Canadians had to make the final decision to stay, therefore, an improvement in actual living conditions was not the immediate reason for *chinjimari* to stay in Canada. The rising living standard was, for them, a reassurance that the decision to stay was right. The betterment of their life functioned as a psychological reenforcement of their Canada-directedness.

Kamata-san was born in 1886, in Makurazaki, Kagoshima prefecture. He came to Steveston before World War I. His wife was born in the same town in 1896, was registered to be married to him in 1916, and came to Steveston, 1918. They were cross-cousins. When she first arrived, the couple began their life in a shabby little cannery house. Mrs Kamata reminisced:

> Through an opening in the floor boards, I was surprised to look into the sea right under my feet. We borrowed a small boat, and we worked hard together to save money to buy a boat.
>
> In 1934, my mother-in-law became ill, and we both went home. But my husband returned to Canada, leaving me alone to take care of the invalid. I spent six years in Japan until the death of my mother-in-law in 1940. My husband, during those years, never sent money to us, so I had to work as a dress-maker to support ourselves and to nurse the sick person at the same time. Thus I experienced a truly hard time in Japan.
>
> It was just a year before the Pacific War started that my husband finally managed to buy a boat. So I went back to Steveston. When the war broke out, we had to sell the boat to make money for travelling expenses for evacuation. The rest of our property was all confiscated. In April, 1942, we were forced to move to Alberta, where we made a contract to work on ten acres of land for 375 dollars. We cultivated sugar beets there. It was very hard toil to cultivate ten acres of land, indeed.
>
> After the war, we returned to Steveston in 1955 and bought this house (a living room, two bedrooms, a kitchen, and a bathroom, with a front garden and two acres of land at the back) where we are living now.
>
> We are grateful now to be free. At the cannery where I work, I can talk freely. I am now living without being worried about what others might think of me. If I were in Japan, life must have been very different. There, we have always to be aware of class distinctions, and to speak and act accordingly. Back at home we are duty bound to restore our ancestral grave, damaged during the war. When it

is done, we are willing to bury our bones in Canada, since this is the place where we have been working most of our life.

Kamata-san, at seventy-three, was still working as a fisherman. He and his wife acquired Canadian citizenship in 1948:

Before the war, I always wanted to go back to Japan. In fact, I made seven trips back. We had two houses built in Makurazaki, so that we might enjoy a good life there after retirement. During the war, however, the houses went into ashes by bombing. That is why we lost our interest in going back to Japan.

This a great country for workers. Since we began to go to church, we have come to feel grateful for our life here. In the fridge we have plenty of fish always on hand. At the back of our house we have two acres of land, where my wife work hard so as to harvest garden radishes and greens twice a year. After all, this is a great country. When the season comes, the Government takes measures to stop fishing to prevent overfishing and to protect the fish for growing.

Although Kamata-san estimated their own living standard to be in a lower bracket, within the context of the Steveston community in 1959, only forty per cent of the Japanese Canadians in Steveston then owned their houses, while the rest were either still living in cannery houses or in apartments. So as far as housing is concerned, Kamata-san was at least in the middle or upper middle bracket.

With reference to income from fishing, however, he is a 'low boat', since he is old, and recently injured himself in an accident. Nevertheless, he was receiving a pension, and his wife was working in the cannery. With their two incomes put together, the couple was leading a stable, if not leisurely, life. Besides, Mrs Kamata's experience of hardship in Japan between 1934 and 1940 contributed, by way of contrast, to their deepening appreciation of their life in Canada.

(3) Children—hope for the future

Mizutani-san, an auto-repair engineer, was born in 1900 in Yuge-chō, Ehime prefecture. His wife was born in the same town, in 1911. Together with their four children, they lived in a handsome house (living room, three bedrooms, kitchen and bathroom) in Richmond, where the majority of the inhabitants were white middle-class Canadians. They owned a second house in Kaslo, B.C., which they said was being rented to a white Canadian family. They estimated their living standard as of the middle rank with reference to the Japanese-Canadian community in Steveston. Both Mr and Mrs Mizutani held Japanese citizenship, while their eldest son and their second daughter had dual citizenship, and the second and third sons held Canadian citizenship. Mizutani-san told me:

My father left for Canada when I was a child, and worked in a saw-mill there. At the age of seventeen, I joined my father to work in the same saw-mill, which was closed when I was twenty-one. Then I went to Vancouver, and got interested in automobiles, since they were running on their own. I had saved the three years' wages I had earned at the saw-mill, and with this money I entered mechanics' school in Vancouver for six months. In 1936, I became the owner of a gas station, hiring men to work for me. From that time on, I have intended to stay here in Canada.

Mizutani-san has, ever since, been consistently Canada-directed. In contrast, his wife intended to return to Japan before, during and immediately after the war. She told her own story of how she came to change her mind:

During the war, my husband was sent to a road camp, and our children and myself were forced to evacuate to Kaslo, where I was asked just before the end of the war, whether I would pledge loyalty to this country or wished to return to Japan. We signed for repatriation. Since my mother-in-law was still alive in Japan, I thought I should go back to Japan to look after her. Before the war, there was such discrimination against the Japanese Canadians that even the college-educated ones among them were not able to get decent jobs. So most of us sent our children back to Japan to be educated. Now that our children may get white-collar jobs here in Canada, according to their qualifications, they do not wish to go back to Japan. This changing situation urged me to change my mind, and I decided to stay here. Besides, the wife of my husband's younger brother reassured me that he would take care of our family back at home. So being freed from obligations to our family at home, I now feel at ease to bury my bones here. When my mother-in-law passes away, we shall apply for Canadian citizenship.

It was the children's career prospects that changed Mrs Mizutani from being Japan-oriented to being Canada-oriented. Her eldest son, after finishing senior high school, worked as a primary school teacher for two years. With money saved from his salary he now attends the University of British Columbia. After graduating from university, he will be qualified to be a high school teacher. The eldest daughter died prematurely; the second son and the second daughter attend high school, while the third son goes to a primary school. On all these children Mrs Mizutani hinges her hopes for the future.

It is also the influence of her children that contributes to her re-evaluation of their war-time experiences. Most of the first-generation Japanese Canadians whom I interviewed complained bitterly about injustices done them during the war by the Canadian government. In contrast, many second-generation Japanese Canadians said that the fact that they were forced to live, during the war, among white Canadians had a 'mixing' effect upon the Japanese Canadians, who had hitherto lived in self-imposed seclusion. According to their evaluation, the mixing had a positive effect on the Japanese Canadians. Mrs Mizutani continued:

> Just at the time when we had finally paid off our debts by working hard for six years as the owners of the gas station, the war broke out, and our gas station was confiscated. We became penniless. When my husband was sent to the road camp, and we were forced to evacuate to Kaslo, I entrusted the key to the custodian to take care of our house and other properties. I made a complete list of the properties we left, for which we had never been compensated. After the war, JCCA (the Japanese-Canadian Association) filed application to the Government for compensation. Some people got some money back while others didn't. We could not afford to submit our case to the court. It costs too much money to do so.
>
> In Kaslo, my boss thought it was not just to separate a husband from his wife, and he managed to get my husband back to live with us in Kaslo. During the war, he worked as a mechanic to earn two hundred dollars a month, which was barely enough to make our living. After the war, he worked in a coal mine in Kaslo for two and a half years, while I worked as a dress-maker for white women. That was the way we bought our present house in Richmond to start all over again.

While she talked, tears overflowed her eyes. But when I asked her for which party she voted in the last election in 1958, her line of thought took another direction.

> I voted for Social Credit [a conservative party].[13] Although I was reluctant, neighbours recommended me to do so, so I did. There are split opinions. Some white people say that the Japanese Canadians were excluded under the Conservative government, so we shouldn't vote for them. Then some Japanese-Canadian friends told me now that the misfortune turned into blessing, we could forget about our past suffering. It is true that thanks to war-time evacuation, which forced us to live among the whites, the second generation Japanese Canadians are now getting good jobs and earning good money. Our children tell us not to make too much fuss about compensation for the injustices done to us. If we do, they are afraid of losing the chances for them to get ahead in Canadian society.

Her attitude toward Canadian society was ambivalent. She was trying, not quite successfully, to suppress her sense of injustices inflicted upon her and her family by the Government, by persuading herself that all's well if it ends well. Unless the traumatic experiences of the Japanese-Canadians, especially those of the first generation like Mrs Mizutani, can be healed, it will be very difficult for them to be Canadian citizens whole-heartedly.

Oota-san, an intellectual and economic leader of the Steveston community, expressed his view on this point:

> During the war, the custodians auctioned the Japanese Canadians' houses and other properties at the rate of one third to one half of the current prices. After the war, the JCCA took the lead to negotiate with the Government. As a result, the Government gave out one million dollars to the Japanese Canadians as a whole. It was much too little. The American compensation to the Japanese Americans was more thorough-going. It was due to the Canadian Government's war-time measure vis-à-vis the Japanese Canadians that almost half a century's hard labour was totally lost. Yet the Government has never admitted its error. Neither the German Canadians nor the Italian Canadians, although they were 'enemy aliens', were treated like the Japanese Canadians. But under the emergency, it could not have been helped. We, on our part, should admit that both police and Mounted Police were kind to us, and we have never experienced any insufferable personal persecution. It is also good that after the war legal discrimination against us was abolished. It is not that the war was good, but the outcome of the war has been good for the Japanese Canadians.

Oota-san makes clear the distinction between what was just and what was unjust. He proposed, as early as in 1956, that the government should publicly admit that its treatment of the Japanese Canadians during the war was unfair, and take some measure to rectify the situation.[14]

On November 21, 1984, the National Association of Japanese Canadians (NAJC) submitted to the Government of Canada the proposal entitled: 'Democracy Betrayed: The Case for Redress'. It reported in detail instances of 'the violation of rights and freedoms of Japanese Canadians during and after World War II', and proposed that the Government should promise to enter into negotiation with the NAJC to redress those violations.[15]

On September 22, 1988, the Canadian Government and the NAJC reached an agreement on redress. It included the following items: the Canadian Government recognized that their treatment of the Japanese Canadians during and after World War II was unjust; a redress payment of twenty-one thousand dollars shall be made to every survivor who is entitled to redress—one who was forced to evacuate or sent to a concentration camp, and whose properties were confiscated; the payment of twelve million dollars shall be made through NAJC, to the Japanese-Canadian communities, for the purpose of carrying out educational, social, and cultural activities and projects to promote welfare and protection of their human rights.[16]

The implementation of the agreement is still under way. By March 31, 1990, out of the 17,974 applications submitted to the Government, 15,570 had received a redress payment. Out of the applications from Canada, ninety per cent were approved, while of those from Japan, thirty-eight per cent have been approved. Out of the applications from Canada, Japan and other places, eighty-seven per cent have been approved.[17]

Recently I telephoned the Canadian Embassy in Tokyo and enquired about 'reparation'. The woman in charge emphatically rejected my wording, saying 'it is not reparation, it is *redress*'. I eventually figured out the difference between reparation and redress: in order to make reparation, one has to make an estimate of the amount of damage incurred. But for redress, it is not the amount of money lost that is important; the payment symbolizes a recognition of the injustices done and the will to rectify the situation so that similar violations of rights and freedoms might not be repeated. Such was exactly what those Japanese Canadians whom I interviewed more than thirty years ago wished to have realized.

Now Japan is faced with similar problems *vis-à-vis* the Koreans, Chinese and other Asian people upon whom we inflicted injustices and calamities during and after World War II. Could we, the Japanese, possibly learn a lesson from the Canadian model of redressing the past?

○

The Missionary Connection

The missionary movement from Canada to Japan made a significant contribution to the development of the Christian movement in Japan during the late nineteenth and early twentieth centuries. Yet the influence of Canadian missionaries also extended far beyond the Christian sphere. Through their educational and social work and their role in introducing new Western ideas and social pursuits, the activities of Canadian missionaries had an impact on many different facets of society and culture in Japan.

Among the many significant activities in which Canadian missionaries were engaged in Japan, the promotion of modern education, especially among women, stands out. Although limited by lack of resources, the social work undertaken by missionaries pioneered work in some hitherto neglected areas. The activities of Catholic missionaries have been described by Joseph Jennes in The History of the Catholic Church in Japan *(Tokyo: 1959) as well as by Otis Carey in* A History of Christianity in Japan *(Tokyo: 1976) and Richard H. Drummond in* A History of Christianity in Japan *(Grand Rapids, Michigan: 1971). In this chapter, Professor Ion focuses on the role of Canadian Protestant missionaries in the formation of early Christian Bands in Tokyo, Shizuoka, Numazu and Kofu during the eighteen-seventies. For it is during those years when George Cochran was teaching at Nakamura Keiu's Dojinsha school and A.C. Shaw at Fukuzawa Yukichi's Keio Gijuku that Canadian influence on Japanese intellectual life was at its most pronounced. Above all, missionaries residing in Japan served as a link between citizens of Japan and Canada and, save for the sole exception of the late nineteen-thirties, acted as trusted interpreters of things Japanese to their home constituents.*

A. Hamish Ion studied at McGill and Sheffield, was a Visiting Scholar at Doshisha University and a researcher at the University of Hokkaido and Tokyo Joshi Daigaku. He currently teaches modern Japanese history at the Royal Military College of Canada, Kingston, Ontario and is the author most recently of The Cross and the Rising Sun: The Canadian Protestant Missionary Movement in the Japanese Empire, 1872-1931 (Waterloo: Wilfrid Laurier University Press, 1990).

AMBASSADORS OF THE CROSS: CANADIAN MISSIONARIES IN JAPAN

A. Hamish Ion

Although Japan had had contact with the West since the sixteenth century, the tempo of Westernization quickened following the Meiji Restoration of 1868. Protestant missionaries from Canada were among those who played an important part in acquainting ordinary Japanese with Western ideas. These Canadian men and women practised international relations of an informal and personal variety, and their experiences at 'the opposite side of the earth' emphasize the human and humanitarian dimensions within the history of the Canadian-Japanese relationship.

Between 1873 and the establishment of the Tokyo Embassy in 1928[1], only a small amount of trade was carried on between Canada and Japan; this slight economic and political involvement did not supply a substantial basis upon which to build mutual understanding. Meanwhile, Canada's policy of restricting Japanese immigration in order to keep Canada a 'white man's country' limited the growth of a Japanese immigrant community in Canada which could act as an alternative means of cultural diffusion. Hence the missionary movement provided the only continuous contact between Canadians and Japanese, and the years between 1873 and 1941 can rightly be termed the 'Missionary Age' in the history of Canadian-Japanese relations.

Peter Mitchell and Margo Gewurtz have observed that 'for sixty years from the mid-1890s, East Asian countries were the setting for the most significant, sustained Canadian overseas endeavour anywhere in the world. Except for the two world wars, this missionary enterprise . . . constituted undoubtedly the largest organized and stable Canadian presence abroad.'[2] Canada's efforts formed a major element in the attempt during the late nineteenth and early twentieth centuries to evangelize the people of East Asia. Only the United States and Great Britain contributed more money and personnel. Counting French-Canadian Roman Catholic fathers and sisters, Canada had by the early nineteen-thirties (according to the Canadian Legation in Tokyo) more missionaries in the Japanese Empire—Metropolitan Japan, Korea and Taiwan—than any other single country.

Before 1941, a missionary from Canada living in a Japanese city was the only Canadian with whom the ordinary Japanese had contact. The missionaries served as living encyclopedias of things Western and models of Canadian society. Their impact was not immediate, but accumulated over time. They linked ordinary people living in small provincial towns in the interior of Japan to the outside world, and were prepared to strive actively to improve ordinary people's material well-being. For many Japanese, the memory of Canadian missionaries who lived in their midst in central Japan during the pre-Pacific War era remains a lasting one,[3] and a legacy of goodwill toward Canada remains one product of the spiritual and secular activities of those Canadians.

The Canadian Protestant missionary experience is typified by the activities of missionaries belonging to the United Church of Canada (and its pre-union Methodist predecessor) and the Anglican Church of Canada. Yet the Canadian presence in Japan went beyond those who worked for the Canadian Methodist and Anglican missions. Some individual Canadians played important roles in the development of other missions. Two graduates of Trinity College, University of Toronto, A.C. Shaw and William Gemmill worked in Japan under the auspices of the Society for the Propagation of the Gospel in Foreign Parts (SPG). Their SPG colleague, Arthur Lloyd, sometime professor at Trinity College and headmaster of its junior school, was another famous missionary with strong Canadian connections. Arthur Lea, a graduate of Wycliffe College, University of Toronto, who served with the Church Missionary Society (CMS), became the Bishop of Kyushu. Benjamin Chappell, a Nova Scotian who worked for the Methodist Episcopal Church, North mission, taught for many years at Aoyama Gakuin in Tokyo. Two Canadian women, Caroline Macdonald and Emma Kaufman, were instrumental in establishing the YWCA in Japan.[4] The distinguished careers of these individual missionaries made a further contribution to the significant influence that Canadians in the missionary movement had upon Japanese society.

THE BEGINNINGS OF CANADIAN MISSIONARY WORK

At the annual meeting of its Missionary Society in October 1871, the Wesleyan Methodist Church in Canada first proposed the establishment of an overseas mission. By the next annual meeting, Japan had been chosen as the mission field, a choice no doubt influenced by the presence of the Iwakura Embassy in North America, which had done much to heighten interest in Japan. On 30 June 1873, the two pioneer missionaries of the Wesleyan Methodist Missionary

Society, George Cochran and Davidson McDonald, and their families arrived in Yokohama.

The Canadian Anglicans began their work in Japan some years later. In 1887, the autonomous *Nippon Seikokai* (Holy Catholic Church of Japan) was formed in Osaka by one American and two British Anglican missions. In response to their appeal for missionary reinforcements, John Cooper Robinson, the first Canadian Anglican missionary, was sent to Japan. A graduate of Wycliffe College and a Low Church Anglican, Robinson worked for most of his career in Nagoya,[5] part of the diocese of South Tokyo. The High Anglican wing of the Church of England in Canada sent their first missionary, J.G. Waller, in 1890. A graduate of Trinity College, Waller established himself in Nagano in 1892.[6]

Very quickly women missionaries extended their work into the mission field. The Woman's Missionary Society (WMS) of the Canadian Methodist Church of Canada owed its genesis in 1880 to the needs of the mission field in Japan. Although independent of the male Missionary Society, even to the point of paying its own missionaries, the WMS was to work in harmony with the authorities of the Methodist Church of Canada—or so it was hoped. Tensions did arise, especially when the women found their male colleagues inclined to disregard the autonomy of the WMS. Rosemary B. Gagan has described the relationship between male and female Canadian missionaries between 1881 and 1895 as 'two sexes warring in the bosom of a single mission station,' but by and large in Japan the WMS and its male counterpart co-operated successfully.[7]

In late 1882 Martha J. Cartmell, the WMS's first missionary, arrived in Tokyo. She was responsible for the establishment of the *Toyo Eiwa Jo Gakko*, the Canadian Methodist school for girls in Roppongi, Tokyo, which opened its doors in 1884.[8] The WMS saw female education as one of the major areas in which women missionaries could play a valuable role. They felt that they could also make an important contribution to evangelistic work, because Japanese women would perhaps be more at ease with a woman visiting their homes.

Coming later into mission work than the Methodists, the Canadian Anglicans saw from the start the need for single female missionaries, and the Anglican Wycliffe College Missionary Society sponsored Miss E.M. Trent in 1894. Among other early Canadian Anglican women missionaries were Miss Louise Patterson, who built St Mary's Church in Matsumoto; Miss Young, who was influential in establishing a kindergarten school in Nagoya; Deaconess A.L. Archer, who was a dedicated evangelist among female factory workers, and Loretta Shaw who taught at the British Anglican Poole Memorial School in Osaka.[9] The major area of endeavour for the Canadian Anglican women missionaries, as with their Canadian Methodist counterparts, was women's education and evangelistic work among women. Although some of the women missionaries had excellent academic credentials, they were prohibited because of their sex from becoming priests. Further, because most, especially those engaged in evangelistic work, were single women, they were expected to endure a degree of isolation and even physical hardship their married male counterparts refused to accept. Without the backbone of self-sacrificing single women missionaries, the Canadian missionary endeavour in Japan would have had little impact beyond the successes of its first years.

EARLY YEARS IN JAPAN

George Cochran and Davidson McDonald arrived in Japan in mid-1873 intending to establish a Methodist Church patterned on the Canadian model. In their determination to duplicate Western church organization as well as the church's theology and discipline, they made few concessions to the sensibilities of Japanese culture and society, and it is somewhat surprising that they were able to make any headway at all. But make headway they did, partly because they responded to an immediate need in early Meiji Japan—the great demand for English-language teachers in schools specializing in Western studies.

Early Japanese converts were drawn to Christianity by five major factors: nationalist feeling, the search for higher moral values, personal ambition, peer pressure, and the personality of the missionary or Japanese mentor. The first Japanese Protestants believed that their conversion would benefit Japan because Christianity was thought to be the essence of Western civilization—a civilization which many felt Japan must adopt in order to hasten its modernization. Many also felt that Christianity offered a higher moral code to fill the vacuum left after Confucianism had been discredited with the fall of the Tokugawa *Bakufu*. Personal ambition also attracted some to Christianity initially, for it became apparent that those who possessed advanced Western knowledge and mastered the English language improved their employment opportunities in the new Japan. For others, the influence of friends and classmates was often a decisive element in their conversion, for Christian ideas were largely disseminated through skeins of friends and acquaintances. The charisma, erudition, and sympathetic personality of the missionary or the example of a Japanese mentor also encouraged the young and often naïve students, who made up the majority of converts, to become Christians. The attraction of Christianity did not lie in its spiritual beliefs or ideas. In this fact as well as in the pragmatic approach of the Japanese to conversion lay the seeds of future disappointment and frustration for missionaries.

During the halcyon days of the mid-eighteen-seventies, the two Canadian Methodist missionaries formed separate groups of Japanese converts: the Koishikawa Band in Tokyo, centred in Nakamura Keiu's Dojinsha School, and the Shizuoka Band, made up of McDonald's students in the city of Shizuoka. From these two Bands came many of the Japanese workers and pastors who contributed to the success of Canadian work in later years. Meanwhile, A.C. Shaw of the SPG, who also arrived in Japan in the summer of 1873, was acting as tutor to the children of Fukuzawa Yukichi and teaching moral science at Keio Gijuku, Fukuzawa's private school.

In the fall of 1873, Edward Warren Clark, an American layman who was a contract teacher at the Gakumonjo school,[10] was to leave Shizuoka for the Kaisei Gakko in Tokyo, the forerunner of the Tokyo Imperial University. The Shizuoka authorities asked George Cochran to replace Clark as English teacher. Cochran declined the offer, but Davidson McDonald consented to go in his stead.

In April 1874, McDonald and his wife arrived in Shizuoka where they would spend the next four years teaching and undertaking medical work. The embodiment of things Western in Shizuoka, the McDonalds and their Ontario school primers helped lay the foundations of English-language education; contributed to the development of Western-style medical practice; aided in stimulating interest in women's education; and influenced a generation of Christians in the city. McDonald built on the earlier work of Clark, who had conducted the first Bible classes in Shizuoka, and his initial success was greatly aided by Sugiyama Magaroku, a Japanese Christian who came from a prestigious family. By 1878, when McDonald left Shizuoka, he had laid the foundation of a church with some sixty members who proved quite capable of continuing the church.

The acquisition of Western learning opened new opportunities for the young converts as English teachers, journalists and pastors. Though very few of them gained national prominence either in the Christian or the secular spheres, these converts did have a significant local impact in Shizuoka prefecture, especially in the development of Western-style education.[11] They had belonged to the losing Tokugawa side in the Restoration struggle, and Western studies provided one means of overcoming the disadvantages of being barred from political power. These opportunities, however, were limited. In any case, for many of the first converts, acquiring the English language and Western knowledge diverted and forestalled whatever secular ambitions they might have had. At the same time as they were learning English from the McDonalds, the first members of the Shizuoka Band members also developed a very strong sense of loyalty to the McDonalds and to their Christian ideas. The early converts became evangelists; some later became pastors, and in doing so consciously chose to forfeit any chance of secular success. In their turn, they attempted to create their own group of disciples who would look up to them as they had looked up to Davidson McDonald.

Just as contact with Edward Warren Clark had led to the opportunity for McDonald in Shizuoka, it was Clark who introduced Nakamura Keiu (Masanao) to George Cochran. Nakamura, a famous Confucian scholar, was searching for a mentor in things Western, and was greatly impressed by Cochran's erudition. He asked Cochran and his family to live and teach at the Dojinsha school, a private school which he had founded in Koishikawa, Tokyo to educate the sons of Tokugawa ex-samurai.

Nakamura was a leading member of the Meirokusha, a learned society devoted both to Japan's modernization and to the campaign for enlightenment. Nakamura's widely-read translations of Samuel Smiles's *Self-Help* and John Stuart Mill's *On Liberty* influenced many Meiji youths in favour of enhanced political freedom and self-advancement.[12] Nakamura had been baptized a Christian while he had been in England during the late eighteen-sixties, and so had some knowledge of Christianity before Cochran came to live at the Dojinsha school. On Christmas morning 1874 Cochran, at Nakamura's request, baptized him. This act encouraged the staff and students at the Dojinsha school to become Christians. Within the space of five years, from 1874 to 1879, an important Christian group was formed. The Koishikawa Band had in Nakamura a man with a national reputation and a leading advocate of modernization in Japan. The Koishikawa Band were his disciples, protected by his prestige; the Band's existence legitimized the conversion of others. As a group identified with Nakamura, the Band also played a part in the educational and intellectual endeavours associated with his name from 1874 until 1879. Among these activities were his writings in the influential journal *Meiroku Zasshi* and in the publication of the *Dojinsha Bungaku Zasshi*, another important magazine. More importantly, they included the establishment of the Dojinsha girls' school in 1875, where Mrs Cochran taught.

George Cochran saw his own role in the context of evangelistic effort, but he acted as a necessary catalyst to the overall activity of Nakamura and the Koishikawa Band. For them, Cochran was essential in two ways: first, as a Christian authority who reinforced their Christian ideas and second, as a living reference book on things Western. Cochran, like McDonald in Shizuoka or Clark before him, stimulated both Christian ideas and other intellectual activities. Though Nakamura developed his interest in the education of women and young children independently, these were precisely the fields in which the Canadian missionaries were also interested. Missionaries realized that the Christian message alone was not enough to attract converts and that they had to become involved in secular activities to enhance the appeal of their religion. Yet to suggest that missionaries were motivated only by pragmatism would be wrong, for most sincerely believed that their role was not only to save the souls of Japanese people but also to improve the conditions of their lives. Their concern with the welfare of the Japanese was one reason why enquirers were attracted to them.

Like Cochran at the Dojinsha, by Christmas 1875 A.C. Shaw had baptized a number of his students at the Keio Gijuku, including Ozakki Yukio who later became an important politician.[13] The student converts formed the nucleus of the congregation of St Andrew's Church, Shiba, Tokyo which opened in the summer of 1876. However, Shaw wrote that the conversion of the Keio students was exceptionally difficult because the school was 'one in which the most advanced opinions on all subjects are held, and in which Mr Mill's and Mr Spencer's writings are used as textbooks.'[14] Shaw also spent some of his time responding to the numerous attacks on Christianity appearing in Japanese papers. His experience was certainly different from that of Cochran at the Dojinsha. Nakamura was already a Christian, and Fukuzawa patently was not; thus Cochran did not have to defend his Christian faith. It was just as well that Shaw did not restrict his evangelistic efforts to students; he also held public meetings which a variety of people attended.

In 1877, Shaw concluded that the evangelization of Japan needed a trained Japanese ministry.[15] By this time, Cochran had also come to realize the importance of training Japanese evangelists. Shaw and other British Anglican SPG missionaries continued to have a close association with Keio Gijuku, but by 1877 Shaw's efforts were directed toward the development of missionary-controlled schools and the training of a Japanese ministry.

While Shaw, Cochran, and McDonald were still working in private schools in Tokyo or Shizuoka, two new Canadian Methodist missionaries, George Meacham and Charles S. Eby, arrived in Japan in September 1876. Within a few weeks Meacham took a contract-teaching position at a private school in Numazu.[16] The crucial conversion of the school's headmaster, Ebara Soroku, in January 1877 opened the way for members of staff and students to convert to Christianity. In his evangelistic work in Numazu, Meacham was greatly helped by some of the Shizuoka converts of McDonald. Indeed, the conversion of Ebara was influenced more by these helpers, who could explain things Christian in Japanese, than by Meacham.[17]

After eighteen months in Numazu, Meacham had gathered around him a group of thirty-seven converts. But in the early summer of 1878, Ebara's school burned down and Meacham was forced to return to Tokyo. Christian work in Numazu continued to be carried on by Japanese evangelists whom Cochran had trained in Tokyo. Once Meacham had returned to Tokyo, he helped form the Shitaya Church, a second Canadian Methodist congregation. Later in the eighteen-eighties, Meacham taught theological students in the Canadian Methodist mission school, the Toyo Eiwa Gakko, and became the minister to the Western congregation at the Yokohama Union Church.

Shortly after Meacham's departure from Numazu, Charles S. Eby, who had remained in Tokyo to help Cochran, was offered a teaching post in Yamanashi Prefecture. The offer stemmed from an evangelistic trip Eby had undertaken with Hiraiwa Yoshiyasu, later an outstanding Japanese pastor, in the summer of 1877 to a small village called Nambu in Yamanashi Prefecture.[18] Although Eby deemed Nambu too small to merit a resident missionary, he decided in 1878 to accept an offer to teach a group of young men in nearby Kofu, the Prefectural seat. It was arranged that Mrs Eby would handle the bulk of the English teaching to leave Eby time to proselytize. Like Meacham in Numazu, Eby was also assisted by Japanese helpers who came from Shizuoka and Tokyo.

From Kofu, Eby made frequent trips into the surrounding countryside, travelling by horse, *jinriksha*, or on foot, and preaching wherever he went. Many years later he recalled that 'In Kofu we put in two and a half of the happiest years of my life'. [19] Despite this, and the fact that over forty converts had been made in Kofu, Eby returned to Tokyo in 1881. The church in Kofu, like those in Shizuoka and Numazu, was developed and continued solely by Japanese pastors. Not until 1887, when John W. Saunby was sent to Kofu, did the Canadian Methodists have a clerical missionary resident in the city.

The churches Eby and Meacham left behind in Kofu and Numazu have certain similarities with the first two mission centres. Like the Koishikawa Band, which had Nakamura Keiu as its leader, the Numazu group was led by Ebara Soroku, a man of local prominence. Also like the Koishikawa Band, the Kofu church expanded as the male members converted their immediate families to Christianity. Before his conversion, Ebara Soroku had decided that Christianity was the best religion in the world, while another convert, Kobayashi Mitsuyasu of the Kofu group, found that 'when reading Wilson's Universal History . . . he discovered the great power of Christianity in promoting the world's civilization'. [20] These men saw Christianity as a great civilizing power and therefore useful for Japan.

Christianity's appeal lay in its moral code. Ebara's and Kobayashi's views of Christianity resembled those of the converts of the Koishikawa Band, for the converts of the first four Canadian Methodist groups were drawn from the same stock of ex-Tokugawa supporters, who looked to the acquisition of Western learning as a means of improving their own and Japan's future. Hence Christianity spread through a tangled web of personal connections, as much as through the force of its ideas. In reality, the ideas of Christianity remained secondary to the relationship between the convert and the group leader. Once the leader had accepted Christianity, his close disciples would eventually follow him. The Shizuoka and Koishikawa Bands were formed during the mid-eighteen-seventies, when the intellectual climate in Japan was sympathetic toward Christianity, but by the time the Kofu group was formed this sympathetic climate was fast disappearing.

The example of the first four Canadian Methodist centres demonstrates that Christianity needed a favourable atmosphere to become established. It also points to the essential role played by Japanese evangelists in expanding the various groups. Finally it suggests that the individual missionary might not always be aware of the reasons for his success or failure. On the other hand, without the missionaries, the four groups of Christians would not have been formed.

EBY AND THE IMMEDIATE CHRISTIANIZATION OF JAPAN

When Charles Eby returned to Tokyo from Kofu, the combativeness in his volatile nature was provoked by the challenge of scientific scepticism. Darwin had gained an enthusiastic following among some Japanese—in part because his theories provided an argument from Western science which could be used to discredit Christianity. Darwin's theories seemed to offer an assurance that Japan's national goals could be achieved, and so were especially popular with Japanese intellectuals. Christianity, meanwhile, became their immediate target, for it was now seen as one manifestation of the foreign interference which hindered progress toward fulfilling those goals.

Concerned missionaries responded by co-operating together to stem the tide of scepticism. In 1881 they began publication of the *Chrysanthemum* magazine, which Eby was to edit until its demise in 1883. During its short life, the magazine provided a significant forum for the views of the Japanese missionary community. A forum was needed to combat attacks on Christianity, for as Davidson McDonald lamented in 1882, 'it seems that every form of unbelief in the Western world is likely to appear in Japan.'²¹ McDonald may have had Nakamura Keiu in mind when he wrote this, for in the early eighteen-eighties Nakamura drifted away from Canadian influence and toward newly introduced Unitarianism.

In 1883 and 1884 Eby arranged a series of public lectures aimed at blunting attacks based on scientific scepticism; he argued that Christianity was necessary for the Japanese to achieve their national goals. Although these lectures received considerable publicity, their lasting influence is uncertain. Nevertheless, by 1884 the attitude toward Christianity had changed, reflecting a new pro-Western mood in Japan, stimulated by preparations for the promulgation of a western-style Japanese constitution.

Though the Meiji Constitution would not be proclaimed until 1889, the five preceding years were marked by a strong pro-Western feeling. This changed mood encouraged much new interest in Christianity, with the change marked by mass meetings of Japanese Christians in Ueno Park in Tokyo during May 1883. It was against this background that Eby delivered a speech calling for a tremendous inter-denominational effort to propagate Christianity. He thought at least a hundred missionaries should be involved in direct evangelistic work, and advocated the establishment of a central Apologetical Institute of Christian Philosophy, complete with lecture hall, library, and publishing house. He also suggested the creation of a national Christian University, which would not only offer more advantages than the Tokyo Imperial University but also rival the best universities in the West.[22] The foreign missionary community enthusiastically approved Eby's ideas, but in the circumstances of the eighteen-eighties they were impractical. Eby failed to get more than moral support from other missionaries working in Japan, and looked to the Canadian Methodist Church to put his ideas into action.

On furlough in Canada in 1886, Eby proposed the formation of the Self-Support Band, to supply auxiliary workers to the Canadian Methodist mission without expense to the Mission Board. In conceiving this idea, Eby was greatly influenced by the marked success of Hudson Taylor's China Inland Mission, which by 1885 had some six hundred and forty missionaries working in all but three of the Chinese provinces.[23] Eby envisioned the Self-Support Band working in conjunction with the Canadian Methodist mission to supply the demand for English teachers in Japanese schools. It was an excellent idea—one that the YMCA and secular organizations in different Western countries later put into general practice. Like so many of Eby's ideas, however, it was ahead of its time. Eby possessed immense charisma, enthusiasm, and dynamism, but he lacked the patience to work out details properly. More than that, he had no sense when it came to money. Opinion among Canadian Methodist missionaries in Japan was divided over the usefulness of the Self-Support Band. The more cautious, headed by Davidson McDonald, feared that Eby's schemes would lead the Canadian Methodist Mission in Japan into difficulties. They did.

Nonetheless, between 1887 and 1891 (when Eby dissolved the Self-Support Band on the grounds of lack of moral support from the Canadian Methodist Missionary Society), twelve volunteers came out to Japan under this scheme. Some, like John W. Saunby, D.R. McKenzie, and Harper H. Coates, would be pillars of the Canadian Methodist Mission for the next thirty or forty years.

Eby's evangelistic leadership stimulated the Japanese desire for greater local autonomy. Given the widespread desire of Japanese Christians for greater independence from missionary control, the Canadian Methodists were quite prepared to go halfway. Their solution was to elevate the Japan mission to the status of a Missionary Conference, which would give the mission in Japan equal status with the various Canadian Conferences within the Methodist Church. There were two exceptions: the Missionary Conference could elect representatives to the General Conference of the Methodist Church only with Mission Board authorization, and it could not interfere in any way with the administration of the Mission Board. The creation of the Japan Conference in 1889 set the organizational structure for the Canadian mission in Japan until, in 1907, the Canadian mission and the two American Methodist Episcopal missions would join to create a united Japan Methodist Church.

In the meantime, Eby began pressing for an evangelistic headquarters in Tokyo, in the neighbourhood of the Imperial University, with the aim of converting students. He wanted this vast church to be an interdenominational endeavour, but he was unable to get financial support from other missions. While in Canada in 1886, Eby began fund-raising for his church project, and in 1890 the Central Tabernacle Church, smaller than Eby envisaged but still with a seating capacity of six hundred, was built close to Tokyo Imperial University. It burned down in 1891 and was rebuilt the same year. It remained the largest Canadian Methodist church in Japan until its destruction in the Tokyo earthquake of 1923. In one sense, the Tabernacle stood as the crowning achievement of the Canadian Methodist mission in the eighteen-eighties, but it also represented the dangerous over-optimism engendered by the growth of that decade. The Central Tabernacle's evangelistic programs never met much success among the student population of Tokyo, but its operation needed amounts of money out of proportion to its achievement, especially judged by the relative successes and costs of smaller churches within the Canadian Methodist mission.

Eby's dreams were too large for a small mission with a small budget, and his excesses led mission authorities to adopt conservative policies. Finally, in 1895, following a special investigation of affairs in Japan, the Mission Board forced Eby to resign from the mission field after nineteen turbulent years. He had been in many ways out of step with his colleagues. During the eighteen-eighties and eighteen-nineties, while Charles Eby devoted his enormous energy to direct evangelism, other Canadian Methodists had begun to concentrate their attention on the development of mission schools.

EDUCATION

Schools for Girls

Female education had, from the outset, been seen as an area in which women missionaries could play a valuable role, particularly because most had teaching diplomas from Canada. During the Meiji period, the Japanese authorities did much less for female education than for male education. While the Educational Code of 1872 made elementary education compulsory for both girls and boys, at no time during the Meiji period did females attend elementary schools in the same proportions as males. Of the private groups involved in female education, the missionary movement was among the most energetic in establishing Western-style educational facilities for girls. By the eighteen-eighties, every major centre had a female mission school, but there was still a great demand for more schools.

In 1884, both a girls' school and a boys' school were established in Azabu, Tokyo. From the start, the Toyo Eiwa Jo Gakko was a resounding success. It opened with Martha Cartmell as its first principal just as the vogue for things Western, typified by the newly opened *Rokumeikan* in Hibiya with its Western-style receptions and entertainments for government dignitaries, took hold. The

Toyo Eiwa Jo Gakko offered to teach Japanese girls all the Western graces, and could compete with the very best girls' schools in Tokyo. While there were other mission schools where girls could learn English and Western manners, many of those schools attracted poor students by offering scholarships—a situation which did not appeal to wealthy parents. At this stage, the perceptive WMS did not provide bursaries, and so the rich, the political and bureaucratic élite came. The Canadian women missionaries proved to be exceptionally canny in their calculations: the decision not to offer bursaries allowed them to remain financially solvent.

The success of the Toyo Eiwa Jo Gakko in Tokyo led to the opening of two other schools, both located outside the capital. In 1887 the WMS opened the Shizuoka Eiwa Jo Gakko with Miss M.J. Cunningham of Halifax as headmistress. In 1889, Miss Agnes Wintemute was sent to open a third girls' school in Kofu in Yamanashi Prefecture. Like the Shizuoka Eiwa Jo Gakko, the Yamanashi Eiwa Jo Gakko was founded following a request from local Christians. It was, as in Shizuoka, a manifestation of the continued Canadian Methodist commitment to their Christian work in that prefecture.

The three Canadian Methodist schools eventually offered education from kindergarten to high-school level, following a curriculum similar to government or other state-recognized schools. The schools offered more hours of English tuition and morals classes than did government girls' high schools.[24] The syllabus of the morals classes extended from the Imperial Rescript on Education to Bible study, the latter receiving particular stress.

As well as providing high-school education for girls, the WMS also wanted to increase women's opportunities for higher education. To meet this goal the Canadian Methodists co-operated with three American missions to found, in 1918, the Tokyo Woman's Christian College (Tokyo Joshi Daigaku). This school remains one of the most prestigious private universities for women in Japan to the present day. These efforts helped create a new and independent class of Japanese women who were relatively well-educated and interested in pursuing their own careers, usually as teachers. The pre-Pacific War Japanese women's movement gained much of its support from the graduates of Christian schools.[25] Secondary education gave individual women a greater degree of independence; meanwhile the unmarried missionary teachers served as examples of single women leading satisfying lives. Although Canadian missionaries considered their mission schools a success as an evangelistic agency, their most important significance may well have been in their contribution to the gradual emancipation of Japanese women.

Schools for Boys

Although the WMS effort in education was marked by growth and sustained success, the results of the Canadian Methodist educational endeavour on behalf of boys were, in the long term, more problematical. The authorities considered male education very important; thus the government was prepared to regulate the curriculum of private boys' schools. The government's attitude did much to undercut mission schools' primary attraction for missionaries—that is, their potential as an evangelistic agency. The girls' schools faced serious competition from only a relative handful of government schools; male institutions by contrast had to compete with an impressively broad range of both state and private schools. While government financing provided state schools with excellent facilities, mission schools lacked such resources, and so by and large came to be second-class institutions which attracted second-class students.

The decision to open a boys' school stemmed from the unsatisfactory experiences of missionaries teaching under the control of Japanese employers. In 1884, a site was chosen in Azabu, Tokyo, and the Toyo Eiwa Gakko was established. George Cochran, the first principal, also taught in the theological department. Robert Whittington, the first of a long line of missionaries whose positions were solely pedagogical, came out to take charge of the lay academic department. Among the Japanese teaching staff were members of the Shizuoka and Koishikawa Bands.

For fifteen years or so the Toyo Eiwa Gakko met with some success as a mission school; by 1899 there were approximately five hundred and eighty students in the academic department. But that same year, the Education Ministry prohibited religious teaching in any school approved to grant government diplomas. The Canadian Methodists felt that to obey the new regulation would be disloyal to their Christian supporters at home. They decided, therefore, to sever their formal connection with the Toyo Eiwa Gakko. A new school company was formed under Ebara Soroku, and the school buildings were taken over at no cost by what now became the Azabu Middle School. The Canadian Methodists continued to provide teaching support and to evangelize the students outside the classroom, but they were no longer financially involved with the school.

Having divested themselves of the Azabu Middle School, the Canadian Methodists were loath for some years to engage in educational work. In 1907, however, with the formation of the Japan Methodist Church, an opportunity for co-operation in educational work with the other two Methodist missions reappeared. In 1909, the Methodist Episcopal South mission invited the Canadian Methodists to join them in the educational project they had begun in Nishinomiya, near Kobe. By 1910, this school, the Kwansei Gakuin, consisted of a middle school and a theological seminary, with a total of more than four hundred students.

The aim of the proposed united educational endeavour was to build a college of higher learning, and a college department which gave courses in literature and commercial science was added to the existing school. This was the first time Canadian Methodists had embarked on a major endeavour which was not completely under their control, and outside their established Tokyo-Shizuoka-Kofu triangle. But while the Canadian Methodists did assist the Methodist Episcopal North mission in Tokyo with the development of Aoyama Gakuin, opportunities for extensive educational co-operation did not exist there.

It was instead the Methodist Episcopal South mission in Kobe that needed financial help from the Canadian Methodists. The Kwansei Gakuin would be jointly managed by the Canadian Methodists and the Methodist Episcopal South mission. Even with the Methodist Episcopal South mission paying for half the expenses, the Kwansei Gakuin proved very costly to develop. This was especially true after 1919 when the Board decided to circumvent even more stringent restrictions on religious education in government-recognized schools by attempting to take advantage of new government regulations allowing a few leading private schools and government colleges outside Tokyo and Kyoto to become universities.

Might the Kwansei Gakuin be recognized as a university? The central objective in the Canadians' aspirations was to defend the school's Christian character, which would be guaranteed by a university constitution. The dream was not impossible. The problem was money. Even though the Methodist Episcopal South mission raised their share of the endowment required by the government before granting university status, the Canadians were unable to raise their half until 1932. Only then did the Kwansei Gakuin finally attain university status. The Kwansei Gakuin was now a denominational college. Among Christian colleges in the Kansai region, it ranked second in importance to Doshisha College in Kyoto, which had attained university status in 1920. But despite its new charter the Kwansei Gakuin remained overcrowded and underfunded, too small to rival the Imperial Universities or the great secular private colleges, such as Keio or Waseda in Tokyo, which also attained university status in the nineteen-twenties.

The Canadian Academy

While the Canadian Methodists largely concentrated on education for the Japanese, one of the most successful of all Canadian missionary educational endeavours was the Canadian Methodist Academy, which opened its doors in Kobe in 1913 to educate the children of Canadian missionaries. The lack of educational facilities for Western children had hampered the Canadian mission in stationing missionaries with families in rural areas, where facilities for their children were unavailable. The creation of the Canadian Academy allowed missionaries preferring to keep their children with them during the crucial years of adolescence to have them educated in Japan, rather than in Canada, up to university age.

The Canadian Academy almost immediately found itself serving a much wider community, with students coming from the Kobe business community as well as from other missions. As a result, the Academy had become, by the nineteen-twenties, a union school supported financially by other missions as well as the Canadian Methodists. The school always remained, however, the preserve of Western children, and it followed the course prescribed by the Educational Department of Ontario for ungraded primary schools. In addition, the Canadian Academy quickly expanded to offer high-school-level courses, which enabled its graduates to enter the University of Toronto.

SOCIAL WORK

Canadian missionaries never engaged in social work on a large scale; what they did undertake usually reflected personal social concern and interest. The most famous of all Western missionaries in Japan during the nineteen-twenties was the 'White Angel of Tokyo', Caroline Macdonald, a Canadian who was instrumental in establishing the YWCA in Japan, and whose name is associated with the rehabilitation of prisoners.[26] Although another Canadian, Arthur Lea, had pioneered penal rehabilitation in Gifu in the eighteen-nineties, it was the activities of women missionaries that tended to attract more publicity. However, the Canadian Anglican Blind School (the Kunmoin) in Gifu exemplified a Christian work that pointed the way for further Japanese government effort in a necessary field of social work. This school began following the great Mino-Hide earthquake in 1891, as a blind men's club. At the time, only one other school for the blind existed in Japan. Until the late nineteen-twenties, when the Kunmoin passed from Canadian Anglican hands into the control of the Japanese government, the Canadian Anglican missionaries provided an extremely valuable service to the community.

One of the major contributions the missionary movement made to Japan was in providing a beginning in, for example, such areas as blind schools and kindergartens. The Canadian Anglicans maintained a kindergarten teachers' training school at Nagoya which attempted to give its young female students, all graduates of a girls' high school, a well-rounded education in which the Bible was emphasized.[27] The Canadian Methodists also trained kindergarten teachers at their three Eiwa schools. Such social-work efforts had an impact far greater than the small scale of the institutions might indicate.

Another area which engaged missionaries was health care. The Canadian Anglicans maintained a sanatorium for tuberculosis sufferers, and by the First World War, social work in the slums of the larger cities had attracted the attention of many missionaries. The Canadian Methodists were especially active in social work in the slums of East Tokyo, which had been created by the large-scale migration of young people from rural areas seeking work in the capital's developing industry. Canadian Methodists began their work by opening a preaching place in Kameido ward and by developing a hostel originally founded by Annie Allen of the WMS in the nineteen-tens for factory women. Slum work represented a clear response to the changing conditions of Japanese society brought about by industrialization. However, the conservatism of missionary societies often stifled innovation, and shortages of personnel and revenue often prevented the inauguration of new projects. Furthermore, as old established areas of work were rarely closed down, new projects were merely added to existing work. As a result, a good deal of missionary effort was expended in specialized work, diverting effort from the expansion of orthodox evangelism. Be that as it may, the personal contact with Canadian missionaries occasioned by such work, perhaps more than the institutionalized schools or social work projects, created feelings of friendship and goodwill that transcended cultural barriers.

THE LEGACY OF THE MISSIONARY AGE

The achievements of the Canadian missionary movement in Japan during close to seventy years were considerable, despite its failure to convert many people to Christianity. Canadian missionaries founded churches, schools, sanatoria and other specialized institutions. The social work of Canadians drew the attention of the Japanese authorities to hitherto neglected areas. At the same time, Canadian missionaries influenced both social and leisure activities. Missionaries introduced the idea of the summer cottage to Japan and encouraged interest in such outdoor activities as hiking, mountain-climbing, and tennis. Dan Norman, a Canadian Methodist missionary, is credited with introducing into Nagano Prefecture both apples (for which it is now famous) and white walnuts. Meanwhile the translation of *Anne of Green Gables* made a story of childhood in Prince Edward Island a favourite for generations of young Japanese girls. Missionaries themselves wrote books, which are still being read, about *netsuke* and Japanese Buddhism, and made sensitive translations of Akutagawa Ryunosuke's short stories.[28]

The scholarship of Canadian missionaries also helped to introduce Japanese culture and society to Canadian audiences. Missionary publications and the deputation work of missionaries on furlough were the prime avenues through which Canadians, at home, especially those in rural areas, could learn about things Japanese. The humanistic outlook of missionary scholarship on Japan continues to be a distinctive characteristic of Canadian academic scholarship on Japan. Indeed, the development in Canada of Japanese studies as a legitimate subject for university study owes much to the missionaries' efforts. While the missionary movement was directed toward the Japanese, it is a moot point whether Japan or Canada gained the most from this overseas Canadian endeavour.

Since Japanese perceptions of foreigners tend to be conditioned by military and industrial power, the Japanese easily distinguished the American and British cultural identities. The existence of a separate Canadian presence was less readily grasped. Even so, Canadian missionaries as a group tended to be distinct: more egalitarian and democratic, more concerned with social justice and more forward-looking than their British colleagues and less closely identified with Imperial political and cultural expansion. On the other hand, unlike the Americans who wanted to see Japan reformed on the American model, Canadians were inclined to be more tolerant and less patronizing. In short, they stood, as ever, between the British and the Americans. Gradually, however, the distinctive Canadian approach came to be recognized. Canadians, to take a single example, characteristically stand up for the underdog and help the underprivileged, as does the traditional Japanese hero. The two best-known Canadians in postwar Japan are probably E.H. Norman and Norman Bethune, both of whom impressed the Japanese because they championed the weak. But there were many other figures of equal stature among missionaries, who contributed to the Canadian legacy in Japan. As a result, there is a deep well of goodwill created by individuals and Canadian-founded institutions which have made significant contributions to the improvement of Japanese society.

Despite obvious achievements and failures, the lasting legacy of the pre-Pacific War Canadian missionary movement remains a controversial one. Within ten years of the Mukden Incident in 1931, the missionary movement had voluntarily withdrawn from Japan, and the world was on the verge of the Second World War. In retrospect, the impact of the missionary movement appears, at first glance, to have been remarkably short-lived. At the same time, Canadian racial hatred toward the Japanese, which manifested itself in 1942 with the forced removal of Japanese Canadians from Canada's west coast, casts doubt on the missionaries' ability to impart understanding about and knowledge of Japan to their compatriots.

From the beginning of Canadian missionary work in Japan, missionaries were deeply committed to and strongly identified with their Japanese converts. But once the East Asian crisis of the nineteen-thirties got under way this same strength turned into weakness, for it came to cloud the missionaries' judgement of events. Even after the beginning of the Sino-Japanese War in 1937, missionaries had difficulty adopting an impartial view of the causes for that war. One of the reasons why the missionaries were less influential in Canada than might have been expected was the obvious pro-Japanese bias of their opinions on the East Asian crisis. Canadian missionaries in Japan can be criticized for not taking a stronger stand against Japanese government policies toward China. Yet, nothing could have prepared the missionaries for the grave challenges of the nineteen-thirties. They were in this sense the first Canadian casualties in a war waged to prevent Western ideas from infiltrating Japanese cultural traditions.

Notwithstanding its failures, the pre-Pacific War Protestant missionary endeavour from Canada was a movement of peace that sought through persuasion and hard work the Christianization of the Japanese. Although the movement failed to achieve this goal, Cochran, McDonald, Shaw and the scores of Canadian men and women who came to Japan as missionaries revealed a genuine and heart-felt concern for the betterment of the physical, material and spiritual lot of ordinary Japanese. By doing so, they contributed in a positive and significant way to the long-term development of relations between the two countries, and left a legacy of memories and connections that continue to link faraway people and places on both sides of the Pacific.

BIBLIOGRAPHICAL NOTE

The most recent academic study of the Canadian Protestant missionary movement in Japan is A. Hamish Ion, *The Cross and the Rising Sun: The Canadian Protestant Missionary Movement in the Japanese Empire, 1872-1931* (Waterloo: Wilfrid Laurier University Press, 1990). A detailed church-sponsored study of the first hundred years of the Japan Mission of the United Church of Canada is G.R.P. and W.H.H. Norman's *One Hundred Years in Japan, 1873-1973* (Toronto: Division of World Out-reach, United Church of Canada, 1981). An earlier Canadian Methodist missionary account written at the time of the Methodist Jubilee in Japan which is of some interest is J.N. Saunby, *The New Chivalry in Japan* (Toronto: Methodist Publishing House, 1923). For A.C. Shaw's career in Japan, see C.H. Powles, *Victorian Missionaries in Meiji Japan* (Toronto: University of Toronto-York University Joint Centre for Modern East Asia, 1987).

○

Among the legacies of Canada's missionary activity in early twentieth century Japan was a generation of men and women born and raised in what was then, for most Canadians, a far-away place in the mysterious East. With their acquired language skills and instinctive understanding of Japanese society, this small group of missionary children—the 'Canadian-Japanese'—were uniquely equipped to bridge the distance between the two cultures. All have made a special contribution to the developing relationship, but perhaps the best known is Egerton Herbert Norman (1909-1957). The son of a Canadian Methodist missionary, E.H. Norman was born in Karuizawa, Nagano Prefecture, studied in Victoria College at the University of Toronto, did graduate work at Cambridge and Harvard universities, and made a name for himself as the author of Japan's Emergence as a Modern State. *In 1939 he entered the Department of External Affairs and served as language officer at the Canadian Legation in Tokyo. After the Second World War, he returned to Tokyo as head of the Canadian Liaison Mission to the Allied Occupation of Japan and developed a close working relationship with the Supreme Commander for the Allied Powers (SCAP), General Douglas MacArthur.*

Despite his credentials Norman was caught up in 1950 in the witch-hunting of the United States Senate subcommittee headed by Joseph McCarthy and accused of being a Soviet agent. Found innocent of the charge after a Canadian government investigation, Norman was posted by Lester Pearson to Cairo as Ambassador to Egypt, where, faced with a second round of nerve-wracking investigation, he committed suicide on the 4th of April 1957. Recently, renewed interest in Norman has resulted in the publication of two scholarly books and prompted the Canadian government to sponsor a further examination of his career and the circumstances leading up to his suicide. In the following chapter Kimitada Miwa, who was among the first Japanese scholars to write of Norman's role in shaping post-war Japan,[1] returns to the subject of his original research to reflect on the enigma of Herbert Norman and to consider the latest controversy. It is clear from Professor Miwa's discussion that the perception of Norman, like Norman himself, is a product of two different cultures. While the attention of Canadians been largely focused on the circumstances of his death—was he a spy?—Japanese writers are more often engaged by the contributions of his life.

Kimitada Miwa completed his BS and MA at Georgetown University and received his PhD in History from Princeton University in 1967. Author of numerous books and articles, his recent publications include Nihon: 1945 nen no shiten *[Japan Seen from the Perspective of 1945]* (Tokyo: University of Tokyo Press, 1985) and *The Ambivalence of Nationalism: Modern Japan Between East and West* (London and New York: University Press of America, 1990.) *The former Director of the Institute for International Relations, he is currently Professor of International History and Director of the Institute for American and Canadian Studies at Sophia University, Tokyo.*

E.H. NORMAN REVISITED

Miwa Kimitada

It seems curious after the passage of so much time that the E.H. Norman 'case' continues to prompt so much controversy. A part of the reason, of course, is politics: for those who wish to use Norman as a stick to beat the current government (and more to the point, government in general) it is imperative that Norman remain an espionage suspect. For its part, the Canadian government would like to see the case closed once and for all, since officials have consistently defended Norman over the years. But although the storm of McCarthyism which blew across the border into Canada from the United States and led to the original charges has long since subsided, questions remain. Two recent books, both published in 1986, sum up the confrontation. The first, by Roger W. Bowen, seemed to finally exonerate Norman, but the second, by James Barros, raised enough doubts that those who wish to continue can find there sufficient ammunition to pursue the case for the prosecution—in the Barros treatment even Lester Pearson emerges as a suspect.[2] Yet even aside from the simple question of guilt or innocence, Norman remains an intriguing figure both as a complex, often enigmatic, personality shaped by the duality of his childhood, and for his impact on the evolution of modern Japan.[3]

My own interest in Norman was stimulated when, in 1976, while researching Japanese images of America during the Occupation, I happened on some documents drafted by Norman among the papers of the Allied Occupation of Japan stored at Stanford University's Hoover Institution and in the archives of the MacArthur Memorial Library in Norfolk, Virginia. Interested in regionalism and localism in modern Japanese history, I was persuaded that the rejection of localism in the building of the modern nation-state had brought about the ultranationalism of the 1930s. Norman's concern for the importance of the aspirations of the common people in shaping history echoed my own, and I was struck by his compassion for the 'lesser names' in history.[4]

Meanwhile John Dower had assembled, as *Origins of the Modern Japanese State: Selected Writings of E.H. Norman*, a collection of Norman's essays and observations.[5] In his lengthy introduction, Dower argued that American historians of Japan, led by Edwin O. Reischauer, John W. Hall and Marius B. Jansen, had judged Norman's studies of Japan largely on ideological grounds and that their condemnation had forced Norman into academic oblivion.[6] Norman had been extremely popular in Japan in the late 1940s, but then had faded from view. The Dower book prompted a burst of renewed interest on the part of Japanese scholars, and a great many articles on Norman soon appeared. Interest in Norman's life and work reached a new peak in 1977, the twentieth anniversary of his death. Coincidentally my original essays came to occupy a place at the foot of this small mountain of material.[7] Although my first interpretation, which pointed up Norman's emphasis on localism in his approach to postwar reconstruction, remains valid, considerable time has now passed and a great deal of subsequent research has been done, much of it in Canada.[8] Perhaps the time has come to revisit the Norman legacy, and to reconsider Norman's unique situation as an interpreter between two cultures from a longer, Japanese perspective.

Returning to Canada and to Norman after the passage of fifteen years is rather like a holiday visit to old friends after a lengthy absence—nostalgia and expectation inevitably make up one's mental baggage.[9] How often on one's arrival, one is surprised. Despite an exhaustive report commissioned by Canada's Department of External Affairs and done by Professor Peyton Lyon of Carleton University, Norman remains under something of a cloud. The Lyon report, 'The Loyalties of E. Herbert Norman', draws on the records of the Department of External Affairs, pertinent documents of the Royal Canadian Mounted Police, and the collection of Norman's personal letters held by the University of British Columbia. The author, a former foreign service officer and colleague of Norman's, concludes that 'not one iota of evidence suggests' that Herbert Norman was a spy:

> Herbert Norman was loyal to the people of Japan, the land of his childhood. He was loyal to humanity, and to the pursuit of historical truth. He was loyal to himself; he never denounced the idealistic youth who misguidedly saw in Communism and the Soviet Union the only hope for civilized man. He was, above all, loyal to his friends and to his country.[10]

Despite Lyon's exoneration of Norman, the suspicions raised by Barros remain current in some quarters. What accounts for such strikingly dissimilar conclusions? The answer appears to lie in differing cultural perceptions and understandings. Barros, an American who has recently returned to the United States after teaching political science at the University of Toronto for many years, tests Norman by an American measurement of national loyalty and condemns him on the basis of 'guilt by association' with some proven Communist Party members.[11] Similar cultural differences explain the otherwise apparently curious fact that despite the controversy which swirls around him in Canada, Herbert Norman continues to be regarded as a genuine Canadian hero by most Japanese.

Consider, as a case in point, the question of Norman's suicide. In Mrs Norman's possession are two recent books by Japanese scholars: *Orimposu no hashira no kage ni* [Behind the Olympian Columns] by Nakazono Eisuke and *H. Noman: aru demokuratto no tadotta michi* [H. Norman: The Fatal Path a Democratic Mind Trod] by Nakano Toshiko, the former a gift through the Japanese Ambassador from two members of the upper house of Japan's National Diet on the occasion of their visit to Ottawa to participate in the 74th convention of the parliamentarians of the world.[12] It is regrettable that Mrs Norman does not read Japanese, for these authors offer a quite different interpretation of the causes of her late husband's death. One might call it an exceptionally 'Japanese' interpretation; certainly it points up the importance of the experience and acceptance of an 'alien' culture in understanding Norman— something stressed by Bowen, Charles Taylor and Cyril Powles but ignored by Barros.[13]

From a Canadian standpoint, Norman's suicide can easily be seen as the act of a desperate man trying to escape the consequences of exposure, and thus it serves as a kind of 'evidence' of Norman's guilt. Yet in the concluding chapter of the Nakano book, the author interprets Norman's action as a consequence of his belief that 'death is also life'—a belief, she notes, common among the Japanese.[14] Indeed, the key to Norman she sees in his life, not his death, for she begins her study by quoting their mother Kate's admonition to Norman and his older brother Howard:

> 'What will people think of Father and me if you do that? Parents are always blamed if their children go wrong.' She was fearful that Father would be misunderstood and frequently tried to restrain him.[15]

Death as life thus becomes a *leitmotif* of the Nakano volume. Bowen refers to the same passage—and in the postlude to her book Nakano acknowledges her indebtedness to Bowen's study—but it appears in Bowen only as a note to a paragraph describing Herbert's early upbringing. Kate, Bowen observes, was overly anxious about public opinion and was 'given to worry and anxiety . . . and may have been too indulgent toward her children. Herbert, for instance, was allowed to sleep with his parents long after infancy, and Kate made a custom of tucking Herbert in' even into his adult years.[16]

In fact, Kate Norman's mothering constituted the most commonplace expression of the ordinary conduct of Japanese people. In assessing E.H. Norman, Nakano Toshiko emphasizes the impact on Norman of his birth in Karuizawa and of a childhood spent growing up in close contact with Japanese children in and around Nagano. The night before his suicide, Norman watched a Japanese movie at the Odeon Theatre in Cairo; given his cultural background, Nakano notes, Norman saw in the film a message that other foreigners would not see, but that Nakano and any other Japanese would readily find. The film, 'Mask of Destiny' [*Shuzenji monogatari*], tells the story of a master artisan commissioned by a nobleman to make for him a life-mask. But no matter how the artisan struggles with the task, none of the masks he constructs come alive. Finally, becoming impatient, the nobleman takes from the artisan a mask which the artisan has not found satisfactory. That night, the nobleman wears the mask and perishes at the hands of assassins. The artisan's daughter rescues the mask from the burning house and proclaims it a masterpiece after all: by it her father had prophesied the nobleman's death.[17]

Nakano observes that foreigners in the audience, with the exception of Norman, were dazzled by the exotic cinematography but could not grasp the film's real point:

> What I got from this movie was the insight that 'death is life.' So did Norman, I believe. As a result, having watched it through to the end, he regained his old

cheerful self, confiding to Irene lightheartedly that 'I received a sign. My own suicide is also a form of living. Death is not only a part of my life, but a part of life contiguous to the lives of many other people.' Having achieved a philosophical attitude toward suicide, Norman felt refreshed and liberated.[18]

In Nakano's interpretation of Norman lies, I think, the secret of his popularity in Japan. It reflects what Ivan Morris identified as the Japanese love and respect for a hero in history elevated by the manner of his death to the 'nobility of failure.'[19]

In addition to the Nakano book, a study of Norman is currently being serialized in the Japanese journal *Sekai*. This series by Kudo Miyoko is entitled 'Habato Noman no shogai' [The Life of Herbert Norman]; the first instalment appeared in the January, 1989 issue and seems to have captured a faithful audience—the eighteenth instalment appeared in the January, 1991 edition of *Sekai*. While Nakano's treatment benefited from her father Yoshio's having known Norman personally during the period when Norman was in Tokyo after the war, Kudo's strength is her command of the archival materials related to Norman held by the Department of External Affairs and the University of British Columbia. Nakano concentrates on the significance of Norman's early life—from birth to the especially sensitive age of seventeen, when he lived in and around Nagano City and Karuizawa. Kudo, by contrast, often draws a credible psychological interpretation from a careful analysis of primary sources left from a later period in Norman's life, occasionally revealing in the process new information on the politics of occupied Japan. Kudo offers some interesting insights into the cause of Norman's fatal depression. In his contribution to Roger Bowen's *E.H. Norman*, Edwin Reischauer recalls the time he and Norman spent as playmates in Karuizawa. Edwin's father, A.K. Reischauer, was also a missionary, but was stationed in Tokyo and taught at the prestigious Tokyo Women's College. When not teaching he spent his time researching Japanese Buddhism, and this led, in 1917, to the publication of his *Studies in Japanese Buddhism*. A.K. Reischauer's scholarship and his Tokyo academic connections made him a sharp contrast with Herbert's father Daniel, whose work was with the people of the countryside. Although the sons played together, especially at tennis in which they were constant doubles partners, and Reischauer came to believe they would be forever friends, in reality this interlude of innocence lasted only from the summer of 1918 to the summer of 1922, from the time Norman was eight to the time he was twelve (Reischauer was a year younger). As teenagers they drifted apart, rarely seeing each other. Both, however, attended Harvard where they had a common mentor, Professor Serge Elisseef. In 1939, both received a doctorate; Reischauer wrote his dissertation on China and Japan in the nineteenth century, while Norman's became the basis for his first book, published the next year by the Institute of Pacific Relations as *Japan's Emergence as a Modern State*.[20]

It is not clear what relationship existed between them. Although Herbert and

Edwin had been childhood playmates, they were also rivals. They met for the first time in many years and for the last time in 1948, when Reischauer, then director of the Yenching Institute at Harvard, visited Norman in Tokyo and was entertained at the palatial Canadian embassy which Norman had rescued from the Occupation. Reischauer's first wife Adrian had died earlier that year.[21] Kudo suspects that the relationship suffered from Norman's brush with Senator McCarthy's committee, whose activities left Norman under a shadow. Herbert Norman, then posted in Wellington, New Zealand as High Commissioner, wrote frequently chiding Reischauer for his negligence in not keeping in touch. When Reischauer married for the second time to Matsukata Haru in 1955, Howard Norman celebrated the nuptial service. But Herbert's letter of congratulation on the occasion of the marriage went unanswered, although he was also personally acquainted with Haru. Despite this snub Reischauer asked Norman to prepare a bibliography on Nakae Chomin (a Meiji period Rousseauite philosopher and parliamentarian) for one of Reischauer's students at Harvard. Neither the student nor her professor, Norman complained to his brother, bothered to write an acknowledgement. Although Kudo cautions her readers not to judge Reischauer too harshly without knowing the full story, she also speculates that if Norman had not been made a target by the Congressional witch-hunters Reischauer might have been less likely to distance himself from his childhood friend. And Norman's somewhat excessive concern over the loss, she adds, may well have reflected the increasingly disturbed state of mind his situation was generating.[22]

Despite his impending estrangement from Reischauer, Norman for the most part maintained close ties with the American Occupation and especially with General MacArthur, who respected Norman's expertise as one of the leading Japanologists in the West. Norman, who believed that great individuals had the power to shape the course of history, was impressed in turn by MacArthur's qualities of leadership. Thanks in part to that relationship, Norman was to have considerable influence over post-war policy in Japan. Arguably Norman's intervention helped forestall the abolition of the Emperor system by focusing attention on the role played by the civilian leadership, and the bureaucracy in particular, in encouraging Japan's ultranationalist imperial ambitions.

Kudo draws special attention to Norman's changing views of the Imperial institution and to the question of Emperor Hirohito's possible abdication. At the ninth Conference of the Institute of Pacific Relations held in January, 1945 at Hot Springs, Virginia, Norman advanced a view of the Emperor system that was much more harshly critical than that held by American policymakers; Norman's ideas at that point were closer to those of the Chinese, who had it in mind that the Emperor might be secretly removed to his Hayama summer house by the sea near Kamakura and a regency committee formed of people innocent of any involvement in Japan's aggressive policies.[23] Half a year later, responding to a questionnaire from the Bureau of Applied Social Research of New York, Norman recommended that the Japanese be encouraged to abolish the Imperial institution because it had been the source of Japanese racism and imperialism; however, he cautioned, the initiative for its destruction must not be taken by the Allies. Instead, he believed that the Japanese intellectuals were flexible enough to respond to the need for changes, and clever enough to make them without creating a loss of face.[24]

But having been posted to Tokyo as the Canadian representative of the Far Eastern Commission soon after the Allied Occupation of Japan began, Norman began to reconsider. Norman arrived in Tokyo via Manila with the U.S. forces, and in a matter of a few days he altered his views. Writing to his wife Irene in Canada, he commented that the Japanese mentality had not changed enough as yet to accept a call for the abolition of the Imperial system. Instead of launching an attack on the Imperial House, Norman observed, it was more important to purge suspect bureaucrats from public offices.[25] Norman's concern with the bureaucracy had surfaced a year earlier in an article published in the September, 1944 issue of *Pacific Affairs* entitled 'The Genyosha: A Study in the Origins of Japanese Imperialism' which examined the role of the ultranationalist organization. The thrust of the article, as John Dower notes, 'was not that the ultranationalist societies led Japan to war, but rather that they penetrated and helped to interlock "the key sections of the bureaucracy" '.[26]

Meanwhile at the American Embassy on September 27, the Emperor met secretly with General MacArthur for the first time. In considering what to do with the Imperial institution, MacArthur shared the conservative views of Joseph C. Grew, former ambassador to Japan and then Undersecretary of State, but Norman may well have played a role in shaping MacArthur's subsequent decisions. Following his conversations with the Supreme Commander, Emperor Hirohito issued on 1 January 1946 an Imperial statement disclaiming the divinity which had always been associated with his person during the militarist years. The Emperor was, at this point, considering abdication and dictated in the spring of 1946 a monologue published for the first time in a Japanese journal in the fall of 1990.[27] Reflecting on his position at the outset of the war, Hirohito remarked that if he had opposed the Government's decision to go to war with the United States, then a rebellion would have taken place—very probably as a result of a court *coup d'état*.[28] Although it has been suggested that in October, 1940 the Emperor sought to keep Prince Takamatsu away from the danger of the battle front to ensure that he would be available to serve as regent in an emergency, Hirohito appears at various times to have been more afraid of a court *coup d'état* led by the Prince and his younger brother Chichibu.[29]

Hirohito thus acceded to war with the United States to protect the 'national polity' and, as is evident in his Imperial rescript to the people in accepting the surrender terms of the Allied Powers, he ended the war in order to preserve it.

But a close reading of his 1946 monologue leads one to the conclusion that what he meant by 'national polity' differed significantly from what the Japanese were educated to understand. Instead of the political structure and values of the Imperial state—the sense in which this phrase would ordinarily be understood—the Emperor was more particularly concerned with the security of the Imperial Regalia, consisting of the mirror, the sword and the beads. These were the symbols of Imperial authority and the source of Imperial legitimacy, indispensable for the Imperial succession. Without them, no one can ascend the Throne. The mirror was in the Grand Shrine of Ise; the sword in the Atsuta Shrine on the outskirts of Nagoya. Both these shrines were located on or close to Ise Bay. According to the monologue, when Hirohito learned that preparations for the defence of the main island were not yet ready, he decided to surrender because:

> If enemy forces landed in the Ise Bay area, the Shrines would soon fall under their control. There would be no time to remove the divine objects [the mirror and sword]. There was no prospect of securing them. Their loss would make the securing of the national polity more difficult. Hence I concluded that in the circumstances, peace should be struck immediately even at the cost of my own life.[30]

To whom Hirohito was addressing this monologue is not yet definitely established, even among Japanese scholars. The Emperor spoke, in three sessions on March 18, 20, and 22, and two further sessions on April 8, to five men: Imperial Household Minister Matsudaira Yoshitami, President of Sochiryo Matsudaira Yasumasa, Vice-Chamberlain Kinoshita Michio, Secretariat Bureau Director Inada Shuichi, and Terasaki Hidenari, who had recently become the official interpreter for the Emperor, and who prepared the manuscript. On January 22, shortly after the Emperor's statement disclaiming divinity, MacArthur had ordered the establishment in Tokyo of an international military tribunal to try Japan's war criminals. In the circumstances, it seems only natural to assume a relationship between the creation of this document and the war crimes trials, which would soon begin.

If the document was produced in anticipation of the trials, the route through which it was to reach MacArthur may well have included Norman, since Terasaki had become friendly with the military secretary of MacArthur, Lieutenant General Bonnar Sellers, when he discovered that Sellers was a cousin of Terasaki's American wife, Gwendolyn Harold.[31] Certainly there is a remarkable correspondence between Norman's views of Japanese military leaders and politicians, and Hirohito's comments in the monologue. Norman, for example, was highly critical of Prince Konoe Fumimaro;[32] indeed, soon after Norman's views became known to the SCAP, Konoe poisoned himself to avoid being arrested by American military police and brought to trial. At the time of the monologue, Konoe had already committed suicide and Hirohito avoided commenting on his character. It is clear, however, from other observations that Hirohito shared Norman's opinion of Konoe.

Admittedly, Konoe was at this point widely unpopular in Japan and the similarity may have been coincidental. But such was not the case with Hirota Koki. Japanese readers, upon discovering that the Emperor laid a large measure of the responsibility for the war on Hirota, and had implied that he might have been controlled by Genyosha (an ultranationalist organization based in Fukuoka, Hirota's birthplace[33]), were very surprised. Did Hirohito's remarks in fact affect the outcome of the trials, perhaps dooming Hirota to a sentence of capital punishment? Professor Ito Takashi of the University of Tokyo, who obtained the manuscript from Gwendolyn's daughter Mariko Terasaki Miller, now living in Casper, Wyoming, suspects that Hirohito came to this idea belatedly 'after the war, when such organizations as Genyosha and Kokuryukai [Black Dragon Society] became archvillains.' On the one hand, there was a relationship between Hirota and Genyosha, and it is not difficult to imagine that the Emperor could have been aware of it. For example, a diary kept by a secretary to Elder Statesman Prince Saionji Kinmochi records that shortly after the fall of Nanking in the China Conflict in 1937, a messenger in the person of a son of Toyama Mitsuru, the President of Genyosha, came to Prince Konoe, the Prime Minister, asking him to 'release Hirota [from his post as Foreign Minister], before he accumulates too much of a bad name.'[34] So it is quite possible that Hirohito had reservations about Hiroto even before the war.

On the other hand, if we accept Ito's argument that the Emperor's remarks amounted to a post-war about-face, then the fact that they bear a striking resemblance to Norman's observations is highly suggestive. Norman had already published the 1944 article on the influence of the Genyosha mentioned above, and the report he wrote for MacArthur, 'Militarists in the Japanese State', took the same line. In his own survey of the International Military Tribunal in Tokyo, Dower notes, Norman put it in even stronger terms:

> it was a civilian Prime Minister, Hirota, who in 1936 set the principles and
> policies for Japan's subsequent open war against China, and . . . Hirota's
> successor, Prince Konoe, had performed the function of 'fusing all of the
> dominant sections of the ruling oligarchy, the Court, Army, Zaibatsu and
> bureaucracy' behind the war program.[35]

In short, Norman rejected the prevailing theory that the military dictatorship had led Japan to war; instead he laid the guilt at the feet of Hirota, who was not a military man but a civilian official at the Foreign Ministry turned statesman. On this point Norman and Hirohito seem to have shared very similar views. In addition, Norman meanwhile, as indicated above, was also becoming persuaded that the Emperor system should be preserved and that Hirohito should remain on the throne, as subsequent events made clear.

On May 3, the International Tribunal duly opened. There had been a tacit understanding between the General and the Emperor that he would not be prosecuted. This became clear when, on June 18, Chief Prosecutor Joseph B. Keenan publicly declared that Hirohito would not be tried. By April, 1948, the Tribunal had completed its deliberations and announced that its verdicts would be delivered late in the fall. In fact, they were handed down on November 9: seven of the chief defendants including General Tojo Hideki, the Prime Minister at the time of the Pearl Harbor attack, and Hirota Koki, who had been Foreign Minister during Japan's aggression in China, were found guilty of conspiracy and crimes against humanity and sentenced to death by hanging. They were executed on December 23 at Sugamo Prison in Tokyo.

Within a month after the Tribunal had concluded its hearings, and before the verdicts were announced, a Japanese weekly reported that the Chief Justice of the Supreme Court, Miubuchi Tadahiko, believed that it would have been a superior moral solution for Hirohito, at the time of Japan's surrender, to have issued an Imperial edict indicating his willingness to accept moral responsibility for the war, and then to have abdicated as Emperor of Japan. English-language newspapers in Japan took this as a cue to circulate the misleading speculation that the Emperor would abdicate on August 24, the third anniversary of Japan's defeat.[36] The English-language papers initially identified the Imperial Household Ministry as their source for this rumour, but very shortly the President of the Imperial University of Tokyo, Nambara Shigeru, also told the Chinese news agency that, in his opinion, Hirohito should abdicate.[37]

Nambara, according to Norman, was very close to Prince Takamatsu, a younger brother of Hirohito who would almost certainly become regent if Hirohito were to abdicate. But the Prince was a dangerously ambitious young man who had surrounded himself with a clique of unpopular men purged from public office. Norman saw behind the rumour of impending abdication the conniving of a gang of conspirators seeking to make Takamatsu regent—a very plausible analysis. More surprising was a suggestion contained in the report Norman despatched to External Affairs on June 17: according to Alvary Gascoigne, the head of the British Liaison Mission to the SCAP, Norman reported that a source in the Imperial Household had told him Hirohito was mentally very disturbed and had sought solace in religion. And further, that one reason why the Emperor had received Cardinal Joseph Spellman of New York at the Imperial Palace the preceding week was to consult him about converting to Catholicism.[38] Immediately afterward, the Minister of the Imperial Household, Matsudaira Yoshitami, and the Grand Chamberlain resigned.[39]

By January, 1948, things had settled down, and Norman was able to report on January 8 that he had visited MacArthur to express personally his New Year's good wishes and that the General had told him that he had assured the Emperor he did not need to abdicate. Norman was pleased at this, since he regarded Hirohito as a far better ruler than Prince Takamatsu, who would have become regent in his place. More importantly, Norman had come to regard the Imperial institution, in the symbolic sense provided for the position of the Emperor in the constitution, as something which needed to be preserved; to force its abolition would, he maintained, deeply wound the pride of the Japanese people.

His assessment of the importance of the Imperial institution is a signal token of Norman's fundamental understanding of the realities of Japan, and his sympathy for the well-being of the Japanese people. His use of the constitutional term 'symbol' in reference to the Emperor's position reflected his perception that in it lay the basis of the Japanese people's national identity. If the Emperor system had been suddenly done away with, the people would have been engulfed in social turbulence and political disorder. The result would have been to exact another, even greater and less bearable sacrifice from them than those they had been asked to make in war. Thanks to the perseverance of this national identity, the Japanese people could endure the onslaught of Americanization forced on them in the name of postwar reforms. Norman's concern for the ordinary Japanese in his approach to this and other problems, his instinctive grasp of the essence of his land of birth, and his ability to translate these insights for other Westerners made him a special figure for the Japanese. Subsequent events, particularly the circumstances of his death, may have tarnished his achievement and gained him an unhappy infamy in Canada. In Japan, by contrast, he remains famous as a respected link between the two cultures; revisiting his life and reviewing his accomplishment only serves to confirm his contribution.

○

Moving Toward Closer Ties

The years between 1921 and 1928 marked an important period in the history of Japanese-Canadian relations. Canada's growing awareness of its interests as a Pacific nation led it to press Great Britain to abrogate the Anglo-Japanese alliance on the grounds that it restricted Canada's freedom to protect its special interests in the Far East. Moreover it threatened to create conflict between Canada and the United States, at a time when the two were moving toward a closer partnership, and interfered with Canada's attempts to restrict Asian immigration. These concerns along with a desire for expanded trade would eventually prompt Canada to establish formal diplomatic relations with Japan in 1928. In the interval, Canadians' attitudes toward Japan and expectations of the relationship were largely shaped by a small group of intellectuals and journalists concerned with international affairs.

Those concerned with Asia, especially Japan and China, found a home for their activities in the Institute of Pacific Relations (IPR) which began as a part of the Canadian Institute of International Affairs. By providing a forum for those with particular concerns about Canada's role in the Pacific region, the Institute focused attention on a few limited aspects of the relationship. The driving force in establishing the Canadian IPR was John Nelson, a resident of British Columbia and a supporter of the anti-Asian movement, whose exclusionist views on immigration had led him to join the international IPR in 1925. Other leading members of the Canadian organization included Newton W. Rowell, a devout Methodist associated with Canadian missionary activity in China, and John Wesley Dafoe, the outspoken and influential editor of the Manitoba Free Press *committed to the cause of collective security. As a result of the activities of the Institute and its members, Ohara argues, Canada's decision to establish formal relations with Japan did not reflect a coherent and realistic assessment of Japan and its importance in the Pacific region, but rather a limited perception of Japan as significant largely as the source of Japanese immigration to Canada, as a base for a Canadian advance into China, and as a problem in international diplomacy. Not until the 1930s would Canadians, guided by the experience of Hugh L. Keenleyside and Henry F. Angus, begin to develop a more realistic understanding of the implications of their Pacific nationhood.*

One of the pioneering Canadianists of Japan, Yuko Ohara received her BA and MA from Saint Paul (Rikkyo) University, and completed a second MA at the University of Victoria, British Columbia, in 1973. In addition to numerous articles, she is the author of Kanada gendai-shi *[A Contemporary History of Canada] (Tokyo: Yamakawa, 1981) and the co-editor of* Gaisetsu Kanada-shi *[A Survey History of Canada] (Tokyo: Yuhikaku, 1984). She also translated, as* Kanada yo towani *(Tokyo: Saimaru, 1984), Ramsay Cook's* The Maple Leaf Forever. *For many years a leading member of the Japan Association of Canadian Studies, she is currently Associate Professor at the University of Tokyo.*

J.W. DAFOE AND JAPANESE-CANADIAN RELATIONS DURING THE 1920s

Ohara Yuko
translated by Peter Currie

Few would argue with the view that John Wesley Dafoe (1866-1944) was the most influential journalist in Canada's history. The comments made during Dafoe's lifetime by University of Toronto historian Frank Underhill, who temporarily put aside his political differences with Dafoe, testify to his importance:

> The Winnipeg *Free Press* is distinguished not for news but for its editorial column. . . . That the *Free Press* has attained the position that what it thinks today, western Canada thinks tomorrow and, after the passage of a number of years, eastern Canada thinks too has become a commonplace over the past generation.
>
> Certainly Dafoe invariably took a firm position regarding anything that happened in the world. And for those whose habit it was to read a number of Canadian newspapers, before making up our minds either to support or oppose on any particular issue, we always waited to see what the *Free Press* had to say.[1]

The stage for Dafoe's activities as an editor was the *Manitoba Free Press* (renamed the Winnipeg *Free Press* in 1931), located in Winnipeg, the capital of the province of Manitoba. From August 1901, when he was invited to become chief editor by the paper's owner Clifford Sifton, until his death at the age of 77, Dafoe was actively concerned as a newspaperman with all the important issues of the day, both domestic and foreign. Despite the paper's name—the *Manitoba Free Press*—under Dafoe's stewardship it became one of only a few Canadian newspapers to consistently exhibit a national view on affairs.

Ramsay Cook's examination of Dafoe's political thinking in *The Politics of John W. Dafoe and the Free Press*[2] has become a classic of Canadian history; to read it is to read nothing less than an account of the political thinking that guided Canadian politics through the twentieth century. As Underhill suggests, Dafoe succeeded in winning widespread support for his views among Canadian voters and thus, given Canada's parliamentary democracy, had a shaping influence on national decision-making. Dafoe's influence is readily apparent in Canada's foreign policy; the convergence between Canada's policies toward Japan in the 1920s and Dafoe's political thinking points up the view of Japan held at that time by thoughtful Canadians, of whom Dafoe was a representative figure.

DAFOE AND THE ANGLO-JAPANESE ALLIANCE

Dafoe's interest in Canadian foreign relations, particularly relations with the U.K., was awakened in 1899 at the time of the Boer War in South Africa. Then the editor of the Montreal *Star*, Dafoe found he could not agree with Hugh Graham, the paper's Conservative owner, in his enthusiasm for the war. As a Canadian of British stock, Dafoe believed that Canada's duty lay in assisting the government of the United Kingdom in South Africa.[3] He did not, however, think such assistance should be rendered automatically as Canada's obligation as a member of the British Empire, in response to a request from the British government. Rather, Dafoe thought that Canada must decide on its own, or, to put it another way, that the decision had to be made by the Canadian parliament.

In a 1917 publication entitled 'Canada's Future in the British Empire', Dafoe outlined the differences between his views, which he called 'National Canadianism', and those of the so-called 'Round Table group', who advocated Imperial centralism. Attempts at greater centralization, Dafoe argued, were bound to fail: 'Whatever shape a reconstituted Empire may take, there will always remain one touchstone. That is, that the lives and the assets of Canadians be entrusted to the hands of a legislature and an administration controlled by Canadians.' Using a specific example to illustrate his position, Dafoe raised the issue of limiting Japanese immigration to Canada, about which, he maintained, the British government properly had no say whatsoever.

In Dafoe's view 'the Empire has only one potential future' and that was to develop in the direction of self-government, with the Dominions enjoying complete sovereignty in a permanent alliance built on common citizenship. That alliance was not to be restricted in meaning to the military or the legal, but was to embrace a broad spectrum of sentiment as an alliance of 'British-style states acting in concert for permanent peace, and taking shape in an atmosphere of hope and expectation.'[4] In expounding his views, Dafoe distinguished sharply between his own position and that of the Canadian independence faction, led by J.S. Ewart and others who strongly opposed Dafoe's version of a 'new imperialism'. However undeservedly, Dafoe founded himself branded with the label of 'colonial nationalist'.

Less easy to dismiss was Dafoe's substantial influence in national affairs. Since encountering Edward Blake in 1884, Dafoe had been drawn toward the Liberal party, and through Clifford Sifton developed close relationships with leading members. Later Dafoe came to a temporary parting of the ways with the Liberal mainstream over the conscription issue during the First World War, and his stance gained him the respect of important Conservatives. Canada had already been at war for eighteen months when, in early 1916, Conservative Prime Minister Robert Borden began to consider adopting conscription.[5] Reluctant to proceed, Borden delayed bringing the conscription bill to Cabinet until its meeting on 17 May 1917. Dafoe, who interviewed the Prime Minister in Ottawa in late January 1917, had meanwhile been arguing for the adoption of conscription as a non-partisan measure in the columns of the *Free Press* since the previous year—arguably initiating public discussion of the possibility of a coalition Cabinet being formed to introduce conscription.[6] It was at this time that a close friendship was formed between Dafoe and Borden.

In 1919 Dafoe followed Borden and the Canadian delegation to Paris for the peace conference ending the First World War. Dafoe would later write that Versailles was the most important conference in the history of constitutional government in Canada.[7] Borden had travelled to London in November 1918 at the invitation of British Prime Minister Lloyd George. On his arrival, Borden immediately argued that Canada should send a separate delegation to the peace conference. 'Lloyd George,' Dafoe observed, 'had absolutely no such idea.' Arriving in London in early December, Dafoe observed Borden's determined efforts to win over the British Prime Minister. Lloyd George finally relented on December 31, in a statement to which Dafoe was a witness: 'Should Canada make such a request, there is only one answer and that has to be "yes".' 'I cannot swear,' Dafoe later recalled, 'whether those were the exact words used or not. I can, however, bear witness without doubt to their purport as to the information supplied. In that instant, the history of the British Commonwealth cleared a hurdle.' Obviously, Canada's independent membership in the meetings of the Peace Conference, and subsequently in the League of Nations and the International Labour Organization, was not secured solely by the efforts of Borden and those around him. As Dafoe himself acknowledged, it was 'the result of a continuous policy of "National Canadianism"' pursued since the days of John A. Macdonald.[8]

That Canada in its newly-won autonomous role played a large part in bringing about the dissolution of the Anglo-Japanese alliance at the Washington Conference of 1922 can be attributed to J.B. Brebner, who advanced the idea with the publication in 1935 of his article 'Canada, the Anglo-Japanese Alliance, and the Washington Conference.'[9] Brebner praised the success of former Conservative Prime Minister Arthur Meighen, who represented Canada at the conference, but argued that 'the clearest voice among those opposing renewal, and the most well-informed, belonged to the veteran Western Liberal editor of the Winnipeg *Free Press*, J.W. Dafoe.'[10]

In strict chronological terms, the first argument advanced against renewal of the alliance was carried by the Vancouver *Province* in December, 1919.[11] But from the spring through the summer of 1922, in the run-up to the expiry of the alliance's term in July, the hottest topic in Canadian political circles was whether it should be renewed or not. On 15 February 1921, the Canadian government formally advised the British government that Canada opposed the renewal.[12] Dafoe first dealt with the issue of the Anglo-Japanese alliance in the editorial columns of the *Manitoba Free Press* on May 16; in this case Dafoe may have missed the mark by joining the discussion rather belatedly. Be that as it may, as Dafoe developed his position on the question of the alliance over the next half year, he drew his arguments, as might be expected, from his earlier pronouncements and in the process gave coherent form to what he believed should be the basic principles governing Canada's foreign relations.

In the autumn of 1920, Clifford Sifton, the long-time owner of the *Free Press* who had withdrawn completely from the world of politics but maintained a continuing interest in immigration questions, had written Dafoe:

> I think the *Free Press* should adopt a stand opposing renewal of any treaty permitting Japanese to emigrate Canada. Any relaxation, however slight, will produce a rush of Japanese into British Columbia and, without question, a serious labour problem will arise.[13]

A subsequent reference to the Anglo-Japanese alliance can be found in the Dafoe papers in early May of the following year. In a letter to Sifton, Dafoe touches on the approaching Imperial Conference of 1921 and reassures Sifton that nothing much can go wrong so long as Meighen retains Loring Christie as legal counsel for the Department of External Affairs.[14] Dafoe's confidence in Christie was echoed in another letter Dafoe received from Canadian journalist John Stevenson about the same time:

I agree completely with your [i.e., Dafoe's] slogan 'status first, discussion after'. The same as you, I firmly believe that Meighen will go along those lines. . . . [Meighen] is a nationalist for a day, then when things get out of hand, he turns to Christie: he's a faithful follower of Borden's. Recently when I talk to Christie, he's against renewal of the Anglo-Japanese alliance.[15]

Dafoe in his reply to Stevenson stressed the need to take an independent stance that reflected Canada's special interests and concerns:

> The time has come for Canada to face the world directly as an independent sovereign state. Establishing such a position means that Canada enjoys full freedom, while with regard to maintaining mutual interests with other British colonies, the only way is through co-operative relations with each one separately that pleases both. . . . In London next month [i.e., at the Imperial Conference in June] I strongly believe in the thinking that holds that Canada's cause will attract much support.[16]

The Imperial Conference that was to decide the fate of the Anglo-Japanese alliance on the British side opened in London on June 20. By the time the conference began the *Free Press* had thrice emphasized its opposition to renewal of the alliance.[17] The reasoning that led Dafoe and the *Free Press* to oppose renewal of the alliance was relatively straightforward. The international situation that had, in 1902, originally made the alliance necessary had changed dramatically; in particular, Germany and Russian were no longer enemies of Japan. Instead, with the formation of the League of Nations, a system of collective security now existed and bilateral military alliances outside that framework ought to be avoided. Moreover, renewal of the alliance would imply that the individual countries of the British Empire, including Canada, sanctioned Japan's imperialist and militarist policies in Korea, China and Siberia. In addition, although the alliance would not apply in the case of conflict between Japan and the United States, it was nevertheless causing tensions in America's relations with both Japan and Britain and was being used by the U.S. as a pretext for a naval build-up. Canada alone among the nations of the Empire was both a North American and a Pacific state. Consequently, Canadian concerns should have first priority in policy decisions which involved possible intervention by the British Empire in the Far East, to the degree that those decisions might affect the interests of the United States.

A week into the conference, Dafoe advanced yet a further objection to renewal of the alliance: the June 27 editorial columns of the *Free Press* raised once again the issue of immigration.[18] All English-speaking countries in the Pacific Basin, the argument ran, agreed on the vital necessity of devising a system to shut out Asians, who could not be assimilated. Although that determination was basic to the foreign policy of each of those countries, Britain was incapable of incorporating a 'whites only' policy into its own. That the senior self-governing dominions, united in opposition to Asian immigration, should make common cause with the United States in defending their interests simply pointed up the compelling importance of their concern for the future of their societies.

Although the Imperial Conference was nominally held in camera, the background for the meetings was covered for Canadian newspapers by Grant Dexter who accompanied Prime Minister Meighen. Through Dexter the *Free Press* learned that Meighen opposed renewal of the alliance in any form.[19] Writing to Sifton, Dafoe applauded Meighen's position:

> The Anglo-Japanese alliance is sure to be abrogated and a large part of the credit for that success can be brought home to Canada. . . . His [Meighen's] intent was that Canadian views should take precedence in the formulation of Imperial policy, particularly in areas where Canada has interests, and that the British government should implement those policies with the advice of the Canadian government. . . . Naturally it is impossible for such an idea to be fully realized, and even to imagine trying is difficult. . . . On the other hand the debate was worthwhile, and all honours should go to Meighen. He showed courage in advocating Canada's right to formulate foreign policy in areas of primary importance to Canada.[20]

Dafoe clearly rejected the notion that Imperial foreign policy should be formulated on the presumption that a 'common interest' prevailed among the dominions. To advance on behalf of the dominions a unified foreign policy in areas where their actual interests were bound to differ was antithetical to the fundamental idea of autonomy to which Dafoe was committed and in the pursuit of which—at least in form—Canada had taken the initiative.

Even before the Imperial Conference closed in mid-August, two critical developments raised questions about the future of the Anglo-Japanese alliance. The first was the announcement on June 28 by U.S. Secretary of State Charles Hughes of the American intention to host a general conference to discuss disarmament. Two days later, Lord Birkenhead made it clear that the British government's understanding was that, unless either side delivered notice one year in advance of an intention to abrogate, the alliance with Japan would be renewed automatically. As Dafoe quickly pointed out, the British position meant that notice of abrogation would have to be given immediately if the alliance was not to be renewed automatically in July 1922, thereby forestalling American intentions.[21]

Dafoe welcomed the American proposal, arguing on several occasions for the importance of holding a wide-ranging conference. His editorial for the July 25 edition of the *Free Press* commented pointedly on the significance of the coming Washington Conference. Observing that unless both Japan and the United States were prepared to reduce their armaments, it would be better not to hold the conference at all, Dafoe argued that the root cause of the antagonism between Japan and the U.S. was not the immigration issue, as many assumed; instead 'the explanation of this clash of national sentiment and interest can be expressed in one word. And that word is "China".' The failure of the Powers to agree to respect the sovereignty of China, the world's most populous nation, and to return to China the various concessions that had been wrested from it, cast a dark shadow over the promise of the Washington Conference. Dafoe returned to this theme in a further editorial on August 22, arguing that Japan's incursions into China were carried out under the security of the Anglo-Japanese alliance; the hope of all those opposed to renewal was that Japan's enthusiasm for colonialist expansion in the Far East could thereby be dampened somewhat.

What exactly was the significance for Canada of the issue of renewal of the Anglo-Japanese alliance? Dafoe could not conceal his disappointment that the Imperial Conference failed to produce any firm resolutions that might serve as precedents. Despite this, however, Dafoe saw the importance of the conference 'less in resolutions actually adopted than in the determination brought on by the light shed on the prospects for development of Imperial relations. That light comes more from what such conferences time and again do *not* do than from what they *do* do.' Canada's concerns over the alliance had been heard. In Dafoe's view, the Imperial Conference of 1921 advanced imperial relations a crucial step forward in that the principle underlying the position put forward by Borden at the Versailles Peace Conference had been recognized at the first postwar Imperial conference, and thus acquired the status of a 'fixed rule'.[22] Accordingly, the Balfour Declaration adopted at the 1926 Imperial Conference was, for Dafoe, merely a confirmation of that principle.

In addition, Dafoe believed that Canada could now play a role as bridge-builder between the United States and Great Britain. As the immediate neighbour of the U.S. on the North American continent and a Pacific nation in its own right, Canada could mediate on the United States' behalf by explaining to the United Kingdom government Pacific issues on which London failed to understand Washington—i.e., immigration, and concerns over China. The existence of the Anglo-Japanese alliance, Dafoe thought, badly damaged Canada's chances of assuming such a role. Accordingly, when the American government failed to send Canada a separate invitation to attend the Washington Conference and instead included Canada as a member of the British Imperial delegation, Dafoe was doubly disappointed. The U.S. action failed to recognize Canada's advancement in two important areas by 1922, for it demonstrated that the U.S. continued to ignore not only Canada's autonomy in foreign affairs, but also its standing as a Pacific nation.[23]

DAFOE AND THE INSTITUTE OF PACIFIC RELATIONS

From the demise of the Anglo-Japanese Alliance through to the establishment in 1928 of formal diplomatic relations between Japan and Canada, the focus of Japanese-Canadian government-level exchanges remained essentially immigration and trade. On the immigration issue, which had been bound up in the abrogation of the Anglo-Japanese Alliance,[24] Canada soon moved to put tight limits on Japanese immigration. Under the 1908 Lemieux agreement—the so-called 'Gentlemen's Agreement'—Japanese immigrants admitted under the domestic help and agricultural labour categories had been limited to a total of 400 a year; that number was scaled back to 150 a year in 1923, and further reduced in 1928 by including dependents (wives, children and parents) who had not previously been counted as part of the quota. Moreover, agreement was reached to put an end to the practice of 'picture brides'. Meanwhile, since Canada had enjoyed a favourable balance of trade with Japan since 1925, it can be said that from the Canadian viewpoint a satisfactory state of affairs had been achieved.[25]

From the time the issue of renewal of the Anglo-Japanese alliance had been raised, Dafoe had concerned himself with defining Canada's status, and emphasizing its role, as a Pacific nation. Despite this, Dafoe in the 1920s was not generally perceived to be actively concerned with Canada and the Pacific region, or in Canada's relations with the various nations of Asia.[26] The fact that Dafoe continued to be interested in Pacific issues, however, can be demonstrated by his participation in the Institute of Pacific Relations. The Institute of Pacific Relations (IPR) was just one among the many private research bodies concerned with international relations that sprang up after World War I.[27] Its mission was 'to collect accurate information about conditions in the Pacific nations, . . . to discuss opinions and sentiments in order to obtain a clear view of mutual relations, [and] to show the way to appropriate activities leading to peace and understanding in the Pacific.' The inaugural conference was held in Honolulu in the summer of 1925 at the initiative of the U.S.[28]

The nine-member Canadian delegation to Honolulu was led by John Nelson, who later joined the steering committee seeking to establish a branch of the IPR in Canada. Nelson was also actively involved in efforts to promote membership of the U.K. in the institute.[29] At that time, there were two other international research organizations active in Canada of a character similar to the IPR: the British Institute of International Affairs (BIIA), Canada group, and the League of Nations Society in Canada (LNSC). Both were located in eastern Canada, however, and were dominated by such men as former Conservative Prime Minister Robert Borden and Liberal leader Newton W. Rowell.

Dafoe had little use for such private research bodies for international relations. Citing 'geographical conditions' and the resultant 'diversity of thinking that can be seen among Canadians', Dafoe argued that such organizations could not be successfully established in Canada. In the same vein, he refused to join the BIIA on the grounds that, as a journalist, it would not be wise to be involved in 'activities that could be seen as a kind of propaganda'.[30]

Rowell, passing through Honolulu on his way to Australia, sat in on the IPR conference for a few hours, and Nelson asked him to become the head of the Canadian IPR committee from November 1925.[31] Although Rowell turned the offer down, saying he was too busy, he proposed that not only should the Canadian Institute of International Affairs (CIIA), the establishment of which was then being planned, absorb the existing BIIA, but that the IPR should also be incorporated into the new organization.[32] In the autumn of 1926, the secretary-general of the IPR on a visit to Toronto met with Canadian members of the Royal Institute of International Affairs (RIIA), as the BIIA was renamed in 1926, and urged that a Canadian delegation be selected to attend the second IPR Honolulu conference. During those talks, it was agreed that the Canadian IPR would be incorporated into the CIIA.[33] At about the same time, Robert Borden assumed the chairmanship of the Canadian IPR, which had got under way thanks to the efforts of Nelson.

The Canadian government also showed considerable interest in the activities of the IPR. Prime Minister Mackenzie King, who acted as his own External Affairs minister, received daily reports through the U.K. government of the activities of the U.S. IPR.[34] O.D. Skelton, Undersecretary for External Affairs, briefed King in June, 1926 on the background of the IPR as well as on the well-known members of the Canadian delegation being sent to the second Honolulu conference in July—a delegation to be led by World War I hero Arthur Currie. As well, the director of the Canadian Bankers' Association, Henry T. Ross, also a member of the delegation to Honolulu, reported back to King with details of conference proceedings. Of the subjects discussed at the conference, Ross pointed to immigration as one which 'I think will arouse the interest of you and of the Canadian government'; he went on to tell King that when the Japanese delegate drew a comparison between Canada and the U.S. in the matter of constitutional rights for Japanese immigrants and their descendants, Canada emerged as the more tolerant.[35]

On 30 January 1928, the CIIA took its first steps in Ottawa under the leadership of Borden, and the Canadian IPR was officially established, with John Nelson assuming the office of CIIA secretary-general.[36] What motive impelled Nelson to take such an active role in the IPR movement? By the time of the first IPR conference in 1925, Nelson had made a name for himself in Vancouver both as a journalist and as a prominent Rotarian.[37] It appears that Nelson's interest in Pacific issues was awakened, in a way not unusual for a British Columbian, by the problem of Asian immigration. In February, 1922, Nelson received a very cordial letter from Loring Christie dealing with the Anglo-Japanese alliance.[38] Nelson subsequently met with Christie and informed him of the direction that opposition to renewal of the alliance was taking in the province of British Columbia; at the same time, he apparently made enquiries about treaties governing immigration between Japan and Canada. Christie told him that the intent of the 1908 Gentlemen's Agreement, the Japan-United Kingdom trade and naval treaty of 1911, and the Anglo-Japanese alliance was to restrict Japanese emigration to Canada; he asked Nelson to keep him informed on the situation in British Columbia.   Nelson made his own position clear in a speech at the first Honolulu conference, in which he argued that British Columbia was threatened with an 'economic invasion' by Asian immigrants. Nelson's position was not simply racist, however; rather, his concern was with the extent to which immigrants who spoke a non-Western language and had different cultural values could be successfully 'Canadianized'. An inability to assimilate meant limits on their political and economic participation were in order. In advancing this argument, Nelson distinguished between Chinese and Japanese immigrants, singling out the latter as particularly unsuitable as immigrants to Canada. In fact, Nelson was quite satisfied with the limitations on Asian immigration then in force; his primary concern was the issue of citizenship for those already in Canada. He believed that civil rights should not be granted until the immigrant had fully assimilated the Canadian way of life, and all of his efforts toward establishing branches of the IPR in various regions of Canada could be said to spring from his wish for a forum in which Canadians and Asian immigrants could further their mutual understanding.[39]

Although Dafoe had avoided forming links with any of the various research institutes, he apparently had had a passing connection with the IPR in its early stages. On his visit to Canada in November, 1926, Davis met Dafoe and later recalled that Dafoe was at that time greatly interested in the IPR. Dafoe's writings, however, suggest that his interest in the Institute developed only after the founding of the CIIA—i.e., from the formal establishment of the Canadian IPR and the installation of Borden as secretary general with Dafoe himself as second in command.

In any event, Dafoe participated in the gathering in Ottawa on 30 January 1928 that took the first steps toward setting up the CIIA. He intended to report on it at a meeting in Winnipeg in February but, prevented by illness from appearing, he prepared a memorandum to be read for him there.[40] The memorandum outlined the activities which had been initiated under the sponsorship of the IPR in Ottawa, Montreal, Toronto and Winnipeg, of which 'Winnipeg was the strongest in terms of the number of people mustered up'. The various branches, Dafoe commented, were all active in one way or another: the members in Montreal, with the exception of Sir Arthur Currie, met once a fortnight and 'are furthering the study of various Pacific issues'. The Ottawa chapter also held weekly meetings, while the Toronto, Winnipeg and

Vancouver branches held study meetings as and when suitable speakers were available.

The third IPR conference was held in Kyoto during October and November of 1929; earlier the same year Canada had opened its first Pacific-region embassy in Tokyo. In the context of the time, the establishment of diplomatic relations with Japan on Canada's initiative was a triumphant follow-through to the adoption of the Balfour Declaration at the Imperial Conference of 1926. The setting up of an embassy in Washington became Canada's first priority.[41] The exchange of ambassadors was delayed, however, partly because of the political situation in Canada and partly because many felt that any problems arising between the two countries could be resolved through the existing mechanism of the International Joint Commission. Finally, in February 1927, the first Canadian ambassador, Vincent Massey, presented his credentials to President Calvin Coolidge.[42]

Soon afterwards, Canada moved to establish diplomatic relations with Japan. In a confidential telegram to London on 22 November 1927, Ottawa expressed its desire to extend its representation to both France and Japan. A month later, on December 22, the British government conveyed Canada's request to the Japanese embassy in London; on January 19 of the following year, the Japanese government announced that it had accepted Canada's proposal for an exchange of ambassadors.[43] The reasons for the choice of France are apparent, but why was Canada eager to establish diplomatic relations with Japan? Mackenzie King had, for the preceding quarter century, largely been engaged by the problems of Europe; nevertheless in the decade of the 1920s he switched the focus of his attention from the Atlantic to the Pacific in the apparent conviction that the new postwar world would centre in Asia. Arguing that diplomacy was shaped by geography, King wrote that Canada, situated equidistant from Europe and Asia, had 'the U.S.A. as its neighbour in North America, France as its neighbour in Europe and Japan as its closest neighbour in Asia.'[44]

Behind King's observations also lay the more pragmatic issues of Japanese trade and immigration, and Canada's interest in China—motives that became apparent when King was forced to defend his initiative. In the House of Commons on 31 January 1928, when questioned by R.B. Bennett, the Leader of the Opposition, about the reasons for establishing diplomatic relations with Japan, King justified his action by pointing to the fact that Japan was Canada's third largest export market (after the U.S. and the United Kingdom), and that Canada's total volume of trade with Japan exceeded that of trade with the U.K. during the Laurier years. Moreover, King continued, Canada would employ all its diplomatic powers to 'limit Japanese immigration to the smallest number possible while continuing friendly relations between Canada and Japan'. In addition, King argued, the new embassy in Tokyo was Canada's 'only window into Asia.'[45] That King was referring to China was signalled by the hurried trip to that country made by Herbert Marler, Canada's first ambassador to Japan, almost immediately upon being installed in Tokyo.[46] Since Chinese immigration to Canada was already limited by law, Ottawa's interest clearly lay in the possibility of expanded trade with Japan's larger neighbour.

Dafoe, who had been much occupied since the early 1920s with choosing a distinctive flag for Canada and with deciding what buildings should fly it as an emblem of Canada's progress toward self-government, welcomed the establishment of formal relations with Japan in the same spirit.[47] The appointment as the first ambassador of Marler, with whom Dafoe had had a warm friendship since first interviewing him in 1922, was to encourage Dafoe to maintain (albeit in a limited way) a continuing interest in the development of Canada-Japan relations. Once settled, Marler wrote to Dafoe thanking him for the coverage the *Free Press* had given the new ambassador. In the course of the correspondence, Marler also reported on the activities and effectiveness of the embassy, passed on information on trade and political issues he had gathered on his trip to South China, and urged Dafoe to visit Japan. As it happened, Dafoe was unable to join the delegation to the IPR conference in Kyoto, but wrote to Borden complimenting the choice of delegates, led by Rowell.[48]

In practice, Dafoe's participation in regular IPR activities was minimal prior to Japan's occupation of Manchuria; writing to Rowell in March, 1932, Dafoe explained that given the pressures of newspaper publishing, IPR business had to be secondary for him.[49] In the interval Canada's chief spokesmen on Pacific issues continued to be Nelson and Rowell. While Nelson was mainly concerned with immigration questions, Rowell's primary interest in the Pacific region had centred for more than twenty years on the problem of establishing stability and order in China—a question he had first raised as moderator of the national congress of missionaries in 1909.[50] An ardent Methodist, Rowell saw Canada's role in the Far East in terms of trade and evangelism. 'The world dramas of our century will be enacted mainly on the Pacific Ocean', he predicted: 'With a face on the Pacific, Canada will surely play a leading role in those dramas.'[51]

Unlike Dafoe, Rowell was also a politician and an active force in the making of Canadian foreign policy. He represented Canada at the first general assembly of the League of Nations in 1920, and sympathy with the League's collectivist spirit shaped his views. Hence, not surprisingly, he argued in the House against the renewal of the bilateral Anglo-Japanese alliance.[52] Rowell also played an active part in the founding of the League of Nations Society of Canada and the CIIA. In 1925, he had travelled for three months in Japan, China, and Australia and his enthusiasm for the future of the Pacific encouraged Borden to chose him to lead the delegation to the Kyoto conference.[53] After a month's return visit to China, Rowell opened the Kyoto conference with a speech emphasizing Canada's main concerns in international affairs: the reduction of military forces, the establishment of a collective security system, and, in the Far East, the future of China and Russia. The focus of hope, he concluded, lay in China, where a new people's government was endeavouring to lead the world's largest population into the modern era.[54]

En route home aboard the *Empress of Canada*, Rowell drafted lengthy letters reporting the results of the conference to Borden and King. The gist of his comments would later take the form of a lecture entitled 'Canada and the IPR'. In Rowell's view, the most urgent of all Pacific issues, the most essential to peace in Asia, and the most complicated was the Manchurian question. Canada, he believed, could play a important role:

> I believe that, just as the 1927 IPR conference is known to have made a significant contribution to better understanding between the United Kingdom and China, so the 1929 IPR conference will be seen as having given birth to a better understanding of relations between Japan and China.[55]

China remained, as it had been twenty years before, the focus of concern in the Pacific. Notwithstanding the changes in international relations wrought by World War I and its aftermath, Rowell worried that affairs in the region remained in their pre-war state. For Rowell the establishment of relations between Canada and Japan could be nothing but a step in the direction of a new age for Canada's relations with the Far East.

CONCLUSION

Canada's expectations for Japan—insofar as there were any—were irrevocably shattered by the Manchurian incident in September, 1931.[56] The Winnipeg *Free Press*, which quickly condemned Japan's actions as 'nothing more than armed oppression', set the tone for subsequent press coverage.[57] Japan's subjugation of Manchuria represented a failure of the collective security system on which Canadians had pinned their hopes since the end of World War I, and signalled the beginning of the end of the promise of lasting peace based on the principles of the League.

In an effort to avert the collapse of the Covenant, and in support of its fundamental principles, Dafoe argued vigorously that 'for countries to settle their disputes with other countries or to extend their interest without reference to a court of law is ultimately and decidedly against the law'. Writing in April, 1932, Dafoe went on to point out the urgency of even greater support and publicity for 'public debate, debate in the parliaments of each country on the decisions of each member of the organization.'[58] Soon afterwards, the Lytton Commission presented its report to the League, and Dafoe held out hope that the Commissioners' recommendations would contribute 'to preserving the rights of China, which cannot be ignored, by abolishing those rights that are the source of dissatisfaction, while protecting Japan's interests in its sphere of influence.'[59] Dafoe was to be disappointed: Japan resigned from the League in March, 1933 when the League approved the Lytton Commission's report.

Nevertheless, Canadians were extremely reluctant to abandon their faith in the League, which they still believed could contain the dangers of Great Power politics. In a lecture entitled 'The Collective Security System and Manchuria' broadcast in March, 1934, Dafoe argued that the danger of a break-down of the League of Nations arose from the Great Powers: from Britain and France, who were members, from Japan which had resigned, and especially from the United States, which had never joined.

> Responsibility for this threatening situation falls on those who failed to support the League at its founding. However, it is possible to recover from this crisis. The peoples of the world who want to be rescued from war by the League must give back to the League the power to do that—it all depends on the strength of public opinion.
>
> Our hope lies in . . . pressing the Japanese government to reverse its policy of armed oppression, and to accept the verdict of world opinion.[60]

The danger, Dafoe continued, 'is that the Japanese people will take any hint of interference by foreign governments as reason to align themselves with those militaristic nations seeking to become great powers.' As Ramsay Cook later observed, Dafoe was unquestionably 'a rigid liberal with no use for institutions that failed to support public opinion.'[61]

In 1936, the year he became chairman of the CIIA, Dafoe took part in the IPR Yosemite Conference and for the first time got on familiar terms with members of the Japanese delegation, led by Foreign Minister Yoshizawa. Dafoe found the experience a bitterly disappointing one, for he concluded that it would not be possible to preserve peace in the Pacific region. The Japanese people, he afterwards told his readers, view themselves as 'a chosen people, a people with a mission to spread their civilization to the outside world.'[62] For Dafoe, a staunch believer in parliamentary democracy and the values of the English-speaking world, Japan no longer held any attraction whatever.

Although the formalization of bilateral relations had promised to usher in a new era of mutual understanding, in fact the cultural gulf which separated Canada and Japan was too great to be so easily bridged. Diplomatic relations had been built on the shaky foundation of superficial mutual interests and limited contacts developed before the exchange of ambassadors. Worse, the two countries had proceeded largely on mistaken interpretations and misplaced expectations of each other. Granted, some good did come out of the new embassies and the activities of the IPR, as is clear if one compares Canada's attitudes to Japan and to Japanese immigration in the early 1920s with those of the 1930s. A good example would be the change of heart shown by John Nelson as early as 1928.[63] Then there was H.F. Angus, deeply involved in the IPR: at the Kyoto Conference he initiated a movement to grant the franchise to Japanese immigrants. Finally there was the first Canadian chargé d'affaires in Tokyo, H.L. Keenleyside. After his return to Canada, Keenleyside spoke up in defence of the rights of Japanese Canadians in the tense period immediately before the outbreak of World War II.[64] However, these men represented only a tiny minority in the 1930s. Indeed, after the Japanese invasion of Manchuria, Canadian attitudes toward the Japanese hardened and from that time on most Canadians distinguished sharply between Chinese and Japanese.

In many respects, Dafoe's interest in Japan and Asia was more representative of the views of the majority of his fellow Canadians—in part because his pronouncements helped shape their understandings and expectations. Although he recognized Japan to be a power to be reckoned with in Asia, its significance for Canada he saw in limited terms: as the source of Japanese immigration, seen as a diplomatic rather than domestic problem, and as the gateway to China. With little first-hand knowledge, he grappled with the presence of Japan largely at a distance, within the framework of his concerns for collective security and the future of the League. A belated familiarity only resulted in shattered illusions. Such views, reflected in the pages of the *Free Press*, formed the backdrop of Canadian-Japanese relations in the 1920s and early 1930s.

○

Although Canada established a fledgeling Trade Commissioners Service in 1886, the Service's mandate restricted its activities to representing Canadian commercial interests abroad. In areas other than trade Canada continued to rely upon the British diplomatic service for representation in international affairs. While quasi-diplomatic offices were established in London (1880) and Paris (1882), they too maintained a very narrow focus for their activities. The Department of External Affairs was officially established in 1909, but confined itself to gathering information and advising the government on international affairs. Meanwhile the large Canadian contribution to the Allied war effort between 1914 and 1918 earned Canada a separate place at the Versailles peace negotiations and accelerated the natural maturing process. When the 1926 Imperial Conference confirmed that Canada and the other British Dominions enjoyed an international personality of their own—equal in status to Great Britain—Canada took the initial steps to establish direct diplomatic relations with foreign states.

As might be expected given its proximity and importance, Washington saw the opening of Canada's first legation in 1927. The following year the government of Mackenzie King announced two further initiatives: the upgrading of the existing commissioner's office in Paris to full diplomatic status and the decision to despatch a Minister to Japan.[1] London, Washington and Paris all represented fixed points on Canada's international horizon; Tokyo, by contrast, was a precedent-setting step in a new direction. The record of the development of an independent foreign policy and its mechanisms have been ably told by others. Less familiar, however, are the efforts of the early members of the Canadian foreign service who, to a great extent, were travelling in uncharted waters. The members of the new Canadian legation in Tokyo were among them. In particular, the contribution of the first Canadian Minister, Herbert Marler, and his staff left a legacy which continues to testify to the long-standing significance of the relationship.

Dr Rice received his PhD in modern history from the University of Toronto in 1974. He joined the Canadian Foreign Service that year and has since been posted twice to the Embassy in Japan. His interest in the origins of the legation was first stimulated by the celebration of the 50th anniversary of diplomatic relations in 1979 when he was Desk Officer for Japan at the Department of External Affairs, Ottawa. He is currently Counsellor (Political) at the Embassy in Tokyo.

SIR HERBERT MARLER
AND THE CANADIAN LEGATION IN TOKYO

Eber H. Rice

When the 1926 Imperial Conference legitimized separate representation abroad by the dominions, Prime Minister Mackenzie King did not hesitate to act. At his urging Canadian External Affairs officials initiated discussion the following year with their Foreign Office counterparts in London concerning King's desire to establish diplomatic relations with Japan. By 1928 there were many good reasons for creating a direct diplomatic link between Ottawa and Tokyo. With total bilateral trade having grown to almost $46 million, Japan represented an important customer for Canadian products, although still ranked an admittedly distant third behind the United States and the United Kingdom. Canada for its part placed sixth among Japan's trading partners, although once again imports from Canada, at $30 million, were a relatively modest three per cent of Japan's total imports.

In addition to a growing trading relationship, there was a particularly sensitive domestic reason for opening a mission in Tokyo. Asian immigration had long been a contentious issue on the Canadian west coast, and the federal Conservative party, seeking to make political capital of this, had adopted a policy of total exclusion. King rejected exclusion on the ground that it amounted to institutionalized racism. But however much he might find the Conservative policy personally repugnant, King was very aware of its potential appeal to certain sections of the Canadian electorate.[2] In response, King and his advisors developed a policy which, they hoped, would counter the popularity of the Tories' exclusionary approach. With a diplomatic mission in Tokyo to screen visa applicants, the Canadian government could control immigration at the source.[3]

In addition to such bilateral issues as trade and immigration which argued in favour of direct relations with Japan, there was a larger, global, perspective to King's decision. By the 1920s, Japan had emerged as a Pacific, if not a world power; King expected the voice of Japan to continue to grow in international affairs. The Prime Minister was convinced that in future the great questions of war and peace would be decided chiefly in Washington, London, Paris and Tokyo. With Canadian diplomatic offices already opened in the first three, he sought to complete the quartet 'to gain the attention of those countries on matters that are of concern' to Canada.[4]

With the agreement of London and Tokyo to a Canadian legation in Japan, King was able to announce to the House of Commons early in 1928 that all governments concerned had given their approval to his proposal. The Prime Minister was delighted that he had been able to keep the announcement a secret from his political opponents. But after the initial surprise wore off, domestic opposition quickly found its voice and the pages of Hansard were filled with criticisms of the Government. In spite of the declarations of the 1926 Conference, a strong body of opinion considered that the welfare of the British Empire required that its various members share a common foreign policy. Such could only be achieved if they worked closely together in harmony with London and avoided actions which might give the appearance of disunity. To those who held this view, the establishment of separate diplomatic missions by Canada, Australia, South Africa, and other dominions was wholly inappropriate. The Conservatives in the Commons together with their supporters among the press railed against King's independent initiative, charging that it threatened to destroy Imperial unity. King had great respect for the Empire—in theory—but he was convinced that too often in practice London took the dominions for granted, and committed them to courses of action which had not been fully debated in each country. He had no desire to undermine the strength of the Empire, but at the same time felt its interests could best be served by recognizing the individual concerns of the senior dominions.

Despite the emotional appeal of the Tories' calls on imperial patriotism, it was difficult to quarrel with King's rejoinder that Canada's principal international interests lay in bilateral concerns rather than in the heady regions of 'imperial' policy. Bilateral issues, he argued, were best dealt with by Canadian diplomats in direct discussion with their foreign counterparts.[5] 'We in Canada',

King observed, 'have just as good material and brains for the foreign service as any other part of the empire.' When London offered no support for the objections, the Conservative thunder quickly subsided and the parliamentary debate made little impact upon King's intentions.

Meanwhile the announcement that a legation would be opened in Tokyo had brought a number of unsolicited nominations for the position of first minister to Japan. King initially offered the job to George Stephens (1866-1942), a Montreal-born industrialist, who had given valuable war and post-war service to Canada and the international community. The multi-lingual Stephens had demonstrated considerable skill as the British nominee to the French-controlled Saar Commission (1923-35), and he had so successfully mediated the conflicting claims of the French and Germans that he had been chosen chairman for a two-year term in 1924. Stephens' nomination received the blessing of the Cabinet, but when King made a firm offer to him, his wife opposed a further period of service outside the country and Stephens regretfully declined.[6]

The Prime Minister then turned to a former political colleague, Herbert Marler (1876-1940). Marler, who was associated with the Montreal law firm of William de Montmollin and H.M. Marler, had been elected to Parliament for the Montreal constituency of St Lawrence-St George in 1921, and King had invited him into the Cabinet as Minister without Portfolio in 1925. Although he was subsequently defeated in the general election of that year, the Prime Minister had developed considerable respect for Marler whom he considered to be tenacious, bright and conscientious, although somewhat humourless.[7] When Stephens reluctantly rejected the Tokyo assignment, King offered it to Marler on New Year's Day, 1929. King feared that Marler in turn would refuse the proposal in order to protect his domestic political ambitions. Marler accepted with enthusiasm, however, and King was delighted. He confided to his diary that he 'will make a splendid Minister, and is just the person to inaugurate the legation in the Orient.'[8] In spite of Marler's undoubted enthusiasm he did protect his future options by extracting from King a promise that he could stand in the next general election, should he so wish.[9]

Marler had virtues and talents which clearly recommended him to King. Marler had proved his business acumen by his contribution to the development of the Marler law firm into one of the most prestigious in the country. His management skills would be of considerable value to the task of setting up a diplomatic mission in Asia. In spite of a pompous personal style of expression, his energy and commitment to his new responsibilities augured well for the success of the Tokyo post. These latter characteristics are those for which Marler is chiefly remembered today, partly because they prompted him to secure for the Canadian diplomatic service one of its finest legation properties.

Marler set about his new tasks speedily and with thoroughness, and within two months of accepting the assignment he had prepared a list of proposals for the Prime Minister's consideration. He first suggested that he travel to London for political and professional consultations with British officials and to purchase suitable clothing and furnishings for the new Legation. Since he believed that 'the work of a Minister lies not only in the area to which he is accredited, but also in the country which he represents', he suggested that he undertake 'a fairly complete tour of Canada' during which he would speak in most of the major cities before local Canadian Clubs or Boards of Trade in order to explain the rationale behind his appointment, and to stimulate interest in the commercial possibilities which he felt awaited Canadians in Japan.[10] This Canadian tour was to be only the first of many.

Marler was also concerned that the staff in Tokyo be the best he could assemble. In spite of his inexperience he had very decided views on how a diplomat should operate. In his own thoughtful, if somewhat pompous, fashion, he told King that a diplomat must never forget that 'every word he utters and every step he takes must be weighted and watched with the most extreme care, so that nothing will occur to mar or diminish the success he hopes to achieve . . . [and] every member of his staff must be fully imbued with precisely the same viewpoint.' He sought to engage only 'those who, by training and temperament, will meet with approval . . . who will be cautious in their demeanour with the people of Japan and who will be discreet and loyal in every respect.'[11] In order to ensure that his staff conformed to his own high standards, and so that he might identify and neutralize in advance any personnel problems, he personally interviewed every candidate for the available positions.

Not surprisingly, Marler's final staff selection highlighted general, rather than specific, skills. His deputy at the Embassy, Hugh Keenleyside, had a doctorate in history, and other staff members had a grounding in the classics and foreign languages.[12] Marler's preferences reflected the values of the time, in that he believed Canada's representatives should have a graceful prose style, a good appearance and excellent manners. Such people, in his view, were those best prepared 'by upbringing and training' to assume the responsibilities of a diplomat. These, he observed, were 'to safeguard the interests and good name of Canada; to cultivate friendly relations; to study economic and political trends which might affect Canadian interests, and to assist in the negotiation of political and commercial treaties'.[13] Whatever one might think of Marler's own prose, his final choices did reflect careful consideration and detailed deliberation in personnel selection.

It was, of course, quite common in the pre-1939 diplomatic profession to find men of independent means who brought their private fortunes to their professional responsibilities. In spite of this, King expressed surprise at Marler's suggestion that he serve in Tokyo without salary.[14] The Prime Minister rejected the suggestion as inappropriate to the professional foreign service King hoped to develop, and Marler was told he would receive a financial package equal to that of the Minister in Washington—a salary of $10,000, allowances of $12,000, and a car allowance of $3,000. Marler, of course, agreed, but he reminded King that he was quite prepared to invest $50,000 annually from his own private fortune to guarantee that Canada was fittingly represented in Japan.[15]

Accommodation in Tokyo was particularly critical because Marler was convinced that his primary purpose of gathering information on his host country could be best achieved 'by social intercourse'—friendly conversation—and by the Minister's taking a personal interest in such things as the arts, the literature, the sports or floriculture of his assigned country. Such things, it is true, might not always appeal to him, but appealed to the nationals of the country whose confidence he hoped to gain, or from whom he sought information on which to base the opinions he passed back to his home government. Given his preferred methods, Marler felt it was most important that he be able to 'suitably entertain, receive and interest those whose friendship and confidence' he would be seeking. While office work must not be neglected, the whole basis of effective and valuable office work had to be 'the gathering of accurate and useful information'[16] Hence the Marlers' concern with creating an appropriate social environment for the pursuit of their objectives.

But Marler had been warned by his business associates that suitable accommodation would be difficult to find due, in part, to the devastation of the 1923 earthquake and fire. With this in mind, early in 1929 Marler had asked a Montreal architect, Kenneth G. Rea, to submit plans for a purpose-built residence and chancery. These were submitted to King within six weeks of Marler's accepting the appointment to Tokyo. The Minister-designate urged the Prime Minister to include in the next national budget sufficient funds to guarantee the purchase of land and the construction of a permanent chancery and residence. While Marler was not to receive permission to proceed on this project for four years, it is not surprising that the Rea plans foreshadowed many of the features incorporated into the final building.

King was particularly pleased with his new appointee's vigour. He agreed that Marler should travel to London and Paris, and tour Canada on his way to Tokyo. But he believed the proposal to build a permanent home for the new Legation was premature and he suggested that Marler proceed to Tokyo and assess the need again after spending some time there.[17]

While the Minister-designate was busy in Europe and Canada, the Government sent Dr Hugh Keenleyside to Tokyo to make advance preparations. Keenleyside was only 30 at the time, and had been hired by the Department of External Affairs the year before, after a short early career in university teaching. He had, in that brief time, impressed the Prime Minister (who, as Secretary of State for External Affairs was Keenleyside's departmental chief) as a 'splendid man . . . who possesses a knowledge of political conditions and has great tact and judgment in the manner of expressing himself'.[18] Upon arrival in early May, 1929, he acquired suitable premises for the Chancery and the residence. He leased offices at No. 5 Nagai Compound for the chancery and, after considerable effort, rented for 12,000 yen annually a house for Marler in Nishi-Machi, Azabu-ku, which had been formerly occupied by Jean Aurèle Vasseiliu, the Romanian Minister to Japan. The temporary chancery opened for business 21 May 1929, and was moved in the autumn to the Imperial Life Building in the Marunouchi district of central Tokyo.[19] On 26 June 1929 the Japanese Government formally confirmed its agreement of the preceding year to the appointment of Mr Marler, and on 9 September 1929 Keenleyside was on the dock in Yokohama, along with representatives from the British Embassy, various Canadians resident in Japan and a collection of journalists, when the SS *Empress of France* arrived with the Marlers and members of their staff, including Mrs Keenleyside, Third Secretary Kenneth Kirkwood, and a Secretary, Miss Marjorie Logan. Marler, never one to ignore an opportunity to make a speech, briefly addressed the welcoming party, and set off by car for temporary accommodation in the recently built Imperial Hotel of Frank Lloyd Wright's design.[20]

An early appointment was sought for the new minister with the Foreign Minister, Baron Shidera Kijuro, for initial introductions and to allow Marler to inquire when he might present his credentials to the Emperor. On September 16, Marler was informed that he would be received by the Emperor the following morning at 10:30 a.m. In spite of the short notice Marler, in full diplomatic uniform purchased during his visit to London, set out the next morning from the Imperial Hotel (which had been bedecked with Canadian and Japanese flags for the occasion) to present his credentials.[21]

From the very beginning the Minister set himself and his staff a strict and vigorous pace.[22] He felt in particular a responsibility to build up a body of information for Ottawa about Japan which, although quite unfamiliar to most Canadians, he believed represented immense potential for Canada. Lengthy and detailed monthly reports were prepared, not only on the economic and political conditions in Japan, but also on China. Typical of these was a 103-page report on Japanese mineral resources and mining, prepared by Kirkwood following an extensive trip into the north.[23] Marler himself travelled extensively throughout Japan to familiarize himself with the country and to visit resident Canadians. In 1930 he and Keenleyside visited China—Marler going to Shanghai, Nanking and Hong Kong, and Keenleyside to Korea, Manchuria and North China—both in pursuit of commercial and political information. Mrs Marler was in many ways no less busy, for in the first year they were in Tokyo the Marlers entertained more than 2,500 guests in their home.[24]

Very shortly the new Minister concluded that his accommodation in Tokyo was inadequate to his professional, social, and hospitality responsibilities.

Upon his arrival Marler had moved the Chancery operation into the then newly built Imperial Life Insurance Building in Marunouchi, but with the centralization of the legation's commercial operation in this main office, its inadequacy was soon obvious. The residence, although comfortable, was very expensive to rent at ¥12,000 a year; it had impossible approaches from the main street and was located in a noisy (albeit prestigious) area. Marler began a search for alternative sites and during 1930 investigated over fifty possibilities.[25] Four sites were short-listed, each to the south or southwest of Roppongi Crossing, and Marler informed the Prime Minister that the price for the land would be close to ¥400,000 (or approximately $200,000). He tried to sweeten this information by noting that in spite of the cost, the final charge to government funds would hardly be more than the continuing cost of rental accommodation.

The Prime Minister, however, could not bring himself to agree. He had recently approved the expenditure of nearly $500,000 for the Legation in Washington, and had been privately shocked by what he considered to be a necessary, but politically sensitive, budgetary outlay. He was relieved that the Washington chancery purchase had drawn no criticism in Parliament, but he was unwilling to risk committing himself to defend yet another major expense for diplomatic premises abroad, particularly with the domestic and international economic situation growing more and more bleak.[26] King's concern was understandable, but could not save him voters angry over the government's cautious response to the deepening depression. The Liberals were defeated in the general election of July, 1930.

The new Prime Minister, R.B. Bennett, chose to continue Marler's appointment to Tokyo, despite his political connections to King and the Liberals. When Marler returned to Canada for a visit in the early summer of 1931, he took the opportunity to raise the matter of a permanent legation with the new Prime Minister. He briefed Bennett on the history of his search for property in Tokyo, and added that with the aid of the Mitsui Trust Company and the architects of the British Embassy, he had identified two more sites. If Bennett were agreeable, Marler could arrange a purchase of one or the other; the first would cost $291,000 including the accommodation Marler proposed to construct, the second site was a bit more expensive and would run $341,000 with the same buildings. Marler was fully aware of the impact of the Depression on the national budget and Bennett's likely reaction to these figures in a period of retrenchment; to soften the blow, Marler offered to personally advance the funds for the purchase of the land and the erection of appropriate buildings, with repayment to be made by the Government over a period of years. Although Bennett was interested, he could not persuade his Cabinet colleagues to agree, and once again Marler returned to Tokyo unsuccessful.[27]

By 1932 Marler had decided that he enjoyed the diplomatic service much more than the perils of the political trail, particularly since the Liberal Party seemed consigned to some years on the opposition benches of the House of Commons. He wrote a personal letter to O.D. Skelton, saying he would remain in Tokyo as long as was desired. But if the Prime Minister agreed that they might stay in place, Marler in turn felt that he and his wife deserved some compensation for the personal sacrifice of the company of family and friends. Once again he raised the question of the new residence and chancery which, he argued, would increase immeasurably their effectiveness—as well as their personal happiness—and compensate for 'all we have given up at home.'[28] Marler was now prepared to make an even more attractive offer to the Government to encourage a positive response. He would purchase land and construct a chancery and residence upon it for a sum not to exceed $200,000 which would be paid back to him by the Government over a period of ten years. The Marlers' own resources did not actually run to this level of generosity; Marler intended to borrow the money from the Bank of Montreal on the strength of his personal credit (which he eventually did). The Minister offered, in addition, to contribute at least $25,000 of his own money to the project.[29] Bennett, not one to reject a good offer, took not only the proposal but, eventually, Marler himself before the Cabinet, and quickly won approval. Formal consent to the agreement was given on 31 August 1932. Both Marler and his wife were delighted. Later in the autumn they were told that property owned by Viscount Tadatoshi Aoyama, last Lord and thirteenth Daimyo of the Sasayama Clan might be available for purchase. The site was larger than Marler had originally considered necessary, but the Minister was able to take advantage of a temporary drop in the value of the yen, so the price was particularly good. The location he thought splendid: it met all of his criteria, was suitable for both chancery and residence, and promised to appreciate in value over the years.

After six weeks of bargaining Mr Langley, the commercial attaché, concluded the negotiations and the deal was closed for ¥425,000–¥25,000 less than originally asked. Some, including Canada's former Ambassador to the People's Republic of China, Arthur Menzies, insist that the favourable price for the land was due to the rumour, then current in Tokyo, that the property was haunted by ghosts and suitable only for foreign occupation. It seems, however, more likely that the Aoyama family preferred to accept a financial loss in order to sell the property to a foreign government rather than to a commercial enterprise.[30]

'I am deciding on what is a very first-class building', Marler informed the Prime Minister: 'I am anxious, as you are aware, to see the Government given an excellent result.'[31] To accomplish this, Marler engaged Kabushiki-Kaisha, Oghayashi-Gumi, the firm which had been the contractor for the American Embassy. Antonin Raymond, a student and colleague of Frank Lloyd Wright, supervised some of the plans and contributed some of the decorative details. Professor T. Naito of Waseda University, an international authority on construction techniques in earthquake-prone areas, was engaged to advise at every stage of construction.[32] The construction phase was notable for Marler's constant supervision of every aspect, and he spent months poring over plans, drawings and samples for furnishings for the new Legation.[33] The latter he sent to London where he asked that Colonel Georges Vanier, on the staff of Canada House, should see that they were promptly delivered to the British purchasing agent.

Construction was barely underway when Marler was stunned to receive instructions from Ottawa that the project should be deferred due to a grave international crisis unless imperative contractual obligations precluded postponement. Curiously the communication to Marler from Ottawa omitted to specify the nature of the 'grave' crisis, and Marler could not judge its 'gravity' for himself. (It was, in fact, the American decision to abandon the gold standard.) He prudently cancelled plans for a cornerstone laying, much to the annoyance of various resident Canadians for whom the ceremony was to have been a great occasion, and hastily consulted with the contractors. Delay was possible, of course, but only at an additional charge of $17,556. In the circumstances and ignorant of Ottawa's reasons for the instruction, the Minister, who had struggled so long get approval for his pet project, concluded that the Prime Minister's telegram provided him sufficient flexibility to proceed. Fortunately the Prime Minister later agreed with this decision.

Following this last threat to the Marlers' dream, the construction phase moved quickly and it was with considerable pride that Marler took possession of the Residence on 2 November 1933, and of the Chancery two days later. The construction of Canada's first permanent Legation had been completed only 64 days behind schedule and at a cost overrun of $549.21. The buildings first conceived by Marler six weeks after his appointment in 1929 and finished four years later served the Canadian government for almost 60 years. Marler himself would leave Tokyo in 1936 to head the mission in Washington, and his place would be taken by Robert Randolph Bruce, the former lieutenant-governor of British Columbia—a reminder of the importance of the immigration question in prompting the original decision to establish formal relations. That question, along with trade and (especially after Japan's occupation of China) the situation of Canadian missionaries would occupy the attention of Bruce and the increasingly experienced staff of career foreign service officers at the legation until the outbreak of war in December, 1941. The buildings themselves would eventually be rescued and restored to Canada at war's end by Herbert Norman, who returned as head of Canada's liaison mission.

The site for the permanent Legation—now Embassy—of Canada in Tokyo had originally been acquired as much because of Marler's pride in Canada as out of necessity. Nevertheless Marler's determination proved prescient. With the brief interruption of the war years, the Canadian presence in Tokyo was to grow steadily as the relationship between the two countries expanded to the point that in 1989, the original Chancery would destroyed to be replaced by an structure of a size that would have astonished Marler. The original Official Residence, for which Marler fought so tenaciously, remains today as a visible symbol of his belief in the importance of continuing and expanded 'social intercourse' between Canada and Japan.

Mio Village, Wakayama Prefecture; more than 5,000 Japanese Canadians have ties to this small village. PHOTO COURTESY S. KOYAMA

The Canada-Mio Village Association office in Steveston, B.C., c. 1900. PHOTO COURTESY S. KOYAMA, MIO MUSEUM

Although not encouraged by the Canadian government, 196 Japanese Canadians volunteered during W.W.I; 147 became casualties. In 1931 the B.C. government granted the survivors the right to vote. PHOTO COURTESY S. KOYAMA

Japanese immigrants found work in the lumber camps of British Columbia. More than one 'picture bride' gave up dreams of prosperity for a job as a camp cook. PHOTO COURTESY S. KOYAMA, MIO MUSEUM

Vancouver parade, 1926: Japanese-Canadian float stresses the importance of Canadian exports to Japan. PHOTO COURTESY CANADIAN EMBASSY, TOKYO

Raising the Canadian flag in Japan for the 1929 First of July celebration. PHOTO COURTESY
CANADIAN EMBASSY, TOKYO

The Kwansei Gakuin today; it is affiliated with Victoria College of the University of Toronto. PHOTO COURTESY KWANSEI GAKUIN UNIVERSITY

Dining out, pre-war style. PHOTO COURTESY CANADIAN EMBASSY, TOYKO

Marler House, Canada's official residence in Tokyo, as it appears today. PHOTO COURTESY CANADIAN EMBASSY, TOKYO

Sharing Canadian culture, c. 1937. PHOTO COURTESY CANADIAN EMBASSY, TOKYO

Evacuation camp for Japanese Canadians in the interior of British Columbia, February, 1942. PHOTO COURTESY S. KOYAMA

Fishing boats of Japanese Canadians, impounded by the B.C. Security Committee, gathered in the Fraser River before being sold. PHOTO COURTESY S. KOYAMA, MIO MUSEUM

*New Canadian Embassy, designed by Japanese Canadian Raymond Moriyama
(Moriyama & Teshima Architects)—opened in May 1991.* PHOTO COURTESY CANADIAN
EMBASSY, TOKYO

○

The Pacific War

In the very early hours of 26 December 1941, a few hundred exhausted Canadian and British soldiers pulled themselves up from their position among the scrub and rocks of Stanley Peninsula on the island of Hong Kong, and stumbled back into that tiny segment of land that was the only part of the Crown Colony not yet in Japanese hands to await their orders. These Canadians were all that was left of the 1st Battalion, Royal Rifles of Canada. The previous afternoon the remnants of the 1st Battalion, Winnipeg Grenadiers had become captives of the Japanese when the rest of the garrison capitulated.

By the time the last Royal Rifleman had passed into Japanese hands, 290 Canadians had died in Hong Kong. A further 267 were to die in captivity. Of the 1418 remaining members of the force who lived to return to Canada there were few who had not suffered physically and mentally from their ordeal. The survivors still bear the scars. What were these Canadian soldiers doing there? Why were almost two thousand men, most of them either from Quebec City and the towns and farms of Eastern Quebec or from the city and suburbs of Winnipeg, fighting and dying thousands of miles from home in the hopeless and unsung defence of an unfamiliar island off the Chinese coast? Despite a subsequent Royal Commission investigation, that question has never been satisfactorily answered. The controversy has flared up periodically, as the surviving veterans have made attempts to have their compensation increased, each time reawakening bitter memories that form a fading but potent counterpoint in the relationship between Canada and Japan. While the Japanese troops of Lieutenant General Sakai's 23rd Army, as Hisashi Takahashi notes in the next chapter, were hardly aware of the Canadian presence among the *defeated garrison, the harrowing ordeal was not easily forgotten by the Canadian survivors.*

Carl Vincent graduated from Memorial University in 1962 and has pursued a subsequent career as archivist, author and publisher. Among his publications is No Reason Why: The Canadian Hong Kong Tragedy (Stittsville, Ontario: Canada's Wings Inc., 1981) from which the following selection has been taken. He is currently on the staff of the National Archives of Canada in Ottawa.

NO REASON WHY:
THE HONG KONG TRAGEDY

Carl Vincent

The colony of Hong Kong was, in 1941, one of the smallest but most valuable jewels in the British Empire's crown. The actual island of Hong Kong had been ceded to the United Kingdom by China in 1842 as part of the spoils of the Opium War. In 1860 the closest portion of the mainland, the Kowloon Penin-sula, and its adjacent islands were ceded to the British, and in 1898 some 360 square miles of territory know as the New Territories were leased from the Chinese government for ninety-nine years, that is, until 1997. During the palmy years of the *Pax Britannica*, Hong Kong was the headquarters and main base of the China Station of the Royal Navy. Even when there was no real military threat there were abundant British political and commercial interests in East Asia that frequently required protection or reinforcement. Hong Kong was therefore maintained in a reasonably high state of defensive preparedness, while troops from its garrison could be conveyed where they were most needed by the long arm of the Royal Navy.

This state of affairs was to last until the end of the First World War. With the added protection to British interests in the Far East afforded by the Anglo-Japanese Alliance of 1904, the Royal Navy was able, during the 1914-18 conflict, to reduce its China Squadron to a minimum. However, by the end of the 'War to End Wars', Great Britain was becoming a little embarrassed by her aggressive *protégé* and was establishing stronger ties with the United States. In the face of the increasing likelihood that the Anglo-Japanese Alliance would shortly be terminated, a 1921 War Office study concluded that 'there was no chance of making Hong Kong sufficiently secure against attack.'[1] Therefore Britain turned to Singapore, where, through the 1920s and 1930s, they constructed a massive and well-protected naval base.

The first attempt to examine Hong Kong in light of the need for defence against possible Japanese attack appears to have been made in 1935. The Inspector of Fixed Defences, General Barron, made a personal inspection of the defences and submitted a report. Barron stated that the defence of Hong Kong posed a different problem from other British-defended ports abroad for several reasons. It was open from attack from the rear either across the frontier or by a landing in the Leased Territories. Its great distance from the United Kingdom meant an exceptionally long period before relief could be expected to arrive. Barron described the Hong Kong defences as 'deplorable' and stated that the island of Hong Kong would be 'easy prey . . . and that in the face of a determined attack by land or sea the fortress could not hold out even for the arbitrary period before relief.'[2]

With the start of the Sino-Japanese war in 1937 the defence of Hong Kong came under increasingly close scrutiny. The Chiefs of Staff made an appreciation of the situation in June 1937 and came to the conclusion that 'the retention of Hong Kong is *not* essential for the security of Singapore, i.e., it should be treated as a valuable outpost only.'[3]

With the feeling being that it would be useless to lock up eight or nine battalions in Hong Kong, the suggestion was made that the garrison be reduced to two battalions, which should be sufficient for symbolic prestige and adequate to maintain law and order.[4] This reduction was never carried out, however, because in the face of the subsequent Japanese aggression it was felt that such a move would be seen as weakness on the part of the United Kingdom. Nevertheless, British policy regarding Hong Kong had by this time evolved to the point where the colony was treated as an outpost—that is, a fortress whose function was to delay the enemy—and it continued to be regarded officially as an outpost right up to the time of the Japanese attack.

In late October, 1940, the Chiefs of Staff Committee on the Far East translated the political situation into military terms:

> Hong Kong is not a vital interest and the garrison could not long withstand Japanese attack. Even if we had a strong fleet in the Far East it is doubtful whether Hong Kong could be held now that the Japanese are firmly established on the mainland of China, and we could not use it as an advanced naval base. . . . we do not recommend that our garrisons in North China or Hong Kong should be reinforced in any circumstances.[5]

When Canadian-born Major-General A.E. Grasett was appointed General Officer Commanding, China in November 1938, he was fully briefed on the new defence policy.[6] Grasett had a low opinion of the fighting quality of the Japanese army; this opinion led him to consider the War Office view a mistake. Accordingly, he attempted throughout his Hong Kong appointment to obtain one or two extra battalions for the Hong Kong garrison, and his perseverance in this crusade after his appointment had ceased was responsible for the involvement of Canadians in the battle for Hong Kong. A new Commander-in-Chief for the Far East, Air Chief Marshal Sir Robert Brooke-Popham, arrived in Malaya in October 1940, and at once had begun to take a more optimistic view of the British position in the area. In late December or early January he had visited Hong Kong, where Grasett, the General Officer Commanding, also was optimistic about the possibility of successfully resisting a Japanese attack.

Grasett does not appear to have convinced Brooke-Popham of the ultimate defensibility of Hong Kong, but he did make the point that reinforcing the garrison would improve the defence capabilities of the colony and would have a desirable political effect. This proposal was sent to the Chiefs of Staff and eventually to General Ismay, Winston Churchill's personal Chief of Staff and Military Secretary, who passed it on to the Prime Minister. Churchill's reply to Ismay showed, in no uncertain terms, that he wholeheartedly agreed with the policy his Chiefs of Staff had maintained until that date:

> This is all wrong. If Japan goes to war with us there is not the slightest chance of holding Hong Kong or relieving it. It is most unwise to increase the loss we shall suffer there. Instead of increasing the garrison it ought to be reduced to a symbolic scale. Any trouble arising there must be dealt with at the Peace conference after the war. We must avoid frittering away our resources on untenable positions. Japan will think long before declaring war on the British Empire, and whether there are two or six battalions at Hong Kong will make no difference to her choice. I wish we had fewer troops there, but to move any would be noticeable and dangerous.[7]

Hence when the Chiefs of Staff communicated their reply to the Commander-in-Chief Far East, they minced no words. No reinforcements were to be allowed:

> We view Hong Kong as an undesirable military commitment but demilitarization is not now possible [due to the political effect on China and Japan]. . . an increase of the regular garrison from four to six regular battalions would unlikely influence . . . the Japanese and could not affect the ultimate result. It would, however, increase the loss should the fortress fall. . . we have no good reason for basing plans on a relief of the garrison being possible.[8]

On 25 January 1941 the Air Ministry passed on this negative response to Brooke-Popham's request.[9] The subject was to lie dormant for another eight months. Unfortunately for Canada, it was then resurrected.

Of all the possible theatres of employment for Canadian troops, the last to cross anyone's mind before the summer of 1941 would probably have been Hong Kong. Anyone, that is, except for one man, Major-General A.E. Grasett, former General Officer commanding at Hong Kong. The twin circumstances of his Canadian birth and his responsibility for the defence of Hong Kong between November 1938 and July 1941 can be held largely responsible for the chain of events culminating in the despatch of Canadian troops to the colony. The defence of Hong Kong was something of an obsession with Grasett. This is neither strange nor particularly reprehensible—the domination of an officer's military thinking by a single tactical problem for nearly three years is bound to make a lasting impression. Unfortunately this fixation was accompanied by an exaggerated belief both in the defensibility of Hong Kong and in the Japanese soldier's lack of fighting quality. Grasett's compulsion to see his theories vindicated was to have a dire effect on almost 2,000 Canadians.

On 19 July 1941, Grasett handed over command at Hong Kong to Major C.M. Maltby and left for England. Whether the route home which took him across Canada was selected for him or was his own choice is difficult to ascertain. Whichever was the case, in August of that year Grasett was in Ottawa where he stopped off to have 'long discussions' with the Chief of the Canadian General Staff, Major H.D.G. Crerar. The two men had been contemporaries at Canada's Royal Military College in Kingston, Ontario, although Crerar, starting out with the Royal Canadian Artillery, had spent his military career with the Canadian forces while Grasett upon graduation had joined the Royal Corps of Engineers and had spent his career in the British Army.

The exact nature and tone of these discussions is unknown, the only information being Crerar's recollections and his testimony at the 1942 Royal Commission investigating the despatch of Canadian troops to Hong Kong. It is certain, however, that one of the topics covered would have been the military situation in Hong Kong. Grasett believed that the defensive capability of the colony had been persistently underrated by his superiors and expressed the view, as Crerar remembered it, that the 'addition of two or more battalions to the forces then at Hong Kong would render the garrison strong enough to withstand an extensive period of siege by such forces as the Japanese could bring to bear against it.'[10] What remains an enigma is the degree to which Crerar encouraged Grasett in his hopes for Canadian participation. In his testimony to the Commission concerning these discussions Crerar never mentioned any suggestion being made that Canada supply the troops Grasett wanted. Conversely, the virtual rubber stamp endorsement given by Crerar to the subsequent British request suggests that it came as no surprise to him.

Grasett was back in London by 3 September, when he reported to the War Office and was present at a meeting of the Chiefs of Staff. In addition to briefing them on his view of the Hong Kong situation, he submitted his proposal that the garrison be increased by two battalions. For the first time, at least in writing, he made the suggestion that Canada might be willing to supply the troops. Major General J.N. Kennedy, Director of Military Operations and Plans, originally drafted a minute on Grasett's proposal for Sir John Dill, Chief of the Imperial General Staff, expressing strong reservations:

> I agree that in view of Mr Mackenzie King's recent speech indicating the desire for Canadian troops to be placed in the front line of battle, and in view of the greater interest now being shown by the Canadian Government in the Pacific, it might now be possible to obtain small reinforcements for Hong Kong.
>
> I suggest, however, that this factor should not be allowed to induce you to reverse your present policy of sending no reinforcements to Hong Kong. The Canadians might never be involved in a front line battle, and, if they are, it will merely mean more forces being locked up in a fortress which at the moment has very little chance of being relieved.[11]

This minute was never sent, but was instead marked CANCELLED. What prompted Kennedy's change of mind is unknown, but his replacement minute of 7 September said only: 'If you think General Grasett has made out a good case, the Chiefs of Staff may wish to submit it to the Prime Minister.'[12]

The note eventually sent to Churchill and dated 10 September read:

PRIME MINISTER

1. On the 3rd of September, the Chiefs of Staff heard an interesting account on the present situation in Hong Kong from General Grasett who had been General Officer Commanding there until July. From this, one important point arose.

2. The present defence policy at Hong Kong is that the Island is to be regarded as an outpost and held as long as possible. In describing the tasks of the force in Hong Kong General Grasett said that of the army garrison of four battalions, one was to be deployed on the mainland and charged with the task of withdrawing to the Island after carrying out extensive demolitions. It is essential therefore that it should be safely extricated from the mainland. He pointed out the great advantages to be obtained from the addition of one or two battalions and suggested that these might be supplied by Canada.

3. The Chiefs of Staff have previously advised against the despatch of reinforcements to Hong Kong because they considered that it would only have been to throw good money after bad, but the position in the Far East has now changed. Our defences at Malaya have been improved and Japan has latterly shown a certain weakness in her attitude towards Great Britain and the United States.

4. A small reinforcement of one or two battalions would increase the strength of the garrison all out of proportion to the actual numbers involved, and it would provide a strong stimulus to the garrison and the Colony. Further, it would have a great moral effect in the whole of the Far East and it would show Chiang Kai Shek that we really intend to fight it out at Hong Kong.

5. The United States have recently despatched a small reinforcement to the Philippines and a similar move by Canada would be in line with the present United States policy of greater interest in the Far East.

6. The Chiefs of Staff are in favour of the suggestion that Canada should be asked to send one or two battalions to Hong Kong, and submit this proposal for your approval. If you agree, the necessary approach would be made through the Dominions Office.[13]

Churchill was prepared on this occasion to accept the recommendation of his Chiefs of Staff, noting on September 15: 'There is no objection to the approach being made as proposed. . .'[14]

No time was wasted once the Prime Minister's approval had been obtained. On 19 September 1941 the following telegram was sent by the Dominions Office to the Canadian Government via the Department of External Affairs:

NO. 162 MOST SECRET

In consultation with late General Officer Commanding who has recently arrived in this country we have been considering the defenses of Hong Kong. Approved policy has been that Hong Kong should be regarded as an out-post and held as long as possible in the event of war in the Far East. Existing army garrison consists of four battalions of infantry and although this force represents the bare minimum required for the task assigned to it we have thought hitherto that it would not ultimately serve any useful purpose to increase the garrison.

Position in the Far East has now, however, changed. Our defenses in Malaya have been improved and there have been signs of a certain weakening in Japan's attitude towards us and the United States.

In these circumstances it is thought that a small reinforcement of the garrison of Hong Kong, e.g. by one or two more battalions, would be very fully justified. It would increase the strength of the garrison out of all proportion to the actual numbers involved and it would provide a strong stimulus to the garrison and the Colony, it would further have a very great moral effect in the whole of the Far East and would reassure Chiang Kai Shek as to the reality of our intention to hold the Island.

His Majesty's Government in Canada will be well aware of the difficulties we are at present experiencing in providing forces which the situation in various parts of the world demands, despite the very great assistance which is being furnished by the Dominions. *We should therefore be most grateful if the Canadian Government would consider whether one or two Canadian battalions could be provided from Canada for this purpose* [underlined in original]. . . .[15]

When the telegram carrying the British request arrived the Minister of National Defence, the Honourable J.L. Ralston, was absent in the United States and the Minister of National Defence for Air, the Honourable C.G. Power, was acting in his place. That morning Power met the Minister of National Defence for Naval Services on the street and they 'discussed the matter at some length.'[16] By the next meeting of the War Committee of the Cabinet they had decided to take on the commitment. Power later testified at the hearings of the Royal Commission investigating the despatch of troops to Hong Kong that: 'I do not think there was ever any question really, or any discussion as between General Crerar and myself as to any reason why we should not take it on.' Power recognized that Hong Kong was in a rather poor position, but 'took it for granted that the military authorities had assessed all that.'[17]

Judging by the minutes, the discussion of the subject at the Cabinet War Committee meeting on 23 September was very short. The telegram was read and agreement in principle was reached. Mackenzie King insisted on first gaining the assent of Ralston, the Minister of National Defence, and obtaining the advice of General MacNaughton in England.[18] The only doubt Ralston had was on the matter of military feasibility. Ralston wanted to reassure himself on this point, as he could 'remember Hong Kong being an outpost to be held as long as possible. I think that was generally understood.'[19] He therefore telephoned Crerar that night to obtain confirmation. Crerar later testified that 'I told him that I had definitely recommended that the Canadian Army should take this on.'[20] Probably the last real chance the government had of going into the request disappeared with these words.

In a study of any aspect of the war in the Pacific, one question that constantly arises is, how much of Japan's intentions did the Western powers know, and how much ought they to have known. One may go on to ask whether the Canadian government should have realized that war with Japan, whether imminent or not, was a strong possibility, and given this, whether or not it was wise to reinforce Hong Kong. In making their critical decision, the leaders of Canada proved to be remarkably uninquisitive. This is all the more surprising considering that the Canadian government *did* have enough information at their disposal to form their own opinions on the matter. Hong Kong defence schemes, intelligence reports, Japanese diplomatic intelligence, and similar relevant material were all in Canadian hands, and a brief glance at the first two in particular would have (or should have) given them pause.

The sources of information available to the Canadian government were varied. The major source for most members of the government was probably the public actions of Japan herself, as reported by the press. Canada also had a legation in Tokyo which, of course, sent many reports back to the Department of External Affairs. There were also sources of information from returning businessmen, missionaries, and officers, which perhaps were not studied as closely as they might have been. Finally the Canadian government had access to almost all of the information available to the government of the United

Kingdom. Military intelligence was exchanged between the War Office and the Canadian Department of National Defence, while the British Secretary of State for the Dominions kept the Secretary of State for External Affairs informed on high diplomatic developments. Not only was all of this information from British sources available at National Defence Headquarters, but a good many of the senior officers there had experience specifically with the Hong Kong problem, as the defence of the colony was considered a 'classic' staff college problem. Some officers, for instance Colonel Macklin, the Director of Staff Duties, had even been to Hong Kong.

It is quite obvious that there was very little information regarding the Japanese threat in general and the defence of Hong Kong in particular that was not available to the Canadian government or its senior military officers at the time the decision was taken to send Canadian troops to Hong Kong. Some two months later, with the force *en route*, a memo from Major General Crerar suggested that the War Office should be asked to supply such papers as a map of Hong Kong (!), Defence Scheme papers and information on artillery forces there (all of which were already available at National Defence Headquarters in Ottawa). Crerar thought that, 'We should keep "up-to-date" on Far East, especially Hong Kong, in view of our particular military commitment there.'[21] It is astounding to contemplate that only after the two battalions had been sent to Hong Kong did it seem desirable to learn something about the place!

Japan was expanding aggressively, and the practically defenceless colony of Hong Kong was in its path. Yet with this knowledge readily available the decision was still made to reinforce Hong Kong with Canadian troops. The only real question after all is said and done is—why?

The Canadian government had agreed in principle to the despatch of two battalions on 23 September, and, after Ralston was consulted, the substance of this decision was communicated to the United Kingdom government. No time had then been set for the actual sailing of the force, but its selection had, to all intents and purposes, already been made. Although the final decision to despatch Canadian reinforcements was not made until 20 October 1941, the Canadian General Staff had commenced preparations well before that date to select the two battalions that would be required. The selection process was set in motion on the day the Cabinet met, by Colonel W.H.S. Macklin, Director of Staff Duties, who requested Colonel J.K. Lawson, Director of Military Training, to prepare a list of battalions within Canada in order of training level. Lawson duly produced the list the next day.

When Canada went to war in 1939 the country's full time army was a tiny Permanent Force totalling little more than 4000 all ranks. This small band of professional soldiers was backed up by the Non-Permanent Active Militia, units whose soldiers trained and served part-time. These units were distributed across Canada—there were 91 infantry battalions alone. On the outbreak of war, many of these Non-Permanent Active Militia battalions were mobilized to form a Canadian Active Service Force and filled their ranks through the recruiting of volunteers. As the war progressed and Canada's military require-ments increased, others of these units were mobilized and brought up to their full wartime establishment. The two battalions which were to form Canada's contribution to the defence of Hong Kong—chosen to represent both Eastern and Western Canada—were, in almost every way, typical of those from which, between 1939 and 1945, Canada created a remarkably successful and formida-ble army.

Both the Royal Rifles of Canada and the Winnipeg Grenadiers had, before the war, been regiments of the Non-Permanent Active Militia, that small but dedi-cated body of men who, on evenings, weekends, and the occasional summer camp, strove to keep Canada's army alive despite lack of equipment, pay, and government and public interest. The Royal Rifles, a regiment which could trace its ancestry back to 1862, had not been one of the militia units selected for mobilization at the start of the Second World War. It must, however, have been regarded as a reasonably efficient unit as it was ordered to prepare for action in late June 1940. Although in most cases battalions were activated in groups to fill the establishment of a larger formation such as a new division, the Royal Rifles was the only battalion mobilized on this date. The battalion was recruited from Eastern Quebec, primarily the Quebec City area, but a consider-able number of Gaspesians and men from northern New Brunswick also enlisted. It was an English-speaking unit but approximately 25% of its strength consisted of bilingual French-Canadians.[22] The Winnipeg Grenadiers were of more recent origin than the Royal Rifles but were also the possessors of a not undistinguished record. Formed as a militia unit in 1908, they had raised the 11th Battalion of the Canadian Expeditionary Force in the First World War, and later carried the battle honours won by this unit on their colours. At the beginning of the Second World War the Winnipeg Grenadiers were one of the units that had been selected for almost immediate mobilization. Recruiting was very successful and by late October 1939 the battalion was up to strength. Most of the officers and NCOs had worked together for years in the Militia unit. Overall the battalion was regarded as an average one—not outstanding, but quite efficient and well disciplined. The officers were seen as 'useful and competent.'[23] At the military level, the logic of training, organization, location and availability had dictated the necessary decisions. Meanwhile, on 9 October 1941 the Dominions Office despatched a telegram to the Canadian govern-ment which informed them that the British government 'now feel that in all circumstances it would be most desirable if the two Canadian battalions could be despatched at an early date.'[24] In response, between 9 October and the end of the month, these two insufficiently-trained units were reinforced, united, and put under the command of a newly organized, unfamiliar, and partly inexperienced Brigade Headquarters, and sent to Hong Kong to fight for their lives. The minutes of the Canadian Cabinet War Committee throughout November and early December reflect a growing concern over the situation in the Far East. The brief period of hope in early October soon died away, and the Allies prepared for war. It was reported at the meeting of 27 November 1941 that the United States Secretary of State, Cordell Hull, had told the United Kingdom that 'the chance of Japanese acceptance of American proposals for a *modus vivendi* was slight. War and Navy Departments [are] impressing on United States Administration the military values of delay.'[25] The news from then on worsened. In all the messages, telegrams, and reports of these last few weeks before war, there is not the slightest suggestion that the Canadian reinforcement of Hong Kong had had any diplomatic effect whatsoever. The strengthening of the colony had not 'tipped the balance' as some had hoped it would. By the time the Canadian arrived the situation had deteriorated irretrievably and the Japanese probably took no notice of the arrival of the Canadian troops whatsoever, except on the most local of levels.

On the political level the Canadian government prepared to reap the political harvest associated with the landing of the troops. The Canadian government wanted a big splash with a long message issued, including the sentence 'Hong Kong constituted an outpost which the Commonwealth intended to hold.' The draft was sent to the United Kingdom for approval, and the Canadians were probably somewhat crestfallen when the reply requested that the communiqué should not 'be on such a scale as to over-emphasize the strength of our defences in Hong Kong.'[26] This should have given the Canadian government pause to think, but there is no indication that it did so. The final statement agreed on was rather bald:

> A Canadian force, under the command of Brigadier J.K. Lawson, has arrived at Hong Kong after a safe and uneventful voyage, the Canadian government announced at Ottawa today. The Canadian troops will serve with other units of His Majesty's Forces making up the Hong Kong garrison. The strength of the force was not disclosed.[27]

The announcement nevertheless went off quite well. Mackenzie King made a little speech saying that defence against aggression anywhere meant protection for Canada.[28] In view of the constant criticism that the government was making a half-hearted war effort, King was delighted to observe all the favourable publicity the announcement received. Canada now had her forces on three continents, and was arguably doing her full share in Commonwealth defence. Meanwhile, as the diplomatic and military prospects continued to darken, the Canadian troops had sailed into a death trap.

The actual battle for Hong Kong, while possessing some interesting features, demonstrated few tactical novelties and progressed to an inevitable conclusion. The Japanese deployed a larger force of better-trained and better-equipped troops, exploited their superior mobility, had the capacity to concentrate against weak points in the defence, and so won the battle. In addition to the perfectly genuine reasons for the Japanese success, a number of rumours and false assumptions were current at the time, many of which continued to exist post-war. For example, the belief persists that the Japanese were headed by 2000 'storm troops'—in reality the invasion troops belonged to an ordinary Japanese division whose previous activities had been garrison and anti-guerrilla duties in South China. The activities of fifth columnists were much exaggerated—one gets the impression that the Japanese were always accompanied by their trusty Chinese guides, whereas the Japanese colonels testified that they made use of none, which, in view of the confusion and control problems they experienced, is probably true. Another rumour was that the Japanese had been sold the demolition plans for the mainland and so were able to cut the lines or have replacements ready. In fact, the rapid Japanese movement of heavy equipment was due partly to hasty demolition and mainly to the efficient Japanese engineers, who could easily deduce what demolitions would be made. A story which gained wide currency was that German officers were the organizers and planners of the expedition, while German pilots were responsible for the accurate bombing. This was too fantastic for Headquarters to give any credence to, but many of the lower ranks believed the tale. This was not surprising—they had been told so often that the Japanese were poorly led, unimaginative, bad flyers, et cetera, that when the battle went so heavily against the defenders, some excuse was necessary.

With the exception of the courage of most of the defenders, there is little that is positive to be gleaned from the defence of Hong Kong. Recognized by informed opinion even before the Japanese attack as futile and wasteful, in the final analysis it remains so. The Canadian soldiers who fought at Hong Kong in December 1941 and either died in the hopeless struggle or else passed into an all too often fatal captivity are the possessors of a unique distinction. They are the only Canadian soldiers and possible the only Commonwealth soldiers of the Second World War who were deliberately sent into a position where there was absolutely no hope of victory, evacuation, or relief. In all, of the 1975 Canadians who sailed with C Force, 557 never returned.

The senselessness of the defence was recognized by the Dominions Office when the battle was nearly over, as a circular telegram to External Affairs states: 'The capture by Japanese of Hong Kong would gain them *some* strategical advantages but would not materially alter the strategical situation of China Sea as a whole.'[29] This was a somewhat sugar-coated version of what the British were admitting to themselves: resistance at Hong Kong was weakening, and the battle would have no 'direct influence in the way of tying up Japanese forces.'[30] After the battle the British official history concluded that the battle (and especially the reinforcement by Canadian troops) represented a 'lamentable waste of manpower'. Since Hong Kong had no strategic importance such a reinforcement was an unnecessary extravagance. Besides, 'the extra few days of resistance which were gained by the presence of the two reinforcing battalions sent at the eleventh hour could not, and did not, have any influence on the course of events.'[31]

During the 18 days of the battle for Hong Kong, people in both Canada and England were almost completely in the dark about the situation in the colony. The situation reports from Maltby's headquarters were markedly vague. Major events, such as the evacuation to the island and the Japanese landings there were, of course, identifiable, but there was little more solid information. It was nevertheless apparent within a short time that Hong Kong was going under.

The Dominions Office had done its part toward calming Canadian storms in the unlikely event that any might arise. On 26 December 1941 the Office sent condolences and thanks to Canada for its part in Hong Kong. 'The defence of Hong Kong will live in History as yet one more chapter of courage and endurance in the annals of the British Commonwealth.'[32] Mackenzie King, for his part, offered the condolences of the Canadian government to the people, especially to the bereaved families. He compared the defenders of the Colony to Dollard des Ormeaux and his men in their stand against the Iroquois at the Long Sault, saving Montreal at the cost of their own lives. Referring to Pearl Harbor and the *Prince of Wales* disaster, he transformed the Hong Kong defence into a delaying action.[33] King's statement appeared to satisfy the Canadian people for the time being.

But soon the whole Hong Kong affair was being used as a political football. In February, 1942 the Reverend B.C. Eckert in Welland, Ontario, charged that the King government was deliberately withholding the casualty lists until after the by-elections scheduled for that month. 'Ottawa knows them', Eckert claimed, 'and more are buried in the blood-stained soil of Hong Kong than are in Japanese prison camps.'[34] This was totally untrue, but there were many who were prepared to believe it. Much of the information that did come in was contradictory and confusing.

By this time all government hopes for a quick burial of the Hong Kong affair had been dashed, and the public, headed by George Drew, Conservative leader in the Ontario Legislature, was beginning to clamour for more facts. Drew had already shown a talent for instigating Royal Commissions. He had accused the government in 1938 of irregularities in awarding a Bren gun contract. The appointment of a Royal Commission had damped down that controversy, and an almost indigestible and incredibly dull report had extinguished it altogether. Once again the King government turned to the device of a Royal Commission to extract it from the controversy. The Commission, with Chief Justice Sir Lyman Duff as Chairman, first met on Monday, 2 March 1942 and closed its hearings Tuesday, 31 March 1942. Nearly 300 exhibits were produced and 60 witnesses called. The Commissioner conducted the hearings fairly in the sense that he put no obstacles in the way of evidence being submitted, but he unfortunately heard (and for the most part believed) testimony from those with an interest in the decision of the Commission.

When Duff's report was published in early June 1942 (it was delayed as Duff was unable to present his argument for some time due to illness) the government was happy, the Opposition disappointed, and Drew furious. Mackenzie King sent a note to Duff, telling the Commissioner that he could not say 'how greatly relieved in mind I am at the conclusions reached. I . . . feel that no finer tribute could have been paid my colleagues in the Defence Department. . . . This report will help to give the people of Canada a confidence in their administration which means everything to the country's war effort.'[35] And there, perhaps, lies the rub: Duff, no matter how impartial, could hardly, in mid-1942, have called into question the entire management of the war. Even a mild censure of the government's role in the affair could have had very wide political repercussions. Nor were the Conservative opposition themselves united on the issue, as some believed that national considerations outweighed political ones. They also did not relish the idea of a Chief Justice of Canada being called in effect a liar or an incompetent, and feared that this would backfire. Thus the controversy eventually died down.

Except for concern for the prisoners, and a very moderate amount of publicity at the time of their return, little more was publicly heard of the matter for a few years. In 1948 the Hong Kong affair was resurrected, but interest quickly petered out. This new eruption had been occasioned by the publication of General Maltby's report on operations in Hong Kong, which, even after deletions made at the request of the Canadian government, seemed to indicate that there was some truth in Drew's original charges. In the immediate post-war years the government exhibited all the defensive reactions of an uneasy conscience as far as the Hong Kong veterans were concerned. The shabby episode of the Pacific Pay entitlement (which was refused to the survivors) occurred at a time when the government was desperately trying to hold the lid down to prevent the whole Hong Kong issue from boiling over again.

In 1948 the Hong Kong Veterans Association was formed. Its members had initially envisioned a social club that would enable survivors to maintain their ties with one another. They soon discovered, however, that they were expressing common complaints and experiencing common problems. It was not long before the Association evolved into an organization primarily concerned with obtaining from the government the benefits and compensation to which its members felt entitled. It is interesting to speculate as to what might have happened if the government had had the courage and integrity to come straight out and admit responsibility and had thereafter tried to compensate the Hong

Kong veterans for the hardships they endured. Possibly the Hong Kong Veterans Association would have remained a social organization. But admission of error has never been a dominant characteristic of politicians, and it took many years of effort and pressure by the Veterans Association, aided by sympathizers in Parliament and by officials in the Department of Veterans Affairs (who have rarely received the acknowledgement they deserve), before full acknowledgement or compensation for their needs was received. The Hong Kong Veterans Association still exists. Its members, a diminishing band of aging men, still bear the external and internal scars of their experience. Few would now recognize that these were once the fine young men of the Royal Rifles of Canada and the Winnipeg Grenadiers who were so casually despatched to the doomed outpost of Hong Kong some fifty years ago.

And what of Hong Kong? Admitted by most informed opinion (including the men who requested that Canadian troops be sent) to be incapable of a prolonged and successful defence, was there any reason why nearly two thousand Canadians should have been caught up in the bloody shambles that marked its fall? Of the British actors in the drama, only Major-General A.E. Grasett appears to have honestly believed that an additional two battalions would markedly upgrade Hong Kong's ability to resist assault. His belief was unfortunately based on a contempt for Japanese military ability, a fixed determination to 'put up a good show', and remarkably poor powers of military appreciation. It is difficult to avoid a grudging admiration for the British Chiefs of Staff and the War Office in the Hong Kong situation. However their judgement may be faulted in other respects, and whatever one may think of their actual motives for requesting Canadian reinforcements for the colony, they were one hundred per cent correct in their opinion of the indefensibility of Hong Kong. They considered that there was no possibility of a successful defence until relief could be expected, they therefore had resolved to treat it as an outpost, they had held to this opinion for a number of years, and at no time changed their minds, even after Canadians were on their way. Events were to prove them absolutely right. The telegram to Canada requesting the troops stated that the 'approved policy had been that Hong Kong should be regarded as an outpost and held as long as possible in the event of war in the Far East.'

Ultimately the politicians in Canada had the final word. They based their decision on two sources of information only—the statement of the United Kingdom that troops were required and it would be desirable that Canada supply them, and the advice of the Canadian Chief of the General Staff that it was militarily feasible to supply the battalions and that Canada should accept the commitment. These statements, and a strong and genuine desire that Canada play her part in the war, led to a practically unquestioning, positive response to the request.

The politicians thus made their decision. What of the role of Major-General

Crerar, the Chief of the General Staff? His duties included 'military policy and strategy' and 'advice as to the conduct of operations of war and orders in regard to military operations', as well as intelligence.[36] He had, in effect, 'advised' the government when asked by Ralston and Power for his opinion. One may, however, question the adequacy of his attempt to consider all aspects of the decision. We have seen that he had conversations with the ex-General Officer Commanding, Hong Kong (i.e., Grasett), a few months before, but other than this Crerar made absolutely no attempt to inform himself on the situation at Hong Kong, preferring to rely completely on the opinions of his old RMC comrade. Crerar did not concentrate on the military aspect of the request in any event, as he later testified:

> the decision for or against the despatch . . . [was] necessarily required to be taken on the highest policy level. The proposed action, whatever the military risks of the enterprise, needed to be examined from the broad view as to its contributory value to the eventual winning of the war. . . . In the case of the despatch of Canadian troops to Hong Kong . . . political and moral principles were involved, rather than military ones, and on such a basis, the matter required to be considered and decided by the War Committee of the Cabinet.[37]

General Crerar was, of course, entitled to his own opinion, but he seems to have forgotten in this instance that his job was to give *military*, not political or moral advice. The problem was therefore a failure to submit to the government for their consideration one of the primary pieces of information involved with the Hong Kong question—that 'it has always been well-known in the Services that there would be considerable difficulties in defending Hong Kong, which presumably had obviously increased by the proximity of the Japanese forces before the war started.'[38]

While there was never any change in the military policy regarding Hong Kong, Britain was determined by September 1941 to present a solid front with the United States against Japan, and also to demonstrate to the Chinese that Britain was still a force to be reckoned with in Asian affairs. There was undoubtedly as well a notion that the current Hong Kong garrison was inadequate to put up the kind of resistance called for by the plans. None of these factors by themselves or in combination was sufficient to persuade the British to reinforce the colony, but they were powerful enough when it was suggested that two battalions could be made available from a 'hitherto unregarded source'—Canada—that the British government abandoned a long-standing military policy based on a succession of intelligent appreciations of the situation, and the two Canadian battalions became the most exposed pieces in a giant game of bluff.

Once having received the request, the Canadian government seems to have assumed that, provided the battalions were available, an affirmative answer was the only one possible. To these busy and sincere men, with neither the knowledge needed nor the inclination to read between the lines or wonder about motivations, the telegram made sense, and unless there were sound military reasons for questioning the request, a yes was automatic. There *were* sound military reasons, but the Chief of the General Staff did not pass these reasons on to the government. There was no reason why Canadian troops should have been despatched to the doomed outpost of Hong Kong—but through a combination of British cynicism and Canadian thoughtlessness, they were sent anyway.

○

In one of the first battles in the Asian Pacific theatre, Japanese and Canadians clashed hand-to-hand over control of the British Crown colony of Hong Kong. Trapped on the indefensible island fortress, the Canadians fought fiercely but were forced to surrender on Christmas Day, 1941. Those who had survived were taken into captivity and imprisoned at North Point Camp, originally built to hold Chinese refugees. The Japanese, who had not anticipated having to deal with large numbers of prisoners, were ill-equipped and disorganized. Poor sanitary conditions and meagre rations led to outbreaks of beriberi and dysentery, and diphtheria raged through the camp. Few medical supplies were available to treat the sick and wounded. Beginning in January, 1943 the surviving Canadians were shipped as forced labour to Japan, where many perished in the mines. Those who survived to be liberated in 1945 carried back to Canada bitter memories of their war-time experience with Japan and the Japanese.

For the Japanese, by contrast, the fighting in Hong Kong was a first step on the road that led eventually to Hiroshima and Nagasaki. Emboldened by the surprising success in Hong Kong, the High Command advanced the schedule for operations against the Dutch East Indies; as a result the Japanese units which had fought at Hong Kong were quickly broken up and scattered to other commands. Few of the ordinary soldiers had enough skill in English to distinguish Canadian from British, and so were hardly aware that their enemies had been Canadians. Most of those who confronted the Canadians at Hong Kong would later be wiped out in the futile defence of Guadalcanal. In the chaotic closing days of the war files were destroyed and records vanished; Professor Takahashi has reconstructed the following account by piecing together the few combat reports and field diaries that remain, and searching out the handful of surviving Japanese veterans to collect their accounts. Little has been published in Japanese on this unhappy encounter; rather than the memories of desperate combat and imprisonment that live on among a vocal part of the Canadian population, most Japanese recall Canada's mediating role during the years of defeat and occupation. Hence a gulf of sympa-

thy and understanding remains from the wartime years that continues as one element in the relationship.

Hisashi Takahashi graduated from Seattle University, and completed his graduate work at the University of Washington and Sophia University's Graduate School of International Relations. Associate editor of Gunji shigaku [The Japanese Journal of Military History], his most recent works include the chapter 'Shinajihen to daihon'ei setchi' [The Outbreak of the Sino-Japanese War and the Establishment of the Imperial General Headquarters] in volume 5 of the Kaigun tsūshi Series [A History of the Imperial Japanese Navy]. Hisashi Takahashi is currently professor of Japanese diplomatic and military history at the Military History Department of the Japanese Defence Agency's National Institute for Defence Studies.

THE CANADIAN EXPEDITIONARY FORCE AND THE FALL OF HONG KONG

Takahashi Hisashi

When the formal surrender of the British garrison took place at the Japanese Command Post in Kowloon's Peninsula Hotel at 1900 hours on 25 December 1941, Hong Kong became the first British colony in the Far East to fall into Japanese hands. The Colony was able to withstand eighteen days of fierce fighting. Together with Singapore and Corregidor, Hong Kong had until that moment of tragedy stood as 'the third leg in a tripod of Anglo-Saxon power and influence in the Far East.'[1]

However, the leg had been so weakened as to be more appropriately called 'Britain's Achilles' heel'. Hong Kong was always regarded as an outpost, ultimately indefensible, though not to be given up without a fight. For example, as early as August 1940, the British Chiefs of Staff decided that since Hong Kong 'could neither be relieved nor be expected to withstand a prolonged siege, it should be regarded merely as an outpost and held as long as possible'.[2] Britain had to accept such a policy in order to meet its overriding strategic need to carry on a struggle for national existence against Hitler's Germany then unfolding in the European theatre.

When Air Chief Marshal Sir Robert Brooke-Popham, the new British Commander-in-Chief in the Far East, pressed the issue of reinforcing the Hong Kong garrison at the beginning of 1941, he received a negative response from his superiors in London. According to the Chiefs of Staff, they viewed the Colony 'as an undesirable military commitment'. Nevertheless, prestige alone demanded that the British should defend the Colony as long as possible with its existing garrison forces.[3] It had been decided, however, to increase the official 'period before relief' for the fortress from 90 to 130 days, and to build up all its reserve supplies accordingly.[4]

Britain's unwillingness to strengthen Hong Kong's defence scheme may be explained by the Colony's tactically hopeless position. The Japanese seemed to be firmly entrenched on the Chinese mainland. There was no adequate fleet in Singapore to extend relief to the Colony. Neither could it be used as an advanced naval base. All major naval vessels had been withdrawn to European waters or to Singapore.

Moreover, the lack of sea power meant that the Colony was always exposed to seaborne assault. This ever-present threat so influenced the garrison's defensive positions that Major-General C.M. Maltby, the General Officer Commanding Hong Kong, was afraid to concentrate his resources against the obvious menace on the north coast. In fact, throughout the siege General Maltby anticipated an enemy landing on the southern shores, which never came to pass. Worse yet, Hong Kong had practically no dependable air support. At its single airfield, Kai Tak airport on the mainland, there were only two amphibians and three torpedo bombers. The nearest RAF base was Kota Bharu in Malaya; the distance of nearly 1400 miles made relief tactically unfeasible. However, British planners still continued to believe that Hong Kong should be able to hold out for a long time.[5]

In addition to the factors of weakness in the defences of Hong Kong, the British Far East Command greatly underestimated the Japanese forces. They were considered to be very poor at night fighting and addicted to stereotyped tactics and planning. The Japanese air force was believed to be much inferior to European standards. In fact, upon arrival in Hong Kong, Canadian officers attended a lecture by a British officer who told them that the Japanese had only 5,000 troops with very little artillery; that their troops were ill-equipped and poor at night fighting; that their aircraft were very mediocre, and their pilots myopic and thus incapable of dive-bombing.[6] It is therefore no surprise that when the Japanese attack started with air raids many of the garrison troops believed that German pilots were actually responsible for the feat.

Partly due to such an unrealistic underestimation of enemy forces, British Intelligence was frequently muddled and remained confused. When General Tojo Hideki became the new prime minister in October 1941, British Intelligence firmly believed that the Japanese would attack the Soviet Union and occupy Vladivostok and the maritime provinces of Siberia. Canada had no intelligence organization of her own to make an estimate of the Far Eastern situation in general, and Japanese forces in particular. She had to depend solely upon London for such information. On 26 October, a most secret message to the Department of National Defence sent by Canadian Military Headquarters, London, contained similar information and the consensus opinion of the British War Office, 'war in Far East unlikely at present'.[7] Sadly, this message was sent the day before the Canadian force sailed for Hong Kong.

Even as late as the beginning of November, the British in the Far East were still optimistic; the report prepared by Intelligence at Hong Kong stated that Japanese preparations were 'more likely part of a general tightening up to concert pitch rather than the final touches for plunging off the deep end'. Only at the end of the month did the British in Singapore finally come to believe that Japan 'might be actually on the verge of starting war'.[8] Accordingly, certain precautionary measures were taken by the garrison troops, such as closing of the harbour at night and close guarding of vital points, etc. By 2 December all troops had been placed on alert.

However, General Maltby had considerable doubt about Japanese intentions even on the eve of the outbreak of war. In spite of the report, on the evening of 6 December, that three Japanese divisions had arrived on the previous day within eight miles of the frontier, plus other indications, he was not completely convinced that war was imminent.[9] Moreover, when the 38th Division launched its surprise attack two days later, General Maltby mistakenly thought that the Japanese came in with three divisions.

Brigadier J.K. Lawson commanded Canada's two battalions, the Royal Rifles of Canada and the Winnipeg Grenadiers. They had been chosen for the defence of Hong Kong to represent both Eastern and Western Canada. The mobilization of both units was rather recent, and prior to assignment to Hong Kong they had had no real combat experience. The Royal Rifles of Canada was mobilized at Quebec City in July 1940; the Winnipeg Grenadiers in September 1939. Both had just returned from peaceful overseas garrison duties. The Royal Rifles of Canada were sent to Newfoundland in November 1940 and returned to Canada in August 1941. The Winnipeg Grenadiers spent over 16 months in Jamaica and returned home in September and October 1941. Since guard duties took up most of their time, both units badly needed refresher training. In the case of the Grenadiers, for example, not one shot was ever fired during the whole time in Jamaica. Moreover, they had received almost no tactical exercises either at a battalion or a sub-unit level. In fact, both battalions were not first class, but belonged to Class C, that is 'those units which, due either to recent employment or insufficient training, are not recommended by DMT (Director of Military Training) to be available for operational consideration at the present time'.[10]

However, there were at that time no other troops in Canada that had attained a commendable standard of field training. Besides, under the arrangement with the British the two units had to be shipped as quickly as possible. However, the question of why they were sent remains to be fully answered. Granted that the Canadian government actually had at their disposal enough information (including the facts about Hong Kong's extremely weak defence position, of course) to make their own judgement as to what fate would befall the selected troops, why were its leaders so 'remarkably uninquisitive'?[11] The fact that a total of 51 men were found to be absent without leave before departure from Vancouver seems to indicate a misfortune awaiting for the motley expeditionary force.[12] Their only hope was that there would be sufficient time to rectify training deficiencies in Hong Kong; in fact, there was no such time.

After an uneventful voyage the Canadians arrived at Hong Kong on 16 November, only three weeks before the outbreak of the Pacific War, and came under the command of General Maltby. Their arrival made the total strength of the garrison 14,554:

British	3,652
Canadian	1,972
Indian	2,254
Local Colonial	2,428
Hong Kong Volunteer Defence Corps	2,000
Auxiliary Defence Units	2,112
Nursing Detachment	136[13]

The Hong Kong garrison was 'extraordinarily' heterogeneous in its composition, and as the C Force report puts it succinctly, it was 'hardly a combination likely to make an efficient fighting force'. In addition to acute shortages of such important weapons as infantry mortars plus ammunition, the garrison in general seemed to be suffering from training deficiencies.[14]

The defence of the Colony was planned in two successive phases: a delaying action on the mainland, followed by a prolonged defence of Hong Kong Island. The garrison was basically divided into the Mainland Brigade under the command of Brigadier C. Wallis and the Island Brigade under Brigadier Lawson. The Mainland Brigade consisted of three battalions (the 2nd Battalion of the Royal Scots Regiment on the left, 2/14th Punjab Regiment in the centre and 5/7th Rajput on the right), supported by three mountain battery and one medium battery troops. The Island Brigade consisted of two Canadian battalions and the 1st Battalion of the Middlesex Regiment, supported by one mountain battery and two medium battery troops.

The Canadians were assigned to hold the south coast, presumably because of their lack of training. The Winnipeg Grenadiers were allotted the south-west sector of the island, the Royal Rifles the south-east. The task was beach defence against enemy landings from the sea. But since there was no seaborne attack from the south, the Canadians were immediately ordered to play a role quite different from that of the original defence plan. Since the details of the battle for

Hong Kong as well as of the battle performance of the Canadians are discussed elsewhere,[15] here I shall briefly deal only with some of the main points.

In the first hours of the battle, the Rajputs were almost wiped out. A large part of the Royal Scots were quickly destroyed after the Japanese carried out an attack against the Shing Mun Redoubt around midnight on 9 December. This famous night assault was initiated by First Lieutenant Wakabayashi Tōichi, a daring and self-sacrificing company commander of the 228th Regiment. Although the redoubt was originally allotted to the 230th Regiment, far-sighted Colonel Doi, commanding the 228th Regiment, decided to let Wakabayashi's battalion launch a surprise attack without authorization from his division commander. Doi disregarded General Sano's frequent orders to withdraw, but with little difficulty he achieved the break-through of the redoubt.[16] The capture of this key position very quickly proved to be a disaster for General Maltby. On 11 December when a prepared position known as the Gin Drinkers Line was hopelessly compromised, Maltby ordered most of the mainland troops to withdraw to Hong Kong Island. In the morning of 13 December all of the remaining troops reached the Island, only five days after the enemy attack.

On the night of 10 December a company of the Winnipeg Grenadiers had been sent across from the Island along with a detachment of the Hong Kong Volunteer Defence Corps to support the decimated Royal Scots. December 11, when the Canadians came under enemy shell fire, marked the first day of action for Canadian infantry in World War II. After withdrawal to the Island there was no one to try to hold the Japanese onslaught except the Canadians. The Royal Rifles carried out more counterattacks at company level or above than the British and Indian battalions combined, while the Grenadiers had the next greatest number. Although the Japanese side might not have been aware of it, wherever they ran into problems it was usually the Canadians who were responsible.[17]

Although it may be a little too much to expect the average Imperial Japanese soldier to possess the ability to distinguish the Canadians from the British across a field of fire—in most cases the Japanese were abysmally ignorant of the Canadians thanks in part to their similar ignorance of the English language— interviews with surviving Japanese officers yielded some interesting comments on the Canadians' role. Kamata Schūichi, whose name will appear again elsewhere, then Second Lieutenant and platoon commander of the 5th Company of the 2nd Battalion, 230th Regiment, vividly remembers almost half a century later how daringly the Canadians fought in the face of the great odds to carry out their counteroffensive in the Kowloon Peninsula. Kamata had been aware of the presence of the Canadians in Hong Kong through frequent briefings he received while in South China. He was able to tell the Canadians from the British by the different helmets they were wearing.[18]

Shortly before dawn of the 25th at 160-Metre Hill in the Stanley Peninsula,

Kamata's platoon was completely wiped out by the Royal Canadians. Kamata himself was badly injured and lost consciousness when he led his men (a little over thirty in all) in their last *banzai* charge against the enemy who were firing from the pillbox on top of the hill near the shore. When Private First Class Hitosugi Jun'ichi saw Kamata, wounded, fall from the cliff, he rushed to Kamata and raised him in his arms. Then both men heard a Canadian, speaking in fluent Japanese shout: 'We are the British Imperial Guards, and we are proud of our age-long tradition and history. Hey, Jap! Come up here!!' Upon hearing these highly provocative words, Commander Kamata angrily got to his feet, gathered the last of his strength, and led the charge up the hill, shouting at the top of his lungs. He was hit a second time by an enemy hand grenade, and fell unconscious where he lay until he was picked up by his comrades-in-arms one whole day later.[19]

The Japanese force assigned to the capture of Hong Kong was the 38th Division under the command of Lieutenant-General Sano Tadayoshi, with Major-General Itō Takeo under him as infantry commander. The division belonged to Lieutenant-General Sakai Takashi's 23rd Army. It was composed of three infantry regiments: the 228th (Colonel Doi Sadashichi), the 229th (Colonel Tanaka Ryōzaburō) and the 230th (Colonel Shōji Toshishige). The division had the usual units of artillery (the 38th Mountain Artillery Regiment of three battalions under Colonel Kanki Takeyoshi), engineers (the 38th Engineering Regiment), transport (the 38th Transport Regiment), signals, ordnance, etc. Attached to this basic division were two Independent Anti-Tank Gun Battalions (the 2nd and 5th), two Independent Mountain Artillery Regiments (the 10th and 20th), the 21st Mortar Battalion, two Independent Engineering Regiments (the 19th and 20th) plus one company of the 14th Independent Engineering Regiment, the 3rd Independent Transport Regiment plus two companies, two River Crossing Companies, etc. In addition, the division was assisted by the entire Army artillery of the 23rd Army under the command of Lieutenant-General Kitajima Kineo. Moreover, strong air support was provided for the Sano Force (34 light bombers, 13 fighters, etc.) The strength of the Japanese ground forces which participated in the capture of Hong Kong was therefore 38th Division, 13,509; attached units, 8,609; total: 22,118.[20]

At this point a summary of Japanese intelligence estimates of the garrison troops before the outbreak of war is in order. They may be compared with the totally inaccurate British assessment of the Japanese troops—5000, with scant artillery—mentioned above. As early as a year before the attack, the 38th Division set up, under the command of Major Noborizaka Susumu, Intelligence Chief, a secret organization with Second Lieutenant Furukawa as its head. This was followed by the setting up of intelligence outposts at Macao (First Lieutenant Yanagihara) in October and at Shenzhen (First Lieutenant Furukawa) in November. The division launched intensive intelligence activities to collect maps and information of all sorts on the Hong Kong fortress. It also sent out on many occasions intelligence officers for reconnaissance, and used many spies.[21] The division estimated that the total enemy ground forces were about ten thousand men, with six thousand infantry and two thousand artillery, including heavy guns, field and mountain guns, and anti-aircraft guns. Enemy air and sea power was considered to be rather weak. The basic composition of the enemy ground forces was estimated at 3,000-4,000 British, 3,000-4,000 Indians, and 1,000 Chinese, or 7,000-9,000 in all.[22] To this were added the Canadians, 'who came in the middle of November 1941 as reinforcements; one to two thousand in number and of low quality'.[23] Thus the Japanese had relatively good knowledge of the enemy troop dispositions.

However, in the course of the campaign, the Japanese acutely suffered from the lack of operational intelligence. For example, General Kitajima commented after the capture of Hong Kong that 'the footnotes to the then available maps were extremely sloppy. The number of enemy pillboxes was counted as 195 in the Kowloon Peninsula, 80 on Hong Kong Island. But the truth of the matter was that there were 86 in Kowloon, and 145 on the Island.'[24] To give one more example of the serious miscalculations on the part of the Japanese, 'The 38th Division Combat Report of the Assault on Hong Kong' specifically states:

> It was generally assumed that since enemy forces were assumed to withstand our attack with full strength by relying on their main defence positions in the Kowloon Peninsula its capture would greatly facilitate the rest of the battle. For this reason information gathering was focused on the peninsula. Not until the seizure of the enemy maps during the battle did we hold even the slightest idea on the existence of such a formidable fortress on Hong Kong Island. Moreover, we had a preconception that once we landed on the Island we would be able to wipe it out in one stroke. . . .[25]

Interestingly enough, 'The Combat Report of the 230th Regiment' gives both a detailed analysis and fairly accurate estimate of enemy forces, more so than the 38th Division's own Combat Report. Here I shall refer only to the Canadians. The regiment estimated the Canadian forces at about two thousand, although they wrongly assumed that the enemy forces were prepared to launch a decisive battle north of the Kowloon Peninsula. It also thought that in terms of the quality of soldiery the Scots were the best of all the enemy units, followed by the Canadians who were generally excellent. The Indians and the Chinese were considered to be generally inferior.[26]

According to Kamata, the 230th Regiment was able to obtain a more accurate picture of enemy troops because it had put more effort into espionage activities. Kamata today recalls that when his regiment was still in South China, he was frequently briefed on the enemy situation and that it was widely rumoured among the Japanese rank and file that the Canadians were a bunch of 'outlaws' (convicts) who would be acquitted of charges if they fought well against the Japanese.[27] Similarly, though the belief still seems to persist among the British and Canadians that the Japanese had 2,000 'storm troops', in fact the 38th Division was just an ordinary Japanese division. The division was mobilized in August 1939. The 228th Regiment was organized in Nagoya, the 229th Regiment in Toyohashi, and the 230th Regiment in Shizuoka. Its previous activities had been strictly garrison and anti-guerrilla duties near Canton in South China. It had previously participated in as many as 390 actions, but they were largely anti-guerrilla activities; its main battle experience was probably the Liang-kou Operation which lasted only from May to June 1940. For the 38th division the Hong Kong Operation was just the beginning of the war, because their next target had been set for the Dutch East Indies.

The Japanese had to pay a considerable price for their victory—683 dead and 1413 wounded.[28] But a far more tragic fate awaited the 38th Division at a later stage of the Pacific War. Most of its officers and men then had to suffer from extreme hunger and tropical diseases under formidable enemy fire, and perish in the jungles of Guadalcanal.[29] The casualties of the British, Colonial, and Indian forces, conversely, are hard to determine. General Maltby's despatch estimates them as having been approximately 955 all ranks killed, and 659 missing. The Canadian losses at Hong Kong were much heavier than those of the other forces—a total of 290 men killed, and 493 wounded.[30] The Canadians even lost their commander, Brigadier Lawson, and nearly all of his staff officers in action. Lawson tried to get out of his shelter to fight it out, and was killed by enemy fire. Because of the deep impression the Canadian contingent left on the Japanese in terms of valour, Colonel Shōji, Commander of the 230th Regiment, buried Lawson with full military honours and put up a monument in his memory. After encampment in Hong Kong until January 1943, where they suffered from the deaths of 182 comrades-in-arms, the surviving Canadians were sent to Japan for forced labour until the end of the war. Of all the Canadians who sailed from Vancouver in October 1941, 557 never returned home.

The Canadian role in the Pacific War was relatively small when compared with the part they played in Europe. But, granted that the presence of the two Canadian battalions sent at the eleventh hour did not have any significant influence on the course of events in Hong Kong, their outstanding combat record speaks for itself. In spite of insufficient training and poor equipment, the Canadians fought extremely well in the face of the seasoned Japanese who outnumbered them and had superior artillery and air power. Considering the smallness of the Canadian forces, their sacrifice at Hong Kong is a source of pride and sadness in the national history of the Dominion of Canada, and has rightfully earned the respect of their wartime enemy. As Winston Churchill later wrote about the defenders of Hong Kong, 'They had won indeed the "lasting honour" which is their due.'[31]

○

Diplomatic Relations

The Far East had a significant impact on Canada during the 1930s. In many ways, developments there posed more perplexing problems for Canada than did the turmoil in Europe. Increasing tension in the Far East threatened to upset trans-Pacific trade (which, though small, was nevertheless important to an economy crippled by the Depression); it also threatened to exacerbate problems surrounding Japanese immigration (a sensitive issue Canadian governments feared might embitter already sour relations between Japan and the British Empire). Moreover, in Europe British and American policies generally harmonized, but in the Far East Britain and the United States often pursued divergent policies—with potentially disastrous implications for Canada's relations.[1] Canadian statesmen, mindful of the way Canadian interests had suffered in the past, recognized the danger of becoming entangled in Anglo-American power struggles. The possibility of war in the Pacific recalled the threat the conscription crisis of 1917 had posed to national unity. Canadian neutrality in the event of an American-Japanese war was theoretically possible, but many believed that Canada might be attacked if war broke out in the Pacific. Military authorities warned the government that if British Columbia was inadequately defended the United States might be forced to step in to ensure American security—violating Canadian neutrality or even threatening Canadian sovereignty.

Canadian officials recognized the dangers—which largely explains their cautious and non-committal approach to foreign policy. Throughout the 1930s they sought to avoid entanglement in Anglo-American conflicts by seeking to promote good relations between Britain and the United States while avoiding any policy that risked *creating what Prime Minister Mackenzie King often referred to in his diary as 'incidents'. At the same time, officials tried to resolve the defence problem—made more acute by the deterioration of the situation in Europe—by giving the Pacific Coast nominal priority over the Atlantic Coast while supporting Britain's European policy of appeasement in hopes of avoiding involvement in a European war.*

A graduate of the University of British Columbia and York University, Gregory A. Johnson has written on various aspects of Canada and the Far East, including Canada and the Far East in 1939, the defence of British Columbia during World War II and, with J.L. Granatstein, the evacuation of the Japanese Canadians in 1942. He is completing a manuscript on the impact of the Far East on Canada's relations with Britain and the United States during the Mackenzie King era. Professor Johnson currently teaches in the History Department of the University of Alberta.

CANADA AND THE FAR EAST DURING THE 1930s

Gregory A. Johnson

A member of the Royal Commission on Dominion-Provincial Relations captured the essence of Canada's position on the Pacific Rim when he remarked that, between the United States and Britain, Canada was like 'a small man sitting in a big poker game. He must play for high stakes, but with only a fraction of the resources of the other players: should he win, his profits in relation to his capital are very large, but if he loses, he risks being cleaned out.'[2] Canadian officials had grappled with the nagging question of what would happen in the event of a Pacific war since the formation of the Anglo-Japanese alliance in 1902. True, there were occasions when the alliance benefited Canada—notably during World War I, when Japan kept German naval forces at bay in the Pacific, thereby allaying fears of a German attack on British Columbia. But the alliance proved on balance to be more of a burden for Canada. Fierce American criticism of Japan's actions during the 1914-18 war, in particular the notorious Twenty-One Demands to China in 1915 and the seizure of Germany's Far Eastern colonies, had raised the question of Japan's desirability as an ally. The alliance, the Canadian naval staff argued in 1919, had 'lost its main value for us, and may be even looked upon more in the light of an encumbrance, as it is a means of embroiling us with the United States.'[3] This danger was Prime Minister Arthur Meighen's chief preoccupation when he argued for the termination of the alliance at the 1921 Imperial Conference.[4]

The replacement of the alliance by the Washington Conference system of

1921-22 somewhat eased the fear of Canada's incurring the hostility of the United States, but there were still those, particularly in the military, who expressed concern over the potential for trouble in the Pacific and the circumstances it would create for Canada. They had reason to be concerned. A naval race between Japan and the United States could easily lead to war; in addition Japanese bitterness towards Britain for abandoning the alliance prompted growing uneasiness.[5] Would Canada get dragged into an Anglo-Japanese war with American abstention? Or an American-Japanese war with British abstention? Could Canada remain neutral if the United States or Britain went to war against Japan? Was Canada even in a position to protect its neutrality in the event of war? Or would Japan attack Canada under any circumstances?

Failure to address these questions adequately during the 1920s and to find answers to them during the 1930s would come back to haunt the government after Japan's attack on Pearl Harbor in 1941. That they remained unanswered in the decade after World War I owed as much to the belief that Canada was 'a fireproof house, far from inflammable materials' as it did to the prevailing mood of optimism over the chances for lasting international peace.[6] The establishment of a Canadian Legation at Tokyo in 1929 reflected the spirit of goodwill. Herbert Marler, a former Liberal member of Parliament and Cabinet Minister, was appointed Minister, a position he would hold until July 1936. His staff was headed by First Secretary Hugh Keenleyside, a native British Columbian who had at one time taught at the University of British Columbia before joining the Department of External Affairs.[7] Japan reciprocated by establishing a Legation in Canada. All the signs pointed to a new era of friendly co-operation. 'Canada and Japan', said I.M. Tokugawa, Japan's first Minister to Canada, upon his arrival in October 1929, 'are marching hand in hand toward the great cause of permanent peace in the region.'[8] British statesman Viscount Cecil expressed a similar sentiment when he told the League of Nations Assembly on 10 September 1931 that 'there has scarcely ever been a period in the world's history when war seemed less likely than it does at the present.'[9]

Such optimism was shattered a week later by a small explosion on the South Manchurian Railway, north of the capital, Mukden. Charging that the blast was the work of Chinese saboteurs, elements of Japan's Kwantung Army clashed with Chinese forces. What had started as a minor incident was soon—quite deliberately—escalated out of control. China took its case to the League of Nations, which appointed a commission under the Earl of Lytton to look into the matter. A crisis might have been avoided had the Japanese not attacked Shanghai in January 1932, but this menacing move threatened the heart of China as well as British and American interests in the region. The American Secretary of State, Henry Stimson, called upon Britain to actively support America's refusal to recognize Japanese claims to any part of China. The British, fearing that they would be pushed out front and then left holding the bag, refused to act on Stimson's proposal. British statesmen, and especially the Foreign Secretary, Sir John Simon, knew very well what would happen if Britain supported the Stimson line. Their fears were confirmed when in 1933 the League accepted the Lytton Commission's report, calling for a policy of non-recognition of Japan's claim to Manchuria. Japan left the League, held Britain responsible for the moral condemnation of its actions in China, and announced its intention, in the 1934 Amau Declaration, to pursue Japan's special mandate in East Asia.[10]

Significantly, Japan's actions did not prompt Britain and the United States to form a common front. Britain had too much, and the United States too little, at stake in the Far East to risk forcing Japan to back down. In addition, the Americans believed Britain's refusal to support the Stimson doctrine amounted to betrayal (Stimson later claimed that Britain, and especially Simon, had 'let America down'). The episode left a legacy of mistrust and suspicion in Anglo-American relations that would last throughout the 1930s and continue into World War II.[11]

Although Ottawa's initial concern was whether the conflict would escalate into a general Far Eastern war through the application of sanctions, Canadian statesmen soon found themselves in the middle of the Simon-Stimson affair. The occasion was a speech which Canada's Secretary of State, C.H. Cahan, delivered to the League on 8 December 1932 in response to the Lytton report. Cahan chose to support Britain by disavowing the report. He questioned the legitimacy of the National Government of China, supported Japan's claim to rights in China, and hinted that Japan had a special mandate to exercise in Manchuria.[12]

The speech angered officials in Ottawa, not so much because of what Cahan said as because of the reaction his remarks provoked in the United States. Canada's Minister to Washington, W.D. Herridge, had overstepped his instructions by assuring Stimson that Canada stood behind America policy. Cahan's speech thus brought a sharp rebuke from the United States. Stimson remarked curtly that the Canadian representative should 'adhere more closely to the letter and spirit of his instructions'.[13] Another American official warned that Washington considered Cahan's action 'a straight double-cross'.[14] Fortunately, Canada managed to escape with only a severe American tongue-lashing.[15] The affair nevertheless demonstrated what could happen if Canada came between Britain and the United States over a Far Eastern issue. It also provided Mackenzie King, then Leader of the Liberal Opposition, with a valuable lesson; namely, that Canada had to be kept out of Far Eastern international affairs.

The controversy over Cahan's speech soon faded, but there were those, notably Major-General A.G.L. McNaughton, then Chief of the General Staff, who were closely following developments in the Far East. When the League (and the Canadian delegate) voted to accept the Lytton report on 24 February

1933, he wrote a long memorandum to Prime Minister R.B. Bennett voicing serious concerns over the League's action and its possible implications for Canada. 'The situation to be appreciated', McNaughton began, 'is that the United States and the League . . . have succeeded in isolating Japan.' He pointed out that Japan and the United States had both recently carried out a number of provocative war exercises and concluded that 'the attitude of these two Powers towards one another is therefore quite definitely one of dangerous distrust and anticipation.' Given that this hostility could lead to war, McNaughton raised the matter of Canada's obligations under the Anglo-American treaty of 1871. That treaty required Canada to protect sections of the Straits of Juan de Fuca which, Japan could argue, were international waters. If Canada failed to prevent the Japanese from utilizing these areas, the Americans could respond with force and, McNaughton feared, might even occupy British Columbia. He therefore recommended that the government increase defences on the West Coast.[16]

The Chief of the General Staff was not simply attempting to exaggerate potential dangers in an effort to wring more money for defence from a stingy government (though this may have played a part).[17] Astute enough to recognize that a Japanese attack on the United States 'would seem the extreme of folly', McNaughton nevertheless correctly observed that 'in the present state of Japanese feeling . . . reason and consideration of future results cannot be relied upon as determining factors.'[18] Even if war did not break out in the Pacific, its possibility threatened to divert British and American attention away from Europe, the real area of concern. '[S]uch detachment [from Europe] on the part of the two States now holding the balance of world power might well result in international chaos', he warned.

McNaughton's remarks partly reflected his distrust of Japan. 'Remember, George', he wrote to one of his staff officers, George Pearkes, in 1929, shortly before he turned over command of British Columbia's Military District Number 11 to his successor, 'keep your eyes on the Pacific. You can't trust those Japanese.'[19] But by 1933 there was a growing realization that the Washington Conference system was not working, the Far East was entering a period of instability (despite the Tangku truce between China and Japan in May 1933), the United States and Japan were eyeing each other warily, and Anglo-American relations had soured. What of Canada's geographical and political position between Britain and America in these circumstances? Here, too, military officials expressed some concern. Colonel H.D.G. Crerar of the General Staff, for example, wrote in March 1933 that 'Canada, by reason of its geographical position alone, is very importantly concerned with the conflict now proceeding between Japan and China. It is moreover vitally concerned with the relations between the United States and Japan and the United States and Great Britain. It follows that the basis of our policy should be to do nothing which will accentuate the difficulties in U.S./Japanese relations, and to do everything which will improve the political understanding between Great Britain and the United States.[20] The role of linchpin was a time-honoured one, though Crerar never explained how Canada should proceed in this situation. Crerar also warned that Canada had to exercise great care in choosing which British policies to support in the Far East or risk coming into opposition with the United States. For instance, when Britain's proposed arms embargo against Japan and China prompted American objections, he argued that Canada should stand aloof because 'it would unquestionably cause undesirable misgivings in American minds as to the attitude and action of Canada . . . in the grave event of hostilities breaking out between the United States and Japan.'[21]

The Americans for their part had doubts about Canada's position, and serious misgivings about the state of Canadian defences. In late April, 1935 Ottawa learned that the United States War Department planned to build air bases in the Great Lakes area which threatened 'to dominate the industrial heart of Canada'. This revelation was followed by a report that the Military Affairs Committee of the House of Representatives had produced a study containing 'provocative references to Canada'; meanwhile others were proposing that a highway be built through British Columbia to Alaska. These schemes occasioned some alarm among Canadian military authorities over their implications for the Pacific Coast and the question of Canadian neutrality. Echoing McNaughton's earlier concerns, the General Staff warned that 'if Canada is unprepared to defend her neutrality in the event of a Pacific war in which the United States is engaged . . ., it is as clear as can be that the Americans will not hesitate for one moment to occupy our country in order to deny potential bases to their enemy.' The proposed highway prompted particular alarm. General E.C. Ashton, Chief of the General Staff, wrote: 'The question of the maintenance of our neutrality in the event of a war between the U.S.A. and Japan—a not unlikely occurrence within the next few years—is a very vital one. The building of a north and south highway through B.C. provides a strong military inducement to the U.S.A. to ignore our neutral rights on the crisis arising.'[22]

Military officials were not alone in drawing attention to the potential dangers Canada faced in the Pacific. In 1935 Lester B. Pearson, in an article in the influential journal *Foreign Affairs*, pointed out that Far Eastern developments contained 'terrific implications' for Canada. 'Canada's position becomes impossible if Great Britain and the United States drift apart on any major [Far Eastern] issue', he wrote. 'Canada is a British Dominion. She is also an American State. She cannot permit herself to be put in a position where she has to choose between these two destinies. Either choice would be fatal to her unity; indeed to her very existence as a State.'[23] Another official in the Department of External Affairs, Loring Christie, warned his colleagues that Canada could not afford to ignore the Far East. 'To what extent', he asked, 'if any, can we expend energy across the Atlantic without weakening our resistance to events impinging from the south or from across the Pacific?'[24] Although military officials, Pearson, and Christie may have been using the Far East to achieve other ends (Christie in particular was attempting to argue that Canada should limit its European commitments and he used Far Eastern developments to make his point), there was nonetheless by 1935 a widespread belief that the horrors of World War I were once again about to descend upon the world and that hostilities might start in the Far East instead of in Europe.

Mackenzie King returned in 1935 to the Prime Minister's office amid this hostile international climate. Five years in opposition had not dulled his political sensitivity, his concern for national unity, or his desire to keep Canada out of another war. Having dealt with Far Eastern issues early in his career, King retained a healthy appreciation of the dangers Canada faced in the Pacific. But for the moment he confronted a number of more pressing domestic problems inherited from the Bennett administration,[25] among them the problem of economic recovery and the Abyssinian crisis, which produced the famous Riddell affair.[26] But he also faced a nasty trade war with Japan.

Only a brief summary need be provided here.[27] By the end of the 1920s trade with Japan, as Mackenzie King bragged in the House of Commons, was 'greater than was the trade of Canada with the United Kingdom at the time the government of Sir Wilfrid Laurier came into office.'[28] In 1896 Canadian exports to Japan had amounted to only $8,148. By 1929 exports had risen to $42,099,968 and Japan had become Canada's third largest importer. Though trade with the Far East represented less than five per cent of Canada's total trade, more important was the fact that Canada generally enjoyed a very favourable balance of trade with Japan (in 1934, for example, Canada exported some $14 million to Japan while importing only $3 million). This favourable balance, along with Canada's protectionist measures to which the Japanese objected, sparked the trade war.[29]

There is little to be gained by assessing blame for the episode. Both Canada and Japan were suffering from a severe downturn in the economy and both countries sought to employ measures that would lead to economic recovery—Canada by using high tariff walls and anti-dumping duties; Japan by embargo-ing gold exports, devaluing currency, and cutting military expenditures. The Japanese fired the first shot in July 1935 when they imposed a 50% surtax on Canadian imports, after charging discriminatory practices by Canada on exchange values of the yen. Japan had gone off the gold standard in 1932, devalued the yen from 49.85 cents to range between 24 and 29 cents, and wanted Canada to accept the current rate of exchange (then 29 cents) on its imports of Japanese goods.[30] The idea, of course, was to increase the level of

Japanese exports to Canada in an effort to correct the trade imbalance. The Bennett government retaliated with a 33^1/$_3$% surtax on Japanese goods and the war was on. Canadian exports dropped in September to a three-year low, from 4,367,000 million yen in 1933 to 2,630,000 million yen in 1935, and overall trade fell 33% between August and December.[31] This, and the subsequent war of words, did neither country any good but the situation remained deadlocked until Mackenzie King returned to office and began negotiations to resolve matters. The trade war ended on 1 January 1936 when both countries cancelled their surtaxes and modified currency exchange values on various exports.[32] Thereafter trade increased, so that by the end of 1936 the Pacific Rim represented more than one-quarter of Canada's total ocean-borne trade. The following year Ian Mackenzie, the Minister of National Defence, confidently reported that 'it is no exaggeration to say that Canada has a $200,000,000 trade interest on the Pacific Ocean.'[33]

The trade war was settled, but very shortly the defence issue reappeared. As O.D. Skelton, the influential Under-Secretary of State for External Affairs and Mackenzie King's closest advisor, commented after the wave of political assassinations that shook Japan in early 1936: 'The establishment of another military dictatorship [in Japan] will not only increase the danger of conflict in China and Russia, but will intensify every other international difficulty. The question of our own Pacific coast defences will undoubtedly be brought up soon.'[34]

It was. When McNaughton retired as Chief of Staff in 1935 he prepared a memorandum outlining deficiencies in Canada's defence system. Mackenzie King did not read the report until August 1936, but what he then read alarmed him. 'The impression left on my mind', he recorded in his diary, 'was one of the complete inadequacy of everything in the way of defence.'[35] The Joint Staff Committee was instructed to prepare a thorough report, which it presented in September 1936. The military officials minced no words: 'the liability of direct attack on Canada by Japanese forces has become a matter requiring urgent consideration and action in view of the menacing situation which continues to develop in the Far East.' As was the case in the past, they stressed the maintenance of Canadian neutrality, Canada's geographical position, and relations with the United States. In each case the message was clear: Canada had to arm and defend its Pacific Coast to fend off both Japanese and American potential encroachment.[36]

The Prime Minister took the military's concerns seriously, especially after President Roosevelt told him in July, 1936 of 'having a number of leading Senators in and asking them the question, what would the United States do if Japan attacked British Columbia. The agreement being instantly, why, of course we would go in and help to prevent her getting a foothold.'[37] A worried Mackenzie King noted in his diary, 'I thought we owed it to our country to protect it in a mad world, at least to the extent of police services, both on sea and in the air, alike on the Atlantic and Pacific Coasts. I stated it was humiliating to accept protection from Britain without sharing in the costs, or to rely on the United States without being willing to at least protect our neutrality.'[38] What King did not like was the cost of implementing a suitable defence program, estimated at about $200 million over five years with an initial outlay of $65 million. Despite the pressure for major improvements, the sum actually allocated amounted to only $36 million, with coastal defence being given priority, the Pacific Coast coming before the Atlantic.[39]

The Canadian government had good reason to place priority on the defence of British Columbia. But in practice the Pacific Coast received little in the way of actual armament until after Pearl Harbor.[40] Moreover, this sad state of affairs continued to concern the Americans. In March 1937, for example, Mackenzie King visited the White House to be told by the President 'that it might be wise for them [the Canadians] to have a certain number of naval vessels in the nature of patrol ships on the west coast.' Roosevelt again raised the subject of the Alaska highway and inquired about 'the possibility of seeing the work eventually carried through.'[41] On this occasion, and others to follow, Mackenzie King remained determined to keep the Americans at arm's length. It was an early indication of his suspicion of American intentions *vis-à-vis* Canada and the Far East. And those suspicions would only increase after full-scale war broke out between China and Japan during the summer of 1937.

The 'undeclared' Sino-Japanese war began on the evening of 7 July 1937 when Japanese and Chinese forces clashed near the Marco Polo Bridge, not far from Peking. Once again, as in 1931, the Japanese used the incident as a pretext to demand disproportionate concessions. This time, however, there was no turning back.[42] Throughout 1937 and 1938 the Japanese inflicted on the Chinese a series of blows, including the capture of such key strategic centres in China such as Canton and Hankow. Japanese forces also savaged Shanghai and Nanking, where the infamous 'rape' is said to have claimed 200,000 lives. Even the Western powers fell victim to the attack. In one incident a Japanese plane strafed the car of the British Ambassador to China, seriously wounding him. Then, in December 1937, Japanese shore batteries on the Yangtze river fired upon the British ships HMS *Ladybird* and *Bee* while Japanese aircraft attacked and sank the USS *Panay* and three Standard Oil tankers. These developments were followed by demands by the Japanese government for the establishment of a 'New Order' in East Asia—one which would not include the Western powers.

By 1939 Japanese forces occupied more than a million and a half square kilometres of Chinese territory and had taken an estimated 800,000 Chinese lives. Nevertheless, Japan had not been able to bring China to its knees. This only served to strengthen the Japanese resolve to deliver a crushing blow. For the remainder of the year Japan sought to tighten its hold on the occupied areas, to weaken China's war effort by undermining the Chinese currency, and to drive a wedge between Britain and the United States in an effort to force Britain into accepting a 'Far Eastern Munich.' Moves in this direction were made with the seizure of Hainan Island off the South China Coast in February and the prohibition of North Chinese currency in March. Japan then began to exert pressure on the International Settlements and especially on the British Concession at the Chinese treaty port of Tientsin. This bold move brought Japan and Britain to the brink of war during the summer of 1939.[43]

The last thing the Canadian government needed was more trouble in the Far East. But trouble there was. The problems were familiar enough: the possibility of becoming drawn into a war and the threat it posed for national unity, the danger of coming between Britain and the United States, and the ongoing dilemma of defence. But the outbreak of the Sino-Japanese war added a new sense of urgency to the resolution of these problems at a time when the government was still struggling with the Great Depression and potential domestic disunity in the face of the ominous situation developing in Europe, an area traditionally of far greater concern.

Initially, Mackenzie King's government tried to ignore the Far Eastern situation. Adopting the Micawber-like approach that constituted King's leadership style, official circles seemed to believe that if the problem was ignored it would somehow go away. That this position was untenable became abundantly clear when, in October 1937, London asked Ottawa for its views on the question of imposing sanctions against Japan.[44] Mackenzie King and O.D. Skelton were violently opposed to such a policy. The Prime Minister feared that Britain was seeking to drag Canada into the Far Eastern confrontation. ' "British interests" in China', he noted sourly in his diary, 'will not be a sufficient ground for our participation in a war in the Orient.'[45] The Under-Secretary, for his part, worried that Britain and the United States might go through another Simon-Stimson affair. Skelton knew that the United States and Britain did not see eye to eye in the Far East, and more importantly, that the Americans were unwilling to give the British a firm military commitment in advance. If Britain pressed ahead with sanctions Canada risked becoming involved in either an Anglo-American squabble or a Pacific war.[46]

If this was not enough, the government now faced increasing pressure on two other fronts: public opinion, and renewed American concerns over Canadian defence. Public opinion had not mattered much in the past, but by the fall of 1937 it had begun to heat up across the country. Archdeacon F.G. Scott of Quebec City, for example, was claiming that Japanese naval officers were living in disguise in Japanese fishing villages on the West Coast. British Columbia MLA Captain MacGregor Macintosh declared that Scott was 'telling the truth' and went on to assert that 'Oriental penetration into British Columbia industry was a real fact.'[47] The situation almost got out of hand when a Vancouver resident, Rolphe Forsythe, tried to blow up the Japanese ship *Hiye Maru* at Seattle, Washington. Fortunately, Forsythe blew himself up instead and Canada managed to escape an international incident with a formal apology to Japan.[48]

In the meantime the Americans were demonstrating increased interest in West Coast defence—in September 1937 President Roosevelt himself paid a visit to British Columbia. He was not impressed. Two months later Norman Armour, the American Minister to Ottawa, noted that Roosevelt had concluded that 'Canadian defenses were . . . not only entirely inadequate, but almost nonexistent' and that he 'felt that more should be done by the Canadian and American governments in developing a co-ordinated plan of defense'.[49] The President followed up his visit with a suggestion that Canada send a couple of officers to Washington for 'off-the-record conversations' on Pacific Coast defence. The Canadians complied, and in mid-January, 1938 the Chief of the General Staff and the Naval Staff travelled separately and incognito to Washington to meet with their American counterparts. But they took with them the familiar instructions from the Prime Minister to enter into 'no commitments.'[50]

Nothing, predictably, came of these talks, but Mackenzie King was becoming increasingly concerned. As he explained to his Cabinet in early January 1938: 'Japan was very dangerous. . . . For us to do nothing was not playing the game. . . . Also that with the United States materially increasing its large war equipment, that for us to do nothing in meeting our own defence was to become increasingly dependent upon the United States with possible serious consequences.'[51] Faced with this prospect, the existing rift in Anglo-American relations, increasing American pressure over defence, and rising hostility in public opinion, the Prime Minister declared in the House of Commons on 31 January 1938 that 'our decision is to be strictly neutral' with respect to the Sino-Japanese conflict. Shortly thereafter he took the lead in killing a Bill to further restrict Japanese immigration to Canada; his government would continue to oppose exclusionist measures in order to avoid provocation. King noted in his diary that he had warned members of the House of 'the position in Japan and the embarrassment which the passing of any exclusion measures would be to the British Government and the danger of the reaction to the parts of the Empire.'[52] Not the most principled policy, perhaps, but it would not offend either the Americans or the British and meanwhile would reassure the Japanese, since Tokyo would presumably read the rejection of the immigration bill as a conciliatory gesture.

Nevertheless, the government's attempts to sidestep the issues were not having the desired effect and Mackenzie King knew it. In August 1938, Roosevelt declared at the opening of the Thousand Islands Bridge at Kingston, Ontario, in a speech that was aimed as much at Japan as it was at Germany, that 'the United States will not stand idly by if domination of Canadian soil is threatened by any other empire.' Mackenzie King publicly assured the United States that Canada's obligations would be met.[53] But privately he was rather disturbed by the President's guarantee. 'I pointed out to the Cabinet', he recorded in his diary, 'that they must not mistake what the President said at the Thousand Islands Bridge; that it was not that the United States would not allow Canada to be dominated by any other Empire or country than the British. That if she had to come here and save [Canada], the Empire being dominated, it would mean that Canada would become a part of America.' This King was determined to resist. He continued to reject American overtures to build the Alaskan highway, claiming that he would not permit 'financial penetration' of Canada.[54]

In an effort to provide at least the appearance of improved defences, the government began to step up rearmament on the Pacific Coast, mostly in the form of artillery. Four of Canada's six destroyers were also stationed there. In addition, a press campaign advertised a well-defended British Columbia. Some of the resulting headlines were rather optimistic. The *Globe and Mail*, for example, ran a front-page story in December, 1938 bearing the headline 'Canada's Pacific Forts Among the World's Finest' while the Toronto *Star* later ran a piece headed 'B.C. Defences To Rank With Best In World'.[55] The federal government, struggling with the economic consequences of the Depression, lacked the means to do all that might be wished. Nevertheless, these measures hardly constituted a reassuring readiness should war come. The continuing failure to deal with defence matters during the 1930s proved, in the event, to be one of the factors fuelling the near hysteria that gripped British Columbia in the aftermath of Pearl Harbor.

Meanwhile, the war in China raged on. As the Japanese became increasingly frustrated in their attempt to bring China down, they began to exert pressure on the International Settlements and particularly on the British Concession at Tientsin. A crisis broke out after the Japanese blockaded the concession on 14 June 1939. Among the issues were the circulation of North Chinese currency, the refusal of the British to give up Chinese silver reserves stored in the Concession's vaults, and anti-Japanese activities carried out from the concession by Chinese guerrillas.

The crisis had menacing implications for other parts of the world and especially for Britain. British policy had been based on the premise that war would break out in Europe first, and then spread to the Far East. But now, as British Prime Minister Neville Chamberlain warned, 'it looked as though it might be the other way round: for, if we sent our fleet to Singapore to deal with Japan, the temptation to the Axis Powers to take advantage of the situation would be almost irresistible'.[56] Moreover, there was the American factor to consider. The British Ambassador to Washington cautioned his government against any policy 'that could be construed as a return to policy of appeasement' (abandoned after the Germans marched into Czechoslovakia in March 1939) since it would alienate the United States.[57]

These developments were viewed with considerable alarm in Ottawa. Once again, the dual fear of an Anglo-American split and of the danger of becoming drawn into a war with Japan dominated Canadian thinking. On 16 June Vincent Massey, Canada's High Commissioner to London, warned that the 'Japanese may have forced [the] issue at Tientsin, where United States interests are not so great, to drive a wedge between the two Governments.'[58] O.D. Skelton agreed with this assessment. Though he believed that Britain would not risk war with Japan without American support, he nevertheless allowed for the prospect of war. 'It would be ironical', he wrote to the Prime Minister, 'if, after declining to take any action against Japan to save the millions of Chinese from slaughter and starvation, we should find ourselves engaged in economic or military conflict in defence of concessions established after the Opium Wars.' The Under-Secretary warned that if Canada were asked to take some form of action, or to participate in economic sanctions, it should have an assurance of support from the United States.[59]

The Americans, however, were not forthcoming. Merchant Mahoney, the chargé d'affaires at the Canadian Legation in Washington, informed Ottawa that the Chief of the Far Eastern Division of the State Department had told him that 'he did not foresee new developments in the Far Eastern policy of the United States'. Meanwhile Escott Reid, Mahoney's Second Secretary, reported that non-interventionist sentiment in the Congress was too strong to overcome.[60] In other words, the Americans would hold their neutralist course and await developments. Without a guarantee of American support, London was forced to instruct its Ambassador to Japan to back down as gracefully as possible. On 24 July Britain accepted the humiliating formula negotiated by Sir Robert Craigie and Japanese Foreign Minister Arita as the basis for a settlement of the crisis.[61]

Not surprisingly, the Americans were disappointed by the British retreat. Secretary of State Cordell Hull later wrote: 'It was disturbing in that Japan had won a victory in her never ending quest for recognition of "special rights", or "special interests", in China.'[62] On 26 July Washington gave Tokyo the necessary six months' notice for the termination of the 1911 American-Japanese commercial treaty. This move came as a surprise to Britain but it was an even greater shock for Japan. Whether designed for domestic political consumption or meant to stiffen Britain's hand, the decision came two days too late. On the whole, the British were delighted, but angry that the Americans had not informed them beforehand of the decision (others, Craigie for example, believed that it was 'just another flash in the American pan').[63]

Whatever prompted it, the American decision forced the British to reconsider the situation carefully. At a series of meetings in early August, Chamberlain's Cabinet discussed the possibility of terminating the Anglo-Japanese Commercial Treaty of 1911, to which Canada was a party. On 16 August Britain asked Canada for its views on the termination of the treaty.[64] Ottawa replied on 21 August, explaining that

> it has not been found possible, in the brief time thus available to secure definitive consideration of the question by the Canadian Government. . . . While we consider it is essential for full understanding of the situation . . . we do not wish to imply that [such considerations] would offset our desire to co-operate with the United Kingdom and the United States in any action which they might take, particularly so in view of the long-range interests involved.

Despite the rather evasive phrasing of this telegram, Canada had acknowledged it would stand by Britain.[65]

The question had, in fact, been very carefully considered by Canadian authorities even before Britain made the request. Skelton, for one, anticipated such a move as early as 1 August. Writing to Mackenzie King he observed: 'It is not our business to offer any advice on the Tientsin negotiations at this eleventh hour, but if negotiations break down and the British decide to follow the United States example in denouncing the treaty, I do not suppose we could do otherwise.' But another factor troubled Skelton: namely, that Japan might retaliate and 'if reprisals are made they will fall largely on Canada, and while I do not think there is any likelihood of reprisals taking a military form it is clear that if they did come in the Pacific the United Kingdom could not give any adequate support.'[66] Skelton's fear of reprisals was not entirely unwarranted. As Norman Robertson, First Secretary in External Affairs, explained, under the Canadian tariff structure Japan would revert to the general tariff instead of the 'most-favoured nation' position. But the same thing would not necessarily happen to Japan's trade with Britain and the United States. Hence Canada could be placed in the position of taking 'what might be regarded as directly punitive measures against Japanese trade at a time when neither the United Kingdom nor the United States were committed to taking similar measures.'[67]

In other words, Canada could be placed in a position where it might be held responsible for creating an incident of the sort King had long feared. This had to be avoided. While Skelton and others believed that Canada had little choice but to follow Britain, they wanted a separate announcement of the termination of the trade agreement. This would demonstrate Canadian independence and would not give the appearance of taking the lead against Japan. Mackenzie King, for his part, agreed. But he was becoming increasingly alarmed over other possibilities. '[W]ith Japan Italy & Germany together in secret conclave', he wrote in his diary, 'it is hard to believe that plans are not already made for simultaneous attacks in the Orient & Europe—a ghastly & appaling [sic] situation.'[68]

The Axis powers were not planning together in 'secret conclave' for simultaneous attacks. But the Prime Minister's fear of becoming drawn into a war against Japan was not altogether removed from the realm of possibility. By the middle of August negotiations between Britain and Japan had broken down. The British decided that the time for conciliation had ended. The danger of alienating the United States, which had shown some signs of adopting a firmer policy, was too great. Chamberlain wrote that Japan 'had made things impossible, . . . & we must deal with the consequences as best we can.' The Japanese were equally determined to pursue their 'New Order' and towards the end of August it seemed almost certain that Britain and Japan would go to war. British Ambassador Sir Robert Craigie later wrote that the younger Japanese officers (who, it is worth noting, often exercised more power than their nominal superiors) 'were determined to exploit the [Tientsin] affair to the point of war' and that Whitehall had information 'showing that the Japanese General Staff had their plans fully laid for a single-handed war with Great Britain.'[69]

The situation was saved, most ironically, by the Germans. The announcement that Germany and the Soviet Union had signed a non-aggression pact on 22 August threw the Japanese into a tailspin. Japanese policy had been based on the 1936 Anti-Comintern Pact, and Germany's betrayal of that pact shocked Tokyo. The Japanese Premier resigned on 25 August, claiming that he had given the Emperor false advice, and his Cabinet fell a few days later. While the Nazi-Soviet pact paved the way for a German attack on Poland, it ensured that there would be would no immediate expansion of the war in the Far East. Germany marched into Poland on 1 September, Britain declared war on 3 September, and Canada followed on 10 September. In the meantime, the new Japanese government declared its intention to remain neutral in the European war and, to the surprise of none, so did the United States.

Despite the fact that Canada's attention had now turned to Europe, the Far East continued to be an area of concern. 'What may the Japanese not do in the Orient!' Mackenzie King recorded in his diary on 6 September. 'There are raiders and submarines on both the Atlantic and the Pacific coasts, and pocket cruisers. I have no doubt that we shall have some bombing of our coast and possibly some inland bombing as well.'[70] Indeed, between 1939 and 1941 Japan continued to menace British interests while the United States stuck to its isolationist course, providing some assistance but no guarantees of armed support. Canadian officials continued to worry about becoming involved in a two-front war without American support at a time when Anglo-American relations were still sour. They also continued to fret over the defence of British Columbia and the ongoing American efforts to have Canada do more to eradicate the problem.

The problems posed by developments in the Far East in the 1930s added another dimension to the complex international situation within which Canadian officials, and especially Mackenzie King, formulated foreign policy. For Canadian statesmen faced not one but three potential outcomes of the growing tension which marked the 1930s. One was a war against Germany, and another a war against Japan. A third was a simultaneous war against Japan and Germany. Viewed in this wider perspective, the Canadian aversion to overseas commitments, in particular King's support for the British policy of appeasement and lack of enthusiasm for collective security are more understandable. The dilemma in Canada's relations with Japan lay not in the bilateral issues of trade and immigration, but rather in Canada's need to maintain its equilibrium within the North Atlantic triangle. The result in practice was timidity. By hesitating and trying to avoid confrontation, Canada surrendered the initiative in Far Eastern affairs to Great Britain and the United States and thereby ultimately placed the protection of its interests in their hands. By doing so, Canada managed to maintain superficially cordial relations with Japan during a divisive decade, but eventually the nation was drawn into the larger conflict it had sought to avoid.

○

Up to the Second World War Canada—as a 'small country' caught between the U.K. and the U.S.—had virtually no presence in international politics. The second war, however, had a revolutionary impact on Canada's foreign policy. With the boom fuelled by military demand Canada experienced economic growth that propelled it into the ranks of economic powers in the postwar period. Meanwhile the decline of the U.K. only strengthened Canada's sense of independence, at the same time that a new self-confidence enabled it to withstand pressure from the U.S. Led by Prime Minister Mackenzie King, Canada sought to establish its credentials as a 'middle power'. Smaller countries, according to this doctrine, should avoid Great Power politics; instead each country should play a part in international politics consistent with its capabilities. Thus Canada's foreign policy shifted from its traditional stance of non-commitment to one of active commitment. In 1948, with the retirement of Mackenzie King, the Louis St Laurent cabinet was born with Lester B. Pearson promoted from under-secretary for foreign affairs to take over the Minister's portfolio. With that, Canada's foreign relations began to change dramatically. Whereas in 1939 Canada had had but seven legations in foreign countries, by 1962 the comparable figure had reached 65. The country played a large part in the establishment of the United Nations and the North Atlantic Treaty Organization, as well as in the restructuring of the British Commonwealth. In addition,

Canada became an active member of the U.N. Atomic Energy Commission and the U.N. Emergency Forces, and contributed to various other international organizations.

Canada's participation in East Asia, meanwhile, began with aid to China during the war (6.5 million dollars), but was largely passive. After the war, with membership in the Far Eastern Advisory Commission (then the Far Eastern Commission) that oversaw the Allied Occupation of Japan, Canada became an active participant in East Asia. In particular, with the establishment of the People's Republic of China and the outbreak of the Korean War, Canada found it could no longer ignore relations with Japan as an important element in its overall foreign policy. This point marks the origins of Canada's new Japan policy and its 'Pacific-area diplomacy'.

Nobuya Bamba received his PhD in history from the University of California at Berkeley, and subsequently taught at Bucknell and McGill universities and Tsuda College. The first president of the Japanese Association for Canadian Studies, as well as a director of the Japan Association for International Relations and president of the Japanese Association for Peace Studies, he was, at the time of his death in 1989, a member of the faculty of the University of Osaka. Among Professor Bamba's published works were Manshu Jihen eno Michi *[Road to the Manchurian Incident],* Japanese Diplomacy in Dilemma, *and* Kanada *(Chūō Kōronsha: 1989), from which the following selection has been taken. Okuma Tadayuki, who edited and abridged Professor Bamba's observations on postwar diplomacy, graduated with an MPA from the Graduate School of Public Administration at International Christian University, Tokyo, before joining the Japan Institute of International Affairs in 1969. After transferring to the Ministry of Foreign Affairs he served at the Japanese Embassy in Ottawa, and subsequently rejoined JIIA as a senior research fellow. The author of* Kanada no Gaiko *[Canadian Foreign Policy], Professor Okuma currently teaches in the Department of International Relations of the Faculty of Law at Hiroshima Shudo University.*

THE POSTWAR YEARS

Bamba Nobuya, adapted by Okuma Tadayuki
translated by Peter Currie

FROM OCCUPATION TO PEACE TREATY

The Allied Occupation of Japan was administered by the U.S., in particular by General Douglas MacArthur as the Supreme Commander for the Allied Powers (SCAP) centring on General Headquarters. Since Canada's Japan policy was more or less in agreement with that of the U.S., it planned to achieve its objectives by supporting the Americans. In general, Canada's basic policy toward Japan during the Occupation reflected three objectives: (1) that Japan never be able to threaten Canada and the world a second time; (2) that Japan be a democratic state; and (3) that Japan be restored to economic health, and the development of Japan-Canada trade in the future supported.

Canada had two main channels to the Occupation authorities. The first ran from the Canadian Liaison Mission, located in Tokyo, to the Far Eastern Commission (FEC). The latter body was ostensibly charged with responsibility for 'policy making in relation to the administration of Japan, authority to investigate U.S. government orders and General Headquarters activities'. With such a mandate, the FEC exerted indirect influence on General Headquarters across a wide range of topics, among them revision of the constitution, legalization of the labour movement, education in democracy, establishing civil liberties, demilitarizing the economy, abolishing monopolies, determining indemnifications, and trying and punishing war criminals. The Canadian representative sat in on all those deliberations, of course, but played a particularly prominent role in reconciling different countries' proposals on constitutional reform. On a wide range of other matters Canada found itself in agreement with the U.K. in advocating a more lenient policy toward Japan, and thus acted as an intermediary between the hard-line faction—the U.S.S.R., Australia, New Zealand and the Philippines—and a U.S. that tended to act arbitrarily and alone.

Canada's other, unofficial, channel of influence was the first head of the Liaison Mission, E. Herbert Norman. Norman was born and raised in Nagano Prefecture, Japan, the second son of a Methodist minister. Well versed in Japanese history and culture, he was hopeful that Japan could be reconstituted as a democratic and peaceful state. As a Japan specialist, Norman was one of a small number of advisers to enjoy General MacArthur's trust. He is widely thought to have played an influential role with the Occupation administration at General Headquarters, particularly in regard to democratic education, agricultural land reform and legalization of the labour movement.

Norman argued strongly for consideration of Japan's historical consciousness and recognition of the 'will of the people' in formulating Japan policy. His standpoint was integrated by the Canadian government into its basic Japan policy, and found its reflection in the views of the Far Eastern Commission. In addition, Norman also sought to protect figures esteemed as democratic leaders from pressure from General Headquarters, succeeding through petitions to General MacArthur in getting Ichikawa Fusae, Inukai Takeshi, Kawakami Jotaro and others removed from the purge list of public officials, and in reducing the severity of sentences on war criminals such as Shigemitsu Aoi and Togo Shigenori.

On 17 March 1947, SCAP announced that, by concluding a peace treaty with

Japan, it intended to wind up the military occupation early. On 11 July the U.S. Department of State instructed the representatives of the member states of the FEC to open preparatory meetings for a peace treaty with Japan on 19 August. The reasons for moving up the peace treaty with Japan included (1) worsening relations between the U.S. and the Soviet Union, (2) increasing unrest among U.S. taxpayers over the mounting burden of the Occupation, (3) SCAP's judgement that a prolonged Occupation would only continue Japan's feeling of dependence and invite a hostile reaction from the people, (4) pressure for an early peace treaty from Canada and the U.K., and (5) the success of the Chinese revolution and the outbreak of war on the Korean peninsula.

Canada had two reasons for preferring to see a peace treaty concluded early on. First, the continued military occupation of Japan made the U.S. by far the leading player, limiting Japan-Canada relations; second, Canada had high hopes for an early revival of commercial relations with Japan. That reasoning had important implications. Already by that time fearful of U.S. dominance in Japan and, in turn, in the Pacific basin as a whole, Canada was showing a strong interest in the region. Thus can be seen elements of Canadian policies in the future: an early pan-Pacific vision, and the idea of distancing itself from the U.S.

Canada's attitude was manifested by its representative at the British Commonwealth meeting in August-September, 1947. Held in Canberra, the meeting centred on deliberations on a peace treaty with Japan. Canada's representative, with Norman attached as adviser, made it clear that Canada had strong reasons for supporting a relaxation of peace treaty conditions with Japan. As a Pacific power and the world's third largest trading country, Canada wanted to see restoration of political and economic stability in the Far East.

The problem in arriving at a peace treaty with Japan was procedural: the U.S. advocated a simple two-thirds majority with no veto powers, while the U.S.S.R. wished to retain decision-making for the Foreign Ministers of the Four Powers—i.e., the Soviet Union, China, the U.S. and the U.K. The two approaches were fundamentally irreconcilable. Although Canada supported the U.S. proposal, it objected to making a peace treaty with Japan that excluded the U.S.S.R. Moreover, although Canada, unlike Australia and New Zealand, was in accord with the U.S. in welcoming the revival of Japan, by no means did it fully back the U.S. approach to political questions. The U.S., eager to make of Japan a military bulwark against the Communists, defended Japanese conservative forces and encouraged a build-up of Japan's military strength. By contrast, Canada hoped that trade could be expanded through a revival of Japan's peacetime industries. That was not because Canada was sympathetic to Communism; rather it was that the two countries did not share the same concern for military security in their interest in Asia.

DEVELOPMENT OF FRIENDLY RELATIONS

The signing of a peace treaty on 8 September 1951 marked the restoration of diplomatic relations between Japan and Canada. In April of the next year, with the upgrading of the Canadian legation in Tokyo to embassy status, Arthur Menzies was appointed temporary chargé d'affaires. Japan reciprocated in June, upgrading its legation in Ottawa to embassy status and naming former deputy foreign minister Iguchi Sadao to the post.

In the years to 1968, which saw the Liberal regime of Pierre E. Trudeau come to power, Canada was ruled by Louis St Laurent's Liberals (1948-57), John Diefenbaker's Progressive Conservatives (1957-63) and Lester Pearson's Liberals (1963-67). Throughout those years, no major political problems arose to trouble Japan-Canada relations, which continued to develop on a friendly basis as the leaders of each country returned the other's visits until the number of prime-ministerial level meetings reached seven.

In addition, there was the trip to Japan by Fisheries Minister James Sinclair for the purpose of concluding the Japan-Canada fishing agreement, signed in May 1952, as well as the visit to Ottawa of the Crown Prince in 1953. The Prince's visit was followed by the signing in June, 1954 by Foreign Minister Okazaki Katsuo and Canadian Ambassador Robert Mayhew of a new commercial agreement between the two countries.

Visits by ranking Japanese cabinet ministers continued throughout the 1950s and 1960s. In 1955, Agriculture Minister Kono Ichiro travelled to Canada to complete a civil aviation agreement [Agreement for Air Services]; in 1958 Foreign Minister Fujiyama Aiichiro went to Canada, as did Finance Minister Sato Fisaku the next year. In January 1960, Prime Minister Kishi Nobosuke and Foreign Minister Fujiyama visited Canada, followed in October by the new Foreign Minister Kosaka Zentaro. That same year, in July, the two countries signed an agreement on the peaceful uses of atomic energy.

Prime Minister Ikeda Hayato and Foreign Minister Kosaka again visited Canada to meet with Prime Minister John Diefenbaker in June 1961, on which occasion a joint communiqué was issued by the two prime ministers. In October of the same year, Diefenbaker returned the compliment by travelling to Japan; this visit too featured a joint communiqué. In November of the following year, Foreign Minister Miki Takeo visited Canada. This series of exchanges culminated in the first Japan-Canada joint cabinet meeting, held in Tokyo in January 1963.

The first joint communiqué between Ikeda and Diefenbaker expressed their agreement on a number of topics, such as continuing co-operation at the U.N., and began laying the groundwork for a joint cabinet meeting in recognition of the growing importance of the bilateral relationship. The communiqué also touched on trade: Japan, for its part, reconfirmed the principle of orderly imports of Canadian products and the export of competitive Japanese goods, while the Canadians on their side voiced expectations that mutual trade would continue to expand. While the joint communiqués focused principally on commercial issues, the cabinet-level meeting in Tokyo looked to continuing mutual visits by top ministers as the times required, and agreed on the exchange of information in economic fields where the interests of the two countries overlapped.

At that time, Japan's principal diplomatic goal was to win re-acceptance as a member of the international order. Canada lent various forms of indirect support to Japan's aims through encouraging her admittance to multinational organizations. For example, in October 1954 at a Colombo Plan steering committee meeting in Ottawa, it was Canada's motion that resulted in Japan being granted membership. With the backing of Canada and the U.S., Japan joined the U.N. on 18 December 1956. Canada was also active in support of Japan's efforts to gain admittance to GATT, which came in 1955, and to the OECD, in 1963.

As the Japanese economy developed and Japan gained in international stature, Japan and Canada reached the stage of exchanging opinions, on an equal footing and at frequent intervals, on the international situation in general, without being limited to their particular commercial concerns. The second joint communiqué by Ikeda and Diefenbaker, for example, revealed that the two prime ministers had discussed a wide range of international issues, ranging from the German question, including Berlin, through the situation in China, Southeast Asia and East Asia, to world economic affairs, particularly trends toward regional economic blocs following the formation of the European Community [then the Common Market].

That communiqué also demonstrated both countries' strong concern over, and deep fears of, nuclear weapons. There was mutual agreement on criticism of the Soviet Union for its renewal of nuclear weapons testing as well on the pressing need for a re-opening of international talks aimed at an absolute reduction of military forces and a petition to the U.N. to hold deliberations on the creation of an effective international monitoring system to work toward the permanent abolition of nuclear weapons tests.

JAPAN-CANADA RELATIONS ENTER NEW PHASE

Canada's attitude to Japan during the Occupation and peace-treaty period could be described as magnanimous but not especially friendly. Nevertheless, when compared to the hard-liners, such as the Soviet Union, Australia and New Zealand, Canada was not anti-Japanese. The reasons for Canada's attitude were three-fold. First, since Canada experienced little direct conflict with Japan during the course of the war, it felt no need to adopt a vengeful attitude. Second, through such figures as Norman and Pearson, Canada had considerable influence on the Far Eastern Commission. Third, Canada's diplomatic policy at the time, built around anti-Communism and the establishment of a collective security system, placed top priority on the United Nations, and policy toward Japan was subsidiary to that concern.

As the relationship between the two countries grew closer, they began to co-operate on matters outside their bilateral concerns, including such areas of international conflict as nuclear testing, arms reduction, and East-West relations. Canada's policy of goodwill toward Japan, looked at from the standpoint of the fundamental policies of both countries, is perhaps best understood as deriving from the intention of nurturing Japan into a significant member of the Western camp during the Cold War.

With the accession to power of the Trudeau administration in April 1968, however, Japan-Canada relations entered a new phase. Prime Minister Trudeau visited Japan twice in successive years: first in April 1969 for the fifth Japan-Canada cabinet ministers' meeting held in Tokyo, and again the next year for Canada Day at the Osaka International Exposition. Beginning in 1971, high-level exchanges between Japan and Canada expanded rapidly. An economic mission headed by Funada Naka, a senior legislator in the Lower House, visited Canada that year; the mission included Foreign Minister Fukuda Takeo, Finance Minister Mizuta Mikio, Ministry of International Trade and Investment (MITI) Minister Tanaka Kakuei, Agriculture Minister Akagi Munenori, and Kimura Toshio, director of the Economic Planning Agency. The Canadian group which returned the visit included Robert Stanfield, then Leader of the Progressive Conservative opposition, J.J. Greene, resources minister and head of the Atomic Energy Commission, and Otto Lang, head of the Canadian Wheat Board.

In April, 1976 a delegation of Canadian parliamentarians from both Houses, including Senate leader Bruno Lapointe and Commons leader James Jerome, paid a joint visit to Japan. Prime Minister Trudeau followed in October of the same year on his third official visit, a measure of how vibrant exchanges had become.

On the trade front, meanwhile, in the ten years from 1964-1974 Canadian exports to Japan jumped nearly sevenfold, and imports from Japan over eight-fold. In this period Japan became Canada's second-largest trading partner, passing the United Kingdom in terms of imports in 1972, and in terms of exports the following year. The structure of Japanese exports also matured along with this growth, with machinery accounting for 65% and fabricated steel products almost 20%, a dramatic change indeed compared with the trade of the 1950s and 1960s, which had been predominately in light industrial goods.

Thanks to high-level exchanges and rapidly expanding trade, Japan-Canada relations assumed a critical new importance in the 1970s. The significance accorded the relationship in the Trudeau era was signalled when the Canadian government began to rank Japan alongside the European Community as a major partner. That the Japan relationship should be put on an equal footing with Europe was indeed an occurrence of historical magnitude.

In the history of Canadian foreign relations there are generally considered to be three turning points. The first was the shift from the prewar period of dependence on the United Kingdom, when Canada was happy to serve as a linchpin between the British Empire and the U.S., to the postwar period of operating under the umbrella of collective security (NATO, NORAD) and in agreement with the U.S. The second occurred during the Trudeau administration, when the policy of pursuing independent diplomacy was born. The third shift, discussed below, would be the move toward North American market integration promoted by the Mulroney administration.

Trudeau's approach was an attempt to roll back Canada's increasing political, economic and social dependency on the United States. The new approach was first promulgated in October, 1972 in an External Affairs white paper as the 'Third Option'. Briefly put, the white paper argued that Canada faced three choices in its relations with the U.S.: (1) to continue the status quo, (2) to press for unification with the U.S., or (3) to strengthen its independence. The Trudeau administration chose the third. In the shaping of that decision, five factors, broadly speaking, were at work in the background: the easing of Cold War tensions which started a movement toward bilateralism in international affairs; a vision of foreign relations that Trudeau derived from his French Canadian ancestry; a desire to escape further Americanization as an expression of the Canadian people's feeling of nationalism; the search for a Canadian identity based on nationalism; and finally, growing interest in the Pacific region, including Japan and China.

For Japan, of course, the last was the most important factor. Canada meant to re-orient itself as a Pacific nation, as can be seen from Trudeau's speech on Canada Day at the Osaka Expo, when he emphasized that the Canadian people should learn to think of the Pacific region not as the 'Far East' but as 'our New West'. Again, the 1970 white paper on foreign relations had placed the Pacific at the top of the agenda. Although the increasing importance of the Pacific to Canada can be seen in the normalization of relations with China as well as in the positive approach taken regarding aid to developing countries in the region, the centrepiece remained relations with Japan. In other words, in taking the 'Third Option' as a way of distancing itself from the U.S., Canada really had little choice but to strengthen its links with the Pacific region, particularly Japan.

The determination by Canada to strengthen its relations with Japan produced joint communiqués on the part, first, of Prime Ministers Tanaka and Trudeau, and subsequently of Prime Ministers Miki Takao and Trudeau, outlining terms for Japan-Canada economic co-operation and creating an agreement to encourage cultural exchange between the two countries. Tanaka and Trudeau agreed, in September 1974, to further expand co-operation in a wide range of fields including politics, economics, technology and culture; to continue close talks between the two governments on matters not only of bilateral, but also of multilateral, concern; to contribute to the development of co-operative relations among the advanced countries of the West in international institutions and conferences; to maintain close consultation between prime ministers on a range of issues facing the Asia-Pacific region; and to promote the development of even freer and mutually beneficial economic and trade relations between the two countries. In addition, the two agreed to support mutual scholarship including establishing a plan requiring the investment by each side of approximately 100 million dollars to promote research on Canada in Japan and research on Japan in Canada.

The joint communiqué issued by Trudeau and Miki did not differ in substance from the earlier one with Tanaka. The one added element was an agreement to set up a Japan-Canada joint committee. Items reinforced included specific agreements on industrial co-operation covering joint ventures and other forms of business, on co-operation in developing and marketing industrial products including raw materials, processed and high-tech goods, and on means of further stabilizing production and supply of agricultural products. The Miki-Trudeau communiqué also referred to some other topics, including the independence and mutual co-operation of the Association of South East Asian Nations (ASEAN), the reform of relations between North and South Korea, and world energy issues. The commitment to scholarly and cultural exchange made at the Tanaka-Trudeau meeting was regarded as essential in order for the peoples of both countries to arrive at a degree of mutual understanding, and was confirmed in the form of an agreement in 1976.

CHANGING CANADA-JAPAN RELATIONS

It is difficult to identify exactly the specific components of Trudeau's Japan policy that mark the shift in Canada's foreign relations. In terms of particular points, a list could be compiled that would include the search for an independent policy which distanced Canada from the United States, the self-proclaimed determination to be a Pacific nation, and an awareness of the usefulness of the 'Japan card' in diplomatic policy. There was also the stress laid on the importance of political and cultural exchanges with Japan, going beyond merely economic ties, along with the renewed realization that both countries could elevate their international standing by co-operating.

Prior to World War II, the primary focus of Canada's relations with Japan lay in missionary activity, immigration, and trade. In the postwar period, trade assumed top priority. But in the second Ikeda-Diefenbaker communiqué, Canada called on Japan to expand links in a number of areas beyond the simply economic. Then, during the Trudeau administration, the scope of discussion of world issues enlarged significantly, with both countries agreeing on positive co-operation and the importance of playing an international role. In sum, Trudeau thought of Japan as not just another country to trade with, but as an important partner in Canada's definition of its identity on the stage of international society through world politics and endeavours aimed at enhancing the prosperity and welfare of people everywhere.

This radical revision of Canada's self-awareness produced in turn a 'spillover' into political, cultural and other aspects of the relationship with Japan. The 1970 White Paper on foreign relations did not venture beyond saying that Japan was important from the standpoint of trade. By the time of the Miki-Trudeau joint communiqué, however, that had been expanded to include agreement on developing a co-operative relationship in order to fulfill responsibilities shared as industrialized democracies. In the 1975 annual report issued by the Department of External Affairs, Japan was given first position in the Pacific section, with 'democracy'—a political, rather than trade, argument—advanced as the most important reason for the primacy of this relationship.

That choice of emphasis illustrates well the maturation of Canada's attitude toward foreign relations. In the postwar period Canada escaped from its timid position of maintaining relations (except for British Commonwealth ties) virtually with the United States only, and effected a confident entrance on the stage of world politics as a full-fledged player. Japan, too, recovering from having been the vanquished in the war, became a country in which Canada could place a part of its hopes for expanded international relationships. In fact, the two countries arrived at similar positions, with both being granted membership in the summit meetings of the advanced industrial countries almost simultaneously.

There was another important factor at work here: a changed perception in Canada of the purposes of relations with Japan. Canada displayed an eagerness to advance co-operation with Japan, and not just to settle problems between the two. Indeed it was on the Canadian side that the idea was born that bilateral co-operation was an essential prerequisite for both countries to make a greater contribution to international society. By contrast, Japan's perception of Canada failed to cross the borders of the pragmatic, the immediate.

In practice, both countries failed to overcome the asymmetrical nature of their mutual perception and understanding. There was, in fact, a yawning communication gap between the two in terms of their perceptions of their own roles, their expectations of each other, and their consciousness of mutual goals in the international political arena. At every stage in the process, from shaping the general outline of the relationship through cultural agreements to joint communiqués, Canada seized the initiative while Japan responded in a passive, reactive way. The feeling in Japan was, generally, that doing so resulted at the least in a step or two forward toward guaranteeing a long-term stable supply of foodstuffs and natural resources.

A variety of reasons can be found for the asymmetry in the Japan-Canada relationship. One would be the difference between the two in their development of a sense of international responsibility as nation states. There is, of course, the difference in starting point between the victors and the vanquished in war; from this standpoint Japan lagged far behind Canada. Moreover, having gone through the bitter experience of failing in its attempt to integrate Asia into a single *bloc*, Japan shifted its concerns to more limited economic goals, and perhaps revealed in the process some of the cunning of the egotistical. In addition, as Japan increasingly moved to giving first priority to the great powers, Canada's hopes for the relationship inevitably suffered some setbacks. In that sense, Trudeau's visit to Japan in 1976 left many on the Canadian side with a feeling of dashed hopes.

In economic terms, Canada certainly realized the indispensability of reaching agreement with the United States long before Japan did. As it entered the 1980s, Canada quietly dropped the 'Third Option' and, under the Progressive Conservative administration of Brian Mulroney that came to power in September 1984, moved to restructure its relations to give top priority to the U.S. Although relations with the United States under the Trudeau administration had verged on the frosty, Mulroney, faced with the impact of an economic downturn in Canada, could hardly escape such a course. Canada's foreign policy for some time to come seems likely to continue to give priority to the U.S. relationship.

Even granting that, however, it would be far from correct to say that the Mulroney administration has taken the relationship with Japan lightly. Upon taking over the Department of External Affairs in December 1984, Joe Clark's first overseas visit was to Japan. Soon after, Prime Minister Mulroney attended the Japan-Canada economic conference held in Calgary in May, 1985. In addition to requesting Japanese direct investment in Canada, the Mulroney administration has exerted itself on every available occasion to further promote Japanese-Canadian relations. However, Mulroney's interest in the bilateral relationship seems limited to economic matters, showing little inclination toward the sort of global philosophical approach to foreign relations favoured by Trudeau.

One aspect of Canada-Japan relations in the 1980s that deserves special mention is the explosive growth in direct approaches to Japan by provincial governments. In 1983, Alberta Premier Peter Lougheed visited Japan, followed in 1984 by Quebec Premier Rene Lévesque, and then in 1985 by B.C. Premier

William Bennett. On the regional level in Japan, meanwhile, a whole host of societies has sprung up to promote cultural, educational and economic exchanges, such as, to give a few examples, the Tokyo Japan Canada Society, the Canada-Japan Society of the Kansai, the Hokkaido Canada Society, the Akita Canada Friendship Society, the Hokuriku Canada Association and the Hiroshima Canada Association.

Given recent developments in Japan-Canada relations, it has now become Japan's turn to ask for 'philosophical relations' with Canada. As Professor James Eayrs, the Canadian author and scholar of international politics, has written, quoting the Canadian prime minister, the age is approaching in which humanity will no longer judge the greatness of a nation simply by measuring its military might or economic power. Rather, the strength of the government of any nation will be shown in the degree to which it succeeds in satisfying its people of the achievement of universal values. Canada has the potential to make the transition from a middle power to a prominent power. And Japan, which has become an economic superpower, should be groping for an identity through an independent foreign policy. As the only country ever to have been atomic bombed, Japan's foreign policy is firmly based on peace. The path toward self-realization for Japan, as perhaps for Canada, lies in rejecting power politics and seeking a 'Pax Diplomatica.'

○

Economic Ties

On 15 January 1988, Prime Minister Noboru Takeshita, the hand-picked successor to Yasuhiro Nakasone, travelled to Canada—the second time in only two years a Japanese Prime Minister saw fit to visit his Canadian counterpart. A new sign of closer Canada-Japan relations? A signal for a stronger diplomatic bridge across the Pacific? A new economic charter further integrating Japan into the North American economy? A deepening of our bilateral relationship? A Canadian opportunity to increase trade with Japan?

For Canadians, accustomed by geography and economics to southward pulls from the U.S., and by history, language, and population to maintaining a diplomatic presence across the Atlantic, recent events have brought home more than ever the new shape of the Pacific era. The impact of this new Pacific century is evident in new thinking about Japan in the high schools and in public opinion, even if more slowly in government bureaucracies and in boardroom management. Canada, having twice as much trade with Japan as with England, four times that with Germany, and six times that with France, has more trade with the Pacific Rim countries than with all of Europe combined. Japan is Canada's second largest trading partner, the United States its first. The economies of both Canada and Japan are undergoing drastic transformations, with implications extending far beyond domestic issues.

What are the next steps? What policies will reinforce the underlying trends to globalization and integration, and what do they mean for Canada? How can Canada capitalize on its own record of economic growth to develop new and better ties to Japan in the period leading up to the next century? It is in this context that current international developments and the long-term potential of Japan-Canada *relations must be assessed. Although circumstances change and our problems may differ, Canada's challenge is similar to Japan's need for industrial restructuring, for diversifying our trade patterns, and for making painful choices for competitive advantage. What Japan and Canada have in common, as economic summit partners and Pacific neighbors, is the necessity of shaping both our economies and our societies to meet the new world of global interdependence in the twenty-first century.*

Charles J. McMillan has taught at the University of Alberta, Laval University, the University of Bradford, and L'Ecole Superieure de Commerce, Lyons, France, and lectured in Britain, Sweden, Poland, France, Italy, the United States and Japan. From 1983-1987, he served as Senior Policy Advisor to Brian Mulroney, Canada's current Prime Minister, and was a member of the Canadian delegation at the Economic Summits in Bonn, Tokyo and Venice. Author of more than sixty articles and six books, including The Japanese Industrial System, *Dr McMillan is presently Professor of International Business at York University.*

BRIDGE ACROSS THE PACIFIC: TRADE AND INVESTMENT

Charles J. McMillan

Canadians have yet to come to grips with the New Japan—the world's new banker, source of technology, generator of new management techniques and, perhaps by the end of the century, a scientific base to rival the United States. But in the larger context, Canadians are even less aware of, much less familiar with, the neighbours of Japan and the rise of the Pacific Rim. Japanese growth rates, doubling real incomes every nine years, have been emulated across Asia based on a relatively straightforward model of development. Simplistically, the model calls for heavy support for agriculture, thereby producing abundant food and domestic savings which then are channelled into market-oriented enterprises forced to compete, in time, internationally. Mass education, on-the-job training and public literacy all reinforce Confucian values of learning and obsession with technology, from whatever source.

Asia, of course, is a diverse region—culturally, socially, politically, and economically. Yet its growth rate is unrivalled and, while the economy is heavily biased towards agriculture and small business, through low taxes, it is increasingly more integrated, partly from the pull of Japanese direct investment and technology, partly by a geography that has diluted European influence. Moreover, much of Asia has all the elements that propel economic growth—raw materials, a highly literate population, a strong university system for undergraduate education, an entrepreneurial class to commercialize technology, and large savings to plough into investment.

Much of Asia is perceived to be in the status of 'developing country'—an ubiquitous term that obscures the difference between countries with $100 per capita incomes and countries like South Korea, which is running a current account surplus approaching $10 billion annually, and has a per capita income expected to reach $6,000 by the end of this decade. Like Japan a generation ago, Asia's Four Dragons—South Korea, Hong Kong, Singapore, and Taiwan—have propelled their economies into the forefront of the industrialized world through a judicious combination of high investment rates, low wages, aggressive marketing of tariff-protected industries, and undervalued currencies. In the past decade, their share of world exports of manufactured goods has doubled, to over ten per cent in 1988.

Because their currencies have been tied to the U.S. dollar, the Four Dragons have not seen their current account surplus fall—indeed, their surplus and foreign reserves have steadily increased. (Taiwan's current account surplus reached 20% of gross national product [GNP] in 1987, five times West Germany's or Japan's; Korea's reached 8% of GNP.) The Pacific Rim countries increased their 1987 current account surplus to $100 billion—Japan alone had a surplus of $82 billion.

The sharp increase in the value of the yen has coincided with a number of related factors, all of which have long-term implications. Japan's efforts to open its university doors to foreign students—perhaps 100,000 by the end of the century—plus generous aid allotments in Asia, occurred at the same time Asian imports started to soar. Japanese manufacturing techniques, automation processes, and personnel practices have become the model for Asian managers, lessening in the process the superior image of U.S. management prowess and underscoring the rising sense of trade interdependence within East-Asian borders—an area with a potential GNP equal to Europe's by the year 2000.

Japan has begun transferring, via direct foreign investment, productive capacity into these countries, for re-import of products, components, and assemblies for Japan's own highly automated factories. Japanese companies have been at the vanguard of transferring technology into these countries (65% of Japan's overseas aid goes to Asia), thereby building up a future export base for Japanese companies and potentially serving as a training ground for expatriate Japanese in a network of overseas subsidiaries.

It is for this reason, i.e., shedding unprofitable and lower value-added productive capacity and sending it overseas via foreign investment, that Japan's adjustment to *Endaka*—the massive and rapid rise in the value of the yen—has not led to the so-called deindustrialization or hollowing out of the manufacturing base experienced by Britain in the 1970s and the United States in the 1980s. True, the Japanese economy is going through a wrenching experience. Unemployment started to climb to new levels—perhaps 3.5% in 1986 and early 1987. The major mass production industries (steel, shipbuilding, petrochemicals, automobiles, textiles, and home appliances) have all seen corporate adjustments—a real and perhaps permanent fall in exports, a new and lasting rise in imports (mainly from other Asian countries), and a dramatic decline in profits or indeed major losses, regardless of currency denomination.

Endaka has opened up a great debate about the future of the Japanese economy, its major institutions and the implications for social cohesion. The threats are obvious. Conflict between small business, less productive and modern, and big business. A breakdown in consensus between government, business, and labour. Threats to Japan's *nenko* system of permanent employment, mainly from changing demographics. Massive upheaval in Japan's traditional rural economy, financed by the industrialized world's most expensive food production support system. And *Nihon No Kazoku*—the Japanese family, the centrepiece of Japanese culture, obsessed with a fiercely competitive education system leading to lifetime careers. Adjusting to the new requirements of imported products and a multinational work system.

Serious Japanese policy-makers are immensely aware of the new challenges. As ever, there are responses of two types—the pessimists and the optimists. The pessimists fear the worst, not only very serious economic dislocations, but an end to the economic miracle, and Japan's post-1945 capacity to maintain its traditional cultural identity and yet remain part of the community of industrialized countries of the West. Japan, after all, is this century's only new superpower.

Manifestations of the pessimists' fear are not difficult to find: invasion of California-style escapist culture, from motorcycle gangs to teenage *anomie*; a new and ominous level of Japan-bashing, from the subtle and the not-so-subtle protectionist initiatives in the U.S. Congress and the threatened boardrooms of Corporate America, to the endless stream of American academics who want to thrust on Japan some of the very worst excesses of North American business sloth.

Some calls for domestic reforms are obviously overdue—reforms to agriculture and the grossly uneconomic rice mountains, property regulations and land use, removal of domestic food subsidies, improved allowances for foreigners living in Japan, and fundamental deregulation of Japanese housing. It is clear that Japan's land-use policy and agricultural reform are priority reforms for North Americans, where comparative advantage in food is clear. Moreover, without domestic land-use reform, including such initiatives as increasing taxation on land held in inventory as compared to saleable land, there will be unfair restrictions on imports of North American lumber and two-by-four house construction technology, to lower building costs and reduced construction time. (For instance, if Japan could divert only 1% of its land use from

Table 1   Comparative Import Quotas and Land Prices

	AGRICULTURAL PRODUCTS (#)	NON-AGRICULTURAL PRODUCTS (#)	TOTAL (#)	URBAN LAND PRICES*
Japan	22	5	27	1400
Canada	4	1	5	200
USA	1	6	7	100
France	19	27	46	n/a
West Germany	3	1	4	150

*$U.S. cost per square metre for ordinary residential districts: cities of Tokyo, Vancouver, San Francisco, and Frankfurt.
Source: Ministry of Foreign Affairs; Foreign Economic Statistics, Bank of Japan.

agriculture to housing and industry, it could increase its housing and industry land by 25%, but decrease farm land by only 7%.) The problem for Japanese agriculture is simple: too many very small farms on widely dispersed acreage, with aged farmers relying on agrochemicals and expensive farm machinery for increased output. As a result, Japan's farm population of 2.6 million small farms, which will decline to about 350,000 in the next century, have one of the highest rates of residual import quotas, a point which adds to trade frictions and cries of trade protectionism.

The domestic path of the Japanese economy over the next dozen years points to opportunities available for Canada, as well as for the steps Canadians must take if those opportunities are to be meaningful. Macroeconomic forces have brought change in Japan to a degree that not many Japanese could have imagined a decade ago. Their collective macroeconomic impact has already accelerated the considerable microeconomic adjustment on Japanese industry. Japanese imports have increased 20% in yen terms between 1986 and 1987 (30% when measured in dollars); Japanese manufactured imports climbed to 42% from 25% five years ago, but this is scarcely half the rate of U.S. manufactured imports.

Increased Japanese imports and industrial restructuring (abandoning sectors no longer competitive; shifting resources into growth markets and new technologies) are the two main forces providing opportunities for Canadian exporters. Trends to falling tariffs and lower import barriers have given added momentum to market liberalization. However, it would be folly to think Canadian or American companies will automatically win the battle for the Japanese domestic market. Super-aggressive Asian exporters have already captured the largest percentage increases in Japanese imports, helped by lower wages, geographic proximity, agile marketing, and undervalued currencies unofficially pegged to the dollar.

The pattern of North American and Japanese responses to recent currency alignments does not provide much optimism for any dramatic lessening of trade imbalances between these two economic blocks. Exports from North America to Japan have not increased in tandem with currency alignments, partly because companies have raised prices to increase profitability rather than market share—the very opposite strategy pursued by Japanese companies. There can be little question of the micro impact of the recent upward valuation of the U.S. dollar—a savage loss of U.S. industrial competitiveness and a dramatic shift of production to offshore markets (and potential re-export back to the U.S.). According to one study:

> This movement to offshore sourcing has developed especially rapidly with respect to Hong Kong, Taiwan, Korea and Singapore—what we designate collectively here as the NICs (newly industrializing countries). U.S. firms are sourcing sub-assemblies from low labour cost countries where usually the exchange rate has moved favourably—that is, where the dollar has remained relatively strong. As a result of U.S. firms' sourcing decisions, the trade balance with the NICs has deteriorated significantly.[1]

No example for North America illustrates the trend better than the car industry, where the weak dollar has not had any appreciable effect on enhancing either market share or profitability of Detroit's Big Three. The car industry is a particularly apt example because it is both a global industry and one subject to managed trade—i.e., a system of quotas restricting imported sales to 2.3 million units (at a potential cumulative cost to North American consumers of $17 billion since 1981). It is also an industry where computer-based technologies and automated equipment—robotics, Computer Numerical Control equipment and microelectronic hardware—have become key to integrated manufacturing. Japan presently accounts for more than two-thirds of all the industrial robots presently in use world-wide. Japan ranks first in the world in the production of numerically-controlled machine tools, and manufactures more than double the volume of U.S. equipment.

To remain competitive, North American companies have to balance two forces in tandem—exchange rate movements, and productivity-enhancing management strategies. To cope with exchange rate movements, American car makers have adopted a strategy of out-sourcing, i.e., closing domestic plants and replacing that capacity either with imports from their foreign plants, or by developing joint ventures with Japanese producers—indeed fully one-third of new Japanese capacity by 1990 was to be with 'Big Three' North American ventures. Moreover, the American manufacturers are reducing their level of vertical integration, i.e., the level of components made in-house, by switching sourcing to external suppliers (General Motors is 70% vertically integrated; Toyota and most Japanese companies are only 30% sourced from within).

But productivity-enhancing measures—adopting state-of-the-art, just-in-time parts delivery, quality control systems, and automated production systems— while significant, have not been sufficiently thorough or widespread among either North American assembly manufacturers or parts suppliers to forestall declining domestic market shares and increased Japanese market penetration. Put differently, the Japanese have managed, despite the high yen, a successful four-part strategy: (1) significant market presence through North American assembly production; (2) shift of Japanese exports subject to the voluntary quota regime away from low value-added commodity products such as small cars into higher profit margin middle-priced models and luxury cars; (3) dramatic increases in sales of Japanese auto parts and components to car manufacturers—American- and Japanese-owned; and (4) using North America as a further springboard in their globalization strategy into other export markets, including Europe and Asia.[2]

Is there a parallel between the recent impact of the high U.S. dollar (and the resulting 'deindustrialization' of smokestack America with loss of production capacity and jobs overseas) and the high value of the yen? What is the impact on Japan and what does this imply for future Canadian trade?

The basic difference is the startling gap in productivity between Japanese manufacturing and North American manufacturing. The combination of minimum productivity growth and decline in trade performance (which is linked to exchange rates) places a severe squeeze on domestic market share. Unit wage costs, the most important (but not only) indicator of productivity, grows with increases in nominal wage costs in manufacturing. Yet since 1979, unit labour costs have been lower in all Western countries relative to the U.S., except Canada. In international comparisons of unit labour costs, Japan has consistently had a better performance in productivity growth in manufacturing compared to the U.S. and Canada. High unit labour costs have contributed to the reduced competitiveness of North American manufacturing relative to foreign companies; coupled with higher exchange rates, the comparative record on productivity has helped increase imports into North America and added to corporate pressures for shifting productive capacity overseas.

For Japan, this process has actually strengthened the long-term competitive position of the industrial structure. Japan's sectors in irreversible decline—coal mining, textiles, footwear, shipbuilding, aluminum smelting, and steel production—have seen a loss of hundreds of thousands of jobs. But the jobs have shifted to new sectors—high technology manufacturing and related service areas. The productivity problem in the North American environment has meant the loss of competitiveness of the high value-added sectors which are key to future competitiveness in long-term productive capacity. As Abegglen notes, 'The U.S. problem is the loss of its manufacturing vitals—machine tools, electronic components, sophisticated metals, key components, and subsys-

Table 2   National Productivity Comparison in Automobiles

	JAPANESE-OWNED IN US	IN JAPAN	AMERICAN-OWNED IN US	IN EUROPE	EUROPE	THIRTEEN-COUNTRY AVERAGE
Worker-Hours of Labour	19.6	20.3	25.8	29.5	39.3	27.7
Defects per 100 Cars	62.1	47.3	88.9	80.9	102	77.6

Source: John Krafcik, MIT

tems. The dramatic example of hollowing out was the report that IBM's PC was imported componentry assembled in the United States.' Further, he adds:

> When the United States exploded its domestic demand through dramatic tax cuts, the factories to supply that demand were not built in the United States. Foreign suppliers filled the market need, and U.S. facilities closed or were never built as national U.S. managers sought supply from foreign sources like Japan. One result is that now, while the fall in the value of the dollar encourages U.S. purchase, U.S. suppliers do not have capacity available—one factor in the continuation of the U.S. trade deficit.[3]

The groundwork for a new stage in North American trade with Japan has now been established. The next step is to marry the Japanese opportunities with Canadian strategies. But there are limits to the potential for Canada's presence in Japan in the short term. In no fixed order, these limits can be spelled out:

1. *Corporate Presence*: Many of Canada's largest companies have offices in Tokyo, but that presence is dominated by the resource companies and the representative offices of the banks and financial houses. Only six Canadian companies are listed on the Tokyo Stock Exchange, including four Canadian banks. While more than a thousand Canadian companies do sales with Japan, Canadian exports are still highly concentrated in traditional resources, although processed food and fish and agriculture products have grown dramatically since 1985. Only 5% of Canadian exports to Japan are manufactured goods. Co-operation among industry associations is relatively weak and dominated by short-run tactical considerations.

2. *Marketing Costs*: Maintaining offices and cultivating the Japanese market is a long-term proposition, prohibitive for small companies, but equally frustrating for bigger companies. Aggressive exporting of Canadian goods by Japan's large

trade houses has helped increase sales, but at a cost of limiting direct contact between Canadians and Japanese businesses. Moreover, Canadian business still concentrate their sales efforts in Tokyo, where competition is fiercest and where chances of short-term success are most limited. The presence of Canadian industry with the greatest potential for market penetration—auto parts, pulp and paper, housing, agriculture, and fish productions—is, at best, thinly spread out. The high yen has substantially increased domestic costs for Canadians doing business in Japan.

3. *Canadians in Tokyo*: Canadian exporters' greatest marketing tool is the Canadian flag and national distinctiveness. Yet Canadian export penetration has hardly kept up to import levels of other European and Australian competitors. Few Canadians study in Japan. Fewer than 200 Canadians per year study Japanese (Australia has 15,000 students immersed in Japanese language training). Canada's diplomatic corps in Tokyo is scarcely a third of the size of the staff in London, Paris, or Rome—capitals which have far less economic and commercial potential for Canada and where science and technology trail developments in the U.S. and Japan by a wide margin.

4. *Ministerial Activity*: Although Japan has had a higher profile in federal government priority-setting in the past few years, this has not translated into a significant re-allocation of bureaucratic effort and Ministerial travel to Japan. Official visits to Japan number only three or four per year, compared to a minimum of two to three dozen Ministerial trips to Europe (where, admittedly, more international organizations are located). Ministerial missions raise the Canadian profile in Japan, add strength to private sector activity, and elevate awareness and Canadian presence within the Japanese bureaucracy and within a new centre of strength in Japan: the policy committees of the governing Liberal-Democratic Party.

At the corporate level, the most important long-term effect of the high value of the yen has been overseas investment and the globalization of Japanese industry. Japanese management, ever poised to long-term growth, recognizes the need to match underlying economic strengths with organizational skills and 'invisible assets'—such as company reputation, customer linkages, brand names, and technologies. The Japanese have advanced their overseas presence in North America as well as in Europe, turning huge segments of domestic manufacturing to foreign subsidiaries and raising Japanese market share directly from new state-of-the-art factories.

These changes mean that the three pillars of Japanese industry are fully positioned in North America: Japanese trading firms, Japanese multinationals in manufacturing, and Japanese financial houses. Each pillar brings in tow a smaller but growing and sophisticated cadre of Japanese professionals (consultants, designers, accountants, lawyers, and engineers), as well as larger groups of small business, component makers, and specialty firms. Together they bring the service supply establishments, ranging from hotels and real estate companies to the construction firms and travel and tourist operators. It adds to a massive Japanese penetration and understanding of the North American market.

Each of these pillars offers unique opportunities for Canadians. Nor have Canadians been slow to develop commercial links to this Japanese inflow. It is in the Japanese market where the Canadian presence is weak. Except in notable areas such as food, fish, and telecommunications, Canadian penetration has not been significant, especially compared to proximate competitors such as Australia and the U.S. Severe bilateral problems exist in several areas—auto parts, coal, and forest products, to cite three notable examples. The larger questions remain: how does Canada organize its trade activities to meet the new Pacific challenge, and does the will exist to make the necessary changes?

THE BILATERAL RELATIONSHIP: CANADA-JAPAN

The steady, if not dramatic, increase in bilateral trade between Canada and Japan has occurred in tandem with a growing number of direct contacts between Japanese groups, industry associations, academic centres, and financial institutions, and their Canadian counterparts. Still, the Japanese presence in Canada manifestly outweighs the Canadian presence in Japan in terms of both people and industrial activity. Unfortunately, the true state of our bilateral relationship, not just in trade terms but the longer term investment of people, is heavily in favour of Japan, to the detriment of Canada. The vast preponderance of Canada-related activity in Japan occurs in Tokyo. Estimates vary, but about 30,000 Japanese nationals now work in Canada. Canadians still view Japan as yet another trade partner and not as the industrial power in Asia and *the* window to the Pacific Rim.

The bilateral relationship has taken a new priority in each country at the government level, partly as a result of back-to-back state visits, first by Prime Minister Nakasone to Toronto, Ottawa, and Vancouver in January 1986, then by Prime Minister Mulroney's official visit after the Tokyo Economic Summit in May 1986 and Prime Minister Takeshita's visit in January 1988.

The Japanese government, for its part, has reorganized the North America desk at the Japanese Foreign Ministry, and in November 1986 the Canadian government announced a Cabinet-approved *Canadian Strategy Towards Japan*. It was one of a series of country strategy documents initiated to bring some focus to specific objectives—e.g., trade, investment, technology, services, small

146

Table 3   Largest Japanese Companies in Canada

NAME	SALES ($000)	INCOME ($000)	ASSETS ($000)	EMPLOYEES	RANK 1987	1986
1. Mitsui Canada	2,608,542	3,796	290,764	135	32	37
2. Mitsubishi Canada	1,368,000	2,176	110,313	n/a	23	39
3. Toyota Canada	1,046,000	8,000	188,000	314	88	112
4. Marubeni Canada	1,010,000	500	37,000	76	94	115
5. Honda Canada	994,706	1,042	560,902	n/a	95	102
6. C. Itoh & Company	769,194	1,534	31,227	70	118	140
7. Nissan Automobile	586,170	9,599	124,494	275	146	185
8. Mazda Canada	415,470	n/a	82,005	115	188	229
9. Westar Mining	370,700	21,700	523,286	1,714	215	174
10. Matsushita	343,286	n/a	108,561	416	231	343
11. Sony of Canada	333,511	942	131,952	911	235	286
12. Kanematsu-Gosho	169,140	355	15,611	35	368	424
13. Crestbrook Forest Ind.	161,669	5,613	138,797	1,298	374	447
14. Yamaha Motor Canada	157,239	5,711	61,688	170	382	449
15. Hitachi Canada	150,000	n/a	n/a	335	392	381

Source: Canadian Business

business, and sectorial relations, such as agriculture, fisheries, forestry, mining, and tourism.

Since 1976, Canada and Japan have held a series of bilateral meetings under the auspices of the Joint Economic Committee, which consists of senior bureaucrats from each country, at approximately 18-month intervals. These talks usually cover (1) thematic bilateral issues such as trade and investment, industrial co-operation and technology transfers, and financial and commercial ties; (2) sectorial issues in the primary, manufacturing, and service fields; and (3) multilateral issues dealing with international economic agenda items such as the GATT, exchange rates and monetary policy, and economic adjustment.[4]

This priority at the government level made a dramatic advance at the corporate level by the publication of the *Kanao Report*, named after Kanao Mimonu, former Chairman of Nippon Kokan, Japan's largest steelmaker, and Chairman of the Canada-Japan Economic Committee of Keidenren. The Kanao economic mission visited Canada 1-10 October 1986. Its report on Canada's big policy changes was in marked contrast to the *Mikita Report* released a decade earlier, which painted a devastating picture of the Canadian economy, characterized by a strike-ridden corporate sector and a fractious system of federal-provincial relations.

The 1986 Kanao Report rightly brought attention to the strong technological potential of Canada, both in the universities and among certain elements of the private sector—particularly small business. Ironically, it took a foreign group—in this case a Japanese industry mission—to highlight this feature of the Canadian economy. Japanese companies are aggressively seeking technology abroad and Canadian technology transfer to Japan is a new symptom of this trend.

Canada is going through a scientific and technological awakening, accepting that the technological and trade status quo is not a viable, long-term alternative. The country is finally shedding its historic approach of relying on research in government and universities as surrogates for private sector research and commercial innovation—a principal factor in Canada's slow rate of technology diffusion and innovation. But the evidence is growing that new attitudes will lead to new structures and methods of organization particularly for technology diffusion and for advancing new technology.[5] There are several features to this dramatic change.

For one thing, the current generation of Canadian industrialists—better educated, more international in outlook—is placing substantially greater emphasis on the technological components of their business, both for value-added and competitive strengths. New forms of technology consortia are developing, from those to maximize technology development in pre-competitive commercialization, to financial syndicates to assist small companies short on capital and weak in management. For the first time, the key national business organizations—the Canadian Manufacturers' Association, the Business Council for National Issues, the Canadian Federation of Independent Business, and, if timidly, the Canadian Bankers' Association—have all highlighted the need for new measures and policies in the private sector and in government. Moreover, the major science and technology industry associations have also started to build consensus among business, labour, government, and academe. However, Canada still has the lowest level of scientists and engineers working in the labour force, a characteristic equally true for the educational background of senior Canadian management, public servants, and politicians.

Second, in the past few years, there has been a new liaison—for fund raising, for research and development (R&D), and for scientific co-operation—between the Canadian university community and the private sector, often in ways that parallel the experience of the U.S. and Japan. The Mulroney government's introduction of a matching-fund formula in the 1985 budget has fostered a new interaction between business and the universities, although the majority of the money raised has been in Ontario, and most of it for science and engineering.

Table 4 Technology Transfers from Canada to Japan (1986)

CANADIAN COMPANY	JAPANESE COMPANY	TECHNOLOGY
1. CWE Hydroponics Inc. Highmark & Resources Ltd.	Japanese Tobacco Sangyo Co. Ltd. (Tokyo)	hydroponic technology
2. Interactive Entertainment Inc., Toronto	Seibu Department Store Co. Ltd.	space amusement system
3. Canpopco	Kato Zoen Landscaping Co. Ltd.	popcorn preparation
4. Roger Rouget Inc.	Dreambed Ltd.	furniture
5. Precision Manufacturing Inc., Lachine, P.Q.	Tokyo Steel Kogyo Corp. Ltd.	partition walls
6. Phillips Cables Ltd. Scarborough	Sumitomo Electric Industries Ltd. (Osaka)	power transmission line technology
7. Atomic Energy of Canada Ltd., Ottawa	Dengen Kaihatsu Ltd.	technological appraisal of Candu system
8. Canadian General Electric Co. Ltd., Toronto	Hitachi Zosen Co. Ltd.	paper making machine
9. Stelco Inc., Hamilton	Kawasaki Steel Corp.	steel reeling
10. Canadian Engine Holdings	Nichimen Co. Ltd. (Tokyo)	fluidized-bed furnace and porcelain enamelled furnace
11. H.J. Langen & Sons Ltd., Mississauga	Dai Nihon Printing Co. Ltd. (Tokyo)	packaging machine
12. Corrosion Services Co. Ltd., Downsview	Daiki Rubber Industries Co. Ltd. (Tokyo)	electric rustproofing equipment
13. 605477 Ontario Inc.	Aski Co. Ltd.	videotext system
14. Logidisk Inc.	Rand Computer Co. Ltd.	educational software
15. Mitsui and Co. Ltd.	Mitsui and Co. Ltd.	videotext software
16. University of Waterloo	Japan IBM	software, computer operating system
17. Watcom Products Inc.	Nichimen Corp. (Osaka)	software
18. University of Waterloo	Japan IBM	prolog interpreter program

Source: Annual Report on the Introduction of Foreign Technology, Science and Technology Agency, FY 1986, Japan.

Third, both the federal and provincial governments are gradually becoming aware of the critical importance of Canada's R&D efforts, not only for international competitiveness but also for manpower and labour policy. This point is illustrated in that all ten provinces and the federal government negotiated the first-ever national science and technology strategy in 1986. Several provinces have started new science and technology initiatives on their own, often to parallel federal efforts to overcome decades of neglect. Canada's ranking and technology competitiveness is still among the lowest of the Western industrialized countries.

Fourth, and most importantly, the Prime Minister has put science and technology front and centre on the national agenda, starting with the 1986 October Throne Speech and the establishment of a new National Advisory Board on Science and Technology. This board, modelled on Japan's Council for Science and Technology, includes a group of outstanding Canadians drawn from industry, finance, labour, the professions, the universities, and the research community. It is undertaking the most thorough review of federal science objectives in Canada's history, examining all aspects of federal spending priorities, and working in tandem with a number of major technology-related initiatives within the federal government. Their initiatives include the National Forum on Higher Education in October 1987, the January 1988 National Conference on Technology and Industrial Innovation, and a basic assessment of Canada's strategic technologies: advanced industrial material, information technologies, and biotechnologies, with implications for their use in Canadian manufacturing and service sectors.

Together with the new Canadian Space Agency, reforms under way in the National Research Council, and major reforms in the delivery of regional development programs, there is an action-oriented renewal to Canada's industry/technology linkages. The National Advisory Board forcefully illustrates the new priority on science and technology, as recognized in the Kanao Report. The pressing challenge is to have these new mechanisms help Canadian industry develop the kind of broad national consensus on long-term technology objectives—the vital key to Japan's success in government-funded R&D programs.

The difficulty is that the available comparative indicators reveal a very weak performance in science and technology, including the number of domestic patents granted to residents per 100,000 population, and the number of Canadian patents filed within Canada. On such a basic indicator as the number of scientists and engineers per 1,000 people in the labour force, Canada has one of the lowest rates, less than half of the U.S. and a third that of Japan. More telling, Canada's weak R&D performance directly relates to Canada's future trade patterns. Canada experiences a negative trade balance in R&D intensive industries; of the leading industrialized countries, Canada's position is least favourable against any two major trade partners.

But the question remains, is Canada doing enough and doing it fast enough? Increasingly, Canada is becoming locked into a three-way trade partnership signalling integration in two-way investment flows across the Pacific. Our two-way trade with the U.S. has increased from $46 billion a decade ago to $170.5 billion in 1986, while our two-way trade with Japan has gone from $3.6 billion to $13.5 billion in the same period. The U.S. has shown an equally dramatic growth with Japan, going from $23.3 billion a decade ago to $108.8 billion.

What those figures fail to show, and what makes trade figures increasingly meaningless by themselves, is that, according to some studies, the largest portion of the Japanese trade surplus comes not from Japanese firms selling abroad, but from foreign-owned affiliates exporting from Japan. It has been estimated that in 1983-84 up to 95% of Japan's bilateral trade surplus with the U.S. came from American subsidiaries operating in Japan.

What does this mean for Canada? What is the impact on Canadian industry, and the potential of our bilateral relationship, in the larger context of the U.S.-Canada-Japan trilateralism? There is no question that Japan has taken a fresh look at Canada—the economy, the political institutions and the investment climate, and the technological potential.

The Japanese, whose R&D statistics and internal performance assessments are second only to the U.S., know of Canada's anemic position in the technology trade balance, an opportunity they see for inward investment. Indeed, the Organization for Economic Co-operation and Development (OECD) calculates that when industries are grouped by high, medium, and low R&D intensity, Canada shows a deficit in both medium and high intensity industry from 1970-1984. Moreover, of Canada's sectors that are science intensive, none are traditional resource industries—an area of supposed Canadian comparative advantage. Yet Canada's R&D strengths are widely recognized, even to the degree where Canadian companies export technology to Japan.

The Japanese have not only taken stock of Canada's national economic policy agenda—downsizing of government, privatization of crown corporations, improving the incentives and the work climate for small business, deregulation of investment, energy, transportation and financial services, new initiatives in intellectual property, trade emphasis with the Pacific Rim. They have taken a fresh look at the Japanese potential in a North American environment of free trade with the U.S., particularly when they have a large production presence strategically positioned throughout North America, including in Mexico.

The Japanese know the importance of an investment presence in the U.S.; they also know the many superior advantages of a Canadian production location with export potential into the U.S., because of such factors as cheaper land prices, lower crime rates, a better educated labour force, and a harmonious

Table 5 Japan's North American Automotive Assembly Production

ASSEMBLER	LOCATION	SCALE	ORIGINAL INVESTMENT	STARTING YEAR
Honda	Ohio	360,000	660,000,000	1982
Nissan (NMMC)	Tennessee	240,000	745,000,000	1983
Toyota (NUMMI)	California	250,000	450,000,000	1984
Mazda	Michigan	340,000	450,000,000	1987
Honda	Ontario	200,000	300,000,000	1987
Toyota	Kentucky	250,000	800,000,000	1988
Toyota	Ontario	50,000	400,000,000	1988
Mitsubishi	Michigan	240,000	500,000,000	1988
Fuji/Isuzu	Illinois	240,000	500,000,000	1989
Suzuki	Ontario	200,000	615,000,000	1989

Source: Nihon Keizai Shimbun, Long Term Credit Bank of Japan, and the Japanese Automotive Manufacturers Association.

multicultural living environment. But it must be recognized that the Japanese emphasis is on fundamentals, namely, the relative cost position of respective investment locations, and the potential for exports as well as production for the local market.

The Canadian assets of Japan's foreign equity investors still amount to only 2% of the total, a figure that will increase marginally in percentage terms, but dramatically in dollar amounts. Indeed, Japanese investors now hold a portfolio of about $36 billion Canadian.[6] The Japanese auto sector will continue to lead investment flows (with perhaps one new major assembly plant in addition to two, possibly three, very large-scale component producers and a dozen medium-size parts suppliers). Japanese producers, armed with joint venture agreements, new state-of-the-art assembly plants, consumer recognition of Japanese quality standards and price competitive models, stand poised to capture up to 40% of the North American automobile market by the start of the 1990s, regardless of government quotas or current trade frictions.

In financial services, financial deregulation measures announced by the federal government in December 1987 allowed further penetration of Japanese securities houses. Japanese Schedule 'B' Banks still have credit ceilings on their corporate lending, although each has grown within the framework of their overseas multi-national presence in New York and London. Long-term investment in energy—particularly gas, petrochemicals, and power equipment for utilities—is only a matter of time, particularly if a new American administration permits exports of Alaskan energy to Japan and further weakens OPEC.

Japanese housing, construction firms, and real estate firms will all develop a

Table 6   Largest Japanese Banks in Canada

	($000)		
	TOTAL ASSETS (1)	INCOME (2)	(2)/(1)
Bank of Tokyo	735,410	2,017	0.29
Dai Ichi Kango Bank	576,333	1,326	0.26
Fuji Bank	482,993	2,459	0.53
Industrial Bank of Japan	495,707	1,131	0.25
Mitsubishi Bank	551,078	1,531	0.32
Mitsui Bank	438,244	1,142	0.29
Sanwa Bank	560,476	1,414	0.31

Source: Annual Reports of these banks.

major Canadian presence, possibly through office developments, engineering infrastructure projects, and hotels. Already Japanese construction firms are active in Ontario-based auto assembly plants. It goes without saying that the wave of more than 300,000 Japanese tourists visiting the Rockies, Montreal, Toronto, and P.E.I. in 1987 was only the start of a dramatic new era of overseas Japanese hotel and tourist development, catering to quality service and mass markets. The Japanese trading firms and their related enterprises have started investing in small and medium-sized Canadian enterprises, particularly those with a technology or marketing edge, especially in areas like aquaculture, pharmaceuticals, lasers, biotechnology, and specialty metals. In these sectors, the Japanese hope to expand their know-how as well as their management skills and, in sectors such as food production, auto parts, electronics, and merchandising, Japan hopes to transfer its skills in automated processes and small lot production technology to the North American marketplace.[7]

In short, the Japanese presence in Canada will be ubiquitous, long-term, and growth-oriented. Obviously, the largest firms will lead the way—the large Japanese trading houses—Mitsui, Mitsubishi, Marubeni, C. Itoh; the major manufacturers, led by auto firms, consumer electronics, and increasingly computers and advanced telecommunications, and the financial houses. Ventures in all areas of resources, commodities, and foodstuffs are evident, potentially where Japanese strengths in marketing and finance combine with Canadian strengths in production, technology, and logistics. Yet without doubt, certain sectors will stand out. The Japanese presence in Canadian energy remains weak and under-developed. Food production and agribusiness remain a natural for Japanese companies, with their R&D strengths and agribusiness interests that have similar applications in all facets of aquaculture and marine biology.

What will dominate the bilateral investment agenda is the automotive industry. It is the largest employer in central Canada and the product area where the larger questions of globalization, yen-dollar exchange issues, and underlying competitiveness come into sharp focus. In stark terms, given the hugely protectionist measures aimed at Japanese auto manufacturers since 1981, can Canadian or American governments, regardless of political stripe, devise measures to increase domestic competitiveness without recourse to imposing obscene protectionist costs on North American consumers? More tellingly, is the auto sector an early-warning case study for future globalization trends in other sectors, from semiconductors to biotechnology and computers to telecommunications?

The Japanese have clearly won the preliminary skirmishes. Auto import quotas in the U.S. and Canada markets actually helped Japanese producers. Quota limits on leading companies like Toyota, Honda, and Nissan, far from restricting competition from GM, Ford, and Chrysler, simply aided North American cash flow and put off market share competition from other Japanese producers. Quotas gave a false sense of market security to North American producers, especially parts makers, with Detroit specifications becoming out of step with international trends in quality, design, and parts delivery.[8]

The predictable consequence of this imbalance—first, on the part of North American producers to fail to stay on top of global trends, in this case, production and parts assembly innovations introduced by the Japanese, and second, on the part of the Japanese, to view import quotas for what they were, a political expedient to sidestep short-term fundamental dynamic forces of shifting comparative advantage—has provided a glaring example of the costly implications of avoiding a global perspective in international markets. In isolation, these responses might not have been significant. In combination, they have introduced a predictable production presence in North America— for Japanese vehicle production, for Japanese-based auto parts suppliers ($10 billion by 1990, up from $3.5 billion in 1986), and massive inroads of Japanese parts suppliers into the North American after-market of the car industry.

In summary, the Canadian potential in the larger framework of the Japan-U.S.-Canada trade triangle requires a new focus. Macroeconomic issues have changed the balance for the next decade. Canadian strengths in raw materials, upgraded resources, and agriculture have never been better, but the competition from countries like France, Australia, New Zealand, and the U.S. will be fierce. Manufactured goods offer Canadian producers unparalleled market access if quality and service needs can be met.

But the 1980s have brought home the reality of Canada's feeble growth in the Japanese market. The bilateral relationship has become asymmetrical—the Japanese penetration of the Canadian economy is robust and dynamic, the Canadian presence in Japan is piecemeal and static. Does the U.S.-Canada bilateral trade initiative provide the catalyst to change these dynamics by the end of the century?

BUILDING TRILATERALISM: THREE-WAY FREE TRADE?

The historical obsession of Japan's post-war leadership has been economic isolationism from the North American and European markets. Japan survives with almost no raw materials: imports account for virtually all energy and commodities, and about forty per cent of its food. Japan has learned to use this peculiar feature of its post-war development as a 'throughput' economy to astonishing heights of success. It has built a trading infrastructure to permit Japan's trading firms—the nine large Sogo Shosha plus the thousands of smaller specialty firms—to scour the global marketplace for competitive imports to supply Japan's voracious manufacturing sector. Aside from the benefits of building a global infrastructure of market intelligence, this approach has actually added to Japan's competitiveness by forcing companies to adjust constantly to international conditions.[9]

With imports so critical, Japan has bought supplies on the open market—which means at competitive prices—rather than relying on cushioned supplies of domestic producers, as most Western countries have done. In other words, most of Japan's manufacturing competitors have bought imports from their own government-supported sectors where prices in such areas as energy, minerals, food, and even intermediate goods like petrochemicals and steel were higher than world prices. The best example, of course, has been energy, where most Western countries, in the name of energy security of supply, promptly turned the post-1973 OPEC crisis into a situation of high-priced domestic energy supply through exploration subsidies, cartel-like price fixing, and tax write-offs. Japan alone bought at world prices.

Japan's industries have adopted two other approaches to retain international competitive strengths. First, most heavy industry activity has been located near deep-water ports, to facilitate global marketing supported by a transportation infrastructure of water transport. Related to this has been radically new inland logistical networks, tying supplier companies to just-in-time delivery to the captive factories. Japan has made its manufacturing sector the centrepiece of its industrial policy—a vital strength now raising questions about the impact of de-industrialization in North America.[10]

Second, Japan policy-makers have made a practice of applying state-of-the-art manufacturing techniques, including factory automation, to big firms and small firms alike. Flexible manufacturing systems (FMS) is the term often used to describe the transformation of traditional assembly lines, using electronics to substitute for mechanical functions, and robotics and intelligent machines to take over many human functions. Indeed, this shift is so widespread now in

Japan that they have invented the word *mechatronics* to describe the link between 'mechanical' and 'electronic' processes. The U.S., Japan, and West Germany all have major research and manufacturing facilities devoted to large, custom-built, flexible manufacturing systems.

Only a minority of Canadian companies have introduced these kinds of management systems into their manufacturing plants. (It is estimated that Japan, with half the population of the U.S., has 50% more flexible manufacturing systems, and 40% more than the U.K., Germany, France, and Italy combined.) Toyota, Nissan, and Honda and the other major automobile manufacturers have introduced these techniques together with the Kanban inventory system of delivering parts 'just in time', such that the same production line can produce not only numerous variations on similar car models but also different models on the same shift. Robotics, the latest embodiment of integrated hardware/software systems, permits the production of an almost infinite range of extras and special features such that mass assembly production can produce truly unique final outputs.

Indeed, for small firms the impact of robotics is no less revolutionary, which is why the Japanese government encourages automation by publicly-supported equipment leasing companies. Small companies will have the opportunity of entering many new market niches normally reserved for larger firms because, within certain volume ranges, automation equalizes costs for big firms and small firms alike. Small firms will no longer be faced with the cost disadvantage of competing against big firms' superior work skills and staff support, yet they can still cope with the small-lot production, cost flexibility, and short production cycles. It is for this reason that while big firms like Olivetti, General Motors, Boeing, Toyota, and Nissan have been in the vanguard of the new production technology, their small business subcontractors, suppliers, and spin-off companies have become key to assuring components with perfect quality, assured delivery times, and long-term pricing arrangements.

But Japan knows that without changes to the trading framework with which it has succeeded in the past three decades, there are limits to its future export success. Increasingly, Japan's exports operate under 'managed trade' and administrative guidance across a wide-range of product sectors.

MANAGED TRADE

The post-war trends reviewed in this study have been predicated on a post-war environment of economic growth, international trade expansion, and U.S.-inspired trade liberalization. The economic environment of the 1990s, based on recent events in the 1980s, threatens to change this course. Countries have erected trade barriers, mainly through overt protectionism, subsidies, and non-tariff mechanisms. Governments, often in the name of industrial policy, have systematically challenged market forces and distorted comparative advantage. Mercantile pressures have increased. Companies and industries have conspired with political forces to manage trade through restrictive measures designed to assist producers to overcome short-term problems. Usually consumers have paid the adjustment burdens through subsidies. Moreover, as the range of tradeable products has grown a whole series of complicating factors has entered into the global trade equation: non-tariff barriers (e.g., customs-clearance measures, safety and health standards), intellectual property (R&D, copyright, patent protection, counterfeit goods), subsidies, international investment, and rules for dispute settlement.[11]

The centrepiece of international trade policy for Canada has been the GATT—the General Agreement on Tariffs and Trade. Started in 1947, the GATT has succeeded to produce on a multilateral basis tariff reductions—through seven rounds of talks—mainly on manufactured goods. Canada, of course, has been a party to these negotiations and has implemented a series of tariff reductions, leading to further product and industry rationalization of the domestic economy, despite the persistence of short product runs and less than optimal economies of scale in most sectors of manufacturing.

In the 1980s, the international trade environment changed dramatically. First, macroeconomic issues—the U.S. government deficit, trade imbalances, low U.S. savings rates and decline in the value of the U.S. dollar—placed enormous political pressure on U.S. politicians for short-term relief for what are essentially longer term problems. The political problem is virulent protectionism in threatened sectors. Second, the post-war trade liberalization measures were essentially limited to merchandise trade, meaning that agriculture and services, two areas of fastest growth, were outside the GATT framework. (It is doubly ironical that while the U.S. led the post-war fight for trade liberalization in manufacturing, the U.S. itself weakened the rules on agricultural trade; the consequence was that Europe, Japan, and, to a lesser extent, Canada, introduced U.S.-style agriculture subsidies first brought on by Congress in the 1950s.)

Thirdly, the post-war economic environment has changed in tandem with the political environment, not only in the rise of the twelve-member European Community, up from the original six in 1958. The same trends have led to a series of economic trading blocks that encompass not just inter-regional trade but as well the policy cross-current of military, political, cultural (i.e., language) and aid factors. The Japanese have pushed this approach in Asia, by promoting a Pacific Rim free trade area and by supporting regional trade blocks like ASEAN.

Trade, in other words, has become truly global despite political boundaries. But the management of trade has been primarily national or regional in scope, with weakened policy co-ordination and dispute settlement mechanisms at the centre. Rules, procedures, and discipline are the underpinnings of liberalized trade. The rise of the European Community and its successive expansions have prompted flagrant violations of the principle of non-discrimination, especially in agriculture and textiles. The U.S. reaction has been to respond in kind, and with bilateral deals. From the U.S.-Japan deal on semiconductors to special measures for Third World textiles, the result is steady and constant compromise of GATT principles.

Severe monetary pressures—structural inflation, exchange rate instability, and huge capital flows—starting in the 1970s but continuing into the recession years of the early 1980s also weakened the resolve of the United States to continue its traditional leadership role in multilateral trade liberalization. While the specific factors are exceedingly complex, and need not be reviewed here, the weakening of GATT discipline and widespread violation of GATT rules has threatened a veritable breakdown in international trade principles, even as world trade volume exceeds $2 trillion annually.

U.S.-CANADA TRADE

For Canada, these developments in the 1980s were particularly ominous. Canada's own competitiveness had seriously deteriorated; unemployment was at historic highs; government deficits and national debt were virtually out of control. Trade blocks, managed trade, and the retreat from multilateral institutions by the U.S. shifted the international economy away from underlying comparative advantage to political power, managed trade, and lessening of international market forces.[12]

In late 1986, as the Canadian government decided to enter into trade talks for a comprehensive free-trade agreement with the United States, the succession of political problems flowing from 'managed trade' began to emerge with force. Japanese-American bilateral disputes added to the tension, especially in such sectors as steel, agriculture, semiconductors, and automobiles. Particular U.S.-Canada bilateral areas of dispute such as carbon steel and softwood lumber added to the stress of the 'managed trade' approach, especially in light of the application of U.S. trade remedy laws, which have the perverse effect of defining unilaterally what constitutes unfair trading practices.

It was in this politically charged climate that Canada and the U.S. negotiated the free-trade agreement between the two countries. The two countries share a huge trade relationship, worth almost $200 billion in 1988. The essence of the deal has been amply reviewed elsewhere, but it suffices to highlight certain features: reduction of tariffs over a ten-year period; free trade over time in energy, certain agricultural products, and services; liberalized investment and government procurement; and new mechanisms for dispute settlement, especially a binational review panel for appeals.

From a Japanese perspective, the U.S.-Canada trade agreement offers a number of signals, some ominous for U.S. perspectives on world trade policy:

1. Is the trade agreement the latest, but most concrete, evidence of American retreat into a Fortress North American policy, reinforced with bilateral agreements with Mexico and Canada? (These agreements followed earlier trade arrangements by the U.S., namely, a bilateral deal with Israel in 1985 and the Caribbean Basin economic initiative.)

2. Is the trade agreement a clear policy alternative to the traditional multilateral approach of trade liberalization, wherein the U.S. negotiates a series of bilateral agreements with like-minded countries? In fact, Treasury Secretary James Baker spelled out this approach quite boldly: 'If possible, we hope . . . liberalization will occur in the Uruguay round. If not, we might be willing to explore a "market liberalization" approach, through minilateral arrangements or a series of bilateral agreements. . . . Other nations are forced to recognize that the United States will devise ways to expand trade—with or without them.'[13]

3. Does the U.S.-Canada free-trade deal launch a new approach, initiating a broader policy framework between the United States and Japan, not only on trade matters, but on the broader agenda of military, political, and technological issues between the world's two largest economies?

There is no question that the U.S.-Canada free trade agreement poses difficult questions for Japan. Indeed, since Prime Minister Nakasone Yasuhiro's January 1986 visits to Washington and Ottawa, the Japanese have made it clear they object to a specific 'Fortress North America' policy framework, where discriminatory measures would be taken against third countries, especially Japan. Yet the Japanese know the underlying bilateral issues facing Canada and the U.S., including the fact that so much of this two-way trade represents trade flows across subsidiaries of companies located on both sides of the border, i.e., within the framework of multi-national subsidiaries. They also recognize that the U.S.-Canada trade accord complements other bilateral agreements, such as the Autopact, NORAD, and the Defence Sharing Agreement.

At present, GATT does not deal with a whole series of fundamental issues in international trade—agriculture, services, intellectual property—and several other areas: subsidies, dispute settlement, and contingent protectionist measures. The U.S.-Canada agreement could serve as a model for multilateral negotiations at the GATT. But will progress at the GATT be sufficiently real to forestall U.S. protectionism? The Europeans, after all, have their own agenda to develop a real, common internal market, perhaps with a common currency and central bank, by 1992.

The Japanese understand, more than most, the American view and attitudes that will be key to the new GATT round. They know that despite public statements in Washington, American trade opinion—in the Congress, in the private sector, and in state legislatures—is at best lukewarm to the hope of any immediate success at the GATT talks. Moreover, the Japanese are privately pessimistic about Europe's industrial potential when compared to North America's. The only alternative for the Japanese is to accept the inevitable, however unpleasant, U.S.-Japan trade negotiations modelled on the U.S.-Canada agreement. The result would be a Japan-North American free trade area,[14] with room to involve other Pacific Rim countries. Japan, after all, proposed this approach in the early 1970s.

The starting points are obviously different. Canada, like most European countries, is relatively trade-dependent, up to 30% of GNP. Canada, alone among the G-7 countries, is heavily dependent on unprocessed raw materials and a limited range of services. With the exception of the automotive sector, Canada has a relatively weak manufacturing base. Moreover, Canada's domestic economy, with high foreign ownership, fragmented provincial economies, strong internal trade barriers, and a small-scale industrial base outside the Toronto-Montreal axis, faces massive adjustment problems in the 1990s. Canada's micro problems are a cumulation of neglect in the past two decades.

Japan has a different set of problems, mostly flowing from strengths. Its export emphasis is mainly a function of its import dependence on raw materials rather than for domestic growth. Its technological infrastructure is second only to the U.S., except that large companies and central government are the leading players, rather than small business, the universities and entrepreneurs, as in the U.S. Japanese entrepreneurship and individual creativity are as yet no match for the U.S. Japan's increasing integration with the U.S. is usually understated, but not to be ignored is the growing integration between Japan and the countries of East Asia, despite the usual caveats of history, culture, and the legacy of Japanese imperialism.

Despite rivalries in manufactured goods, technology and, increasingly, services, especially banking, Japanese and American trade is fundamentally complementary. The respective comparative advantage of each country's economy is far greater than say the U.S. and West Germany, or Japan and Britain. Even in such contentious areas as electronics and autos, national rivalry gives way to mutual advantage when so many large corporations like IBM, Texas Instruments, Honda, Matsushita, and NEC have investments in each market.

Moreover, relatively little analysis has been done on the potential trade diversion between Japan and the U.S. from and to Canada as a result of trade and investment conflicts arising between industry interests in Washington and Tokyo. Very little of Canada's trade with Japan is immune to potential trade diversion by American sources, especially in such contentious sectors as softwood lumber, coal, fish, aluminum, and steel. Japanese trading houses, which dominate Canadian imports to Japan, have a vested interest in preventing such trade diversion, but the potential nonetheless remains, especially without a trade agreement ratified by Congress and Parliament. Further, Japanese out-sourcing to other Asian countries will accelerate the shift of the trade deficit away from Japan *per se*; increasing imports from Asian countries to North America will add to the complexity of managing and anticipating trans-Pacific trade conflict.

The U.S.-Canada trade deal meets three tests. First, it helps Japan if this bilateral deal advances negotiations at the GATT. In fact, the U.S.-Canada agreements break new ground on tariff barriers, investment, agriculture, and services. Second, this bilateral initiative can be trade-creating, rather than trade-destructive, because it advances trade rationalization. Domestic subsidiaries on both sides of the border, rather than closing, as apocalyptic views have argued, will be led to product specialization and new market niches. Third, because exchange rates will be the primary factor determining investment flows, rather than trade barriers, further Japanese and North American integration will increase trade as each country adjusts its industrial structure based on real comparative advantage.

The potential for a triangular Canada-Japan-U.S. free trade agreement, while remote, is not without mutual gains. After all, Canada and the U.S. started trade talks in 1982 only to see them fail. They restarted in 1985 and led to an agreement in 1987. In these same five years, the respective economic strengths of the U.S. and Japan have changed, with Japan, the traditional protectionist, running huge trade surpluses and assuming the role of creditor nation.

Japan, like Canada, needs to develop its international voice through multilateral institutions. Japan's economic strengths are still dependent on an open world trading system with rules which prevent governments from imposing discriminatory measures in the name of 'fair trade', particularly when the domestic costs of protectionism can be made so transparent. Moreover, the artificial nature of trade surpluses and deficits, made so because of exchange rate imbalances, transforms the open trading system into a neo-mercantilist collection of bilateral contracts. Japan and the U.S. are at the centre of this challenge to open trading. American desires for a focused, discriminatory and retaliatory trade policy, specifically aimed at Japan, is not without support in U.S. business circles.[15] Only leadership on both sides can produce breakthroughs in the continuing GATT talks.

The themes of this study can be stated simply. The global economy is moving faster than the political mechanisms to manage it. Bilateral relations and managed trade have become the preferred approaches to what are essentially multilateral problems needing multilateral solutions. Multilateral leadership has given way to the historical turbulence of trade politics.

At the same time, technology, communications, and severe financial imbalances have all thrown the global economy into a wrenching dilemma first witnessed by the 1973 Oil Shock and repeated by the 1986-1988 dollar crisis. The problem is simple: can political management of international economic affairs help or hurt international adjustment? For those in government, large corporations and the banking establishment, the answers are clear. The political resolve and policy discipline are less certain.

For Canada, these issues come together in very direct ways. Almost 90% of Canada's trade dependent economy is with two countries—the United States and Japan. These two countries are not only the two largest economies, but they themselves share a degree of integration and interdependence which Canadians should see as both a strength, because they have a mutual interest in continued growth, and an opportunity, because Canada can share in that growth with the world's two most dynamic economies. But Canadians must run faster to stay even.

This study has reviewed Canada-Japan relations. The starting point obviously is the steady build-up of two-way trade between what is essentially a large resource-based country and a large 'throughput' economy dependent on imports and manufactured exports to pay for them. But the dynamics of this fundamental relationship are changing. Japan's phenomenal post-war success in manufacturing, technology management, and organization has now produced a new era—a financial powerhouse of global importance and a centre of technological excellence. Japan's adjustments to a rising currency and import protectionism are themselves profound, setting in motion a number of new Japanese strengths for the decade ahead.

Canada stands at an important threshold. U.S.-Canada relations are only one side of an important policy triangle linking the capitals of Washington, Tokyo, and Ottawa. The U.S.-Canada trade agreement will provide enormous job and investment opportunities on both sides of the border, but the adjustment pressures for competitiveness are no less important nor can they be lessened by global trade patterns, by defensive posturing, or by transplant protectionism.

Japan offers a new opportunity, both at home and in Canada. As a result, Canadians must think carefully about the place of Japan in its future. The Japanese presence in Canada is here in strength and it is growing. The weakness in the bilateral relationship is in the Canadian presence in Japan. While our joint problems may be bilateral, our relationship is asymmetric—Japan is the larger power, and it is Japan that is shaping the outlines of what will become the new Pacific Century. Canada's choice is one as simple as it is challenging: to alter traditional habits of thought and ways of doing business to respond to the changes or to ignore them and be left an economic outpost.

Acknowledgements
This study, conducted with interviews in Japan, Canada and the U.S., as well as primary and secondary sources in Tokyo, owes thanks and appreciation to many people. In Tokyo, I particularly want to thank many Japanese executives who spoke with honesty and candour. I single out senior officials at the Keidanren and Yamakoshi Atsushi, who helped arrange meetings. Ambassador Barry Steers and Dr Peter Eggleton, Science Counsellor at the Embassy were singularly helpful.

At the Canada-Japan Trade Council, I wish to salute Jack Struthers for his support and assistance. For superb research assistance and help, I wish to thank Nigel Wright. Responsibility for any error or questions of interpretation remain with the author.

As usual with her special help and devotion, I thank Kazuyo, to whom I dedicate this study.

○

Although the 'Pacific Century' referred to in the preceding chapter is fast becoming a reality, its promise for Canada is tempered by the realities of Canada's position in the international trading system. Although Japan has become Canada's second largest trading partner, Canada is much less important from a Japanese perspective. Moreover, both countries are heavily dependent on the United States for markets and security. Canadian trade policy in the 1970s and 1980s put heavy emphasis on developing the so-called 'Third Option' of expanded economic relations with the Pacific Rim. At the same time the success of those efforts was limited by the perception that Canada continues to rely on its special relationship with the United States, and tends to ride on the coattails of the U.S. in its efforts to influence Japanese policy and gain greater benefits from the relationship.

The presumption on the part of Japan that the United States continues to be the real priority of Canada's international trade policy was confirmed by the signing of the Canada-U.S. Free Trade Agreement, which went into effect in January, 1989. While Professor Sato notes that it is still too early to measure the impact of the FTA on Japan-Canada economic relations, one can at least say that so far it appears to have resulted in little in the way of concrete damage or benefit. Since the agreement was signed, Canada's trade with Japan has increased marginally, with Canadian exports rising from U.S. $8.3 billion in 1988 to U.S. $8.6 billion in 1989. Meanwhile, Japan's direct investment in Canada increased substantially from U.S. $626 million in 1988 to U.S. $1,362 million in 1989. But the size of Japanese investment in Canada remains only 4% of that in the United States, far below the 10% ratio equivalent to the relative size differential between the Canadian and U.S. economies. Given the United States' declining economic influence in the world, Sato *argues, expanding and diversifying Canada's economic relations must be a goal to be actively pursued; the pursuit of that goal through expanded economic relations with Japan need not, he concludes, be incompatible with closer trade relations between Canada and its southern neighbour.*

Hideo Sato received his BA from the International Christian University in Tokyo, and his MA and PhD from the University of Chicago. He has been an Associate Professor of Political Science at Yale University and a Research Associate at the Brookings Institution, and has authored or co-authored eight books including The Textile Wrangle *(Cornell University Press, 1979) and* Taigai Seisaku *[Foreign Policy] (Tokyo University Press, 1989). An authority on International Political Economy, he is currently Professor of Political Science and Dean of the College of International Relations at the University of Tsukuba.*

CANADIAN-JAPANESE ECONOMIC RELATIONS: A JAPANESE PERSPECTIVE*

Sato Hideo

Japan is the world's second-largest market economy after the United States. Canada has a much smaller economy but, as one of the seven most important industrial nations, it is still a major actor in the international economic system. Japan is Canada's second-largest trading partner, while Canada ranks ninth among Japan's trading partners. Consequently, the Canadian-Japanese economic relationship is important in itself and deserves serious attention. In analyzing this relationship between the two countries, one could treat it as a kind of 'dyad' by focusing on their individual characteristics and on the pattern of their past interactions without paying attention to any other international interaction. Such a 'dyadic interaction' approach often explains much of the variation in the two countries' behaviour; indeed, virtually all existing studies on Canadian-Japanese economic relations implicitly adopt this approach.[1]

Both countries, however, have major economic and political ties with the United States. Thus, any analysis of the Canadian-Japanese relationship that is unmindful of the role of the United States may constrain substantially our understanding of the nature of that relationship. As one observer has noted, 'For both countries, the United States—like it or not—is the most important political and economic partner. Consequently, the U.S. factor is considered primary by both countries and decisions made by one or the other are often viewed through the U.S. lens.'[2]

This 'triangular' relationship is particularly meaningful in a multipolar world in which the United States no longer has undisputed hegemony. Like Great Britain in the nineteenth century, the United States in the postwar era played a preponderant role in the creation and maintenance of a free-trade regime. Since the late 1960s, this authority has declined; the United States gradually has lost the power to sacrifice short-term national interests for the systemic objective of maintaining a free-trade regime by itself. At the same time, the relaxation of Cold War tensions has reduced the United States' incentive to make short-term sacrifices for the sake of the 'free world'.[3] In short, the United States has now become much more sensitive to its interdependence with its postwar allies, including its two largest trading partners, Canada and Japan.

Yet U.S. primacy in the two countries' foreign relations is undisputed and suggests that any examination of Canadian-Japanese relations should be a function of relations both have with the United States. The trade flows in Figure 1 illustrate the magnitude of the triangular economic relationship. The purpose of this study is to examine Canadian-Japanese economic relations in the context of political relations between the two countries. Three strands of Canadian foreign policy make up this context: Canada's historical interest in the so-called Third Option, its perceived tendency to ride on the coattails of the United States, and its tendency to rely on a special political relationship with the United States.

JAPAN AS CANADA'S 'THIRD OPTION'

Japan has long maintained a somewhat ambivalent attitude toward the United States. On the one hand, it has sought to capitalize on its close historical, cultural, and economic relationship with its giant neighbour. On the other hand, it has sometimes tried to preserve its cultural and economic autonomy by diversifying economic relations to reduce excessive reliance on the United States. The latter type of foreign policy posture, favoured by the Trudeau government after it came to power in 1968, became known as the Third Option—the First Option consisting of maintaining the status quo with the United States and the Second Option consisting of closer integration with it. Canadian articulation of its Third Option coincided with the pronouncement in the United States of the Nixon Doctrine, itself a manifestation of the United States' desire to lessen its foreign policy burdens as its hegemonic position became increasingly undermined.

It was as part of the Third Option that Canada took greater notice of the Pacific area in general and Japan in particular. Canada consciously sought to expand trade and investment relations with Japan during the Trudeau years. An opportunity for Canada to put substance into the Third Option policy appeared in the wake of the Nixon administration's decision in 1971 to impose a surcharge on imports and to take the United States off the gold

Figure 1   Trade Flows Among Canada, Japan, and the United States, 1984

(Can. $ billions)

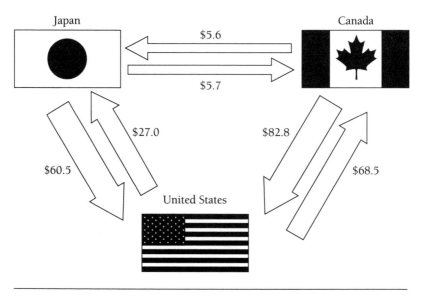

Source: Wendy Dobson, 'Canada, Japan, the United States, and the Triangular Economy' (Background paper prepared for the Canada-Japan Business Co-operation Committee, Nagoya, May 19, 1986), pp. 22-3.

standard. As a result of this 'Nixon shock', Japanese government officials and leaders feared that Japan might lose an important share of its North American market unless it opened its own market to foreign imports. Consequently, Japan made an unusual effort in 1972 to sell Canadian manufactured goods in Japan, even though these goods competed directly with Japanese products.

It was clearly in Canada's interest to seize this opportunity to market its manufactured products in Japan to correct what was seen as an 'undesirable' structure of trade between the two countries. Canadian exports to Japan had consisted mainly of raw materials and agricultural products, whereas imports from Japan had been almost exclusively manufactured products. As far as Canadians were concerned, this qualitative trade imbalance had left Canada 'in a position of a less-developed country in relation to Japan.'[4] What was worse, manufactured imports from Japan had tended to concentrate in Quebec and Ontario, where competing products were manufactured. In Western Canada—and in British Columbia and Alberta in particular—the situation was quite

Figure 2   Canada's Trade with Japan, 1965-84

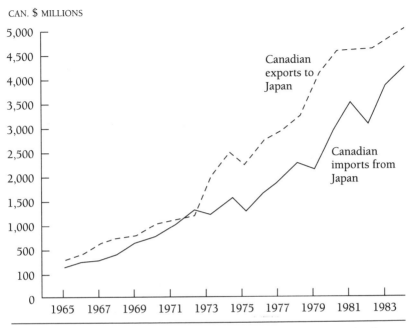

Sources: Statistics Canada; and the Japan Tariff Association. The figures after 1981 are based on Japanese statistics.

different. These provinces had benefited directly from large exports of raw materials and agricultural products to Japan. As a result, a serious conflict of interest existed between Western and Central Canada over Japanese trade. The Canadian federal and provincial governments sent various sales missions to Japan in attempts to increase manufactured exports to that country, but these missions did not bear much fruit. Canadian businessmen largely failed to follow up with initiatives of their own, and those who did were importers of Japanese products who had frequently visited that country without any Canadian or Japanese government assistance.[5]

As Figure 2 shows, Canadian exports to Japan increased steadily after 1972, creating a substantial trade surplus that persisted until recently. It should be noted, however, that the exports which increased most rapidly were such raw materials and agricultural products as coal, lumber, rapeseed, and woodpulp, as is evident in Figure 3. In other words, Western Canada benefited from increased exports to Japan while Ontario and Quebec continued to suffer from serious trade deficits (see Figure 4). The share of Canadian finished manufactured products (or end products) in total Canadian exports to Japan hovered around the 2-4% range, in marked contrast to the structure of its trade with the

United States, where the share of end products was as high as 34% in 1981 (see Figure 5).

It is of no consolation to Canada that the United States has had the same kind of problem in its trade with Japan. As shown in Table 1, more than sixty per cent of U.S. exports to Japan consist of industrial supplies—such as coal, logs and lumber, raw cotton, and hides and skins—and agricultural products, while more than sixty-five per cent of U.S. imports from Japan consist of automotive products and capital goods (machinery and transportation equipment). The United States, too, has long complained about this situation. As a U.S. congressional report stated a few years ago, 'we are a developing nation supplying a more advanced nation—we are Japan's plantation: haulers of wood and growers of crops, in exchange for high technology, value-added products. . . . [T]his relationship is unacceptable.'[6] Consequently, the United States has been anxious to increase its manufactured exports to Japan.

One major obstacle to increased Canadian exports of manufactured goods to Japan is the fact that several Canadian industrial sectors that could export competitively to Japan are dominated by subsidiaries of U.S. firms. When spotting a prospective sale in Japan, the U.S. parent company tends to shift the order to the United States, racking up a credit for that country instead of for Canada.[7] But even Canadian companies that are not dominated by U.S. capital and are not U.S. subsidiaries do not seem to compete well against U.S. rivals for Japanese markets. Former Canadian Ambassador to Japan, Barry Steers, in attempting to explain this phenomenon, has observed, 'The problem with the "third option" was that Japan's most important relationship was with Washington.'[8]

As an example of how this process has worked, Canada has been trying to sell its Candu heavy water nuclear reactor to Japanese utilities for many years, but has had no success because Japan uses U.S.-made light water reactors. Similarly, Canada has tried to persuade Japan Air Lines and other Japanese companies to purchase the Canadian-made Dash short-to-medium range commercial airliner, but the Japanese have favoured U.S. aircraft.[9] A notable exception to this trend may be the Japanese decision in 1985 to place an order worth U.S. $250 million for telecommunications equipment with Northern Telecom, a subsidiary of Canadian-owned Bell Canada Enterprises Inc. The purchaser, Japan's NTT (Nippon Telephone and Telegraph Co.) settled on Northern Telecom after looking at open bids from that company, U.S. giant AT&T, and four Japanese companies. In the United States, though, it was emphasized that Northern Telecom is also a U.S. company, with headquarters in Nashville, Tennessee, and that the switching systems for NTT would be produced at a plant near Raleigh, North Carolina.[10]

In the final analysis, Canada' attempt to increase manufactured exports to Japan as part of the Third Option has not produced any spectacular results.

Figure 3   Major Canadian Exports to Japan, 1974 and 1980

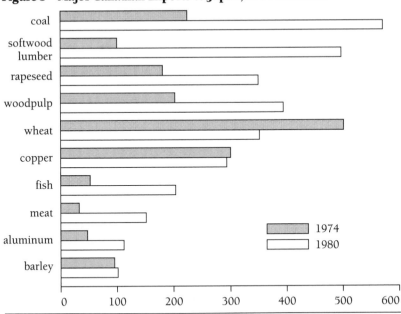

Sources: K.A.J. Hay and S.R. Hill, Canada-Japan: The Export-Import Picture 1975 (Ottawa: Canada-Japan Trade Council, 1976), p. 10; and idem. 'Canada-Japan Trade Statistics.' Canada-Japan Trade Council Newsletter, March 1981, p. 5. This particular figure was prepared by Robert Blain for his MA thesis at York University, Toronto.

Moreover, Canada's trade surplus with Japan, once as high as Can. $1.8 billion, shrank during the 1970s and early 1980s because Japanese demand for Canadian raw materials slowed down and because Canadian imports of Japanese value-added manufactured products, including automobiles and parts, telecommunications equipment, and electronics, increased dramatically. By 1984, Canada had a trade deficit with Japan of Can. $82 million, which increased to between Can. $100 and $200 million in 1985.[11]

Canada has also tried to induce direct Japanese investment, particularly in manufacturing. Indeed, the amount of annual investment did increase to Can. $500 million in 1979 from Can. $194 million in 1972. But the amount of cumulative investment is not particularly large. In 1985, just Can. $1.6 billion of Japan's total overseas direct investment was located in Canada, a fraction of the Can. $19.9 billion invested in the United States and well behind the Can. $3.2 billion directed to Australia, a country with political and economic concerns toward Japan similar to those of Canada.[12]

Not only is Japanese investment in Canada limited, but it is heavily concentrated in resource development, much to the chagrin of Canadian policy-

Figure 4   Canada's Trade with Japan, by Region, 1982

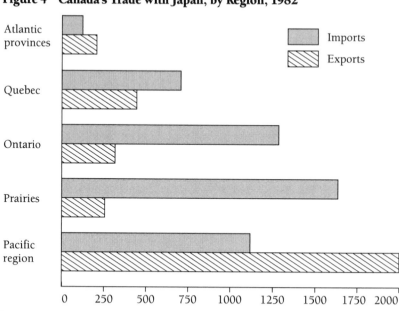

Source: Kokusai Keizai (Tokyo), No. 256, 15 December 1984, p. 72. Based on data from Statistics Canada.

makers who have been severely critical of decisions to put money into such areas as coal mining and tar sands development at the expense of job-creating investments in manufacturing. There are, of course, a few important exceptions, including Mitsubishi Electric's television tube plant in Midland, Ontario; Honda's investment in the auto assembly plant in Alliston, Ontario; Toyota's investment in the aluminum wheel plant in Delta, B.C., and its decision to build an auto assembly plant in Cambridge, Ontario; and Suzuki's decision to build an auto assembly plant in Ingersoll, Ontario, in a joint venture with General Motors.

One of the bottlenecks for Japanese investment in Canada was the disposition of the Foreign Investment Review Agency (FIRA). The agency was designed to encourage foreign investment while preserving Canadian policy objectives of fostering economically desirable projects, such as manufacturing and additional processing of mineral resources. But FIRA came to be perceived as a political bureaucracy shrouded in red tape and hostile toward potential investors. Japanese business interests saw the Trudeau government itself, especially in its later years, as unstable and unnecessarily combative, particularly toward the United States. Such a perception also might have acted as an impediment to Japanese investment in Canada.[13] Under the Progressive Con-

Figure 5   Composition of Canadian Trade with Japan and the United States, 1981

(A) *Imports from Japan and the United States*

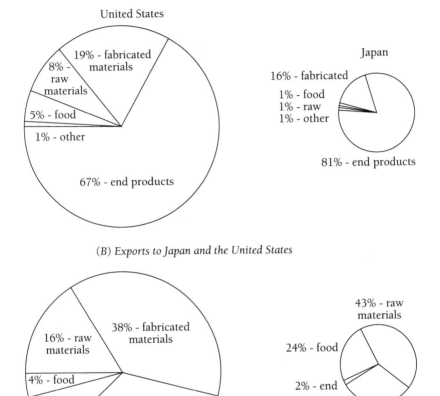

(B) *Exports to Japan and the United States*

Source: Richard W. Wright, Japanese Business in Canada: The Elusive Alliance (Montreal: Institute for Research on Public Policy, 1984), p. 16.

servative government led by Brian Mulroney, FIRA has been reorganized and renamed 'Investment Canada', promising greater assistance to potential investors with fewer strings attached. While apparently retaining the spirit of the Third Option, the Mulroney government seems eager to improve relations with

Table 1   U.S. Trade with Japan, 1985

	U.S. $ MILLIONS	PERCENTAGE
U.S. exports to Japan[a]		
Industrial supplies	$8,679.9	38.4%
Capital goods	5,938.6	26.2
Food & feed	5,000.7	22.1
Consumer goods	1,415.5	6.3
Other	1,596.1	7.0
Total exports	*22,630.8*	*100.0*
U.S. imports from Japan[b]		
Automotive products	24,980.0	36.3
Capital goods	21,515.7	31.3
Consumer goods	14,017.2	20.4
Intermediate goods	7,035.3	10.2
Other	1,234.7	1.8
Total imports	*68,782.9*	*100.0*

[a]*F.a.s. value basis*   [b]*Customs value basis.*
Source: JEI Report *(Washington, D.C., Japan Economic Institute), no. 19A, 16 May 1986, and no. 24, 27 June 1987.*

the United States. Consequently, more Japanese investment in Canada and more trade between the two countries can be expected in the future, with the high value of the yen providing an additional incentive. It may be unrealistic, however, to expect very dramatic changes in the short term, for the reasons discussed above.

CANADA'S RIDE ON THE COATTAILS OF THE UNITED STATES
Another strand in Canadian foreign policy has been its tendency to ride on the coattails of the United States in influencing the policies of other countries. Canada by itself is not powerful enough to exert much influence over Japan. Instead, it has often relied on the leverage created by its close relationship with the United States to induce Japan to impose export restraints and to increase direct investment. This tendency has become increasingly evident since the late 1960s as the United States has gradually lost patience with Japan over bilateral economic issues and has pressured Japan to restrain its exports to the United States. For Canada, it has become an urgent necessity to follow the U.S. example and seek Japanese export restraints, because 'when goods destined for the United States are blocked or restricted, it is convenient to divert them to the

Canadian market, which can easily be flooded because of its much smaller size."[14] Japan, for its part, has found it difficult, once it has acceded to a U.S. request for export restraints in a particular sector, not to accept a similar request from Canada.

An appropriate example is Japan's voluntary export restraints (VERs) on automobiles. During the 1979-80 period, following the second oil price shock, Japanese exports of small cars to North America substantially increased, while sales of larger, less fuel-efficient U.S. and European cars declined. Under these circumstances, in early 1980 the United States launched an intensive campaign, spearheaded by UAW President Douglas Fraser, to get Japan voluntarily to restrain its auto exports to the U.S. market, as well as to build auto manufacturing plants there.[15] Soon after, Canada followed suit. Herb Gray, then Canadian Minister of Industry, Trade and Commerce, even 'went to Washington in April, 1981 in an effort to concert policy with the United States'.[16]

The United States and Japan came to an understanding in May 1981, with the latter agreeing to limit auto exports to the U.S. market to 1.68 million units in fiscal year 1980-81, a decrease of 7.7% from 1980. Within a month of this agreement, Japan consented to reduce its auto exports to Canada by 6% in the current fiscal year.

It is important to note that the terms of Japan's agreement to restrain auto exports to the Canadian market were relatively milder than those of its agreement with the United States. While the Canadian-Japanese agreement led to a decline in auto exports to Canada during fiscal year 1980-81, exports actually increased about ten per cent during calendar year 1981 because of the flood of cars in the first three months of the year. Canadian auto industry and labour leaders criticized the agreement, arguing that the United States had obtained much better terms in its agreement with Japan—greater restraint for a three-year period, instead of just for one year.[17] Thus, while the Canadian strategy of riding on the coattails of the United States is a successful one, Canadians do not necessarily win Japanese concessions strictly equivalent to those made to the United States. Japanese auto industry representatives apparently are much more susceptible to U.S. demands and are inclined to make greater concessions to the United States because of that country's importance for Japanese economic and foreign policy.[18]

Even after obtaining Japanese export restraint concessions, Canada has not found it easy to extend such restraints. In fact, the two countries went through very difficult negotiations in 1982 over extension of the VERs. Japan agreed to an extension of only six months after Canada slowed down customs clearance of Japanese autos at Vancouver for several months (just as France let imported Japanese video cassette recorders pile up at Poitiers between 1982 and 1983).[19]

Japanese auto restraints were extended further in 1983 and 1984, after another strenuous negotiation. In early 1985, suggestions that Tokyo would not continue voluntary controls raised a furore in Canada. But again, right after announcing the extension of the VERs for the U.S. market in late March, Japan agreed to 'a vaguely worded arrangement' to limit its exports to 18% of the Canadian market for the 12 months ending March 31, 1986—an arrangement not fully satisfactory to Canadian auto producers and workers.[20] In February 1986, the Japanese government announced the continuation of restraints for the U.S. market for a year beyond April. But a similar announcement did not immediately follow for the Canadian market, in part because the Japanese came to worry about the rapidly increasing share of South Korean cars imported into the Canadian market free of tariffs and quotas. It was only after protracted negotiations that Japan agreed to extend restraints for another year with Japanese autos being allowed 21% of the Canadian market.[21]

In addition to depending on its leverage with the United States, Canada has used the threat of unilateral action to induce Japanese direct investment in the auto industry. This action sometimes has included harsh pressure tactics, such as the 1982 slowdown of customs clearance at Vancouver mentioned above and the 1983 recommendation by a federal task force that Japanese autos sold in Canada should have at least sixty per cent Canadian content. Japanese auto manufacturers, however, have been reluctant to invest in production in Canada for a number of reasons. One is the small size of the Canadian market. In order to make a profit in Canada, a Japanese manufacturer would have to sell at least 50,000 units per year. If each of seven or eight Japanese companies produced 50,000 per year, the Canadian market would not be able to absorb them. For their part, Canadian officials argue that the North American market is a single entity and that autos produced in Canada can be sold in the U.S. market as 'made in North America'.

Geographically speaking, it is true that autos produced in Ontario can be more easily delivered to Chicago or Cleveland than to Vancouver or Edmonton. But apart from the local-content provisions of the 1965 Canadian-U.S. auto pact, Japanese manufacturers seem to be afraid that assembling autos in Canada—instead of producing additional autos in the United States itself—might antagonize the UAW and policymakers in Washington. Indeed, some people in the U.S. auto industry are said already to be worried about the possible 'backdoor entry' into the U.S. market of Japanese autos produced in Canada.[22]

Japanese investors in general have preferred to commit investment dollars in the United States rather than in Canada for three reasons. First, they perceive that the United States is more committed to capitalism than is Canada; second, they consider the United States to be more politically stable; and third, the demarcation between federal and state governments in the United States is clear, while the relationship between the Canadian government and the provinces 'is sensitive', according to Nakamura Kunio, executive director of the Japan Information

Centre in Toronto.[23] Recently this view seems to have changed somewhat, with relatively more attention being paid to positive factors about Canada, such as long-term lower operating costs (including Canadian labour and utility costs) and the generally reliable quality of Canadian workers. There is some growing interest among Japanese auto parts producers to invest in Canada and a number of them have already established joint ventures and technology transfer arrangements with Canadian counterparts, either on their own initiative or through Pacific Automotive Co-operation, created in Toronto in 1984 by a consortium of Japanese auto manufacturers to facilitate technology transfers between Japanese and Canadian auto parts makers. Moreover, Nissan is planning to build an auto parts manufacturing plant in Canada to supply its auto assembly plant in Tennessee.[24]

In any case, it was the threat of protectionism through continued restraints and unilateral action that persuaded Honda and Toyota to build their auto plants in Canada.[25] Explaining why Japan acceded to protectionist threats by increasing automotive investment in Canada is difficult, since Japan is economically more powerful and less dependent on the Canadian economy that it is on the U.S. economy. One may say that Canada rode on the coattails of the United States again, though the evidence is not as clear as in the case of Japanese auto export restraints. What Keohane and Nye, two U.S. political scholars, have said about Canadian-U.S. trade relations may be applied to Canadian-Japanese trade relations as well:

> Although Canada depended on mutual trade more than the United States, Canadian trade was important enough to the United States that Canada had a potential weapon for retaliation. The deterrence value of Canada's ability to inflict pain on the United States would depend on her will to suffer great pains herself and she was often willing to do that because of asymmetric salience: the relationship was more important to Canada than to the United States.[26]

Canada, along with the United States and Australia, is one of Japan's most important suppliers of raw materials and agricultural products. One could argue, therefore, that Japan made concessions in auto investment for fear that Canada might restrict its supply of these materials. But one should recall that western provinces such as British Columbia and Alberta, which provide most of the Canadian raw materials and agricultural products exported to Japan, have been generally happy with their trade with Japan and would have objected to such linkage between two policy issues. The Japanese knew this. Thus, it would be more realistic to conclude that Canadian pressure on Japan on autos was not linked to possible retaliatory action in the other sectors.

Apart from trying to increase policy independence from the United States and occasionally using U.S. leverage in dealing with other countries, there is a third strand of Canadian foreign policy relevant to Canadian-Japanese relations. Canada has tried to obtain a special exemption from restrictions that the United States has imposed on its allies and trading partners. In 1963, for example, the United States imposed the so-called interest equalization tax on its economic partners to prevent further capital outflow because of lower U.S. interest rates. Canada was granted an exemption 'after Canadian officials showed their American counterparts that the two capital markets had become so integrated that the damaging effects in Canada would feed back into the American economy.'[27] Canada was similarly exempted from two other measures intended to restrict foreign access to U.S. capital: the 'voluntary co-operation program' of 1965 and the 'mandatory direct investment guidelines' of 1968.[28] Immediately after President Nixon announced his new economic policies in August 1971 and imposed a 10% surcharge on all imports, Canada tried, but failed, to obtain a special exemption from the surcharge. Because Canada wanted to secure U.S. concessions for itself alone, Canadian officials were not particularly receptive to the idea of Japan and Canada joining ranks to pressure Washington, as suggested by then Japanese Foreign Minister Fukuda Takeo.[29]

Another example occurred in late 1977, when the United States decided to impose so-called trigger prices on steel imports. Canadian steel producers sought and obtained 'preclearance' on their steel exports to markets in the U.S. Great Lakes states and were able to expand exports to the United States.[30] In early 1983, the protectionist movement in the United States picked up momentum, reflecting a steadily increasing U.S. trade deficit brought about by high interest rates and the U.S. budget deficit. Canada began calling for a bilateral free-trade agreement with the United States, hoping, at least in part, to be exempted from harsh protectionist measures that the United States might impose on Japan and other trading partners. And anticipating the protectionist sentiment that flared up in the U.S. Congress in 1985, Canadian officials seriously took up the free-trade issue at the highest levels of both provincial and federal governments.[31]

Japan has been distinctly nervous about Canada's moves to explore a closer trading relationship with the United States, fearing that it could be a prelude to a united and more protectionist North America.[32] In his January 1986 meeting with Prime Minister Mulroney, Prime Minister Nakasone said Japan would not object to a Canadian free trade agreement with the United States if it would promote freer trade globally.[33] David Culver, chairman of the Canada-Japan Business Co-operation Committee expressed a similar view from a different angle: 'Japan-U.S.-Canada trade is a triangular event. We cannot maximize our trade unless the whole triangle is trading freely.'[34]

A key question is not why Canada seeks special treatment from the United States, but why the United States often provides such treatment to Canada and not to Japan or its other major trading partners. Hobart Rowen, of the *Washington Post*, raised a similar question in August 1985: 'Strange, isn't it, that the United States last year had a [U.S.] $20 billion trade deficit ($22.2 billion in 1985) with Canada—exactly the size of the deficit with Japan the year before—but no one in Congress . . . stands up to say that Canada is a threat.'[35]

Three explanations are possible. The first is that Japan has had the largest bilateral trade surpluses of any country in recent years. But one should also note that, given the much smaller size of the Canadian economy, Canada's per capita trade surplus with the United States is far larger than Japan's, and that Japan's share of the United States' global trade deficit declined to about 30% in 1984 from over 45% in 1982.

A second explanation could be that the United States regards Japanese trading practices as particularly 'unfair'. Such a perception could be related to the U.S. frustration that Japan, as the second largest market economy, is not carrying out international responsibilities commensurate with its economic power.[36]

The third possible explanation is that the United States is willing to take a tougher stand in its trade relations with Japan because of a large asymmetry in economic interdependence between the two countries. Within the existing structure of Japanese-U.S. trade relations, the United States could produce virtually all of the things it buys from Japan and, therefore, could terminate trade with Japan if it wanted to. It would be next to impossible, however, for Japan to find a replacement for the United States as a large and stable export market and as a reliable supplier of raw materials and agricultural products. The same thing cannot be said of the Canadian-U.S. economic relationship. Because of the closely interlocking nature of the two economies and the extent to which U.S. capital is heavily involved in Canadian industries, there is more symmetry in the economic interdependence between the two countries.[37]

A final and somewhat related factor is that, to a substantially greater degree than are Japanese-U.S. relations or even European-U.S. relations, Canadian-U.S. relations are based heavily on multiple channels of private-sector, personal, and intergovernmental networks. Therefore, Canadian interests are more effectively communicated to the U.S. side. And despite the obvious disparity in Canadian and U.S. economic (and military) capabilities, Canada has been able to influence U.S. policy much more frequently than might have been expected.[38] By contrast, the U.S.-Japanese relationship is influenced more directly by the underlying power structure, reinforced as it may be by greater cultural distance. One should note, however, that because of its declining industrial competitiveness and deteriorating macroeconomic position, the United States has become less capable and less willing of late to give special treatment even to Canada. This change is reflected in its attitude toward the softwood lumber, and shakes and shingles issues, its decision to subsidize

grain exports to the Soviet Union and China, and its tendency to seek reciprocity in the current free-trade negotiations with Canada.

CONCLUSION

Canada has not been very successful in expanding its manufactured goods
exports to Japan as part of the historical Third Option. It has been slightly more
successful in obtaining Japanese concessions in the form of VERs by riding on
the coattails of the United States whenever convenient. It has also managed to
induce some Japanese manufacturing investment in the Canadian market,
perhaps because it has been willing to suffer great pains to achieve this
purpose. Canada has often succeeded—although with increasing difficulty of
late—in obtaining special treatment from the United States because of the
relatively close formal and informal ties between the two countries. Canada's
tendency to ride on the coattails of the United States and to count on a special
relationship with that country can be understood in the context of the historical First Option of maintaining the status quo with Washington, although the
Canadian decision to conclude a bilateral free trade arrangement also could be
linked to the Second Option of greater integration with its giant neighbour.

In view of declining U.S. economic influence in the world and a dynamically
changing international economic environment, it will no longer be feasible or
possible for Canada to remain passively dependent on its southern neighbour.
While continuing to maintain its relatively heavy reliance on the U.S.
economy—which may be unavoidable for geographical and historical
reasons—Canada would do well to diversify its foreign economic relations.
Such a policy does not have to conflict with Canadian efforts to further
strengthen its economic relations and institutional linkages with the United
States while retaining its cultural identity and political sovereignty. In short, if
interpreted flexibly, the Second and Third Options can be compatible and
need not be mutually exclusive.

Japan is now under unprecedentedly strong pressures to open its domestic
market to foreign goods and services, to increase manufactured imports, and to
expand direct investments abroad. It can no longer count on export-led economic growth without being branded as 'neomercantilist'. The high value of
the yen is obviously an additional constraint. Under these circumstances,
Japan is in the throes of having to implement basic structural adjustments to its
economy along the lines of those recommended by the Mayekawa Report.
Canada now has an important and timely opportunity, much more so today
than in the early 1970s, to expand its economic relations with Japan, to
promote Canadian investment and manufactured exports across the Pacific, to
invite Japanese direct and indirect investment to Canada, and, with the United
States, to maintain free trade through multilateral negotiations. While one

cannot and should not expect any dramatic results in the short term, as suggested earlier in this paper, it would certainly be worthwhile for Canada to pursue a very active and persistent economic diplomacy toward Japan, both at governmental and at private levels. The opportunity should not be missed again.

O

Considerations and Reconsiderations

There were, argued R.B. Bennett, the leader of the opposition, obvious reasons why Mackenzie King's decision to establish diplomatic relations with Japan was a grotesque mistake. First, it was a pretentious assertion of independence which would send the wrong signals to the world and threaten the unity of the Empire-Commonwealth. While the Caucasians in Washington, where a Canadian minister had resided since 1926, or Paris, where an embassy was established in 1928, might understand the subtleties of Canada's subordinate position in the British Commonwealth—and where special geographic, economic, and cultural relations perhaps justified separate representation—the Oriental mind certainly could not, and the Japanese would conclude that Canada was in fact a sovereign state. Second, the creation of an embassy would mislead Canadians. 'Where are our fleets . . . our cruisers abroad?' Bennett demanded to know: 'This is putting on a show, a pretence, without having behind us the power, authority or means to assert ourselves.' Opening a Tokyo embassy amounted to a 'false representation of sovereignty' which Canada did not possess. No historical or cultural ties linked Canada with Japan. More trade commissioners and simple bilateral discussions as the occasion demanded were all that was needed.[1]

John Saywell argues that Bennett was right. The history of Canada-Japan relations has been, in his reading, almost exclusively focused on the flow of resources—human and material—across the Pacific. In this lies the continuity which, from the Osaka Industrial Exhibition of 1903 to the 'Pacific 2000' strategy of 1989, is signalled on the Canadian side by the endless reiteration of the promise of wealth to be gained by closer ties to Japan. The discontinuity is owed to Japan. From the turn of the century to 1945 Canada did have a foreign policy in the northern Pacific because of our unique relationship in the North Atlantic triangle. But the Pacific War brought that chapter in Canada-Japan relations to an end. Finally there is the matter of asymmetry. Symmetry is a word suggesting balance and mutuality, interdependence and reciprocity. But the bilateral relationship—in trade, investment, scientific and technological exchange—has become increasingly unbalanced, dependent.

Author of numerous books and articles, including most recently Making the Law *(Copp Clark Pitman:1991) and* Just Call Me Mitch *(University of Toronto Press: 1991), John Saywell has lectured at more than forty Japanese universities and was from 1979-81 the Visiting Professor of Canadian Studies for Japan. A graduate of the University of British Columbia and Harvard University, where he completed his PhD in History and International Relations, Professor Saywell currently teaches at York University.*

CONTINUITY, DISCONTINUITY, AND ASYMMETRY IN CANADA-JAPAN RELATIONS*

John T. Saywell

Assured that the twentieth century belonged to them, Canadians had given little thought to the emergence of Japan as a modern industrialized power, and not until Japan's striking victory over Russia in 1904-1905 was there any concern about Canadian security in the Pacific. However, the Anglo-Japanese alliance of 1902 meant that Japan was an ally, and Canada welcomed the renewal of the alliance in 1911. The First World War brought a less than subtle change of opinion—and policy. Although Japan sent a battleship and cruiser to ward off a possible attack on the west coast by the German Pacific squadron, her conduct during the war and after—the demands on China in 1915, intervention in Siberia, claims to the former German colonies in the Pacific, the earlier occupation of Korea, Taiwan, the Pescadores, and (temporarily at first), the Liaotung Peninsula in Manchuria—fuelled deep suspicions about her territorial ambitions. With a major shipbuilding program under way at the end of the war, Japan 'was no longer a client of the English-speaking world, no more a co-operative middle naval power and docile partner of the British Empire.'[2]

Between the wars Canada was forced to fashion the rudiments of a Pacific foreign policy based on its own analysis of the geo-politics of the north Pacific and on its delicate, and unenviable, position in the North Atlantic Triangle. The United States, too, was suspicious of Japanese intentions and regarded the

Anglo-Japanese alliance, up for renewal in 1921, as a threat to its security. Great Britain, on the other hand, saw its renewal as a safeguard against its own growing international impotence and the security of Australia and New Zealand—as did they. Well aware of American opinion, Prime Minister Arthur Meighen went to the 1921 Imperial Conference determined to prevent its renewal. The alliance, he argued, had not kept peace in the Pacific and Japan, far from being a loyal ally, was guilty of 'exceeding her rights, violating her covenants, committing acts of aggrandizement, and being prepared to repeat the performance in the next twenty years.' Moreover, the renewal of the alliance would 'jeopardize Anglo-American accord, anger American public opinion . . . and be regarded as a provocative rebuff to the United States.' In the end the alliance was not renewed, and a year later a five-power treaty established the paper façade of the naval status quo in the Pacific.

The Canadian government watched the unfolding tragedy in the Pacific in the 1930s with increasing anxiety. Although suspicious of Japanese intentions in Manchuria and towards China after the Mukden incident, the Bennett government preferred equivocation to condemnation and its delegate to the League of Nations spoke, as one contemporary observed, 'strongly on both sides.' But with the evidence of Japanese aggression so clear and the United States vigorous in its condemnation, Canada could not remain on the fence. It endorsed the Committee of Nineteen Report in 1933, which in effect meant censuring Japan, but, like the rest of the League, was willing to go no further.[3]

While Canadian public opinion was inflamed by the open invasion of China in 1937 and the atrocities that followed, reports from the Ministry in Tokyo seemed sympathetic to the Japanese rationale. With Britain unwilling to act— certainly not without the United States—Roosevelt unwilling to take any initiative that could involve military action, and the Japanese refusing to attend, the Nine Power Treaty Conference in Brussels was doomed to failure. Canada supported the conclusion neither to coerce nor condemn, but to call for an end to the war and peaceful negotiations.

Canadian policy from 1937 to December 1941 was an amalgam of a number of concerns. As usual, at the centre was Prime Minister W.L.M. King's determination to do nothing if at all possible. Given that, however, his obsession was that somehow the Pacific war would involve either Britain or the United States but not both. Could Canada remain out of an Anglo-Japanese war if the United States remained neutral? Could Canada remain neutral if Japan attacked the United States and Britain remained neutral? Could Canada protect its own territory in the event of a war in the Pacific, or would the United States demand that its forces occupy Canadian territory for the defence of North America? And finally, could Canada avoid imposing economic sanctions on Japan which would invite retaliation and damage Canadian trade? The answer to each question was to attempt to march hand in hand with Britain and the United States, an extraordinarily difficult task since the Americans and the British were deeply suspicious of each other and often marched to different drummers.[4]

In 1937, the government gave pride of place to the Pacific defences, as much to deter the Americans as the Japanese, and it remained a priority (if only on paper) until the outbreak of the European war. Little in fact was done until June 1940 when it appeared that Japan contemplated taking advantage of Britain's situation in Europe to force the hand of Britain and France in the Far East. The Cabinet War Committee, without alarming the public, quietly moved some troops from Dundurn and Shilo to the Pacific.[5]

Although unwilling to proceed as fast and as far as the British demanded, and concerned about the American position and possibility of provoking Japan, Canada began to impose export restrictions on steel and scrap iron in October 1939, followed by nickel and zinc in February 1940, aluminum in August, and copper in October. With the Japanese movement into Indo-China in the summer of 1941, Britain and the United States froze Japanese assets, ending all trade, and Canada followed suit at once. King dismissed the Japanese Minister's protest, that the advance into Indo-China was no different than the American presence in Iceland and Greenland, as the difference between offence and defence.[6]

Although King constantly cautioned Britain against a provocative course in the Pacific and there was some concern in London that Canada might remain neutral, there was no doubt in King's mind that if Britain was at war in the Pacific Canada would be involved. When Baron Tomii raised the question over dinner at Kingsmere King replied: 'We were opposed to dictatorship and recognized democratic ways of life were at stake. I believed that today we were prepared to fight in any quarter of the globe where the British Empire was threatened. . . . I thought it more likely the U.S. would be fighting for the preservation of democracy and that the fight would be kept up until democracy was saved.'[7]

Three weeks later Japan signed the Tripartite Pact with Germany and Italy pledging joint action if any member went to war with the United States. The British at once informed Canada that they would go to war if the Americans were attacked in the Pacific and asked King for a statement of Canada's position. Although some members of the War Cabinet felt the reply was automatic, King's paranoia prevented such an easy decision. For Canada to base its decision 'solely upon North American considerations' such as the joint defence agreement with the United States, he told the Cabinet War Committee, 'would create a major political division in Canada and the government would be criticized for throwing in our lot with our new friends and forswearing our old.' As O.D. Skelton laboured over a draft despatch, King warned him that

great care must be taken to link up Canada's position in the closest possible way with what arises out of United States action to assist the United Kingdom and other parts of the British Commonwealth in the present conflict against Germany and Italy, and to avoid so wording the despatch that it could be construed as a commitment on the part of Canada to go to war with Japan simply because of war between the United States and Japan regardless of the circumstances which might occasion it. . . .

We have to be careful I think not to have it assumed that because there are joint plans for defence between the United States and Canada we are thereby committed in advance to active participation in every war in which the United States may be concerned, any more than we can be regarded as committed to participate in any war in which Britain may be involved, merely because we are part of the British Commonwealth of Nations.

It was classic King, but despite the qualifications, the tortured logic and semantics, Canada's answer was yes.

Yet King himself remained tortured until the very end that Canada might find herself in the position where Japan somehow divided the members of the North Atlantic Triangle. December 7 was almost a welcome deliverance. 'It was an immense relief to my mind to know that their attack had been upon the U.S. in the first instance', he confided to his diary, 'and that the opening shots were not between Great Britain and Japan.' Pearl Harbor ended the painful dialectic in Canadian Pacific policy, and Canada was the first western nation to declare war on Japan. Soon other shots were fired between Britain and Japan, however, and on December 18 the untrained and ill-equipped Canadian regiments that had been sent to Hong Kong in the fall tasted battle. A week later the British and Canadians surrendered. Of the 1975 Canadians, 575 either were killed in battle or died in Japanese prison camps and coal mines.[8]

Canada was not a major participant in the Pacific war, and the Japanese surrender made unnecessary preparations to send an army division and units of the navy and air force to participate in the final invasion. Nor did Canada play a major role in the Pacific peace, accepting with some hesitation the American invitation to become a member of the Far Eastern Advisory Commission, later the Far Eastern Commission. On the whole Canada supported the American view of the necessary democratic, economic, and spiritual remaking of Japan. But it had been an American war and Canada was content that it be an American peace. And the obvious lack of desire among the Japanese to emigrate to Canada in large numbers after 1945 meant that the emerging bilateral relationship would not be troubled by the flow of human resources.

THE CHANGING PATTERN OF TWO-WAY TRADE
At the 1903 Osaka Industrial Exhibition the Canadian display won rave reviews and a visit from the Emperor. The stellar attraction was bread freshly

baked from Canadian wheat, eagerly sampled by visitors and a hit in Osaka restaurants. Returning from Osaka, the minister of agriculture was convinced that the forty million Japanese were a promising market for fish and fruit, pulp and newsprint and, with modest dietary changes, Canadian wheat and meat.

It had not been the dream of markets but the lure of silk that had drawn the Canadian Pacific steamers across the Pacific fifteen years earlier. Their holds largely empty on the outward passage, the sleek white empresses returned to unload their cargo onto silk trains waiting to speed to New York, Chicago and Montreal. After the Osaka success the despatch of a Trade Commissioner to Yokohama and repeated government exhortations did little to develop an export market. Not until the eve of the First World War did exports reach a million dollars, about one third of the imports of silk, tea and rice. The trade was so paltry that the Japanese government spurned the proposal of a separate commercial treaty, although they had appointed a Consul in Vancouver in 1889.[9]

Yet, if not sufficient, the trade was so potentially profitable that the Laurier government had no desire to antagonize the Japanese by yielding to demands from British Columbia to arbitrarily and draconically restrict Japanese immigration. Moreover, Canada was bound by the 1894 Anglo-Japanese Treaty which gave the citizens of each nation 'full liberty to enter, travel or reside in any part of the dominions and possessions of the other contracting party'. Nor did Japan have any desire to encourage emigration, its energy being directed towards the settlement of Hokkaido, and was prepared to 'voluntarily' limit emigration if it could be done by regulation and without any suggestion of racial discrimination.

The fluctuations in immigration, the anti-oriental movement in British Columbia, the federal government's use of the power of disallowance to kill Victoria's anti-Oriental legislation, and the negotiation of the 1908 Lemieux Agreement are too well known to need repetition here. It is interesting to note, however, that Laurier suggested that in the interests of trade and the British alliance it would be much better if Japan voluntarily negotiated a restrictive agreement than have it imposed. Immigration continued to plague the two governments, particularly in the 1920s. After prolonged discussions, in 1928 Mackenzie King was able to persuade the Japanese government again to accept voluntarily a limit of 150 emigrants a year, to exclude picture brides, and to place the granting of visas in the hands of the new legation in Tokyo.[10]

By then the trans-Pacific trade had become more important. Industrial expansion, a growing population, and destructive earthquakes enlarged the market for Canadian wheat, lumber, pulp, newsprint, lead and zinc, electrical equipment, and even the Canadian automobiles that attracted attention at Tokyo's annual motor show. By 1929, when the exchange of ministers underlined the growing importance of bilateral relations, Japan was taking over three per cent of Canadian exports, ranking in fifth place fractionally below Germany and the Netherlands. The balance of trade had swung decisively in Canada's favour in 1922, and remained between three and five to one in the inter-war years.

Trade plunged during the Depression (from a high of $42.2 million in exports and $12.9 in imports in 1929 to a low of $10.3 and $3.3 in 1933). The drop was precipitous in part, at least, because of Bennett's high tariff policy, the application of exchange rate compensation and anti-dumping provisions after Japan depreciated the yen in 1932, the decreased demand for silk, and the shift in the composition and source of Japanese imports. The intensification of the bitter trade war in 1934-35 ended only with King's victory in the fall of 1935. Exports picked up in 1937 when Japan began to import large quantities of raw materials to feed its military machine, but the composition switched dramatically when the Japanese government restricted imports of commodities not essential for its military build-up. Silk still dominated the import picture—the last silk train left Vancouver in 1939—but the heavily protected Canadian textile industry was charging that Japanese cottons were a threat to its survival. In 1939, in response to domestic pressures and in retaliation for Japanese import restrictions, the King government raised the tariff on Japanese cottons. By then, with 90% of Canadian exports in minerals and metals the question had become whether the country should continue to provide an obvious aggressor and a likely enemy with the sinews of war.[11]

The war over, despite the pessimism in General Crerar's 1948 report about the inability of Japan to finance large-scale imports, and the prospects of fierce competition from the United States, trade with Japan recovered reasonably quickly. Even before the Allied occupation ended and the peace treaty was signed, a Japanese trade mission had visited Canada in search of raw materials to fuel industrial recovery and help feed the population. A commercial agreement signed in 1954 provided for most-favoured nation treatment, gave Canada unconditional access to the Japanese market in nine important export areas, and lowered the duties on Japanese imports, particularly textiles, but with safeguards to protect domestic producers against disruptive competition.[12]

There was a natural complementarity between resource-poor and resource-rich countries. The value of exports doubled in the 1950s, tripled in the 60s, and quintupled in the 70s. Japan became the fourth largest market in 1954 with 2.5% of Canadian exports and in 1973, when it passed Great Britain to become our second largest trading partner, took an all-time high of 7.2% of our exports or one-fifth of all exports not headed to the United States. By then the composition of Canadian exports had become established, with wheat yielding first place to copper and then to coal as lumber, wood pulp and rapeseed moved up the export ladder. The value of exports continued to increase in the 1980s, but as a percentage of our exports the Japanese market declined to under six per cent and dipped under five in 1985 before recovering to over 5.08% in 1986 and 1987. However, in 1988 Japan still took about 2.5% of non-American exports.

There was a corresponding increase in Japanese exports to Canada, although the balance of trade, with the exception of 1972, remained strongly in Canada's favour until the mid-1980s. But the composition of Japanese exports changed dramatically, and repeated assaults on domestic producers in Canada created major internal and bilateral problems. The rapid increase in Japanese textile and footwear imports in the late 1950s forced Canada to follow the United States in asking for voluntary restraints, and over the next few years to secure 'negotiated agreements' concerning some textiles, footwear, consumer electronics, and plywood. By 1962, when Canada enjoyed a two-to-one trade advantage, there were restrictions on two-thirds of Japanese exports to Canada.

By 1970 automobiles had become Japan's leading export to Canada, capturing 10% of the market. Sales declined during the recession, but soon jumped back and the sale of 120,000 cars in 1977 represented 13.3% of the market. After another drop in 1979 sales increased to 150,000 in 1980 and showed no signs of diminishing. Canada followed the lead of the United States in 'accepting' export restraints in 1981, and they were extended annually until 1985 when they were allowed to lapse. But the value of cars, trucks and parts continued to increase and in 1985 were over 3 billion, or 34% of Japanese exports to Canada. By then, however, the Japanese industry had moved some manufacturing and assembly capacity to Canada which eased some of the domestic protectionist pressures. Yet it did little to diminish the growing Canadian concern that the soaring export-import figures masked some very serious immediate and even more serious potential problems.[13]

By the mid-70s it had become clear to those responsible for managing the bilateral trading relationship that Canadian exports were not keeping pace with the growth of the Japanese economy. The Canadian share of the market reached 7.2% in 1973, but by 1980 had fallen below 4% and has remained about 4% ever since.[14] Even more disturbing was the decline of market share in commodities in which Canada had traditionally held a very strong position, such as copper and aluminum. Only the sudden and dramatic expansion of coal exports after 1972-73, made possible by heavy Canadian public-sector investment in infra-structure, disguised the drop in other key commodities. However, the volume of coal exports remained reasonably steady over the past decade; it was the dramatic increase in price, a trend now reversed, that led to the increase in the value of coal exports.

The relative decline in Canadian exports reflected a change in the composition of world trade generally, but was more specifically due to industrial restructuring in Japan. In world trade the share of agricultural commodities fell from 21% to 14% between 1973 and 1985, and the share of minerals fell from 28.5% to 22.2% between 1980 and 1985.[15] In Japan the relative and absolute decline, or static growth rate, of such energy, labour and raw materials intensive industries as shipbuilding, aluminum refining, and steel lessened the demand for raw material inputs. The oil shocks and the rising costs of labour also stimulated great increases in efficiency throughout the manufacturing sector. By 1984, Japan was consuming only 60% of the raw materials consumed in 1973 for every unit of industrial production, and productivity has continued to improve. In addition, Canada was facing increasing competition from lower cost producers, particularly in the Pacific basin.

The almost complete reliance on natural resource exports became a matter of serious concern, particularly as the share of raw materials in world trade was declining. In its trade with Japan, Canada it seemed was locked inexorably into the staple trap. With less than five per cent of its exports in a fully manufactured form, and much of that low value-added, while its imports from Japan were almost exclusively very high value-added end products, Canada was in fact exporting much of its comparative advantage.[16]

Canada was not alone in pressing the Japanese to open their markets in all areas and particularly to ease the restrictions on manufactured goods. Yet despite the real and alleged obstacles to entry, the complex distribution system, consumer preferences, government procurement, and a host of other non-tariff barriers, the Japanese market for a middle range of manufactured goods was expanding. But Canada, it seemed, was not benefiting from its expansion. Manufactured exports, in fact, declined in value and as a percentage of total exports in the early 1980s, and Canada continued to export a lower percentage of manufactured goods to Japan than to other countries.

The end of the trade surplus removed the last comforting pacifier in an increasingly uncomfortable bilateral relationship. The relative decline in price and volume of exports compared to imports, the contrasting elasticity of demand for exports and imports, and the low proportion of high value-added goods in the export mix all contributed to the gradually whittling away of the surplus. By 1983 it had almost vanished; a small deficit in 1984 increased five times in 1985, and another five times to reach $1.7 billion in 1986. In 1987 Canada suffered a $1.3 billion deficit in merchandise trade valued at $15.3 billion, but took heart in 1988 when the deficit fell to $600 million on $18 billion in trade. There seemed to be few objective market factors other than the appreciation of the yen to suggest any reversal in the short term. And while the appreciation of the yen has made some Canadian products more competitive in Japan, in the long run, it accelerated the decline of heavy industries which have been a major consumer of Canadian industrial raw materials.

THE UNCHANGING PATTERN OF INVESTMENT

By the 1980s it was also depressingly clear that Canada was not receiving its 'share' of Japanese foreign direct investment (FDI). Like all investors, Japanese corporations look for low-risk, high-opportunity countries and create rough equations from such factors as political stability, economic performance, easy access to resources, market potential, labour supply and stability, government regulatory policies (and their general predictability), political and cultural receptiveness and whatever political and economic leverage the host country may possess. The relative weight of those factors changes, as do the regional targets, in response to domestic demands and international restraints and uncertainties. Although Canada would appear to be a low-risk and high-opportunity country with ample natural resources, a small but affluent market, and a stable political environment, it has not proven to be a powerful magnet for Japanese FDI. Indeed, the conclusion is inescapable that Canada has been, and remains, on the investment periphery.

For the first twenty years after the war when Japan was experiencing severe balance of payments problems, the modest investment of $10 million was largely in the establishment of a trading network and investments in west coast mining and some food processing. By the early 1970s, with some pressures on its supply network, much of the investment of about $300 million was in western resources: lumber, pulp and paper, mining, and coal with some expansion of the consumer marketing network, assembly and processing. The oil shock shifted the emphasis to a consideration of energy supply and diversification—coal, frontier oil, oil sands, uranium exploration, and liquified natural gas (LNG)—but with the crisis over (and the negative impact of the National Energy Program) Japanese interest lapsed.

It was in the early 70s, too, that Japanese direct investment took off, exceeding $2 billion in 1972 and $3 billion two years later. However, the slow economic growth of the late 60s and early 70s, the combination of high unemployment and soaring inflation, labour unrest, low productivity, federal-provincial disputes over the constitution and energy policy, the menacing shadow of the Foreign Investment Review Agency, and the uncertainties inherent in the rise and election of the Parti Quebecois did nothing to enhance Canada's attractiveness to Japanese investors. The report of the 1976 Makita Mission made that painfully clear as it cited labour costs, crippling strikes in the private and public sector, low productivity, government regulations, high taxes and the small market as barriers to higher levels of investment.[17]

Canada's lack of appeal as an investment target, particularly for manufactured goods—compared to Southeast Asia, the United States and Australia, in particular—became increasingly disturbing as Japanese investment strategy turned sharply in the mid-1980s and the volume increased dramatically. As

Japan's soaring trade surplus became increasingly unacceptable in the United States and western Europe, Japan countered with a new wave of direct investment in manufacturing where the protectionist sentiment and the political leverage was strongest and the economic advantages the most obvious. Yen appreciation since the G-5 meeting in 1985 also altered production costs and made even further Japanese offshore investment imperative.

But Canada remained an unattractive host. Between 1951 and 1986 Canada was host to 1.8% of Japanese FDI, ranking thirteenth. In 1985 it received only .8%, in 1986 only 1.2% and in 1987 around 2%. Direct investment in the United States was 46% of the total in 1987 and Australia, a smaller market and competing economy, maintained its share of 4%. With Japanese FDI expected to grow by more than 15% annually, with Japanese firms by 1995 producing goods worth $75 to $100 billion overseas that were previous export items, and with projected investment of $5 billion annually in North America to implement the production transfer strategy it became imperative that Canada reap more of the benefits. Free trade made the task more challenging, to the optimistic more promising, and certainly more uncertain.[18]

Portfolio investment provided a much rosier picture as Japan became banker to the world. Initially, at least, Japanese investors favoured the debt instruments of the United States, Canada, and Australia which absorbed 90% of the total in 1984, with Canada securing 28% and the United States 40%. The volume of investment increased rapidly between 1984 and 1988 when it reached an estimated $35 billion, but declined to about 6% of the total in 1986 with the United States deficit absorbing 56% of the total. However, a survey carried out by the Canadian Embassy in Tokyo in September 1988 suggested that investors had decided to reduce their relative share of Canadian holdings 'because of concerns over excessive concentration in U.S.A. and Canadian bonds' and to diversify their portfolios by additional purchases in other regions, particularly western Europe. The 1989 survey would appear to confirm that analysis, although the Embassy's rough estimate suggested that investment may have increased by as much as $6.5 billion to reach a total of $40 billion. Not surprisingly, Government of Canada bonds account for 61%, provincial bonds 17%, provincial government enterprises 9.8%, and private corporate bonds 6.9%. Major Japanese life insurance companies hold over 60% of the total, with the rest divided among the Postal Life Insurance Bureau, trust companies, marine and fire insurance companies, and banks (the smallest investors with 1.2 billion or 3.4%).

While Japanese portfolio investment has helped the Mulroney government cover the deficit, it is not without risk. A 1986 study for the Canada-Japan Trade Council, a government of Japan funded organization, observed that 'should Japanese bond holders decide to disinvest rapidly, the Canadian bond market would almost certainly be thrown into chaos' and quoted one Canadian bond dealer as saying 'Japanese investors actually own Canada's long-term future.' The observations, however exaggerated, were to the point for without Japanese portfolio investment, or with its withdrawal, there would be more than a blip on the bond market, interest rates, and the value of the dollar. Even without such a worst-case scenario, the drain of $3.4 billion in investment income is a not inconsiderable loss to the economy.

There would be much more to cheer about if the men with the yen, to use Zavis Zeman's phrase, invested in the Canadian economy. Acquisition of equities was virtually non-existent until 1986 when Japanese investors acquired $294 million in Canadian stocks, or 26% of all net stocks sold abroad. In 1989 the Embassy estimated Japanese holdings at $400 million, with life insurance companies holding about three-quarters of the total.[19]

For all but accounting purposes Canadian investment in Japan can be ignored.

THE CONTINUITY OF CANADIAN POLICY

This evolving and shifting pattern of trade and investment provided Canada with an oscillating mixture of opportunities and challenges, and Canadian policy—strategy and tactics—evolved either in anticipation of or in response to the prospects and problems inherent in the increasingly asymmetrical and critically important relationship. Inevitably the emphasis changed as the mix of trade and investment and the structure of relations changed, but policy objectives remained reasonably constant.

For the first two decades after the war Canadian policy concentrated on assisting Canadian exporters to secure greater access to the Japanese market (at the same time containing some of the more disruptive effects of Japanese competition in sensitive domestic markets) and encouraging modest investments in export-related resource industries. Japan and the Pacific received new attention with the election of the Trudeau government in 1968. The major thrust of the subsequent foreign policy review (1970-1972) was to reject Pearsonian internationalism—Canada as the 'helpful fixer'—in favour of a more functional policy based on the limits of Canadian capacity and the principle that 'External activities should be directly related to national policies pursued within Canada, and serve the same ends.' Among the principal objectives of Canadian policy was the sustained and balanced growth of the Canadian economy.[20]

The review forecast that Japan would be an increasingly important global economic and financial power, and would probably become Canada's second largest one-country market. In very pointed language, however, it observed that Canadian exports were limited to industrial raw materials, often derived from Japanese direct investment, which while 'advantageous to the development of Canadian resources' involved their export 'in their rawest transportable and least profitable form' Access to the Japanese market for manufactured goods, on the other hand, was limited by a 'broad range of direct and indirect import restrictions . . . no longer relevant in view of Japan's domestic prosperity and the strong external payments position. Despite Canadian and other efforts, the pace of liberalization remains slow.' While Japan had to be pressed to open its markets, 'Other clear needs, however, are to overcome the lack of familiarity, imagination and aggressiveness on the part of Canadian businessmen in the area, and to attack the general problem of lagging scientific and technical innovation in Canadian industry.'[21]

Although not made explicit until 1972, the 'Third Option' of lessening dependence on the United States was implicit: 'Active pursuit of trade diversification and technological co-operation with European and other developed countries will be needed to provide countervailing factors.' The Nixon 'shock' of 1971 encouraged both Canada and Japan to intensify efforts to expand trade and investment, and pursuit of the Third Option led to an unprecedented parade of Canadian missions to Japan. The persistent refrain of federal-provincial and industrial missions became all too familiar in Tokyo and Osaka: the demand that Japan open its markets to more processed natural resources and fully manufactured goods; the request for more investment in Canadian processing and of joint ventures in the resource field; the removal of restrictions on semi-processed agricultural, fisheries, and forest products; and the pressure for an enlarged share of certain imports. Canadian spokesmen attempted to counter what was seen as Japan's 'resource diplomacy' where Canada was viewed as an 'open-pit mine' by offering the alternative image of a country with a high level of sophistication in transportation equipment, nuclear energy (including the Candu reactor), automobile parts, aerospace and telecommunications.[22]

The culmination of Canadian efforts was the Framework for Economic Co-operation, signed in October 1976. The Framework called for trade liberalization and expansion, and measures to minimize the fluctuations in supply and demand. The two countries promised to co-operate in the development of marketing and further processing of resources, to co-operate in the high tech field, and to increase 'mutually beneficial' investment. The Framework provided for the creation of a Joint Economic Committee (JEC) which would meet periodically to review progress made under the agreement. However, the Makita report observed that, while a solution to the many problems demanded government involvement, much might be gained if businessmen from the two countries took a greater and more consistent interest in the development of new policies and trade and investment interaction. The result was the formation of the Canada-Japan Business Co-operation Committee whose annual meetings alternate between Canada and Japan, with presumably beneficial results.

Experience also revealed that sectoral consultations and working groups at the bureaucratic level were an important mechanism for resolving bilateral questions and promoting mutually advantageous relations. By the early 80s there were such mechanisms in fisheries, forestry, housing, agriculture, canola, nuclear energy, science and technology, and resource processing. The latter working group was proposed by Canada at the 1980 meeting of the Joint Economic Committee, the objective being to encourage government-to-government dialogue on the advantages of further processing Canadian raw materials destined for Japan and the potential that existed for further Japanese investment in resource-processing industries.

Yet despite all the initiatives and mechanisms, the structural composition of trade and investment remained largely unchanged at a time when Japan was rapidly becoming a leading actor on the global economic and financial stage. While the volume and value of Canadian imports increased, exports to Japan as a per cent of GDP fell from 1.5% in 1974 to 1.2% in 1985. Despite the rhetoric of the Third Option, imports to the U.S. had risen dramatically from 13.4% in 1972 to 20.3% in 1985.

In May 1985 the new federal government released a discussion paper entitled *Competitiveness and Security: Directions for Canada's International Relations*.[23] The paper was a sobering document as it underlined the critical importance of international trade, capital investment, and the importance of technology development and transfer to Canada's competitive position. Yet it scored with telling effect the declining comparative advantage in global trade in raw materials, the growing market penetration of imported manufactured goods, Canada's declining world share of manufactured exports, and the mounting deficit in the trade in medium and high technology products. The questions were brutally asked. The answers, or the failure to find them, were implicitly and menacingly present. In the fall the government followed with its National Trade Strategy and in October 1986 with the announcement of its Japan Strategy.

The October 1, 1986 throne speech stated that the government intended 'to improve Canada's status as a trading nation among our major partners. Particular emphasis will be placed upon trade with Japan and other Pacific Rim countries.' A month later the cabinet gave formal approval to the Japan Strategy which described the challenges and opportunities facing Canada as Japan achieved economic and financial superpower status and established Canadian priorities that were to be rigorously pursued through an intensification of current activities and new initiatives. The government realized that there were no quick fixes. Reaching an optimal economic relationship with Japan would be a long-term process, perhaps even more difficult in the future than in the past as other nations with enormous trade deficits sought to use their superior leverage to gain access to Japanese markets and induce or compel greater Japanese direct investment.

But the general objectives were clear: to press Japan towards greater market liberalization through ministerial visits, focused parliamentary missions, bilateral meetings, and multinational trade negotiations; to maintain and improve Canada's position as a stable supplier of industrial raw materials and food products and increase the market share of commodity exports; to secure a better balance in the bilateral trade by increasing the sale of both value-added resource commodities and fully manufactured goods; to stimulate both direct and portfolio investment in Canada and increase Canada's share of the direct investment flowing to North America; and to enhance Canadian productivity by securing access to Japanese production technologies. To provide a more solid foundation for the purely economic and financial relationship the strategy envisioned increased political consultations and interaction, the enhancement of cultural and social relations, and a heightened Canadian presence in the Japanese media. The government realized that it was not the only Canadian actor on the Japanese stage, and the strategy assumed co-operation and co-ordination of federal, provincial, business and labour activities in Japan. Soon after the strategy was launched the Secretary of State wrote to each provincial government offering reciprocal support and soliciting advice.

The government had already announced or implemented many of the new initiatives, for the Japan Strategy was part of the more general National Trade Strategy (NTS) initiated in the fall of 1985 which had declared Japan to be a priority target. The NTS had identified five major areas as promising for Canadian exports: *power*—hydro, thermal, and nuclear; *transportation*—highway systems, rail systems and urban transport; *telecommunications*—office switching, data transmission, satellite communications; *oil and gas* technology and skills—drilling, offshore exploration, transportation and processing; and *resource development* skills and technology. The NTS also suggested that Canada had real export possibilities in computerization, aerospace, processed foods, some lines of consumer goods, and automotive parts among others.

Steps were soon taken—some of them long advocated by those in the field but rejected in Ottawa—to provide more and better points of contact. In Canada the creation of the International Trade Advisory Committee with 300 members from the private sector was designed, through fifteen sectoral groups, to provide an ongoing information flow between government and the private sector. The creation of the Canada-Japan Interparliamentary Group was designed to strengthen consultations at the political level, and the first delegation from the Commons in March 1987 was encouraged to raise direct and concrete questions with their counterparts in the Diet. To further improve contacts in the Diet, as decision-making seemed to be shifting from the bureaucracy to the officers of the Liberal Democratic Party and key Diet committee members, a new office was established in the Embassy to monitor the Diet and establish personal contacts with Diet members in positions of influence. To prove that Canada was indeed 'open for business', the cabinet not only changed FIRA to Investment Canada but approved the appointment of investment counsellors to posts in priority targets. The task in Tokyo was less to deal with the super-companies, who knew only too well the opportunities or lack of them in Canada, than the thousands of small and medium-sized firms that lacked direct economic intelligence. Finally, the opening of a consulate in Osaka gave Canada a window on Kansai, a region with a population of 22 million which accounted for 20% of Japanese GNP.

At the centre of the new strategy was a concerted program to acquire and apply Japanese production technology. Canada's lack of international competitiveness in world trade in manufactured goods had long been a matter of comment and concern. The greatest increase in world exports is now in industries characterized by significant economies of scale, pervasive product differentiation, or high levels of Research and Development (R&D). Canada's performance was at best mixed in its share of exports in these most rapidly growing sectors of world trade. Moreover, its share of exports in R&D-intense industries was well below the OECD average and last among the seven summit nations, and its expenditure on R&D as a percentage of GNP was dismally below other advanced industrial nations. Japan, on the other hand, had become the world leader in the commercialization of pure and applied research and development. Science and Technology (S&T), government and the private sector agreed, would be the real gold standard of the future.[24] Japan's R&D expenditure has expanded about 7% annually over the past decade, and by 1989 was 2.8% of GNP—over 85% of which was in applied research (25%) and development (61%), most of which was by the private sector.

Although Japan has still a deficit in technology exchange, since 1972 it has been a net exporter of new technology, and advanced technology lies at the heart of Japan's industrial restructuring. Moreover, a survey of Japanese technology exports in 1985 revealed that 23.7% went to the United States and only 2.2% to Canada (and the United States supplied 68.6% of Japanese imports and Canada a minuscule 0.3%). Since Canada produces only 2% of its technology requirements, access to advanced Japanese technology seemed not only the course of wisdom but, perhaps, of survival.

In the early 1970s the government of Canada had taken the initiative to promote bilateral industrial and S&T co-operation in resource exploration and development, and biennial consultations to review co-operative projects provided the basis for more formal and elaborate agreements. In 1985 the Ministers of Canada's Department of Regional and Industrial Expansion (DRIE) and Japan's Ministry of International Trade and Industry (MITI) signed an Industrial Co-operation Arrangement designed to develop more balanced bilateral relations and, in the process, provide greater access to Japanese technology. The role of government was to foster an environment conducive to the smooth expansion of industrial co-operation. Nine sectors were proposed for joint action: advanced manufacturing technology, ceramics, microelectronics, advanced industrial communications, information technology, artificial intelligence, agriculture, insect control, robotics, plastics, biotechnology and biosensors, and wastewater treatment. Finally, in May 1986, a formal Science and Technology Agreement provided an umbrella for a wide range of collaborative activities in the public and private sectors. When the first meeting of the Joint Committee for Science and Technology was held later in the year there were seventy projects on the table for review and eight new projects were approved. What remained to be seen was whether Japanese corporations or research institutes were prepared to share information on leading edge technology which the Canadians so desperately needed.

There was a disconcerting asymmetry in the Japan Strategy, for Japan's role seemed to be one of passive acquiescence with Canada the ardent suitor. The new Canadian initiatives, as well as the changed economic climate in Canada, however, were praised in the report of a major economic mission to Canada in 1986 organized under the auspices of the Japanese government. The Kanao report underlined the importance of the trade in raw materials, heralded the new approach to foreign investment, endorsed technological exchange and joint ventures in domestic and third country markets, highlighted the high-tech areas in which Canada excelled or showed promise, and reported positively on the 'New Canada' they had discovered as a host for direct investment.

Yet despite the flurry of Canadian missions, the heightened rhetoric of prospects and possibilities, tours of Canada by the Tokyo and Osaka Chambers of Commerce, the arrival of Japanese auto assemblers, and a steady stream of reports of new investments and joint ventures, very little appeared to change. The trade imbalance remained in value and structure, direct investment remained dismally low, and portfolio investment levelled off. It was certainly no time to stand still. In 1989, cabinet approved another package labelled 'Pacific 2000', one of the three pillars of a new comprehensive policy called 'Going Global'. Pacific 2000 was designed to permit Canada to pursue the following objectives:

a. to build on the benefits of enhanced competitiveness under the FTA and to demonstrate sensitivity to the fears of Canadians that the magnetism of the 'American Dream' will reduce our independence;

b. to develop new markets for Canadian exporters, and to prevent the erosion of market share for traditional exports;

c. to attract our share of the booming Asian investment;

d. to acquire new technologies;

e. to improve Canadian ability to deal with Asia and in Asian markets;

f. to establish Canada as a significant player in the region.

Pacific 2000 was to have four basic components:

a. An enhanced *Pacific Trade Strategy* to better enable Canadian business to compete in the expanding markets of Asia Pacific. *Five-year budget: $14 million.*

b. A *Japan Science and Technology Fund* to strengthen Canada's scientific and technological base through co-operation with Japanese research institutes. *Five-year budget: $25 million.*

c. A *Pacific 2000 Language and Awareness Fund* to stimulate the acquisition of Asian language skills and awareness so that Canadians can better deal with the region. *Five-year budget: $14.6 million.*

d. A *Pacific 2000 Projects Fund* so that Canada can better project its presence in Asia Pacific. *Five-year budget: $11.5 million.*[25]

It was not difficult to believe that much of Pacific 2000 was simply old wine in new bottles or, if that was too cynical, an improvement in the vintage but by no means a new cellar. Although the amounts seemed superficially impressive, how much new money was allocated was never made clear. Three million dollars a year for language and culture spread across the country along five levels, for example, is not likely to have much impact and the program (expanded upon in an External Affairs press release) suggests that Ottawa was unwilling or unable to target specific categories.

NOT BY BREAD ALONE

Nevertheless, the Language and Awareness Fund was a continuing indication that the government realized that healthy bilateral relations cannot flourish on bread alone. What had long been needed was an expansion of the political dialogue on national and international affairs, closer personal contact between élites, and an expanded cultural diplomacy to alter the perception and enhance the presence of Canada in Japan. Not only would this more rounded diplomacy better suit our self-perception, it would also provide a more appropriate context for the evolving economic relationship.

Little thought had been given to the formulation of a Pacific foreign policy in the years after the war. Canadian involvement in the Korean war and the International Control Commission in Vietnam was a reflection of middle-power internationalism and our relations with the United States rather than the belief that Canada should be involved with security and strategic issues in the Pacific. There were, indeed, no strategic interests to defend other than across the Arctic, and the only national self-interest lay in the promotion of trade and investment. However, although its performance (other than the recognition of the People's Republic) never measured up to the promise that Japan and the Pacific should be seen as Canada's 'New West' rather than the 'Far

East', the Trudeau government did begin annual foreign policy consultations with Japan at the official level in 1972. And in 1980 the foreign ministers began to meet annually for a wide-ranging discussion of bilateral, multilateral and international issues.

The 1985 foreign policy review, *Competitiveness and Security*, made no reference to Pacific security, and while the Special Committee noted the importance of Pacific stability to Canada's economic interests it observed that Canada's 'military resources are insufficient to consider a direct contribution to maintaining security in the region.' However, in December 1986 while emphasizing the centrality of the multilateral approach to managing world affairs, the government stated that 'In Asia and the Pacific we must seek to intensify our links with an economically vibrant but diverse area, and to play a more active consultative role on regional security issues.'[26]

In 1986 Prime Ministers Mulroney and Nakasone agreed that consultations on aid policy, first started on Japan's initiative in 1982, should be revived and approved annual consultation at the senior official level on arms control, disarmament, and terrorism. The initial discussions were fruitful, and those on arms control ranged over the whole field of international security concerns. The government's declared policy is to develop a dialogue with Japan on these issues, as well as on east-west security concerns, NATO and other international issues, and make the consideration of each other's views a more automatic part of policy formation.

Yet the asymmetry in our relations with Japan and the Pacific remains; there is a lack of balance between our economic interests and ambitions and our participation in the wider range of affairs central to the concerns of other countries on the Pacific Rim. If Canadian traditions are not overcome by a heightened sense of self-interest the asymmetry will remain.

The new strategy of the 1980s also called for a broadening and deepening of cultural relations involving personal contacts, academic relations, the creative and performing arts, and sports. The Special Committee had observed that although it was 'essential to build an economic and political relationship' with the Asia Pacific nations, 'a third layer, based on cultural ties will be needed to put the relationship on a solid long-term footing.' The government agreed, and announced that the Department of External Affairs 'intends to more than double the funding devoted to arts promotion, academic relations and exchange programs in the Pacific countries in the year ahead, with further increases thereafter.'

It was time. There had long been—and still is—a beautiful symmetry in the history of cultural relations, distinguished as they were by an indifference on both sides that only a few found disconcerting. Whatever interest the Japanese had in Anglo-American society, culture, and language did not extend to the Canadian linguistic or cultural dialect. And when Canadians could be persuaded to look across the Pacific it was the Men of Han rather than the children of the Sun Goddess who captured their imagination. The curriculums of schools and universities avoided the study of each other's country with a determination that has proven to be difficult to overcome.

In 1970, when Japan was already emerging as our second most important trading partner, it ranked sixteenth in the budget for cultural and academic relations. The bulk of the appropriation went to western Europe, where France ranked a healthy first, and the United States stood in tenth place. By 1975, when the trading pattern was set, Japan had risen only to twelfth while the United States stood a distant second behind France.[27]

By then it was reasonably clear that the Japanese perception of Canada could be a barrier to trade and investment. Anecdotal evidence, confirmed a decade later by a major survey of university students, suggested that Canada was regarded as a northern appendage of the United States. The Japanese view of Canada was the view from the Rockies or Niagara Falls, and the best known Canadian was the fictional Anne of Green Gables. Canada was a land known for its 'mighty nature', its clean and crime-free streets, and its apparently inexhaustible supplies of raw materials for Japanese industry. It was a land without culture, with a low level of scientific and technological accomplishments, and an educational system that lacked distinction. There was virtually no mention of Canada in the high school curriculum and few courses on Canada in the five hundred colleges and universities.[28]

In 1974 during his visit to Canada, Prime Minister Tanaka announced a one-million-dollar endowment for the promotion of Japanese studies in Canadian universities. The Canadian government responded with a pledge to spend one million dollars over a five-year period on both Canadian studies in Japan and Japanese studies in Canada. That commitment was not only realized but exceeded. At the same time under the Government of Canada Awards Program, which is operated on a reciprocal basis, Japanese graduate students were to receive scholarships to study in Canada and by the 1988-89 academic year 25 scholarships were available annually.

In a 1976 cultural agreement, Canada implemented support for Canadian studies in Japan by the appointment of visiting professors, translation of books, a library support program, grants for Japanese faculty to study in Canada, and support for the Japanese Association of Canadian Studies founded in 1977. On the government's initiative and promise of financial support, and with the additional assurance of provincial government and private sector contributions, the Asia Pacific Foundation was established in 1983, mandated by federal statute to enhance both the awareness of Asia Pacific within Canada and of Canada in Asia Pacific. Although the impact of the Foundation is difficult to assess and some contributors have been unhappy with their own rudimentary cost/benefit analysis, Ottawa clearly intends to keep it alive.

During his visit to Japan in 1984 Prime Minister Clark announced an annual $50,000 grant competition for research on Canada or Canada-Japan relations. Prime Minister Nakasone's gift of another million dollars in 1986 for Japanese studies was reciprocated by the doubling of funds for cultural relations in Japan. By 1985-86 Japan received 5.7% of the cultural relations budget (the US had 23% and France 18%) and with 7.2% of the budget was second only to the United States in grants for the promotion of Canadian studies.

In 1986 Canada became the third country, after the United States and Australia, to have a working holiday agreement with Japan, and Japan agreed to include Canada as a source of anglophone language teachers in its public schools. The government has also realized that a showroom for Canadian culture is a necessity in Japan, and the new chancery on Aoyama Dori in downtown Tokyo has facilities for art displays, films and small concerts, and a good working library. There is also a commitment to the staff expansion necessary to invigorate a more sharply focused public affairs, cultural, and academic program to increase Canada's visibility in Japan and help to bring Japanese perceptions into line with what Canadians, at least, believe to be reality. But as those of us who have taught and worked in Japan—and in Canada—know only too well, the task of bridging the cultural gap and dismantling the barriers of ignorance and indifference will be a long and lonely task, for objective market forces work in the cultural and educational fields as well.

Canadian policy towards Japan has moved from complacency to anxiety as Japan has emerged from post-war poverty to alarming affluence. There has been a striking continuity in Canadian attempts to reap the maximum benefit from the economic relationship, but the rhetoric and exhortations, the appeals to the Japanese to look more kindly towards us and to the private sector to try harder have not altered the fundamental asymmetry in the bilateral relationship. Given the enormous difference in size and wealth, level of technological achievement, and the preoccupation of both with their relations with the United States, things are not likely to change. It is best to acknowledge the asymmetry and lack of interdependence for what it is: to call a spade a spade. If Canada wants to change the structure of exports to Japan it must realize, as the Americans have, that the old policy of the 'manufacturing condition' may have to be imposed despite screams from the provinces and the private sector: for example, the Japanese may have to be told that logs, pulpwood and pulp are out and newsprint and paper are in. It may be prudent sometimes to leave resources in the ground. National treasures, natural or historic, may have to be taken off the auction block.

The alternative is to accept things much as they are—to realize that the past really is prologue. Indeed, it may be that we have to run very hard to stand still in the fields of trade and investment. But if so we should acknowledge the way it is and not boast of a quadrupling of exports when so much of it is an increase in value not volume and when we have failed to maintain market share and keep up with the growth of the Japanese economy, or boast of new investment which is little more than a continuation of our traditional policy of trading away our comparative advantage. Above all, we should have a national day of mourning for the officers in External Affairs and the external trade offices in the provincial governments who like Sisyphus must feel that they have been condemned to push that heavy rock up the steep hill forever.

○

Recent Scholarship

Canada's contact with Japan began with an eccentric and little-known adventurer named Ranald MacDonald. MacDonald, born to the factor (or supervisor) of a Hudson's Bay trading post in 1823, became convinced that his native Indian mother's family had come from Japan and smuggled himself into Hokkaido in 1845 to seek his roots. He was sent to Nagasaki where he became the first teacher of English in Japan and helped train, among others, the interpreter who served the Japanese when Commodore Perry arrived in 1853. MacDonald died in 1894, unable to convince anyone that his stories of Japan were true. Regular contact between Canada and Japan had to await the completion of the Canadian Pacific Railway in 1886. Travelling via passenger ship and the Canadian transcontinental railroad became the fastest way to reach Japan and the rest of East Asia from either Europe or North America.

But despite Canada's early links with Japan, interest in things Japanese remained largely confined to missionaries, diplomats, and others with a special interest in the island nation. Systematic and sustained study of Japan at Canadian institutions of higher learning started with the arrival of Ronald Dore at the University of British Columbia in 1956. There he lectured on Japanese language and society. In the subsequent three decades, governments and private institutions have funded the development of four centres for teaching and research, with less comprehensive instruction in an additional thirty-three colleges and universities. Two university research institutes and a number of private research organizations also deal with Japan. Three Japanese prime ministers—Kakuei Tanaka, Masayoshi Ohira and Yasuhiro Nakasone—made major gifts on the occasion of official state visits to

Canada to encourage Japanese studies. All Canadian specialists on Japan stand in debt to the government of Japan and the Japan Foundation for these benefactions. John Howes received his BA from Oberlin University, and his MA and PhD from Columbia University. A specialist in modern Japanese intellectual history, he is the author of Pacifism in Japan: The Christian and Socialist Tradition (University of British Columbia Press: 1970) as well as Tradition in Transition: The Moderniza-tion of Japan (Macmillan: 1975), and adapted and translated, with Nobuya Bamba, Hideo Kishimoto's edited volume of essays Japanese Religion and the Meiji Era (Obunsha: 1956). He has taught at Columbia and the University of British Columbia, where he was associated with the Institute for Asian Research, and is currently Professor of Japanese History and Director of the Japan Studies Program at Obirin University.

JAPANESE STUDIES IN CANADA

John F. Howes

Canada established diplomatic relations with Japan when it opened a Tokyo consulate in 1928. There two of its first representatives, Hugh Keenleyside and Russell Kirkwood, wrote important monographs on Japanese history and so continued the British tradition of scholarly diplomats. Meanwhile Canadian missionary scholars had already started to publish studies in what amounted to a reversal of their primary mission—the propagation of information about Japan and its religions in the English language. The warm relations which had developed between the two nations for the most part because of the work of missionaries ended in the hysteria of the Pacific War. A network of Japanese-language schools which had been established by immigrants broke up when the Canadian government, fearing sabotage, moved all those of Japanese ances-try away from the coast. One of the few good results that have come out of this wartime experience is the dispersion of the Japanese Canadian community throughout Canada and the very high levels of education that many of its members have received.

Two other results of the War were the introduction of the study of the Japanese language among the members of the majority population and the extension of American cold-war hysteria into Canadian politics. The outbreak of the Pacific War in 1941 caught both the United States and Canada with almost no individuals who could speak Japanese and at the same time gain the confidence of the authorities. Public hysteria meant that those of Japanese descent, whatever their citizenship, were not trusted, yet the need for interpretation and translation was great. Out of this necessity, language courses were established in Ottawa and Vancouver in 1943. They were administered and in part taught by missionaries at home because of the war. Graduates of these programs formed the nucleus for postwar Canadian expertise on Japan.

The second result of the war is symbolized by the tragic death of the Canadian scholar/diplomat Herbert Norman. Norman, the son of Canadian missionaries, had published his seminal *Japan's Emergence as a Modern State* (Institute of Pacific Relations, 1940; rpt. in John W. Dower, *Origins of Modern Japanese State: Selected Writings of E.H. Norman*, Random House, 1974) immediately before the Pacific War. He entered the Canadian diplomatic corps and in 1947 became the chief Canadian diplomat in the Occupation of Japan. After the Communists took over China, unscrupulous American politicians tried to advance their own careers by claiming that traitors had 'sold' China into Communism. Norman, sympathetic to the common people and for a short time as a student at Cambridge University a Communist, became the target of these irresponsible accusations. As the United Nations' representative in the attempt to solve the Suez Crisis of 1957, he took his own life. The suicide became a major irritant between the United States and Canada. It is one of the points in which Canadian attitudes and institutions with regard to the study of Japan differ from those in America. This history, though important in shaping Canadian attitudes toward Japan, bears very little on the teaching and research that takes place in Canadian institutions now. It is increasingly shaped by the current relationship with Japan which now affects most areas of Canadian life.[1]

INSTRUCTION

Discussion of instruction in Canadian universities must start with mention of the responsibility for higher education under the Canadian Constitution, for Canadian policy on education differs from that in many more centralized societies. In part because one quarter of the Canadian population was French, the framers of the Canadian Constitution in 1867 left the control of education in the hands of the provincial governments. The francophone population centred in Quebec, and provincial responsibility for education allowed Quebec to preserve its pattern of instruction linked closely with the Catholic church. The founding fathers did not envisage the importance that higher education would assume, with the result that they also left it under provincial auspices. Now representatives of the federal government can talk about a national policy to better educate Canadians about Japan, but implementation remains the domain of the provincial governments. Material about Japan must be introduced in each case not only in competition with the normal inertia inherent in fixed curricula, but also to reflect each provincial government's estimate of the importance of Japan to itself.

Provincial control over the priorities of education and the great distance between major educational institutions in the east and west hampers co-ordinated development. Four thousand kilometres separate the two major Canadian centres of instruction on Japan, in Vancouver and in Toronto; the third centre, Montreal, lies over five hundred kilometres to the east of Toronto; and the easternmost point where there is instruction on Japan is more than 1200 kilometres farther east. The next largest centre of instruction on Japan, Edmonton, lies almost thirteen hundred kilometres northwest of Toronto and similarly distant from Vancouver to the southwest. Thus distance adds to the difficulty in the development of a coherent national plan caused by Canada's political framework.

A further impediment to an integrated national program is that Canadian centres of culture are usually at least as close to similar centres in the United States as they are to other Canadian centres. Montreal is about equidistant from Boston, New York, and Toronto. Toronto is much closer to Buffalo than to Montreal, and Seattle is much closer to Vancouver than the closest Canadian cities of any size east of the Rocky Mountains: Edmonton and Calgary. The physical proximity of large population masses in the United States leads urban Canadians to think in regional north-south rather than national terms.

Within this pattern of provincial responsibility for education and strong foreign regional influence, a 1972 report of the Senate of Canada first set forth what would become a pattern for Japan studies. It recommended the development of 'centres of excellence (perhaps one each in British Columbia, Ontario, and Quebec)' around which regional colleges and universities could develop programs on Asia, including Japan.[2] Later decisions fleshed out this concept with the ultimate development of the current centres of strength.

When the members of Senate considered the development of such centres, they thought primarily of language instruction, and with some notable exceptions, strengths in Japan Studies have developed where students are encouraged to master the Japanese language. All well-established programs on Japan include Japanese language. A number of other institutions are beginning language instruction; if they follow earlier precedent, they will establish related courses on Japanese culture as the language program grows. Twelve Canadian universities and colleges now offer language instruction: Toronto, York, McGill, Montreal, British Columbia, Alberta, Victoria, McMaster, Windsor, Capilano College, Douglas College, and Vancouver City College.

Among the institutions that teach Japanese language, two are distinguished by the length of their commitment to Asian Studies, the sophistication of their study programs, their facilities for research, and the volume of research results. The first is in Toronto and the second is in Vancouver. Two other centres are rapidly developing, one in Montreal and the other in Edmonton. In the case of each of these centres, instruction in languages, literature, and culture is the responsibility of a program organized along area lines, while other instruction and research on Japan takes place in departments throughout the university. Thus, the history of Japanese literature is taught in the same department as Japanese language, while the politics of Japan is taught in the department of political science. The division of the study of Japan among the various parts of the university helps integrate the Japanese experience into areas where the overwhelming bulk of the empirical data is taken from Western Europe and North America. At the same time, it means that the specialist on Japan in any given department may find himself isolated. A proven method to offset this effect is to have a committee or institute that co-ordinates all the research in a university that deals with a certain geographical area. All four of the large Canadian centres have such organizations.

RESEARCH

Although, for most universities, commitment to Japan studies starts with instruction, those trained in research who also teach must continue to seek new understandings of their subject matter. Most Canadian research in Japan studies is carried on by single investigators, as with other fields in the humanities and social sciences. Because individuals find their own topics and pursue them in their individual ways, joint research is relatively infrequent. When it exists, such co-operation usually results from the spontaneous coming together of individual investigators who discover they have common interests. Such researchers in tandem often produce results more noteworthy than the sum of the individuals' work.

Consequently, it is important to identify such nodes of activity and excellence. To recognize them in Canadian Japan studies is particularly important because the total number of Japan specialists is small and the number of fields within Japan studies in which Canada can make an important international contribution is limited. A survey of research in progress in 1987 across Canada indicated that eight fields of study merit notice. These are business, prehistory, law, cultural anthropology, linguistics, modern literature, intellectual history, and the Japanese-Canadian experience. In each of these fields researchers in a number of institutions regularly work together on common problems.

Japanese business and economy

Of those responding to the survey from Ontario, thirty-five indicated a research interest in the business and economy of Japan. They worked at eleven universities. Only thirteen of the total listed publications that appear to have come out of their research. This indicates that for the others the research interest is relatively new. Only seven reported a knowledge of the Japanese language, so one can further assume that those with no language rely either on

Western-language sources or on those who can do their reading in Japanese for them.

Although the percentage of researchers with a knowledge of the language was low in comparison with other areas of research among Japan specialists, the fact that more than thirty of these Ontarians identified Japanese economics and business as a field of interest indicates a significant concentration of talent in one area of Japan studies and one area of Canada. Further, members of the group concentrated their attention in fields, like statistics, where cultural variables make relatively little difference. The resultant findings can be easily compared with those of other economies and integrated into comparative courses.

Individual Ontario researchers who identified Japanese business or economics as an area of investigation were in the following universities: Carleton, Ottawa, Toronto, Osgoode Hall, York, McMaster, Guelph, Queen's, Western Ontario, Wilfrid Laurier, and Windsor. Topics of research, as reflected in publications, included, all with reference to Japan, international economics and business transactions; macroeconomics; technology transfer; overseas investments, particularly in Canada; public sector management; management style; banking systems; and the importation of Canadian manufactured goods.

The three among these universities whose faculty members do research on Japanese economy and business with the greatest concentration of expertise are York, McMaster, and Carleton. Considerable co-operation has existed between the relevant faculty members in these institutions over a number of years. Though no mechanism exists to explore the extent of co-ordination between these researchers, it is clear that Ontario has the necessary numbers and community of interest for continuing fruitful collaboration. If they could overcome the obstacles posed by distances, the individual scholars with similar interests in Quebec, Manitoba, Alberta, and British Columbia might join with those in Ontario to form a Canadian organization for the study of Japanese business. A possible locus for this interest is the newly formed Japan Social Sciences Association of Canada.

Prehistory

In Japan, prehistory, defined as the time before written records exist, continues into the eighth century. A horde of material artifacts compensates to some extent for the lack of written records. Most scholars in this specialization work, of course, in Japan. A high proportion of the remainder teach and do their research in Canada. The work of Fumiko Ikawa-Smith at McGill is well known. Gary Crawford teaches at the University of Toronto and studies the prehistory of Hokkaido, as does William Hurley, also on the faculty at Toronto. B. Chisholm now studies in Japan after having finished a dissertation at Simon Fraser University. Richard Pearson at the University of British Columbia includes detailed research on Japan in his more general interest in the prehistory of Northeast Asia.

The breadth of Canadian interest in this period of Japanese history has been illustrated in the definitive *Windows on the Japanese Past*, which Pearson edited and published in 1986 (Ann Arbor, The University of Michigan Center for Japanese Studies). It consists of contributions of scholars from across the world with a number from Canada. The work's high standards and innovative approaches demonstrate how a few Canadian scholars have organized research in a carefully defined field and orchestrated fruitful collaboration.

Law

The study of Japanese law in Canada has developed largely at the University of British Columbia although recent initiatives at Osgoode Hall in Toronto indicate a developing interest in eastern Canada.[3]

The UBC program developed after a short visit across Canada by Morishima Akio, a professor of environmental law at Nagoya University. Morishima spent one week in Vancouver at the time on a trip financed by the Japan Society for the Promotion of Science and the Canadian Social Sciences and Humanities Research Council. During that interval, an enthusiastic law student, Wilfred Wakely, persuaded a far-seeing dean, Kenneth Lysyk, to meet with Morishima. The program began from that chance meeting. Morishima returned in 1980 to teach for six months. Sufficient interest developed at UBC during that time so that the Law School could persuade Malcolm Smith to accept a position in Japanese law in 1981.

In the succeeding six years, Smith developed a full program of teaching and research on Japan. It utilized visiting professors from Japan, involved Canadian professors of law in co-operative research projects with colleagues in Hokkaido University, assisted Japanese graduate students who wanted to study Canadian law, and produced a first generation of young lawyers competent in Japanese language and equipped to work on projects that involved both countries. When Smith left to return to his native Australia and the University of Melbourne, the UBC program enjoyed the support of all the members of the faculty. Because of the collaborative work with Hokkaido, half of them had worked in Japan and enjoyed an acquaintance with its legal system.

In the fall of 1987, Stephen Salzberg replaced Smith. Salzberg, trained in Japanese and Chinese literature as well as law, plans to build on the foundation which Smith built. One of the major elements of his program will be to demonstrate how the relations between Japanese law and Canadian law, as part of the British common-law tradition, differ from those which characterize the relation between Japanese and American law. While it trains Canadians to deal with Japan, the program will also promote the understanding of Japanese law in the many nations more familiar with Commonwealth traditions than those of the United States.

While UBC moves ahead with a general program in Japanese Law, Jean-Gabriel Castel of Osgoode Hall, the law school of York University, reports that he has organized an exchange of instructors with the Faculty of Political Science at Kobe University. It is possible that this may develop into further cooperation which would provide training in Japanese law close to Canada's major population centres.

Anthropology

Four anthropologists with a speciality on Japan in Montreal provide another node of particular Canadian competence. Fumiko Ikawa-Smith heads McGill's Centre for East Asian Studies and its Department of East Asian Languages and Literatures. Her work in Japanese prehistory has already been mentioned. Margaret Lock at the same university works in medical anthropology with a Japanese speciality. Clare Fawcett is finished her doctorate in anthropology at McGill and will move to l'Université de Montreal as a postdoctoral fellow, where she will work with Bernard Bernier. These four anthropologists working within a few kilometres of each other constitute part of a larger complex that includes anthropologists who specialize on a number of Asian countries. This group shows signs of great promise.

Linguistics

In western Canada, a number of specialists work on the structure, tense, aspect, and modality of the Japanese language. Those at the University of British Columbia include Soga Matsuo and Bernard St Jacques. Members of the group at the University of Alberta are Fujimura Taiji, Kawashima Michiko, Ohta Kaoru, Terakura Hiroko, and Sonja Arntzen. These researchers meet regularly to compare the results of their studies which have wide-ranging implications for our understanding of the Japanese language and how best to learn it.

Modern Literature

Scholars at a number of institutions have specialized on modern, and particularly twentieth-century, literature. They include Kathy Merken at McGill, Anthony Liman and Tsukimura Reiko at Toronto, and Tsuruta Kin'ya at the University of British Columbia. The research that results from the studies of members within this group is characterized by a concentration on language and style. With careful analysis and attention to details, the general meanings and themes of a work of literature become apparent. This dependence on specifics provides for a greater assurance that the author's intentions have been recognized than more impressionistic searches after themes usually provide.

Modern History

Several historians at universities across Canada have co-operated for a number of years on the intellectual history of modern Japan and in particular Western influences on modern thought. They include Yuzo Ota of McGill, Hamish Ion of the Royal Military College in Kingston, Cyril Powles of Trinity College, the University of Toronto, Sinh Vinh of the University of Alberta, and John Howes at the University of British Columbia. Until they moved to Japan, Bamba Nobuya and George Oshiro worked with members of the group. Co-operative studies have included work on pacifism and Christianity in Japan along with the intellectual legacy of Nitobe Inazo. The experience of immigrants and their families has been the subject of several volumes of essays issued under the leadership of K. Victor Ujimoto.

PROSPECTS

Discussion of university research on Japan naturally leads to a consideration of the future directions of study. The results of Japan Studies programs in Canada are now becoming apparent. Canadian-trained Japan specialists work in Australia, New Zealand, the United States, Japan, and Canada itself. They have worked as trilingual—for Canada has two national languages—guides, entertainers, and Pavilion officials in international exhibitions—Tsukuba Expo 85 and Vancouver Expo 86. One became the first Canadian-born official interpreter for a Japanese minister of state during a visit to Canada. Another has chaired the Vancouver city committee to chart new directions for economic growth. A number are now employed in Japanese consulates in Canada. Younger students are inspired to study the Japanese language by the success of these individuals.

The list could go on. All those concerned with the training of these individuals feel justifiable pride. Yet the small number of people involved and their almost exclusive location in Vancouver demonstrates the need for future development. After all, the responsibilities of interface between Canada and Japan which these Canadians have now started to share have been handled for more than a century by Japanese. In comparison to the Japanese, who flock to Canada to learn English, the few who trickle in the other direction to further their knowledge of Japanese seems woefully inadequate. Yet their value is great. The complexity of the relations between the two countries and the contribution Japan makes to world culture increase daily. The responsibility to ensure that representatives of the two societies get together for the common good has become too great to entrust to either side alone.

It is clear that efforts to train oncoming students in the language and culture of Japan must increase. First, the curriculum in the public schools throughout Canada must gradually adapt to the reality that Canada faces west across the Pacific as well as east toward Europe. Relatively little has been accomplished to date in this level of basic reorientation. Secondly, research must continue to discover more effective means of Japanese-language instruction. Twenty-year-olds are no longer told, as I was informed by a well known American Japanologist when I started Japanese in 1945, that the Japanese language 'is impossible to learn but you should try your best'. One can learn Japanese as a young adult, but not without great effort and perseverance. Research to improve instruction and financial assistance to those who start must continue to have priority. At British Columbia, Alberta, and Toronto in particular, Japanese-language specialists work continuously to improve texts and methods of instruction. The results are apparent in the well known text by Matsuo Soga of the University of British Columbia, *Foundations of Japanese Language*. Toronto's innovative course by Nakajima Kazuko utilizes new technology like the Xerox Star. Second, the need for those well trained in Japan and its language is spreading east across Canada from the West Coast. Japanese plants in Canada's manufacturing heartland require individuals who can assist the inevitable adjustments as quite different customs and values take root in Canadian soil. More people able to work intelligently within Japan and Japanese culture must be trained throughout Canada, but particularly in eastern Canada.

Another question requires reference to history. In the mid-nineteenth century, both the Japanese and Westerners considered their nations distinctly different. The Japanese quickly responded to the Westerners' interest in what seemed strange. They liked what appeared most at variance with what they knew at home. This led the Japanese to a kind of ethnographic approach to their own nation.

The ethnographic view of Japan's culture as unique has continued. As most specialists will agree, this interpretation no longer fits. Take the example of the Noh drama, according to the old view peculiarly Japanese and in need of special explanation if non-Japanese were to understand it. Now Noh has become part of the world understanding of drama. Western playwrights and authors borrow from its techniques and make them their own. Those with little understanding of drama still find Noh opaque, but those who understand theatre accept Noh as part of man's common tradition of drama, no more in need of special explanation than other classical forms tied to distant cultures.

The understanding of Noh is not a unique case. The same is true of other elements of Japanese culture. In this way, 'Japan studies' has changed greatly. This is not to say that the study of those peculiarly Japanese elements, like Noh, Kabuki, Gagaku, Haiku, and numerous others, no longer require support. Rather, it is to say that they no longer require support because they are uniquely Japanese but because they form an important part of man's common cultural heritage. To master them still requires great application and patience, whether the student be Japanese or non-Japanese, and study of them still results in new understanding of man's common cultural legacy.

At the same time as it continues to fit traditional Japanese culture into a world context, 'Japan studies' must encompass a whole new world of research and teaching to help those within and outside Japan come to grips with Japan's new international role as a major element in the evolving world culture and economy. Japan Studies has developed significantly in the past thirty years in Canada, and Canadian specialists look forward to working with colleagues throughout the world as a new concept of Japan Studies emerges. As Japan Studies in Canada develops, Canadians must find better ways to encourage and support their nucleus of informed specialists and dedicated students interested in areas other than Europe and North America. Only then can the significant achievements of the last thirty years mature to meet the needs of the future.

○

Before World War II, few serious books about Canada were available in Japan, other than various official surveys or reports prepared by the Japanese Ministry of Foreign Affairs and its posts in Canada, plus a small number of stories about Japanese emigrants in Canada, often including their personal observations. Kunpei Matsumato's 1903 book Beifu-Oun-Roku *[American Winds, European Clouds] based on Prime Minister Hirobumi Itoh's earlier trip to North America and Britain,* Keikoku Kashiwamura's North America: A Field Survey *(1913), Tamiji Naito's* The World through a Camera: Canada and Latin America *(1916), Jinshiro Nakayama's 2,037-page* Kanada-no-Hoko *[A Canadian Encyclopedia] (1922), and Takashi Ito's* The Canadian Federation *(1941) provided the first descriptions of Canada to Japanese readers. These were supplemented by highly specialized publications such as* Canada's Steel Industry *by Manabu Sano (1919) and* The Establishment of a Central Bank in Canada: Its Process and the Problems Encountered *(1935) by Teruo Nishimura. While the post-war years saw the publication of a handful of additional titles and surveys by government and trade institutions such as the Japan External Trade Organization (JETRO), only illustrated coffee-table publications and travel books, which helped to promote Canada's image as a 'country of forests and lakes', were commonly available.*

Indeed, until the 1960s and 1970s, serious interest in Canada was limited to a small number of diplomats, researchers, businessmen and travel writers. But in 1977, a small group of academics formed what eventually became the Japanese Association for Canadian Studies (JACS). The development of the field since then has been so impressive, in terms of both quantity and quality, that it is now difficult to imagine that Canadian Studies, as an academic subject, was virtually non-existent in Japan until the mid-1970s. While translations and adaptations of Canadian books and papers constitute the majority of Japanese works related to Canada, new material based upon field studies and original research and analysis is now being increasingly produced.

After graduation from the University of Missouri, Kensei Yoshida became Tokyo correspondent for the Associated Press and later Newsweek. In 1975 he joined the staff of the Canadian Embassy in Japan, first as media relations and publications liaison and subsequently as academic relations officer. Co-author, with John Saywell and Suzanne Firth, of Kanada wo Shiru *and a contributor to* Motto Shiritai Kanada, *he has also translated numerous Canadian books and articles for Japanese readers. Professor Yoshida currently teaches in the School of International Studies at Obirin University.*

CANADIAN STUDIES IN JAPAN*

Yoshida Kensei

In the immediate postwar years, Japan was so preoccupied with the United States that Canada received very little attention. But with the improvement of trade relations, interest in Canada began to grow. In his essay *Land of Canada and Friends of America* (1954), Tanaka Kotaro, the Chief Justice of the Supreme Court, described Canada's political system and constitution. On a more popular level, *A Country Called Canada* (1955), by Azuma Ryozo, provided a general, if occasionally impressionistic, view of Canada's geography, history, society, and relations with Japan. It remained one of the most popular books about Canada for nearly two decades. In 1963, the Institute of World Economy published *The Study of Canada*, perhaps the first objective and comprehensive review of Canada's various aspects, particularly its economy, industry and relations with England and the United States, ever to come out in Japan. Another, less well-known, book was *Canada* (Life World Library Series, 1964) which was translated by Yoshizawa Seijiro, a former Japanese Ambassador to Canada. Yoshizawa also contributed a chapter about Canada and its relations with Japan to *North America, Australia and New Zealand: Modern World 1* in the Area Studies Lecture Series (Tokyo: Diamond, 1970). Miyake Takeo published *The Canadian Economy* in 1968.

Until the 1960s and early 70s, Canadian Studies, as such, remained in an embryonic stage. Gradually, however, several Canadian authors were introduced to Japanese intellectuals through translations of their works. The most notable examples included George Woodcock's two-volume *Anarchism* (1968),

Northrop Frye's *The Modern Century* (1971), *The Critical Path: Essays on the Social Context of Literary Criticism* (1974), *The Educated Imagination* (1969), and *Anatomy of Criticism: Four Essays* (1980), and *The Scalpel, the Sword* by Ted Allan and Sydney Gordon (1974). Important historical and philosophical works about Japan by E.H.Norman[1] also appeared in translation. Although these books probably had little direct impact in Japan on the development of Canadian Studies *per se*, they contributed to the growing interest in Japan as a result of the fact that the authors (and the subject, in the case of *The Scalpel, the Sword*) were Canadians. Seymour Lipset's *Revolution and Anti-Revolution* (1972), which discussed major sociological differences between Canadians and Americans, was one of the most important books dealing with Canada to be translated into Japanese during this period.

The turning point in the development of Canadian Studies in Japan occurred in 1977, when the predecessor of the Japanese Association for Canadian Studies (JACS), the Kanada Kenkyu-Kai (Association for Canadian Studies), was organized. The same year saw the publication of five scholarly articles about Canada in *Kokusai Mondai*, a monthly magazine published by the Japan Institute of International Affairs (which began to publish a series of pamphlets on Canada for the Japanese Foreign Ministry around 1970). These essays covered Canada's relations with Japan, federalism, politics and government, foreign relations, the economy and race relations. Subsequent publications of note included the translation of three textbooks for Japanese university students: *The Pelican History of Canada* by Kenneth McNaught, *The Canadian Economy: Structure and Development* by Ian M. Drummond and, in 1978, *How Are We Governed?* by J. Ricker and J. Saywell. The Canadian government subsidized these textbooks which were distributed to many Japanese academic institutions and scholars. They became essential reading for both Japanese-Canadian specialists and their students and, in many respects, provided the cornerstone for the development of Canadian Studies in Japan. Also in 1977, the four-volume *Complete Collection of E.H. Norman's Works* was translated by Okubo Genji and published by Iwanami Shoten.

Between 1978 and 1982, a number of other important books about Canada were translated, including J.M.S. Careless's *Canada: A Story of Challenge*, John Saywell's *Canada: Past and Present*, Paul Blanchard's *Le Canada Français*, *Introduction to Canadian Politics and Government* by W.L. White, R.H. Wagenberg and R.C. Nelson, and *Our Nature—Our Voices* by D.M. Tomkings and others. Two historical documents were translated, with extensive annotations, during this period: Ranald MacDonald's *Japan, Story of Adventure of Ranald MacDonald, First Teacher of English in Japan, A.D. 1848-49* and Jacques Cartier's *The Voyage of Jacques Cartier*.

CONTRIBUTING FACTORS

Several factors explain this growing interest in Canada. E.H. Norman, considered by many Japanese intellectuals to have been a particularly astute and sensitive Japanologist as well as a highly capable diplomat, inspired a number of Japanese scholars to become interested in his (and his Methodist missionary family's) role in Japan and his country as well. In addition, this period followed Canada's widely-publicized international peacekeeping activities, the awarding of the Nobel Peace Prize to Lester Pearson in 1957, Canada's Centennial and the World Exposition held in Montreal in 1967, and the Quebec crisis of 1970. The 100th anniversary of the arrival of the first Japanese emigrant in Canada took place in 1977, and the 50th anniversary of Japan-Canada diplomatic relations in 1979 resulted in further publicity about Canada. With the election of the colourful and charismatic Pierre Trudeau and his 'Third Option' foreign policy, as well as the establishment of diplomatic relations with the People's Republic of China, Canada began to attract much greater attention among Japanese scholars. Trade relations between the two countries had developed enormously. In every respect, Canada waited to be studied more carefully.

This emerging interest was stimulated by the *Report of the Commission on Canadian Studies* (commonly known as The Symons Report)[2] and a joint communiqué issued in Ottawa by Prime Ministers Tanaka and Trudeau in September 1975. The communiqué committed each government to donate $1 million for the promotion of Japanese Studies in Canada and Canadian Studies in Japan. This step paved the way for Canada's Department of External Affairs to establish a Canadian Studies course at Tsukuba University and Keio University in 1976. Funds became available for the translation of the three university-level textbooks already mentioned, as well as a number of scholarship and research programs for Japanese graduate and post-graduate students. These included the Faculty Enrichment Program, and a book donation program to the National Diet Library and selected universities in Japan. External Affairs also contributed to the establishment of the Japanese Association for Canadian Studies.

These efforts produced some highly rewarding results. Successive visiting professors, from Vivian Nellis of York University to John Schultz of Mount Allison University, have lectured at Tsukuba and Keio universities, as well as at International Christian University, Tokyo University, Sophia University, and many other Japanese institutions. They have also served as resident advisors on Canadian Studies and as a convenient link with the Canadian academic community for Japanese researchers. One result is that Tsukuba now has several Canadianists in its area studies and other programs. The 'seed' was considered to have developed so much that, in 1988, External Affairs transferred responsibility for the visiting professor program to the Japanese Ministry of Education. The translation of textbooks on Canadian history, politics and economy provided Japanese researchers interested in Canada with the first authoritative books in their own language and helped to spawn many valuable papers and books.

The various other government-supported programs have given many Japanese researchers the opportunity to visit Canada and make first-hand observations, gather research materials, establish contact with Canadian academic institutions and scholars and develop Canadian-content courses, or hold study sessions. These visits and seminars have led to the publication of a considerable number of papers, The book donation program has made Canadian reference materials and books available to Japanese researchers. No doubt, these programs have contributed substantially to the development of Canadian Studies in this country.

The establishment of the Japanese Association for Canadian Studies (JACS) was significant in many respects. It united more than 100 Japanese researchers studying particular aspects of Canada in isolation or in small groups scattered throughout Japan. Many of them had considered (many still do) Canada only as a marginal extension of their primary specialties.

The birth of JACS provided a central organization. With a current membership of about 250, the Association now holds an annual conference and a number of regional study seminars. Its *Annual Review of Canadian Studies*, inaugurated in 1979, provides a forum for academic discussions about Canada or Canada-Japan relations, and its *Newsletter* describes the various activities of the Association and its four regional chapters. JACS has published collections of academic essays, entitled *Various Issues in Canadian Studies* (1987), *Introduction to Canadian Studies* (1989), and a three-volume bibliography of Japanese books and papers on Canada. A group of JACS members in eastern Japan has also compiled a bibliography of foreign-language books on Canada in their collections. Moreover, the Association has established a research award for outstanding papers by students and young scholars.

As noted, with the exception of a few pioneering works such as *The Study of Canada*, Canadian Studies in Japan essentially began with a series of books translated from English or French into Japanese in the 1970s and the early 1980s. Even today, works of translation abound: Hugh L. Keenleyside's *Memoirs of Hugh L. Keenleyside: Vol. 1, Hammer The Golden Day* (1984), Ramsay Cook's *The Maple Leaf Forever* (1984), F. Henry Johnson's *A Brief History of Canadian Education* (1984), Marcel Mauss's *Essai sur les variations saisonnières des sociétés Eskimos: Etude de morphologie sociale* (originally published in 1906), *Politics, Law and the Constitution: The Canadian Experience* by John Saywell (1987), John W. Holmes's *Life with Uncle: The Canadian-American Relationship* (1987), *Approaches to Canadian Politics* edited by John H. Redekop (1989), and *Federal-*

ism and the French Canadians by Pierre Trudeau (1990). These translations have provided important resources for Japanese students of Canada. (Although, strictly speaking, not falling under the category of Canadian Studies, the following translations of Canadians books are also worthy of note: John O'Neill's *Sociology as a Skin Trade: Essays Toward a Reflexive Sociology* (1984), *Institutional Care of the Mentally Impaired Elderly* by Jacqueline Singer Edelson and Walter H. Lyons (1986), several books by Marshall McLuhan such as *The Extensions of Man* and *The Gutenberg Galaxy*, R. Murray Schafer's *The Tuning of the World* (1986), and several books on Glenn Gould including Tom McGreevy's *Glenn Gould Variations* and Geoffrey Payzant's *Glenn Gould: Music and Mind*.)

Compared with the number of translated works, the number of original books about Canada by Japanese is relatively small, although it has been growing in recent years. However, a large number of papers have been published on subjects ranging from multi-cultural education to labour law, local government and literature. Few generated much interest beyond a small circle of experts in the respective fields. Nor is the academic standard of these works considered sophisticated enough for them to be published in Canada, with a few notable exceptions concerning Japanese Canadians and Canada-Japan relations.

Among these exceptions are several books and papers by the late Bamba Nobuya, who was instrumental in establishing the Japanese Association for Canadian Studies, and Ohara Yuko, a leading Japanese authority on Canadian history and historiography. In addition to acting as supervising editor of the Japanese version of *The Pelican History of Canada* and co-translator of *How Are We Governed?*, Bamba wrote or edited several other works, including *International Politics of Identity*, which provided an analysis of the Quebec question; *Canada: A Country of the 21st Century; Diplomacy of Middle Powers*; and *Political Science Series IV: International Relations* and *General Survey of Canadian History*. Among his many papers on Canada are 'Development of Canada-Japan Relations', 'An Introduction to Canada-Japan Cultural Exchanges: Canada Methodist Mission and Japan's Meiji-Era Thinkers', 'Japanese Occupation and (E.H.) Norman', 'Canada's New Identity', and 'From Big-Power Diplomacy to Co-operative Diplomacy: Middle Powers Such as Canada and Japan Should Co-operate'.

Ohara Yuko, translator of Ramsay Cook's *The Maple Leaf Forever* and co-translator of *The Pelican History of Canada* and Careless's *Canada: A Story of Challenge*, has written *A Modern History of Canada* and co-authored *The General Survey of Canadian History*, regarded as one of the best introductory books about Canada available in Japanese. It covers Canada's history from the time of New France and outlines various postwar issues such as the search for a national identity, Quebec, regionalism, and the country's economic development. Ohara has also produced a number of important analytical papers, including 'The Decision on the "National Policy" and John A. Macdonald', 'National Policy and the American System: A Preliminary Comparative Historical Study of Canada and the United States', 'Canada's Role in the Abolition of the Anglo-Japanese Alliance and Japan's Reaction', '"National Policy" and the Development of Nationalism in Canada's Historiography', and 'A Case Study: Separatism in a Modern Country'.

Other highly qualified observers of Canada include Okamoto Tamio who has written extensively about Canada's welfare system and recently co-authored *Canada's Social Security*. In 1973, Kuwahara Masahiro co-authored *Development of Public Service Labour-Management Relations: The Situation in the U.S. and Canada* and in 1985 wrote *Operating Standards of Sexual Employment Equality Laws in Canada, the United States and Japan*. He and his colleague at Niigata University, Kunitake Teruhisa, have been particularly interested in Canadian labour relations and labour law. In 1989, Kunitake produced *Canada's Labour Relations and Law*, a comprehensive historical and constitutional analysis of Canada's labour relations and federal labour laws. Ito Katsumi's *Study of the French Canadian Question: Minority Problems and Their Challenge to the Canadian Federation* (1973), based upon his PhD dissertation, was perhaps the first academic study of the Quebec situation by a Japanese. Okuma Tadayuki, who recently joined the faculty of Hiroshima Shudo University from the Japan Institute of International Affairs, has been closely following Canada's economic and diplomatic relations with the United States and the rest of the world.

Kimura Kazuo of Tsukuba University, who has long been interested in Canada's economic history, particularly in connection with nineteenth-century British imperialism, has written an important analytical survey of Canada from the 1840s to the 1890s under the title *The Birth of the Dominion of Canada* (1989). Sekiguchi Reiko of the University of Library and Information Science has written extensively on multiculturalism and multicultural education. She edited *An Interdisciplinary Study of Canada's Multicultural Education* (1985). Her more recent work includes *Canada and Japan: A Comparison of Life Culture* (1990), a study of women at different stages from birth to death. Ayabe Tsuneo of Tsukuba University has co-authored and edited two important books. One of them, *A Study of Canada's Ethnic Cultures: Multiculturalism and Ethnicity* (1988), is based upon field surveys by Japanese and Canadian anthropologists. *More about Canada* (1989) analyzes Canada's history and geography, social and cultural make-up, education, politics, economy and relations with Japan.

Iino Masako of Tsuda Women's College, who has written numerous academic papers on Japanese Canadians, has co-written *Mutual Hostages* (University of Toronto Press, 1990) with J.L. Granatstein, Patricia Roy, and Takamura Hiroko. This book deals with Japanese Canadians in Canada and Canadian civilians and prisoners of war in Japan during World War II. Iizawa Hideaki of Yamagata University has written a number of papers on Canada's economy and economic policy. Takenaka Yutaka of Caritas Women's College has a special interest in the history and culture of French Canada.

Other major works of study on Canada by Japanese researchers include *Introduction to Canadian Commercial History* (1981) by Toyohara Jiro, *American and Canadian Geography* (1985) by Masai Yasuo, *General Overview of Canadian Law* edited by Morishima Akio and Kenneth Lysyk (1982), *Ecology in Canadian Forests* by Kojima Satoru (1986), *To Know Canada* by Yoshida Kensei, John Saywell and Suzanne Firth (1985), *Contemporary Quebec: French Culture in North America* by Osabe Shigeyasu, Nishimoto Koji, Higuchi Yoichi, et al. (1989), *Political Analysis of Canadian Federalism with Special Reference to Inter-governmental Grants* (1985) by Iwasaki Mikiko, *Structure of the Canadian Society* by Shimpo Mitsuru (1989), and *Group Rights, Democracy and the Plural Society* by Kato Hiroaki.

Other specialists of note include Kobayashi Junko (education), Osanai Satoru and Suzuki Kenji (law and the Constitution), Murai Kohei (divorce laws), Suzuki Toshikazu (language rights), Sakamaki Toshio (company laws), Sato Sadayuki (economy), Sato Hideo (U.S.-Canada-Japan economic relations), Uchida Masahide(Canadian Methodists in Japan), Toyohara Jiro (economic history), Tabayashi Akira (agricultural geography), and Sasaki Tetsuro (the co-operative movement in Nova Scotia).

Over the years dozens of papers have been presented at JACS conferences and study sessions and published in the *Annual Review of Canadian Studies*. As mentioned earlier, in 1977 *Kokusai Mondai* published five scholarly articles on Canada, while the Japan Association of International Relations featured the 'Historical Evolution of Canada-Japan Relations' in its 1985 issue of *International Relations*. The National Institute for Research Advancement devoted an entire issue of its magazine, *NIRA*, to 'The Future of Canada and Japan' in 1988; 'Recent Policy Issues in Canada' was the publication's theme in 1989.

Some of the above books and papers exhibit an especially high level of scholarship and insight. Professors Bamba and Ohara, in particular, have contributed greatly to improving the standard of Canadian Studies in Japan, both in their respective areas of specialization and in other fields. Generally speaking, however, with the exception of Japan-Canada relations and the history of Japanese Canadians, and works by several specialists in other fields, Japanese research has fallen short of the standards that would qualify for publication in Canada.[3] Many articles are little more than adaptations of Canadian publications with little new insight or analysis to offer. Some researchers, out of affection for Canada, have even painted overly biased and romantic pictures of the country.

JAPANESE CANADIANS AND NATIVE STUDIES

In contrast, many excellent, original surveys about Japanese Canadians and native Canadians have been produced. This tradition began in 1962 when a group of Japanese and American social scientists published *The Japanese Village That Crossed the Ocean*, a highly praised socio-cultural field study of Japanese Canadians in Steveston, British Columbia. This was followed by *Indians in the Far North* (1965), based on on-site observations of the Hare Indians by the anthropologist, Hiroko Sue (Hara); *Canadian Indians: A Dying Minority People*, a description of the social changes taking place among Indians on reserves by Shimpo Mitsuru (1968); and *Canadian Eskimos*, a detailed documentary of the lifestyles of the Inuit by journalist Honda Katsuichi (1972). Irimoto Takashi's studies of native ways of life and folklore are described in the book, *From the World of Canadian Indians* (1983). Miyamae Hiroshi documented his life with Indians on reserves in two separate books published in 1983.

Not surprisingly, within the area of Canadian Studies, Japanese researchers have demonstrated special interest in the subjects of Japanese Canadians and Canada-Japan relations. Substantial literature on Japanese Canadians had been produced before the war, either by emigrants such as Nakayama Jinshiro or by the Japanese-Canadian newspaper *Tairiku Jiho [Continental Times]*. After 1945, discrimination against Japanese in Canada was the focus of much study. Shimpo Mitsuru of Waterloo University has written extensively, and sympathetically, about this situation in *As if Chased Away with Stones: Social History of Japanese-Canadians* (1975), *History of Discrimination against Japanese Emigrants* (1985), and several other books and papers. Iino Masako and Takamura Hiroko have written several more objective papers on Japanese emigrants to Canada. Others have studied the demographic and social impact of emigration on Japanese villages or analyzed the history and content of Japanese-Canadian newspapers and Japanese-Canadian literature. Writer Kudo Miyoko has documented the experiences of Japanese Canadians in books such as *The Yellow Soldiers* and *The Picture Brides*.

While no definitive study of Japan-Canada relations is available, the subject has been surveyed extensively from several angles. The May 1985 issue of *International Relations* included eight related articles, many of them based upon original research: 'The Anglo-Japanese Treaty of Commerce and Navigation and the Japanese Emigration Problem in Canada' by Iino Masako, 'John Wesley Dafoe and Japanese-Canadian Relations during the 1920s' by Ohara Yuko, 'Canada-Japan Trade Conflicts during the 1930s and the Japanese Motion for Invoking Trade Protection Law' by Ohata Tokushiro, 'Canadian Attitude toward the League of Nations during the 1930s' by Unno Yoshiro, 'Canada and the Pacific War' by Shiozaki Hiroaki, 'Universalism in Canadian Foreign Policy and Japan: Canadian-Japanese Relations 1946-1968' by Okuma

Tadayuki, 'Prime Minister Trudeau and the Development of Canadian Relations with Japan and the Pacific' by Mito Takamichi, and 'Canadian Political Dynamics and Canada-Japan Relations: Retrospect and Prospect' by John Saywell. As already mentioned, Bamba Nobuya has written a number of articles on Canada-Japan relations, including the contributions of Canadian Methodist missionaries in the early nineteenth century and, more recently, concerning economic and political ties.

LITERATURE

Japanese research in the field of Canadian literature deserves special mention. Although few Canadian novels have been translated into Japanese,[4] there is growing interest in Canadian literature. A group called the Canadian Literary Society of Japan has been meeting regularly since 1982 and publishing *Studies in Canadian Literature* annually since 1986.

The pioneer in the field is Hirano Keiichi, a Canadian-born professor of literature who started teaching Canadian literature at the University of Tokyo in the 1950s. He was one of the first Japanese introducing this subject in academic journals during the 1960s and early 1970s. As a result, Japanese readers and critics were exposed to a wider selection of Canadian literature.

In 1983, Hirano co-authored *Literature of Commonwealth Countries* and, in 1986, *Anthology of Canadian Short Stories*. Tsutsumi Toshiko has written a number of papers on Margaret Laurence, Alice Munro, Joy Kogawa, W.O. Mitchell and others. In 1982, Asai Akira published *An Introduction to Canadian Literature* and in 1985, *Modern Canadian Literature: An Overview, Writers and Their Works, References*. Also in 1985, Asai co-edited, with Tsuruta Kinya of the University of British Columbia, *Cherry Blossoms and Maple Leaves: Comparative Study of Japanese and Canadian Literature*. A pioneering work in the field, this book includes contributions by six Japanese and nine Canadian scholars. Minami Ryosei has shown a particular interest in George Ryga, Tamura Kenji in Susanna Moodie, and Chida Akio in Hugh MacLennan.

While most Japanese experts on Canadian literature have focused on such themes as the Canadian search for national identity, national and individual survival, regionalism and ethnic consciousness, *Cherry Blossoms and Maple Leaves* was an interesting departure. Not only did it result from the collaboration of both Japanese and Canadian researchers, but the contributors made an effort to compare seemingly incomparable world views, literary styles and themes as expressed by the novelists of both countries.

PROBLEMS AND PROSPECTS

The field of Canadian Studies in Japan, which before the 1970s was something of an oddity, has grown tremendously in less than fifteen years. No longer is it confined to examining the problems of Japanese Canadians or limited to books translated from English or French.

The number of Japanese researchers interested in Canada has been steadily increasing and, with more of them having the opportunity to study or conduct research in Canada, the quality of Canadian Studies in Japan continues to improve. Another positive development has been the participation of an increasing number of specialists in the areas of law, history, economics, geography, international relations, social security, anthropology, English literature, etc. Research on Japanese Canadians and Japan-Canada relations is particularly advanced.

More and more universities and colleges, including Tsukuba, Kwansei Gakuin, Sophia, Hokkai Gakuin, Daito Bunka, Tsuda, Caritas and Obirin, offer at least one introductory course on Canada. Many academics include some Canadian content in their lectures and some universities occasionally offer seminars or lecture series on Canada. In addition to the annual conference of the Japanese Association for Canadian Studies, colloquia are held by the organization's regional chapters and the Canadian Literary Society. Academic papers on Canada now appear in many publications including JACS's *Annual Review of Canadian Studies* and *The Journal of American and Canadian Studies* published by Sophia University's Institute of American and Canadian Studies. The Canadian government helps to finance major research projects and the publication of books dealing with Canada or Canada-Japan relations through a number of programs. As a result of these and other efforts, the number of Japanese graduate students interested in Canada has increased significantly in recent years.

Less encouraging is the fact that demand for Canadian specialists at Japanese universities is still very limited. Also, Canadian Studies have yet to be recognized as an independent field of research as have for example, American Studies. This probably explains why there are so few Japanese researchers wholly involved in Canada. The Japanese market for academic books about Canada remains so small that most publishing houses hesitate to publish them without some kind of university or government subsidy. Research material about Canada is still difficult to obtain. Although many Canadian books and government documents have been donated to Japan's national library and the libraries of several leading universities, there is yet no comprehensive index to indicate their availability and location.

While Ottawa's financial assistance is extremely useful in promoting Canadian Studies in Japan, the requirement of producing a publishable manuscript on the basis of a three-to-five-week visit makes it difficult for most recipients to conduct extensive and accumulative research. The Japanese government also provides various research grants, but thus far only a few Canadianists have received such assistance. Canadian government scholarships and fellowships have permitted many young Japanese scholars to enroll in graduate and post-graduate programs at Canadian universities, but all too few of them have returned home with degrees and few have found teaching positions at universities.

In spite of these problems, Canadian Studies in Japan can be expected to expand, given the rapid increase in the number of original papers published in recent years. In order for the field to develop, however, Japanese researchers will need to improve the quality of their scholarship to the level where they can compete or work collaboratively with Canadian researchers in the areas including, but not limited to, Japanese Canadians and Japan-Canada relations. The final test will be whether their books and papers are considered worthy of publication in Canada.

NOTES

PREFACE

1. Charles J. McMillan, *Bridge Across the Pacific: Canada and Japan in the 1990's* (Ottawa: Canada Japan Trade Council, 1988), p. 51.

2. Quoted in Margaret Atwood, *Survival: A Thematic Guide to Canadian Literature* (Toronto: Anansi, 1972), p.49.

PATRICIA E. ROY

1. *Illustrated British Columbia* (Victoria: J.B. Ferguson, 1884), p. 273.

2. For a fuller history of British Columbia's early attitudes to both Chinese and Japanese immigrants see Patricia E. Roy, *A White Man's Province: British Columbia Politicians and Chinese and Japanese Immigrants, 1858-1914* (Vancouver: University of British Columbia Press, 1989).

3. Vancouver *Daily News-Adverstiser*, 4 May 1889.

4. Vancouver *News-Advertiser*, 16 June 1893.

5. Vancouver *World*, 6 July 1896.

6. Nanaimo *Free Press*, 13 August 1895.

7. Victoria *Colonist*, 28 March 1897.

8. *World*, 29 April 1897; Executive Council of British Columbia, Minute Approved by the Attorney General, 30 April 1897, copy in National Archives of Canada (hereafter NAC), Department of Immigration Records, file 9309.

9. *News-Advertiser*, 10 February 1899.

10. While visiting a museum of the Ainu people in Hokkaido, I was struck by the similarities between their artifacts and those of the northwest coast Indians found in Canadian museums.

11. Canada, *Report of the Royal Commission on Chinese and Japanese Immigration* (Ottawa: King's Printer, 1902), p. 347.

12. Ibid., p. 340.

13. New Westminster *British Columbian*, 1 June 1893.

14. *Report of the Royal Commission on Chinese and Japanese Immigration.*

15. Francis Carter-Cotton to Lieutenant-Governor in Council, 13 February 1899, British Columbia, *Sessional Papers*, 1900, pp. 497-9. See also Carter-Cotton's comments in his newspaper, the *News-Advertiser*, e.g., 20 January 1899.

16. *Report of the Royal Commission on Chinese and Japanese Immigration*, p. 327.

17. *Colonist*, 3 May 1900.

18. J.B. Whitehead (Tokyo) to Marquis of Salisbury, 19 May 1900, NAC, Department of Immigration Records, file 9309; *Colonist*, 8 August 1900.

19. British Columbia, *Statutes*, 64 Vict., c. 11. The Act was named after the British colony in South Africa which earlier devised a language test to limit immigration from India.

20. S. Shimizu to Governor General Minto, 1 September 1900, NAC, Governor General's Records, A1 series, vol. 97, file 1600.

21. Quoted in A. MacLean to F.C.T. O'Hara, 11 February 1905, NAC, Laurier Papers, #95432-3.

22. *Report of the Royal Commission on Chinese and Japanese Immigration*, pp. 329 and 389.

23. Vancouver *Province*, 8 July 1903.

24. *Colonist*, 23 April 1905.

25. Vernon *News*, 1 October 1903.

26. *British Columbian*, 24 September 1903.

27. W. L. Mackenzie King, Royal Commission into the Methods by Which Oriental Labourers Have Been Induced to Come to Canada, *Report* (Ottawa: King's Printer, 1908), p. 3.

28. Nelson *Daily News*, 11 July 1907.

29. *Province*, 13 August 1907.

30. Nanaimo *Free Press*, 22 August 1907. Such claims were not mere newspaper rhetoric. See, for example, the letter of R.G. Macpherson to the editor of the *Canadian Courier*, 31 July 1907, NAC, R.G. Macpherson Papers, vol. 1.

31. *Province*, 9 September 1907.

32. *Semi-Weekly World*, 16 August 1907.

33. Nosse to Grey, 7 October 1907, NAC, Governor General's Records, G21 series, vol. 199, file 332/1.

34. W.L.M. King to Richard Jebb, 30 December 1907, NAC, King Papers, #6149-50.

35. *News-Advertiser*, 31 October 1907.

36. *Colonist*, 3 January 1908.

37. Fred Yoshy to W.L.M. King, 7 February 1908, NAC, King Papers, #9846.

38. Canada, House of Commons, *Debates*, 11 January 1909, p. 61.

39. *Saturday Sunset*, 2 December 1911.

40. W.D. Scott to Mr Cory, 14 April 1916, NAC, Department of Immigration Records, vol. 61, file 9309/7.

41. Victoria *Times*, 14 March 1919; F.S. Barnard to Secretary of State, 1 April 1919, NAC, Robert Borden papers, vol. 41.

42. Vancouver *Sun*, 15 April 1919; *Province*, 11 April 1919

43. *World*, 28 December 1920.

44. House of Commons, *Debates*, 8 May 1922, p. 1509.

45. For further details on this legislation and its background, see Patricia E. Roy, 'The "Oriental Menace" in British Columbia', in S.M. Trofimenkoff, ed. *The Twenties in Western Canada* (Ottawa: National Museum of Man, 1972), pp. 243-58.

46. Joseph Pope to Governor-General's Secretary, 23 July 1923, NAC, Governor-General's Records, G21 series, no. 332, vol. 17b; Consul General Ohta to J.A. Robb, 22 August 1923, NAC, King Papers, J4 series, vol. 80, file 636.

47. New Westminster *News*, 6 June 1914.

48. *Sun*, 8 June 1921.

49. *World*, 9 July 1923.

50. Percy Reid to A.L. Jolliffe, 30 July 1924, NAC, Department of Immigration Records, vol. 61, file 9309/12.

51. *British Columbian*, 18 July 1925.

52. British Columbia, Legislative Assembly, *Journals*, 17 December 1924, p. 6.

53. Deputy Minister of Immigration to W.L.M. King, 20 February 1925, NAC, Department of Immigration Records, vol. 61, file 9309/12.

54. British Columbia, *Journals*, 29 February 1928, pp. 4-5.

55. O.D. Skelton to W.L.M. King, 23 March 1926, NAC, King Papers, #C61214.

56. E.g. British Foreign Office to Sir J. Tilley, Ambassador to Tokyo, 30 April 1926, copy in NAC, Governor-General's Records, G21 series, no. 332, vol. 18.

57. O.D. Skelton, Memo on Japanese Immigration [after an interview with Mr Matsunaga], 10 September 1925, NAC, King Papers, #C61278.

58. A copy of the agreement may be found in A.L. Jolliffe, 'Confidential Memorandum Relating to Japanese Immigration', NAC, Department of Immigration Records, vol. 62, file 9309/13.

59. W.L.M. King, Diary, 25 May 1928, NAC, King Papers.

60. Vancouver *Star*, 18 June 1928.

61. *Star*, 18 June 1928.

62. H.M. Marler to King, 5 September 1919, NAC, King Papers, #140108-124.

63. Nanaimo *Free Press*, 17 November 1937.

64. T.D. Pattullo to W.L.M. King, 26 January 1938, NAC, King Papers, J2 series, vol. 293.

65. King Diary, 16 February 1938.

66. House of Commons, *Debates*, 17 February 1938, p. 574.

67. Minutes of Interdepartmental Committee, 7 March 1938, NAC, Department of External Affairs Records, D1 series, vol. 16. Keenleyside's recollections of this investigation may be found in Hugh L. Keenleyside, *Memoirs of Hugh L. Keenleyside: Vol. 1 Hammer the Golden Day* (Toronto: McClelland and Stewart, 1981), pp. 479-82.

68. Vancouver *Sun*, 26 April 1938.

69. Government of British Columbia, *British Columbia in the Canadian Confederation* (Victoria; King's Printer, 1938), p. 353.

70. House of Commons, *Debates*, 24 May 1938, p. 3200.

71. King, Diary, 26 August 1938.

72. 'Confidential Report to Council on The Oriental Problem in Canada', [30 August 1938], NAC, King Papers, #210488-99 (italics in original). The proposal would also apply to China as there was considerable pressure within Canada to treat China and Japan equally.

73. Randolph Bruce to O.D. Skelton, 13 December 1938, NAC, King Papers, #C122612-3.

74. Bruce to W.L.M. King, 16 December 1938, NAC, King Papers, #C122614-6; Canadian Minister to Japan to King, 30 January 1939, NAC, Department of External Affairs Records, G1 series, file 799-25.

75. King, Diary, 31 January 1939.

76. King, Diary, 10 January 1939.

77. House of Commons, *Debates*, 4 August 1944, p. 5916.

78. House of Commons, *Debates*, 16 June 1952, pp. 3300-2.

79. Minister of Citizenship and Immigration, Memo to the Cabinet, 18 April 1955, Department of External Affairs Records, file 989-40.

80. Memo, 17 November 1952; Secretary of State for External Affairs to Canadian Ambassador, Tokyo, 5 March 1954, Department of External Affairs Records, file 9890-40; Memo on Japanese Immigration prepared for Mr Howe's visit, 8 October 1956, all in NAC Department of External Affairs Records, file 9890-40.

81. A.M. Nicholson, House of Commons, *Debates*, 15 January 1958, p. 3384.

82. Quoted in Klaus H. Pringsheim, *Neighbors Across the Pacific: The Development of Economic and Political Relations between Canada and Japan* (Westport, Conn.: Greenwood Press, 1983), pp. 134-5.

83. One discriminatory feature remained. Asians were at a disadvantage in sponsoring distant relatives as immigrants.

84. House of Commons, *Debates*, 14 August 1964, pp. 6823-4.

85. *Financial Post*, 15 August 1965; C.M. Isbister to the Minister of Citizenship and Immigration, 6 December 1965, NAC, Department of Citizenship and Immigration Records, vol. 128.

86. *Financial Post*, 22 August 1970.

87. Pringsheim, *Neighbors*, p. 211.

KAZUKO TSURUMI

1. Masao Gamō, 'Sutebusuton no Nikkeijin Shakai' [The Japanese-Canadian Community in Steveston], in Gamō, ed., *Umio Watatta Nihon no Mura* [The Japanese Village that Crossed the Ocean], Chūōkōronsha, 1962, pp. 14-15.

2. Kazuko Tsurumi, 'Kizokukan' [Sense of Belongingness], in Gamō, ed., *Umio Watatta. . .*, p. 201.

3. Forrest E. La Violette, *The Canadian Japanese and World War II* (University of Toronto Press, 1948) p. 280, footnote.

4. '[T]he decision to liquidate [Japanese property] without consent of the owners was essentially a political one and was based upon the War Measures Act.

'Decision to liquidate all Japanese properties, except liquid assets such as stocks and bonds, was made in January, 1943. . . . Prior to January, 1943, no property, except for fishing boats and automobiles, had been sold without the consent of the owner.' La Violette, op.cit., p. 208.

5. Ibid., p. 96.

6. Gamō, 'Ijūsha no Ayunde Kita Michi' [The History of Immigrants], in Gamō, ed., p. 45.

7. Mio Tomekichi, 'Kanada no Nikkei wa Kōfuku' [The Japanese Canadians in Canada are Happy], *Tairiku Jihō* [The Continental News], 3 November 1959.

8. La Violette, op.cit., p. 248.

9. Ibid., pp. 258-70.

10. Ibid., p. 273.

11. W.A. Carrothers, 'Oriental Standards of Living', in *The Japanese Canadians*, by Young, Reid and Carrothers (Toronto: University of Toronto Press, 1939) pp. 224-82.

12. In 1958, the income of the fishermen in Steveston according to our survey was as follows:

highest (minority)	about $12,000 - $15,000
middle (majority)	$ 8,000 - $ 9,000
lowest (minority)	$ 3,000 - $ 4,000

13. As for the voting behaviour of first- and second-generation Japanese Canadians in Steveston, the highest percentage of them voted, in the 1958 election, for the CCF (the socialist party). The reasons given were: 'they stand for fishermen's interest'; 'they are fair to the minorities, including Japanese Canadians'; 'during the war they were thoughtful to the Japanese Canadians', etc. In comparison, Mrs Mizutani's voting for the Social Credit Party was not representative of the political attitudes of the Japanese Canadians in Steveston.

14. All the interview materials used above are quoted, except for otherwise noted, from chapters on 'Chinji-mari-kō (1) and (2), Kazuko Tsurumi, Sutebusuton Monogatari [Steveston Stories], (Chūōkōron-sha, 1962), pp. 116-56.

15. Democracy Betrayed: The Case for Redress, National Association of Japanese Canadians, 1985; Justice in Our Time: Redress for Japanese Canadians, National Association of Japanese Canadians, 1988.

16. Shinichi Tsuji, Nikkei Kanada-jin: Redressing the Past: Self-Portraits of Japanese Canadians (Shōbun-sha, 1990) pp. 19-24.

17. The New Canadian, 13 July 1990.

A. HAMISH ION

1. Sir Herbert Marler to Secretary of State for External Affairs, 22 May 1936, RG 25 G1, vol. 1668, file 537, National Archives of Canada, Ottawa (hereafter NAC).

2. M.S. Gewurtz and P.M. Mitchell, 'Canadians and East Asia: The Missionary Experience' (typescript in the possession of the author, dated 1981), p. 1.

3. See Matsuzawa Hiroaki, 'History and Prospect of Canada-Japan Relations: Through My Personal Experiences', Hokudai Hogaku Ronshu 36 (October, 1985), pp. 623-40, 643-4.

4. See Nihon YWCA hachijunen shi henshu iin kai, Mizu o Kaze o Hikari o Nihon YMCA Hachijunen Shi 1905-1985 (Tokyo: Nihon YWCA, 1987), especially pp.30-6 and pp. 48-9.

5. See Mayama Mitsuya, Owari Nagoya no Kirisutokyo–Nagoya Kyokai no Sosoki (Tokyo: Shinkyo Shuppansha, 1986), p. 67.

6. Ushiyama Setsuai, Kirisutokyo Shinko Dendo Shi: Wara Choro, Dendo no Kiseki (Nagano: Ginga Shobo, 1980).

7. Rosemary B. Gagan, 'Two Sexes Warring in the Bosom of a Single Mission Station: Feminism in the Canadian Methodist Japan Mission, 1881-1895', unpublished 31-page typescript in the author's possession. As the text suggests, it would be mistaken to overemphasize gender warfare in an attempt to see in the mission station a microcosm of the confrontation of feminism and patriarchy in late Victorian Canadian society.

8. Toyo Eiwa Jo Gakuin hyakunen shi hensan jikko iinkai, Toyo Eiwa Jo Gakuin Hyakunen Shi (Tokyo: Toyo Eiwa Jo Gakuin hyakunen shi hensan jikko iinkai, 1984), pp. 17-18.

9. Ushiyama, pp. 35-9.

10. For Edward Warren Clark and Canadian missionaries, see A. Hamish Ion, 'Edward Warren Clark and the Formation of the Shizuoka and Koishikawa Christian Bands (1871-1879)' in Edward R. Beauchamp and Akira Iriye, eds, Foreign Employees in

Nineteenth Century Japan (Boulder, Colo: Westview Press, 1990), pp. 171-89.

11. See Iida Hiroshi, *Shizuoka Ken Eigaku Shi* (Tokyo: Kodansha, 1967).

12. Kuranaga, Takeshi, *Kanada Mesojisuto Nihon Dendo Gaishi* (Tokyo: Kanada Godo Kyokai Senkyoshikai, 1937), p. 20.

13. Nippon Seikokai rekishi hensan iinkai, *Nippon Seikikai Hyakunen Shi* (Tokyo: Nippon Seikokai kyomuin bunshokyoku, 1959), p. 60.

14. Unpublished letter to Secretary of the Society for the Propagation of the Gospel in Foreign Parts, 27 December 1875, quoted in Carmen Blacker, *The Japanese Enlightenment: A Study of the Writings of Fukuzawa Yukichi* (Cambridge: Cambridge University Press, 1969), p. 150.

15. *Mission Field* (June, 1877): 422, cited in Grace Fox, *Britain and Japan 1858-1883* (Oxford: Clarendon Press, 1969), p. 31.

16. Kuranaga, p. 108.

17. Ebara Sensei denki hensan iinkai, *Ebara Soroku Sensei Den* (Tokyo: Ebara Sensei denki hensan iinkai, 1924), p. 205.

18. 'Interesting Journal of a Missionary Tour in Japan', *Missionary Notices*, third series, no. 3 (1877): 258.

19. C.S. Eby to A. Carman, 31 August 1898, H13 F1, Folder 3, in United Church of Canada Archives (hereafter UCCA), Victoria College, University of Toronto, Toronto, Canada.

20. *Minutes of the Japan Conference of the Methodist Church of Canada, 1899*, p. 16.

21. *Fifty-seventh Annual Report of the Missionary Society of the Methodist Church of Canada* (Toronto: Methodist Church of Canada, 1882), p. xxxi.

22. Charles S. Eby, *The Immediate Christianization of Japan: Prospects, Plans, Results* (Tokio: Japan Mail, 1884).

23. C.S. Eby to A. Carman, 31 August 1898, H13 F1, Box 3, UCCA.

24. Shizuoka Eiwa Jo Gakuin hachijunen shi hensan iinkai, *Shizuoka Eiwa Jo Gakuin Hachinen Shi* (Shizuoka: Shizuoka Eiwa Jo Gakuin, 1971), p. 189.

25. Kano Masanao, *Nihon no Rekishi 27: Taisho Demokurashii* (Tokyo: Shogakukan, 1979), pp. 43-4.

26. M.S. Murao and W.H. Murray Walton, *Japan and Christ: A Study in Religious Issues* (London: Church Missionary Society, 1928), p. 57. See also John McNab, *White Angel of Tokyo* (Toronto: Centenary Committee of the Canadian Churches, n.d.). While another Canadian, Arthur Lea, had pioneered penal rehabilitation in Gifu in the eighteen-nineties, the activities of women missionaries tended to attract more attention.

27. John G. Waller, *Our Canadian Mission in Japan* (Toronto: Joint Committee on Summer Schools and Institutes of the Church of England in Canada, 1930), p. 20.

28. *Hell Screen*, W.H.H. Norman, trans. (Tokyo: Hokuseido, 1948). Other important missionary writings include: Egerton Ryerson, *The Netsuke of Japan* (London: G. Bell, 1958); H.H. Coates and Ryugaku Ishizuka, *Honen, the Buddhist Saint* (Kyoto: Chionin, 1924); Robert Cornell Armstrong, *Just Before the Dawn: The Life and Work of Ninomiya Sontoku* (New York: Macmillan, 1912); and Armstrong, *Light From the East: Studies in Japanese Confucianism* (Toronto: Toronto University Press, 1914).

MIWA KIMITADA

1. His original articles—'Nihonshika Noman no hakken: kaikyu shikan de ha nai dochaku e no shiten [The Discovery of E.H. Norman, Historian of Japan: A Perspective on the Indigenous vs. the Class Conflict Theory] and 'Shinsyu no nomin to Noman' [Farming People of Nagano Prefecture and E.H. Norman]—are collected as chapters 9 and 10 of Miwa Kimitada, *Kyodotai ishiki no dochakusei* [The Indigenous Character of a Community], (Tokyo: Sanichi Shobo, 1978).

2. Roger W. Bowen, *Innocence Is Not Enough: The Life and Death of Herbert Norman* (Vancouver: Douglas and McIntyre, 1986); James Barros, *No Sense of Evil: The Espionage Case of E. Herbert Norman* (New York: Ivy Books, 1987).

3. Norman was wont to say of himself 'I also come from Nagano Prefecture', both as a way of pleasing members of his audience from Nagano and as a means of surprising his listeners and thereby capturing their attention. In a talk entitled 'People Under Feudalism', which he gave in Nagano City on the occasion of the memorial service for his father, the Reverend Daniel Norman, Herbert Norman began thus and then went on to pay tribute to nationally renown local leaders of the nineteenth century Liberty and Popular Rights movement, reminding his audience that they, too, could contribute greatly to the reconstruction of Japan as a democracy. Although the date on the copy of the manuscript of this talk sent to General MacArthur is 21 June 1947, the jubilant report of his homecoming carried by the prefectural newspaper *Shinano Mainichi* makes it clear that the ceremony was actually held June 22. It was the manuscript of this talk, found in the MacArthur Memorial Library, that prompted my initial essays on Norman.

4. See Maruyama Masao, 'Affection for the Lesser Names: An Appreciation of E.H. Norman', *Pacific Affairs*, XXX, No.3 (September, 1957): 249-53.

5. John Dower, ed., *Origins of the Modern Japanese State: Selected Writings of E.H. Norman* (New York: Random House Pantheon Asia Library, 1976).

6. See F.G. Notehelfer's review in *Monumenta Nipponica*, XXX, No.4 (Winter, 1975): 471. Nevertheless, Jansen concluded his own introduction to the *Cambridge History of Japan, Volume II: The Nineteenth Century* by acknowledging Norman's pioneering work: 'A field that E.H. Norman, almost half a century ago, described as fertile and awaiting cultivation, has brought different harvests for workers in many seasons, but its riches are far from exhausted.'

7. Okubo Genji, ed., *Habato Noman zenshu* [The Complete Collection of E.H. Norman's Works], Volume IV (Tokyo: Iwanami Shoten, 1978), p. 531.

8. Although my research took me in other directions, Norman continued to hold an important position in my perception of Japanese-Canadian relations. Speaking at the Department of External Affairs on 21 March 1985, for example, I pointed out that although in the prewar period Nitobe Inazo had tried to create a 'bridge across the Pacific' without succeeding, Norman had contributed very substantially to just such a construction. See Miwa Kimitada, 'Canada and Japan in the "Pacific Age"', *Journal of American and Canadian Studies*, No.1 (Spring, 1988): 59-60.

9. This rewarding trip was made possible through the support of many people, especially Mr Furushima Norio, Director of the Japan Foundation in Toronto, who together with Mr David Moore of his staff and Mrs Fukuroi Mariko, First Secretary at the Japanese embassy in Ottawa, provided me with a copy of the Peyton Lyon report

and arranged interviews with both Professor Lyon and Mrs Irene Norman, the widow of Herbert. I was also able to speak with Professor A. Hamish Ion of the Royal Military College, Kingston, and with Professor Cyril Powles in Toronto, the son of a Canadian Anglican missionary, who was also born in Karuizawa in the same decade as Norman.

10. Peyton Lyon, 'Loyalties of E. Herbert Norman', a report prepared for External Affairs and International Trade, Canada, 18 March 1990, pp. 2-3.

11. Paul Gassell, writing in the Ottawa *Citizen* for 31 March 1990, suggests that more than scholarly differences are involved, pointing to the relationship between 'the role. . . . Barros played in trying to tarnish Norman's name and the influence Barros has had over some Conservative MPs'.

12. Nakazono Eisuke, *Orimposu no hashira no kage ni*, 2 vols. (Tokyo: The Mianichi Press, 1985); Nakano Toshiko, *H. Noman: aru demokuratto no tadotta michi* (Tokyo: Libroport, 1990).

13. In addition to the Bowen volume cited above, see Charles Taylor, *Six Journeys: A Canadian Pattern* (Toronto: Anansi, 1977) and Cyril Powles, 'E.H. Norman and Japan' in Roger Bowen, ed., *E.H. Norman: His Life and Scholarship* (Toronto: University of Toronto Press, 1984).

14. Nakano, p. 285.

15. Howard Norman, 'Norman of Nagano', quoted ibid., p. 33.

16. Bowen, *Innocence*, p. 26.

17. Nakano, p. 284.

18. Ibid., p. 285.

19. Ivan Morris, *The Nobility of Failure: Tragic Heroes in the History of Japan* (New York: Holt, Rinehart and Winston, 1975).

20. Bowen, ed., *E.H. Norman*, pp. 5-6.

21. *Sekai* (January, 1991): 317.

22. Ibid., 319.

23. *Sekai* (January, 1991): 317.

24. Ibid.: 319.

25. Ibid.: 323.

26. Dower, op. cit., p. 27.

27. It appeared in the December, 1990 issue of *Bungei Shunjyu*. Advance reports of its sensational content appeared in the Japanese mass media, with the result that the December issue sold out completely on November 9, the first day it went on sale, despite the fact that the print run had been increased to 900,000—300,000 more than usual.

28. *Bungei Shunju* (December, 1990): 119.

29. *Bungei Shunju* (January, 1991): 138.

30. *Bungei Shunju* (December, 1990): 141.

31. Ibid.: 99.

32. Okubo Genji, *Noman zenshu*, p. 531.

33. *Bungei Shunju* (December, 1990): 119.

34. Harada Kumao, *Saionji-ko to seikyoku* [Prince Saionji Kinmochi and Political Situations], vol. 4 (Tokyo: Iwanami: Shoten, 1951) pp. 129, 132.

35. Dower, op. cit., p. 27.

36. *Sekai* (May, 1990): 369.

37. Ibid.: 371.
38. *Sekai* (May, 1990): 370.
39. Ibid.: 376.

OHARA YUKO

1. Frank H. Underhill, 'Canadian Writers of Today: J.W. Dafoe', *Canadian Forum*, 13,145 (Oct. 1932): 23.
2. Ramsay Cook, *The Politics of John W. Dafoe and the Free Press* (Univ. of Toronto Press, 1971 [1963]).
3. Ibid., pp. 13-14.
4. John W. Dafoe, 'Our Future in the Empire: Alliance under the Crown', in *The New Era in Canada*, ed. by J.O. Miller (Dent, 1919), p. 290-9.
5. Cook, op. cit., p. 24. Robert Craig Brown and Ramsay Cook, *Canada, 1896-1921: A Nation Transformed* (McClelland and Stewart, 1974), p. 264.
6. Robert Craig Brown, *Robert Laird Borden: A Biography*, vol. II, 1914-1937 (Macmillan of Canada, 1980), p. 84; Cook, op cit. pp. 73-5.
7. John W. Dafoe, 'Canada and the Peace Conference of 1919', *Canadian Historical Review*, 24,3 (Sept. 1943): 233-48.
8. Dafoe, 'Our Future', pp. 287-8.
9. On Canada's role in the abrogation of the Anglo-Japan Alliance and for an appraisal of it, consult author's manuscripts, *viz.*, 'The role taken by Canada in the Anglo-Japanese Alliance abrogation issue and Japan's reaction', *Journal Proceedings of Kokugakuin University*, vol. XV (1977): 197-220, and 'North Atlantic Nation Canada—Canada's attitude to Japan as shown in the Anglo-Japanese Alliance abrogation issue', Japan Association for Canadian Studies, *Annual Report on Canadian Research*, No. 2 (1980): 119-26.
10. John Bartlet Brebner, 'Canada, The Anglo-Japanese Alliance and the Washington Conference', *Political Science Quarterly*, 50,1 (1935): 50.
11. Author's manuscript, 'Anglo-Japanese Alliance abrogation issue', p. 206.
12. Canada, Department of External Affairs, *Documents on Canadian External Affairs*, Vol. 3, pp. 162-3.
13. Ramsay Cook, ed., *The Dafoe-Sifton Correspondence, 1919-1927* (Manitoba Record Society, 1966), p. 41. Sifton to Dafoe, Nov. 18, 1920. In this regard, consult John S. Ewart, *Independence Papers* (Ottawa, 1921), pp. 131-6, 152-9.
14. *Correspondence*, p. 69. Dafoe to Sifton 2 May 1921. The majority of scholars now agree in the assessment that Christie was responsible for devising, organizing and implementing policies opposing the Anglo-Japanese Alliance. See Robert S. Bothwell, 'Loring Christie: The Failure of Bureaucratic Imperialism' (Ph.D. thesis, 1972) Chapter VII.
15. Dafoe Papers, John Stevenson to Dafoe, 13 May 1921.
16. *Correspondence*, pp. 72-3. Dafoe to Sifton, 18 May 1921.
17. *Manitoba Free Press*, 16 May, 31 May, 17 June 1921.
18. *Manitoba Free Press*, 27 June 1921.
19. *Manitoba Free Press*, 30 June 1921.
20. *Correspondence*, pp. 77. Dafoe to Sifton, 30 June 1921.

21. *Manitoba Free Press*, 6 July, 14 July, 25 July 1921.

22. *Manitoba Free Press*, 22 August 1921.

23. *Manitoba Free Press*, 4 July, 1 Sept., 13 Sept., 14 Oct. 1921.

24. Regarding the movement in British Columbia to exclude Asian immigrants, the usefulness of the Anglo-Japanese Alliance becomes clear if one compares the exclusion of the Chinese with that of the Japanese. On this point many historians of Asian immigration to Canada agree: for example, see Donald Avery and Peter Neary, 'Laurier, Borden and a White British Columbia', *Journal of Canadian Studies*, 12,4 (Summer, 1977): 23-4.

25. Kunihira Haraguchi, 'Considerations on Japan-Canada Relations: the dispute over renewal of the 'Lemieux (Gentlemen's) Agreement', *International Politics (Kokusai Seiji)*, No. 58 (1978): 45-68; Klaus H. Pringsheim, *Neighbors across the Pacific: Canadian-Japanese Relations, 1870-1982* (Westport, Conn.: Greenwood Press, 1983), p. 30, note 17.

26. Although it might be going too far to assert this without reference to the *Manitoba Free Press*, nevertheless, for a similar impression see Cook, op. cit. and Murray Donnelly, *Dafoe of the Free Press* (Macmillan of Canada, 1968).

27. For the Pacific Problem Commission, see Mori Nakami, 'The Pacific Problem Commission and Japanese Intellectuals', *Shiso*, No. 728 (1985): 104-27.

28. Institute of Pacific Relations: *Honolulu Session*, June 30-July 14, 1925 (Greenwood Press, rep. 1969), p. 14.

29. Edward D. Greathed, 'Antecedents and Origins of the Canadian Institute of International Affairs' in *Empire and Nation: Essays in Honour of Frederic H. Soward*, ed. by H.L. Dyck and H.P. Krosby (University of Toronto Press, 1969), pp. 91-115.

30. Rowell Papers, Dafoe to N.W. Rowell, 22 March 1921, in Greathed, op. cit., p. 100; ibid, Dafoe to N.W. Rowell, 16 April 1921.

31. Margaret Prang, *N.W. Rowell: Ontario Nationalist* (University of Toronto Press, 1975), p. 415.

32. Nelson Papers, Rowell to John Nelson, 21 November 1925. Greathed, op. cit., p. 102.

33. N.A.M. (Norman A. Mackenzie), 'The Canadian Institute of International Affairs', *Canadian Forum*, 9,106 (July, 1929): 339.

34. Mackenzie King Papers, British Consulate General, San Francisco to His Majesty's Ambassador, British Embassy, Washington, 20 April 1925.

35. Ibid., O.D. Skelton to Prime Minister, 1927; Henry T. Ross to Mackenzie King, 31 August 1927.

36. N.A.M., op. cit., p. 340. Greathed, op. cit., 111-12. Dafoe Papers, Memorandum, Winnipeg, 23 Feb. 1928.

37. Greathed, op. cit., p. 96.

38. Christie Papers, L. Christie to J. Nelson, 21 Feb. 1921.

39. John Nelson, 'Canadian View of Pacific Relations', *Institute of Pacific Relations: Honolulu Session*, pp. 65-8; see also John Nelson, 'Shall We Bar the Yellow Peril', *Maclean's Magazine* (15 May 1922): 13-14, 50, and Greathed, op. cit., p. 105.

40. According to Dafoe, Memorandum (see Note 36), the date was January 31, almost certainly an error by Dafoe.

41. C.P. Stacey, *Canada and the Age of Conflict*, vol. 2: 1921-1948, *The Mackenzie King*

Era (University of Toronto Press, 1981), p. 89.

42. See Peter C. Kasurak, 'The American Dollar Diplomats in Canada, 1927-1941: A Study in Bureaucratic Politics', *The American Review of Canadian Studies*, 9 (1979): 57-71.

43. *Documents on Canadian External Relations*, vol. 4, pp. 30-1.

44. W.L.M. King, 'Canada's Inter-Imperial and Foreign Relations: Address at the Toronto Board of Trade, November 22nd, 1928; reprinted in *Empire Review* (February 1919): 94.

45. Mackenzie King Papers; Debates of House of Commons, 31 January 1928, Unrevised *Hansard*, p. 68.

46. Dafoe Papers, Herbert Marler to Dafoe, 18 April 1930.

47. M. Donnelly, op. cit., pp. 107-8; *Correspondence*, p. 110. Dafoe to Sifton, 30 March 1922.

48. Dafoe Papers, op. cit., Herbert Marler to Dafoe, ibid., Dafoe to Robert L. Borden, 7 Sept. 1929. Dafoe held high hopes of John MacKay, the rector of Manitoba College who had lived in Vancouver and travelled in Asia, becoming the spokesman for the Winnipeg chapter of the IPR. Dafoe to Norman Mackenzie, 16 November 1928.

49. Ibid., Dafoe to Rowell, 14 March 1932.

50. Newton W. Rowell, 'Canada Looks Westward: Opening Address at the Kyoto Conference', *Foreign Affairs*, 3,1 (January 1930): 28.

51. *Canada's Missionary Congress* (Toronto, 1909), pp. 39-47; Prang, op. cit., p. 81.

52. *Debates, House of Commons*, 27 April, 1921, pp. 2647-58.

53. Rowell Papers, R.L. Borden to N.W. Rowell, 7 May 1929.

54. Rowell, 'Canada Looks', pp. 27-33.

55. Rowell Papers, Rowell to Robert Borden, 27 Nov. 1929. Rowell to W.L. Mackenzie King, 28 Nov. 1929, 'Canada and the Institute of Pacific Relations', p. 18. According to Prang, in the few weeks after his return to Canada, Rowell delivered lectures on the Far East issue in major cities from Vancouver to Montreal. Prang, op. cit., p. 456.

56. The report on the Japanese invasion of Manchuria submitted by the Canadian Embassy in Tokyo is notable in that it was 'the first instance in Canadian history of a Canadian embassy reporting that its host country had gone to war with a third country.' To measure the depth of Keenleyside's interest in the Japanese invasion of Manchuria, see Hugh L. Keenleyside, *Memoirs of Hugh L. Keenleyside* (McClelland and Stewart, 1981) trans. Iwasaki Tsutomu, *Tokyo no sara ni Kanada no hata wo* (Tokyo: The Simul Press, 1984), pp. 256-74.

57. Winnipeg *Free Press*, 31 December 1931, cited by Lower, op. cit., p. 34.

58. Winnipeg *Free Press*, 2 April 1932. W.L. Morton, ed., *The Voice of Dafoe: A Selection of Editorials on Collective Security, 1931-1944* (Macmillan of Canada, 1945) pp. 18-22.

59. Winnipeg *Free Press*, 10 December 1932; in *The Voice of Dafoe*, pp. 21-5.

60. 'The Collective System and Manchuria', *Interdependence*, vol. XI (April, 1934): 65-9. Broadcast from Winnipeg 4 March 1934.

61. Cook, op. cit., p. 25.

62. Winnipeg *Free Press* 'Problems of the Pacific', 1, 3, 6, 8, 10, and 14 October 1936.

63. John Nelson, 'Canada's Concern in the Pacific', *Maclean's Magazine* (1 November 1928): 15-16, 56, 58.

64. To cite one example, see Henry F. Angus, 'Urges Votes for Japanese', *The Daily*

Province, 27 March 1934; see also Hugh L. Keenleyside, *Memoirs of Hugh L. Keenleyside*, vol. 2: *On the Bridge of Time* (McClelland & Stewart, 1982), pp. 168-81.

N.B. The author wishes to thank Esso Seikiyu K.K. and the Japan Society for the Promotion of Science, without whose generous funding research trips to Canada in 1981 and 1983, respectively, would not have been possible. In the absence of the original sources, English-language quotations have been translated as accurately as possible from the author's Japanese publication.

EBER H. RICE

1. See in general John Hilliker, *Canada's Department of External Affairs, vol.I: The Early Years 1909-1946* (Montreal and Kingston: McGill-Queen's University Press, 1990).

2. 'The problem of immigration from the Orient can be solved with satisfaction', King had observed, '. . . if it is dealt with as an economic problem, which it is: not as a problem of race, or colour, or creed, which it is not.' William Lyon Mackenzie King, *Industry and Humanity* with introduction by D.J. Bercuson (Toronto: 1973), p. 59.

3. Hilliker, p. 112; W.L.M. King Diary, 18 October 1927.

4. Canadian House of Commons *Debates*, 11 June 1928.

5. Commons *Debates*, 8 April 1930.

6. W.L.M. King Diary, 15 November 1928.

7. 'Marler is conscientious, lacks humour somewhat, will do well'—an interesting juxtaposition of characteristics for a diplomatic representative. In his diary for 12 January 1929, King expressed considerable pleasure that his appointment of Marler drew almost universal praise from many sides, including opposition politicians who opposed the opening of the Legation itself.

8. King Diary, 5 January 1929. King was an astute judge of men and he made the characteristic comment to his diary on this day that 'It is quite clear that it is the social significance of the position which appeals to him and his wife, as well as the opportunity for public service. He is a little too effusive about his desire to meet *my* [underline in original] wishes, to do what I want, etc, but his willingness to use his own means to the extent of $50,000 a year in addition to his salary shows how pleased he is to have the opportunity.'

9. W.L.M. King Papers, King to Marler, 5 January 1929, National Archives of Canada (hereafter NAC), MG 26 J1/58.

10. Marler Proposal Document. A copy of this remarkable document is maintained in the archives of the Canadian Embassy in Tokyo. A second copy is available in the National Archives in Ottawa.

11. Ibid.

12. Hugh L. Keenleyside, *Memoirs*, vol. I: *Hammer the Golden Day* (Toronto: McClelland and Stewart, 1981), chapter 5.

13. Marler Proposal Document, p. 16.

14. King Diary, 5 January 1929.

15. Ibid.

16. Marler Proposal Document.

17. King Papers, 'Memorandum', 5 January 1929, NAC, MG 26 J4/58.

18. King Diary, 30 June 1929.
19. King Papers, Marler to King, 2 October 1929, NAC, MG 26 J1/58.
20. King Papers, Marler to King, 2 October 1929, NAC, MG 26 J1/165. All was not happy upon the arrival of the Marlers, as King notes in his Diary on 15 October: 'Received a letter from Marler, the first from Japan, a rather homesick sort of note—conditions anything but joyous, arrived in a typhoon, etc.'
21. King Papers, Marler to King, 2 October 1929, NAC, MG 26 J1/165.
22. Ibid., King to O.D. Skelton, 25 June 1929. 'It is not my intention', Marler had assured Skelton, 'when we are established at Tokyo to sit down and wait for work to come in. I intend to be as active as possible in gathering information and in assisting in trade matters.' The voluminous reports sent to Ottawa from the Legation throughout Marler's tenure testify that he proved to be a man of his word in this regard.
23. Keenleyside, chapter 12.
24. R.B. Bennett Papers, Beatrice Marler to Bennett, 6 November 1930, NAC, MG26 Series F/249.
25. King Papers, Marler to King, 2 October 1929, NAC, MG 26 J1/165.
26. King Papers, King to Marler, 12 May 1930, NAC, MG26 J1/165.
27. See Bennett Papers, Marler to Bennett, 19 August 1931, NAC, MG26 Series F/249 for details of Marler's proposal.
28. Ibid., Marler to O.D. Skelton, 3 June 1932.
29. Ibid.
30. Mrs Marler subsequently suggested the most plausible explanation for the advantageous purchase—at least when judged from the standpoint of contemporary business customs in Japan. 'We really got it', she wrote to former Prime Minister King, 'because we play golf with Viscount Aoyama.' King Papers, Beatrice Marler to King, 2 January 1932, NAC, MG26 J8/26.
31. R.B. Bennett Papers, Marler to Bennett, 22 December 1932, NAC, MG26 Series F/ 249.
32. Ibid., J. Langley to Secretary of State for External Affairs, 22 May 1933: 'Prior to the execution of the work, steel bars and concrete were tested in the laboratory of Waseda University and field tests of concrete for each floor was conducted as the work progressed. As the floor heights of this building are comparatively high, special care was taken in mixing and placing.'
33. 'The Legation is getting on splendidly, surprisingly so, thanks to the time Herbert spends there every day. What would happen if he did not understand buildings and gardening I hate to think.' King Papers, Beatrice Marler to King, 1 January 1934, NAC, MG26 J8/26.

CARL VINCENT

1. Canada, Department of National Defence, Directorate of History (hereafter DHist), file 840.013, 'Far East Defence, 1921-39'.
2. Great Britain, Public Record Office (hereafter PRO), WO106/2364: 'Report of Defenses 1937'.
3. PRO, WO106/2366: 'July 1938 Notes Major General Grasett'.
4. DHist, file 840.013: 'Far East Defence 1921-39'.

5. Canada, National Archives of Canada (hereafter NAC), J.L. Ralston Papers, MG27 III/B11/46.

6. PRO, WO106/2366.

7. PRO, WO106/2409: 'Policy Re Hong Kong'.

8. Ibid.

9. Ibid.

10. NAC, H.D.G. Crerar Papers, MG30/E157.

11. PRO, WO26/2409.

12. Ibid.

13. Ibid.

14. Ibid.

15. Ibid.

16. Charles Gavin Power, *A Party Politician: The Memoirs of Chubby Power* (Toronto: Macmillan, 1966).

17. NAC, Duff Royal Commission, RG33/120.

18. NAC, Cabinet War Committee, RG2/7/C4653A.

19. NAC, RG33/120.

20. Ibid.

21. NAC, Department of External Affairs, RG25/2865: 'Canadians at Hong Kong'.

22. The regiment also had some powerful political friends, among them the Honourable C.G. Power, Associate Minister of National Defence, who represented a Quebec City riding and had a son in the regiment. Major John H. Price, the regiment's second-in-command, wrote to Power on 13 September to complain that the unit was fed up with 'just killing time' and was anxious to be put to use. Power replied on 22 September to assure Price that he had made 'certain representations' and had 'some hope that events overseas may soon develop to the point that it will be possible for your lot to have the opportunity it deserves.' There seems little doubt that Power exerted his influence when the battalions were being selected, for Mackenzie King in his diary for 19 December, when Hong Kong was under siege, noted that 'Those who have been so keen to send our forces overseas realize the kind of reaction likely to follow in the country where losses occur. . . . It was Power himself who was keenest on having the Quebec Regiment go, he mentioning at the time that his own son was a member of it.' DHist 111.1009/D2, 'Defence in the Far East 1929-1939'; King Diary, v. 394.

23. NAC, RG33/120.

24. NAC, RG33/120.

25. NAC, Cabinet War Committee, RG2/7/C4654.

26. DHist, file 593.013/D5: 'Canadian Reinforcements'.

27. Ibid.

28. NAC, W.L.M.King Papers, MG26/394.

29. Ibid., MG26/407.

30. DHist, file 593.013/D21: 'Hong Kong Policy'.

31. J.R.M. Butler, ed., *History of the Second World War*, vol. 1: *Grand Strategy* (London: HMSO, 1956).

32. W.L.M. King Papers, MG26/394.

33. Ibid., MG26/369.

34. NAC, Ralston Papers, MG27/III/71.

35. NAC, King Papers, MG 26/395.

36. NAC, Duff Royal Commission, RG 33/120.

37. NAC, Crerar Papers, MG30/E157.

38. NAC, Duff Royal Commission, RG33/120.

TAKAHASHI HISASHI

1. K.D. Bhargava and K.N.V. Sastri, 'Campaigns in South-east Asia', in *Official History of the Indian Armed Forces in the Second World War, 1939-44* (New Delhi: Orient Longmans, 1960), p. 8.

2. Major-General S. Woodburn Kirby, et al., *The War Against Japan*, Vol. I, *The Loss of Singapore*, in *History of the Second World War*, United Kingdom Military Series (London: Her Majesty's Stationery Office, 1957), p. 34.

3. J.R.M. Butler, *Grand Strategy*, Vol. II, *September 1939-June 1941*, in *History of the Second World War* United Kingdom Military Series (London: Her Majesty's Stationery Office, 1957), p. 495.

4. Colonel C.P. Stacey, 'Six Years of War: The Army in Canada, Britain and the Pacific', in *Official History of the Canadian Army in the Second World War* (Ottawa: Queen's Printer and Controller of Stationery, 1955), p. 439.

5. Ibid., p. 456.

6. Kirby, pp. 116-17; Bhargava and Sastri, p. 21. General Maltby later recorded that 'the efficiency of the enemy air force was probably the greatest surprise to me'. See Carl Vincent, *No Reason Why* (Stittsville, Ontario: Canada's Wings, 1981), p. 204.

7. Stacey, p. 452.

8. Ibid., pp. 454-5.

9. Kirby, pp. 117-18. Despite his sanguine view of the situation General Maltby did not dare to take risks before the attack. At Hong Kong, every battle position was manned and ready for action before the Japanese attacked.

10. Vincent, p. 45 and pp. 51-2. For details of their training and equipment, see also Stacey, pp. 446-50.

11. Vincent, p. 32.

12. Stacey, p. 448.

13. Bhargava and Sastri, p. 20.

14. Stacey, p. 457. Even the Official British Military History frankly admits that 'the British forces consisted mainly of units employed overlong on garrison duties, indifferently equipped, lacking experience of warfare and even of battle training, and hastily formed into *ex tempore* formations.' See Kirby, p. 146.

15. Stacey, pp. 461-88. For the Japanese side of the story, see Bōeichō Bōeikenkyūsho Senshishitsu [War History Office, National Defence College], ed. *Hong Kong, Chōsa sakusen* [Assault on Hong Kong and Chang-sha], in *Senshi Sōsho* Series [Official History of the Second World War in Asia and Pacific Series], Vol. 47 (Tokyo: Asagumo shinbunsha, 1971).

16. In Canton where the 23rd Army's headquarters was located, General Sakai became furious at the report of this *dukundan senko* or 'field initiative'. Pedestrian Sakai ordered his staff officers to 'pull out the troops at the earliest time and punish

the responsible officers severely by courtmartial'. Sakai even flew to the 38th Division's headquarters to scold them for their indiscipline. See Bōeichō Bōeikenkyūsho Senshishitsu', pp. 151-2. For details of this incident, see also pp. 142-50.

However, this case of serious infringement on command was later settled in a most Japanese-like way. It was decided by the high command of the 23rd Army and the 38th Division that credit was to be given to Wakabayashi and that this problem would be forgotten once and for all. Thus Wakabayashi was made an overnight hero, when he was mentioned in despatches from the Commanding General of the China Expeditionary Army.

Wakabayashi later died a hero's death at Guadalcanal, and for this he was mentioned in despatches for the second time.

17. Vincent, pp. 202-5.

18. Interview with Kamata Shūichi, 16 and 17 Feb. 1991.

19. Ibid.; Interview with Hitosugi Jun'ichi, 17 Feb. 1991. Also see Hohei Dai-230 Rentai Dai-5 Chūtai [The 5th Company, 230th Infantry Regiment], ed., *Michishirube* [The Guidepost: A History of the 5th Company, 230th Infantry Regiment], Shizuoka (not for sale), 1990, pp. 142-4.

20. Fujita Kiyoo, 'Aa Hong Kong kōryakusen' [The True Story of the Capture of Hong Kong], *Renge* [Lotus Flowers] (May 1968): 53-8.

21. For the outline of such intelligence activities, see Sec. 3 of Chap. 2 in 'Dai-38 Shidan Hong Kong kōryakusen sentō shōhō' [The 38th Division Combat Report of the Assault on Hong Kong], Military History Archives, National Institute for Defence Studies, Tokyo.

22. Ibid., Chap. 3

23. Ibid.

24. Bōeichō Bōeikenkyūsho Senshishitsu, p. 322.

25. 'Dai-38 Shidan Hong Kong kōryakusen sentō shōhō', Chap. 9.

26. Dai-38 Shidan Hohei Dai-230 Rentai [The 230th Regiment, 38th Division], 'Hong Kong koryakusen sento shosho' [Combat Report of the Assault on Hong Kong], Pt. 1, Military History Archives. See also Hohei Dai-230 Rentai Dai-5 Chūtai, pp. 116-18.

27. Interview with Kamata, 16 Feb. 1991.

28. Bōeichō Bōeikenkyūsho Senshishitsu', p. 320.

29. The history of the two regiments of the 38th Division is now available. See Hohei Dai-228 Rentaishi Hensan Iinkai [The 228th Infantry Regiment History Editorial Committee], ed., *Hohei Dai-228 retaishi* [The 228th Infantry Regiment History] Nagoya (not for sale), 1973; and Hohei Dai-229 Rentaishi Hensan Iinkai [The 229 Infantry Regiment History Editorial Committee], ed. *Hohei Dai-229 rentaishi* (The 229th Infantry Regiment History) Nagoya (not for sale), 1981.

30. Stacey, pp. 488-9.

31. Winston S. Churchill, *The Second World War*, Vol. 3, *The Grand Alliance* (Boston: Houghton Mifflin, 1950), p. 635.

GREGORY A. JOHNSON

1. This has been demonstrated most persuasively by Christopher Thorne, *The Limits of Foreign Policy: The West, the League and the Far Eastern Crisis of 1931-1933* (London,

1972) and *Allies of a Kind: The United States, Britain, and the War against Japan, 1941-1945* (London, 1978); S.W. Roskill, *Naval Policy Between the Wars*, Vol. 1 (London, 1968).

2. Quoted in J.B. Brebner, *North Atlantic Triangle* (Toronto, 1945), p. 315.

3. National Archives of Canada (NAC), Department of National Defence Records (DND), vol. 5696, file NS 1017-31-2, Naval War Staff, 'Occasional Paper No. 1 Remarks on a Canadian Naval Base in the North Pacific', 28 May 1919. See also Roger Sarty, ' "There will be trouble in the North Pacific": The Defence of British Columbia in the Early Twentieth Century', *BC Studies* 60-63 (1983-84): 3-29.

4. See Documents on Canadian External Relations (hereafter DCER): III, p. 163ff.

5. On this see Hosoya Chihiro, 'Britain and the United States in Japan's view of the International System, 1919-37', in Ian Nish, ed., *Anglo-Japanese Alienation 1919-1952* (Cambridge, 1982); H.P. Willmott, *Empires in the Balance* (Annapolis, Maryland, 1982).

6. Senator Raoul Dandurand to the League of Nations, League of Nations, Official Journal, Special Supplement No. 23, Records of the Fifth Assembly, 1924, p. 222.

7. Some interesting details surrounding the establishment of the Legation can be found in Klaus H. Pringsheim, *Neighbors Across the Pacific* (Westport, Conn.: Greenwood Press, 1983), pp. 32-8.

8. Ottawa *Citizen*, 21 October 1929.

9. Quoted in Thorne, *The Limits of Foreign Policy*, p. 4.

10. Ann Trotter, *Britain and East Asia, 1933-1937* (Cambridge, 1975), p. 72.

11. On this see Thorne, *Allies of a Kind*, passim, and 'The Shanghai Crisis of 1932: The Basis of British Policy', *American Historical Review* 75 (1970): 1616-39.

12. Cahan's speech in Walter A. Riddell, ed., *Documents on Canadian Foreign Policy, 1917-1939* (Toronto, 1962), pp. 516-22.

13. DCER: V, p. 329.

14. Quoted in Richard Veatch, *Canada and the League of Nations* (Toronto, 1975), p. 121.

15. Historians remain divided over responsibility for the incident. F.H. Soward, 'Forty Years On: The Cahan Blunder Re-examined', *BC Studies* 32 (1976-77): 126-38 lays the blame on Cahan while Donald C. Story, 'Canada, the League of Nations and the Far East, 1931-3: The Cahan Incident', *International History Review* 3 (April, 1981): 236-55 argues that Cahan essentially acted in accordance with his instructions and the will of the League. For other examples of Stimson's anger see DCER: V, pp. 317, 329.

16. Ibid., 337ff. See also Stephen J. Harris, *Canadian Brass: The Making of a Professional Army, 1860-1939* (Toronto, 1988), pp. 179-80.

17. It should be pointed out, however, that there is to date no evidence to suggest that military officials were deliberately exaggerating the situation in the Far East.

18. In the view of the present writer, 'correctly' is the apt term. During the period before Pearl Harbor, many believed that the Japanese were not capable of waging a first-class war because they were racially inferior. For an example of how this racialism influenced Whitehall see Peter Lowe, 'Great Britain and the Coming of the Pacific War, 1939-1941', *Royal Historical Society Transactions*, Fifth Series, 24 (1974): 43-63; Thorne, *Allies of a Kind*, pp. 3-6. In Canada, however, there was, if anything, a tendency to overrate Japanese capabilities.

19. Quoted in Reginald Roy, *For Most Conspicuous Bravery: A Biography of Major-General George R. Pearkes, V.C., Through Two World Wars* (Vancouver, 1977), p. 100. See also John Swettenham, *McNaughton, Volume 1: 1887-1939* (Toronto, 1968), p. 182.

20. DCER: V, p. 346.

21. Ibid. See also Patricia Roy et al., *Mutual Hostages* (Toronto, 1990), p. 33, when McNaughton raised these concerns with Sir Maurice Hankey, the secretary of Britain's Committee of Imperial Defence, in 1934.

22. NAC, Department of External Affairs Records (DEA), vol. 744, file 163, General Staff Memo, 'Canada and the United States Security Measures Against Air Attack', 29 April 1935; DCER: V, pp. 256-7, 265.

23. Published under the pseudonym 'T', 'Canada and the Far East', *Foreign Affairs* 13 (1935): 388ff. A copy of this article denoting Pearson as the author is in NAC, H.D.G. Crerar Papers, vol. 13, file D.M.C. & I9A.

24. Quoted in J.L. Granatstein, *The Ottawa Men* (Toronto, 1982), pp. 72-3.

25. See R. MacGregor Dawson, *William Lyon Mackenzie King: A Political Biography, 1874-1923* (Toronto, 1958), pp. 146-64; NAC, W.L. Mackenzie King Papers, Diary, esp. February, March 1908.

26. See C.P. Stacey, *Canada and the Age of Conflict, Volume 2: 1921-1948, The Mackenzie King Era* (Toronto, 1981), chap. 5.

27. Alan Mason, 'Canadian-Japanese Relations, 1930-1941' (University of Toronto Research Paper, 1973): 46-72; M.G. Fry, 'The Development of Canada's Relations with Japan, 1919-1947', in Keith A.J. Hay, ed., *Canadian Perspectives on Economic Relations with Japan* (Montreal, 1980), pp. 26-34. See also DCER: V, pp. 715-56.

28. Riddell, *Documents on Canadian Foreign Policy*, p. 281.

29. Fry, 'The Development of Canada's Relations with Japan', pp. 54-5 for figures.

30. Ibid., p. 30.

31. Mason, 'Canadian-Japanese Relations', p. 69.

32. Stacey, *Canada and the Age of Conflict*, vol. 2, p. 192.

33. NAC, King Papers, vol. 237, ff.203757ff., Mackenzie to King, 26 May 1937.

34. Ibid., vol. 211, file 1678, Skelton Memorandum for King, 26 February 1936.

35. Quoted in James Eayrs, *In Defence of Canada, Volume II: Appeasement and Rearmament* (Toronto, 1965), p. 138.

36. This document is reproduced in Eayrs, pp. 213-22.

37. NAC, King Diary, 31 July 1936.

38. Ibid., 10 September 1936.

39. Eayrs, *In Defence of Canada*, II, pp. 139-40.

40. For an idea of just what was done see T. Murray Hunter, 'Coast Defence in British Columbia, 1939-1941: Attitudes and Realities', *BC Studies* 28 (1975-76): 3-28.

41. United States National Archives (USNA), Washington, D.C., Records of the Foreign Service Posts of the Department of State, RG 84, vol. 287, Memorandum of Interview with Mr King, 22 March 1937. I am grateful to Alan Mason for providing me with this reference. See also NAC, King Diary, 5 March 1937.

42. On the Sino-Japanese war see Bradford Lee, *Britain and the Sino-Japanese War* (Oxford, 1973); Peter Lowe, *Great Britain and the Origins of the Pacific War* (Oxford, 1977); Nicholas R. Clifford, *Retreat From China: British Policy in the Far East, 1937-1939* (Seattle, Wash., 1967); Saburo Ienaga, *The Pacific War, 1931-1945* (New York,

1978); D. Borg, *The United States and the Far Eastern Crisis of 1933-1938* (Cambridge, Mass., 1964); Jonathan G. Utley, *Going to War With Japan, 1937-1941* (Knoxville, Tenn., 1985).

43. Lee, *Britain and the Sino-Japanese War, 1937-1939*, p. 274ff; Kyozo Sato, 'Japan's Position before the Outbreak of the European War in September 1939', *Modern Asian Studies* 14 (1980): 179-83.

44. DCER: VI, p. 1024.

45. NAC, King Diary, 3 September 1937.

46. DCER: VI, pp. 1026-8. Even stronger warnings of this were coming from Loring Christie. See DEA Records, vol. 723, file 64 (1-2), Christie Memoranda, 'Note on Departmental Conference', 20 October 1937 and 'Consultations on Far Eastern Situation', 21 October 1937.

47. Vancouver *Sun*, 17 November 1937; Patricia Roy, 'Educating the "East": British Columbia and the Oriental Question in the Interwar Years', *BC Studies* 18 (Summer 1973): 50-69. See also USNA, General Records of the Department of State, RG 59, 842.00 PR/117, Armour to Hull, 4 December 1937; material in Public Record Office [PRO], London, Admiralty Records, ADM 178/178. It is now known that in 1932 the Japanese navy secretly sent two intelligence officers to the West Coast of North America, where they operated under the direction of the military attaché at the Washington Embassy. See Roy et al., *Mutual Hostages*, pp. 46-7.

48. DEA Records, vol. 2453, 'Secret Files 1938', Skelton to Marler, 18 February 1938 and Skelton to Kinoshita, 11 February 1937. See also PRO, Foreign Office Records, FO 371/22192 F10150/941/23, Paul Mason to C.W. Dixon, 10 February 1938.

49. DCER: VIII, 150-2; Records of the Foreign Service Posts of the Department of State, vol. 284, box 1486, Armour Memorandum, 9 November 1937. I am indebted to Alan Mason for providing me with this reference.

50. NAC, King Papers, vol. 157, file 1411, Ashton Memorandum, 'Conversations on Defence Questions', 25 January 1938 and Nelles Memorandum, 'Conversations held in Washington, D.C., on the 19th and 20th January 1938.' See also Eayrs, *In Defence of Canada*, II, pp. 180-3.

51. NAC, King Diary, 11 January 1938.

52. Canada, House of Commons, *Debates*, 1938, vol. 1, 66; King Diary, 10, 30 January 1939. One immigration bill was stopped on 18 February 1938 and another in 1939. The British also breathed a sigh of relief over this. See FO 371/23560.

53. Quoted in Eayrs, *In Defence of Canada*, II, pp. 183-4; King Diary, 20 August 1938.

54. Ibid., 27 January 1939; Eayrs, *In Defence of Canada*, II, p. 178.

55. *Globe and Mail*, 3 December 1938; Toronto *Star*, 15 July 1939.

56. Quoted in R. John Pritchard, 'The Far East as an Influence on the Chamberlain Government's Pre-War European Policies', *Millennium* 2 (1973-74): 18-19.

57. Documents on British Foreign Policy [DBFP]: third series, vol. IX, pp. 227-8.

58. DEA Records, vol. 723, file 64 (1-2), Massey to King, 16 June 1939.

59. NAC, King Papers, vol. 211, file 1678, Skelton Memorandum for King, 19 June 1939.

60. DEA Records, vol. 1754, file 804 (XIII), Mahoney to King, 20, 26 July 1939; NAC, Escott Reid Papers, vol. 5, file 2, Draft Telegram of 20 July 1939.

61. DBFP: third series, vol. IX, p. 313.

62. Cordell Hull, *The Memoirs of Cordell Hull*, Vol. 1 (New York, 1948), p. 635.
63. DBFP: third series, vol. IX, p. 313. See also Lee, *Britain and the Sino-Japanese War*, p. 196; Hull, *Memoirs*, I, p. 636; Utley, *Going to War with Japan*, pp. 62-3.
64. FO 371/23567, Circular B. No. 273, London to Ottawa, 16 August 1939.
65. Ibid., No. 46, Ottawa to London, 21 August 1939.
66. NAC, King Papers, vol. 211, file 2011, Skelton to King, 1 August 1939.
67. DEA Records, vol. 723, file 64 (1-2), Skelton Memorandum for King, 19 August 1939; King Papers, vol. 211, file 2011, Robertson Memorandum, 5 August 1939.
68. NAC, King Diary, 21 August 1939.
69. See Lee, *Britain and the Sino-Japanese War*, p. 201ff; Robert Craigie, *Behind the Japanese Mask* (London, 1946), pp. 73-4. Efforts to turn up this sort of evidence in the PRO have so far been unsuccessful. But much of the high-level information in Britain falls under the fifty and even the seventy-five year rule and many records are still held by the originating departments, which greatly hinders access to records in Britain.
70. NAC, King Diary, 6 September 1939.

CHARLES J. McMILLAN

1. F. Finan et al., 'The U.S. Trade Position in High Technology: 1980-1986', Report prepared for U.S. Congress (Washington: Joint Economic Committee,1986) pp. 30-1.
2. Kenneth S. Courtis and Paul A. Summerville, 'Beyond Trade: A New Phase in the International Competitive Position of the Japanese Automotive Industry', *Journal of American Chamber of Commerce in Japan* (Oct. 1986): 33-8.
3. James C. Abegglen, 'Hollowing Out', *Tokyo Business Today* (Oct. 1987): 6.
4. Hon. Pat Carney, 'Seventh Canada-Japan Joint Economic Committee Meeting's *Communiqué* (Ottawa: April 1, 1987).
5. National Research Council, *A Practical Perspective* (Ottawa, 1986).
6. For an analysis of Japanese financial flows and the impact for Canada, see J. Ariadne Hawkins and Keith Hay, *Canada-Japan: The Money Business* (Ottawa: Canada-Japan Trade Council, 1986); see also Richard Wright, with Susan Huggett, *A Yen For Profit* (Montreal: IRPP, 1987), Chapter 2.
7. Canada and Japan signed an industrial co-operation agreement in September 1985. Canada has sought industry missions and exchange of information and research contacts in fine ceramics, advanced production manufacturing, microelectronics, aircraft and aerospace, and biotechnology.
8. See *Ward's Automotive International*, Vol. 2 (Dec. 1987): 9-10; 'The American Car Industry's Own Goals', *The Economist* (6 Feb. 1988): 69.
9. See James C. Abegglen and George Stalk, Jr, *Kaisha, The Japanese Corporation* (New York: Basic Books, 1985) chapters 1-5.
10. James Brian Quinn, 'The Impacts of Technology in the Services Sector', in Bruce Guile and Harvey Brooks, eds, *Technology and Global Industry* (Washington: National Academy Press, 1987); Stephen Cohen and John Zysman, *Manufacturing Matters* (New York: Basic Books, 1987).
11. I.M. Destler, *American Trade Politics: System Under Stress* (Washington: Institute for International Economics, 1986), especially chapters 8 and 9.
12. G.E. Salembier, Andrew R. Moray, and Frank Stone, *The Canadian Import File:*

Trade, Protection and Adjustment (Montreal: IRPP, 1987), Chapter 8; Richard G. Lipsey and Murray G. Smith, *Taking the Initiative: Canada's Trade Options in a Turbulent World* (Toronto: C.D. Howe Institute, 1985).

13. Quoted in 'A Test For Free Trade', *Wall Street Journal*, 28 Dec. 1987.

14. For related views, see Peter Morici, *The Global Competitive Struggle—Challenges to the United States and Canada* (Toronto: Canada America Committee, 1984); Wendy Dobson, *Canadian-Japanese Economic Relations in a Triangular Relationship* (Toronto: C.D. Howe Institute, 1987).

15. Robert T. Green and Triana L. Larsen, 'Retaliation Will Open Up Japan', *Harvard Business Review* (Nov.-Dec. 1987): 22-8.

SATO HIDEO

*This study was made possible by the Canada-Japan Research Award of 1985 from the Department of External Affairs, Government of Canada. The author wishes to acknowledge valuable comments and suggestions by Dr Wendy Dobson and Professor Frank Langdon on an earlier version of this paper, originally published in Wendy Dobson, ed., *Canadian-Japanese Economic Relations in a Triangular Perspective* (Toronto: C.D. Howe, 1987).

1. See, for example, Klaus H. Pringsheim, *Neighbors Across the Pacific: Canadian-Japanese Economic Relations, 1952-1983* (Westport, Conn.: Greenwood Press, 1983); Frank Langdon, *The Politics of Canadian-Japanese Economic Relations, 1952-1983* (Vancouver: University of British Columbia Press, 1983); and Keith A.J. Hay, ed., *Canadian Perspectives on Economic Relations with Japan* (Montreal: Institute for Research on Public Policy, 1980).

2. Michael W. Chinworth, 'Japan-Canada Relations', *JEI Report* (Washington, D.C., Japan Economic Institute), No. 30A, August 9, 1985, p. 8.

3. Hideo Sato, 'The Political Dynamics of U.S.-Japan Economic Conflicts', *Journal of Northeast Asian Studies 3* (Spring 1984): 5-7.

4. Richard W. Wright, *Japanese Business in Canada: The Elusive Alliance* (Montreal: Institute for Research on Public Policy, 1984), p. xvi.

5. Langdon, *The Politics of Canadian-Japanese Economic Relations*, p. 76.

6. United States, Congress, House of Representatives, Subcommittee on Trade of the Committee on Ways and Means, *United States-Japan Trade Report* (Washington, D.C.: U.S. Government Printing Office, September 5, 1980), p. 5.

7. Chinworth, 'Japan-Canada Relations', p. 7.

8. David Stewart-Patterson, 'Japan nervous over Canada's moves toward U.S', *Globe and Mail* (Toronto), 10 December 1984, p. R3.

9. Chinworth, 'Japan-Canada Relations', p. 7.

10. Interview with NTT officials, San Francisco, 13 March 1986; and Edmund B. Fitzgerald, Chairman, Northern Telecom Inc., Statement before the U.S. Senate Finance Committee, Subcommittee on International Trade, Washington, D.C., 3 May 1985, pp. 15-17.

11. Ann Walmsley, 'Canada's Tense Trade Ties with Tokyo', *Maclean's* (22 April 1985): 35; and Brian Milner, 'Yen's rise cited as reason to end Japanese car import restrictions', *Globe and Mail* (Toronto), 21 February 1986, B4.

12. Chinworth, 'Japan-Canada Relations', p. 4.

13. These perceptions are drawn from a survey by Tsukuba University of 182 Japanese companies investing in Canada (with a response rate of 39%); and from Chinworth, 'Japan-Canada Relations', p. 2.

14. Langdon, *The Politics of Canadian-Japanese Economic Relations*, p. 30.

15. For details, see Gilbert R. Winham and Ikuo Kabashima, 'The Politics of U.S.-Japanese Auto Trade', in I.M. Destler and Hideo Sato, eds, *Coping with U.S.-Japanese Economic Conflicts* (Lexington, Mass.: D.C. Heath, 1982), pp. 73-120.

16. Langdon, *The Politics of Canadian-Japanese Economic Relations*, p. 50.

17. Ibid., p. 51

18. Interviews with Japanese auto industry representatives, Tokyo, 25 June and 22 November 1985.

19. Langdon, *The Politics of Canadian-Japanese Economic Relations*, p. 510.

20. Chinworth, 'Japan-Canada Relations', p. 7.

21. *Nihon Keizei Shimbun* (Tokyo), 21 August 1986.

22. Interview with a Canadian auto industry official, Toronto, 2 August 1986.

23. Gail Lem, 'Canada luring diverse investment from Japan', *Globe and Mail* (Toronto), 28 October 1985: E14.

24. *Nihon Keizei Shimbun* (Tokyo), 16 September 1986.

25. Interviews with Japanese auto industry representatives, Tokyo, 25 June and 22 November 1985; and Ken Romain, 'Imported car distributors hope for end to curbs', *Globe and Mail* (Toronto), 17 December 1984: B8.

26. Robert O. Keohane and Joseph S. Nye, *Power and Interdependence* (Boston: Little, Brown, 1977), pp. 203-4.

27. Ibid., p. 203.

28. Charles F. Doran, *Forgotten Partnership: U.S.-Canada Relations* (Baltimore: Johns Hopkins University Press, 1984), p. 21.

29. Langdon, *The Politics of Canadian-Japanese Economic Relations*, p. 74.

30. Hugh Patrick and Hideo Sato, 'The Political Economy of United States-Japan Trade in Steel', in Kozo Yamamura, ed., *Policy and Trade and Issues of the Japanese Economy* (Seattle: University of Washington Press, 1982), p. 216.

31. A.J. Sarna, 'The Impact of a Canada-U.S. Free Trade Area', *Journal of Common Market Studies 23* (June 1985): 299-318.

32. Stewart-Patterson, 'Japan nervous over Canada's moves toward U.S.'

33. Jeff Sallot, 'Nakasone qualifies free-trade support', *Globe and Mail* (Toronto) 15 January 1986: A1-A2.

34. Walmsley, 'Canada's Tense Trade Ties with Tokyo'.

35. Hobart Rowen, 'Low Point in Japan-Bashing', *Washington Post*, 1 August 1985.

36. Hideo Sato, 'Japanese-American Economic Relations in Crisis', *Current History 84* (December 1985): 406.

37. Keohane and Nye, *Power and Interdependence*, p. 203.

38. Ibid., pp. 24-37.

JOHN T. SAYWELL

*This selection first appeared in *Discovering Japan: Issues for Canadians*, Donald J. Daly and Tom T. Sekine, eds (Toronto: Captus University Publications, 1991).

1. Canada, House of Commons, *Debates*, 1928, pp. 28ff, 3484, 4152-67.
2. The best account of Canada-Japan relations between the wars is Michael G. Fry, 'The Development of Canada's Relations with Japan, 1919-1947', in Keith A.J. Hay, ed., *Canadian Perspectives on Economic Relations with Japan* (Montreal 1980), pp. 7-67. See also his *Illusions of Security: North Atlantic Diplomacy 1918-1922* (Toronto).
3. Hugh L. Keenleyside, *Memoirs*, vol. 1, *Hammer the Golden Day* (Toronto, 1981), p. 405.
4. The best study of King's concern about the Pacific, in the context of Anglo-American-Japanese relations, is Gregory A. Johnson, 'North Pacific Triangle?: The Impact of the Far East on Canada and its Relations with the United States and Great Britain 1937-1948' (Doctoral dissertation, York University, 1989).
5. National Archives of Canada (NAC), Minutes, Cabinet War Committee, 20 June 1940.
6. Ibid., 13 August, 1 October, 1940; Fry, 'Canada's Relations with Japan', p. 41.
7. NAC, King Diary, 7 September 1940.
8. NAC, King Diary, 8 October 1940; Minutes, Cabinet War Committee, 8 October 1940; King Papers, King to Skelton, 11 October 1940, cited in Johnson, 'North Pacific Triangle?' p. 174; King Diary, 7 December 1941.
9. R.J. Gowen,: 'Canada and the Myth of the Japanese Market', *Pacific Historical Review* (February 1970): 63-83; O. Mary Hill, *Canada's Salesmen to the World* (Montreal 1977). Canada, Sessional Papers, *Report of the Department of the Secretary of State* (1893) states that Fukashi Sigimura was appointed Consul in Vancouver in 1889.
10. See Peter Ward, *White Canada Forever: Popular Attitudes and Public Policy Towards Orientals in British Columbia* (Montreal 1978); Klaus Pringsheim, *Neighbors Across the Pacific: Canadian-Japanese Relations 1870-1982* (Westport, Conn.: Greenwood Press, 1983); Fry, 'Canada's Relations with Japan', p. 15ff.
11. On the pattern of Japanese foreign trade see William E.R. Lockwood, *The Economic Development of Japan* (Princeton 1968). The best study of the trade war is Fry, 'Canada's Relations with Japan', pp. 29-38.
12. On post-war economic relations see Frank Langdon, *The Politics of Canadian Japanese Economic Relations 1952-1983* (Vancouver 1983). Dates on bilateral trade and investment, unless otherwise cited, are those used by the Department of External Affairs as provided as a rule by Statistics Canada.
13. Clyde Prestowitz interprets the Japanese offer of voluntary restraint which was accepted by the Americans as a shrewd and calculated negotiating strategy. If the Americans imposed quotas they would determine volume and duration, and could even impose tariffs and reap the benefits of price increases. But if the Japanese 'voluntarily' limited exports, he writes, 'the shipments, the amounts, duration, and conditions would all be subject to negotiation and thus be much more under Japan's control.' *Trading Places: How We Allowed Japan to Take the Lead* (New York 1988), p. 253.
14. On a customs basis the share was 3.76% in 1988 (*Canada's Balance of International Payments* 1988).
15. GATT, *International Trade*, various years.
16. It is worth noting that the share of manufactured products in Japanese exports is 97% compared to the OECD average of between 60 and 70%. The share for Canada is

45% including the automobile trade. Left out of all calculations are Japanese exports of high-tech consumer durables through offshore manufacturing in Taiwan, and other Asian countries.

17. The unilateral imposition of a ban on uranium exports in 1976 (two months after Framework for Economic Co-operation was signed) did not improve Canada's image. The agreement on atomic energy co-operation two years later removed that irritant, but the exclusion of Japanese fishermen from the 200-mile zone at the same time substituted another.

18. See Keith A.J. Hay and S.R. Hill, *Canada-Japan Trade and Investment* (Ottawa 1979); Richard W. Wright, *Japanese Business in Canada: The Elusive Alliance* (Montreal 1984): Langdon, *Canadian-Japanese Economic Relations*, Chapter 7. Data for the 1980s are those used by External Affairs.

19. Canadian Embassy, Tokyo, Japanese Portfolio Investment in Canada, Canadian Embassy Survey (September 1988, October 1989); Canada-Japan Trade Council, *Canada-Japan - The Money Business* (Ottawa 1986), p. 13; Statistics Canada, *Security Transactions with Non-Residents*. various issues; *Quarterly Estimates of the Canadian Balance of International Payments. 4th Quarter. 1988*. There is no need to point to the arrival of eleven Japanese banks with their enormous assets or the presence since 1987 of Japanese securities firms on the Toronto Stock Exchange, led by Nomura with more capitalization than the entire Canadian industry. In all probability the financial flows will be increasingly managed by Japanese financial institutions.

20. *Foreign Policy for Canadians* (Ottawa 1970).

21. Standing Senate Committee on Foreign Affairs, *Report on Canadian Relations with countries of the Pacific Region* (March 1972).

22. 'Smiling diplomacy', Derek Burney, now Ambassador to Washington, termed it. Burney told Klaus Pringsheim in 1977 that: 'We want more out of the relationship with Japan. I'm not convinced that the Japanese are reciprocating. They're reciprocating to the extent that it serves their immediate interests, as they always will. But I don't think their attitude is changed all that much', (Pringsheim, *Neighbors Across the Pacific*. p. 168).

23. On Canadian competitiveness see a number of articles by Donald Daly. On science and technology see Charles J. McMillan, *Investing in Tomorrow: Japan's Science and Technology Organization and Strategies* (Canada-Japan Trade Council, Ottawa, 1989) and Michael W. Donnelly and John Kirton. *The Potential for Partnership: Canadian-Japanese Investment and Technology Relation* (Policy Studies, No. 3, Joint Centre for Asia Pacific Studies, Toronto 1988).

24. Masanori Moritani, 'Japanese Technology', *Journal of Japanese Trade and Industry* No. 3 (1982): 26-8. By 1980, he reports, exports of technology totalled ¥74,263 billion compared to imports of ¥27,675.

25. Summary statement and 'Going Global' press release provided by the Department of External Affairs. A report by the Science Council late in 1989 identified six areas of science and technology for bilateral cooperation; advanced materials and biomaterials, biotechnology and biosciences, oceanography and ocean engineering, space science, advanced manufacturing (artificial intelligence, robotics, microelectronics, communications and photonics), and sustainable development and environmental management. The report, under study by government, called for an emphasis

on young researchers and creative ideas (*University Affairs*, December 1989).
26. For the recommendations of the Special Committee and the government's response, see *Canada's International Relations Response of the Government of Canada to the Report of the Special Joint Committee of the Senate and the House of Commons* (Ottawa, December 1986).
27. Foreign policy as an extension of domestic policy, with a vengeance!
28. John Saywell, *How Japanese Students View Canada*, Working Paper Series No. 54, University of Toronto-York University Joint Centre for Asia Pacific Studies, 1988. The article includes a brief survey of Canadian content in Japanese school texts and curriculum, brief because there is virtually nothing.

JOHN F. HOWES

1. See John F. Howes, 'Review of Japanese Studies Abroad (19): Japanese Studies in Canada', *Japan Foundation Newsletter*, 61 (April-May 1978): 10-18, reprinted with additional information as *Directory of Japan Specialists in Canada*. Directory Series, no. 3 (Tokyo: The Japan Foundation, rev. 1983).
2. *The Standing Senate Committee on Foreign Affairs, Report on Canadian Relations with the Countries of the Pacific Region* (Ottawa, 1972), p. 4.
3. This section is based in part on Malcolm Smith, 'Japanese Law in Canada: 1980-1987', thirty-four page typescript double spaced; available from the author, The Asian Law Centre, Law School, University of Melbourne, Parkville, Victoria 3052, Australia.

YOSHIDA KENSEI

*This is a revised version of a paper originally prepared for the International Council for Canadian Studies. I would like to express my gratitude to ICCS for granting permission to publish it in this format, to Professors John Schultz and John Saywell who provided valuable comments on the original manuscript, and to my friend and English teacher, Glen Jones, for his editorial remarks. Needless to say, I am solely responsible for any injustice, oversight or omission committed. English titles of Japanese books and articles are mine.
1. Although, strictly speaking, the works of E.H. Norman do not fall under the heading of Canadian Studies, for many Japanese intellectuals he remains one of the most highly respected foreign observers of Japan and in some ways represents Canada. Norman was the focus of a special issue (1977) of the monthly magazine *Shiso*, mainly in connection with his contributions to Japanese historiography and his role in the American occupation policy immediately after World War II. His life, beliefs and activities have been documented extensively in a number of articles and books, including a long series in the magazine *Sekai*, a semi-fictional novel, and a recent biography.
2. For an abridged version of volumes 1 and 2 of *To Know Ourselves, The Report of the Commission on Canadian Studies*, see *The Symons Report* (Toronto: McClelland and Stewart, 1978).
3. Among the exceptions are Bamba's *Japanese-Canadian Relations: An Overview* (Downsview, Ontario: University of Toronto-York University Joint Centre on Modern

East Asia, 1983) and several papers by Hideo Sato on Japan-Canada economic relations. Masako Iino contributed the article 'Japanese Immigration and Canada-Japan Relations in the 1930s' to J. Carlsen and J.M. Lacroix, eds., *Canadian Society and Culture in times of Economic Depression* (Ottawa, 1987) and, as noted, co-authored *Mutual Hostages* with Patricia Roy, J.L. Granatstein, and Hiroko Takamura. The aforementioned *Cherry Blossoms and Maple Leaves: Comparative Study of Japanese and Canadian Literature* is another example of collaborative research.

4. In the field of literature, Japanese translations include Louis Hemon's 1921 classic *Maria Chapdelaine* and Lucy M. Montgomery's *Anne of Green Gables* and its sequels, Farley Mowat's many books from *The Dog Who Wouldn't Be* to *The Siberians*, Mordecai Richler's *St Urbain's Horseman*, James Houston's *The White Dawn: An Eskimo Saga*, Joy Kogawa's *Obasan*, William Stephenson's *A Man Called Intrepid* and Anthony Hyde's *The Red Fox*. Although not novels, G. Kingsley Ward's *Letters of a Businessman to His Son* and its sequel, *Letters of a Businessman to His Daughter*, are extremely popular in Japan, the former having sold more than a million copies. While Margaret Atwood has finally been introduced to Japanese readers through the translation of *A Handmaid's Tale*, most other top Canadian writers such as Robertson Davies, Hugh MacLennan, W.O. Mitchell, Morley Callaghan, Margaret Laurence, Gabrielle Roy, Pierre Berton, and Anne Hébert remain virtually unknown in Japan.

O

Index